DOCTOR WILLIS AT HOME

Wedgwood plaque on bright blue jasper ground,
commemorating the King's recovery, 1789

George III and the Mad-Business

BY IDA MACALPINE
& RICHARD HUNTER

> *We are not ourselves*
> *When nature, being oppress'd, commands the mind*
> *To suffer with the body.*
> KING LEAR, ACT II, SCENE 4

PANTHEON BOOKS
A DIVISION OF RANDOM HOUSE, NEW YORK

Contents

List of Illustrations

Foreword

We became interested in George III's illness when our researches in the history of psychiatry taught us how much its development had been stimulated by the recurrent attacks which deranged his mind. Indeed the royal malady seemed to be a watershed between the old and the new. However when we wanted to learn more about the illness itself and its symptoms we found to our surprise that there was no reliable account of all the attacks on which a modern clinical judgement or diagnosis could be based. No attempt had been made to use the many new sources which have become available or to review the illness in the light of advances in scientific medicine. What there was seemed challengingly unsatisfactory, long on interpretation and speculation but short on fact. A fanciful picture of a weak and neurotic personality prone to 'mental' breakdown had been constructed on a mixture of nineteenth-century historical and twentieth-century psychiatric bias and by sheer weight of repetition had been generally accepted.

Once we had assembled from primary manuscript and printed sources an authentic account of all attacks, the King and his sufferings – among which his treatments must be counted – appeared in a very different light. The pattern fitted that of a rare metabolic disorder which has only recently been recognized. Because it is heritable it was possible to obtain confirmation of our diagnosis from the family history. Strangely, the new facts bring George III very much more alive as a human being than the psychologizing mythology which has been spun around him.

This study is not a biography of England's and psychiatry's most famous patient, but it contains material basic to one. It tells for instance, for the first time and from sources never before consulted, the incredible story of what happened during the attack of 1801 – and what did not happen in 1765.

The medical problems raised by the attack in which mental derangement first appeared, that of 1788–9, stirred the profession, and its impact on the general public led to an upsurge of humanitarian concern for the fate of the mentally ill. The spotlight thrown so glaringly on the obscure 'mad-business' of ill-repute brought about its gradual transformation into a respectable branch of medicine. The lines along which psychiatry has developed since, from Georgian days to our own, can be traced in what later generations of doctors made of the illness. Unexpectedly, it turns out, the King's own physicians, in their unsophisticated way, had a better grasp of the nature of the royal malady than those who followed.

Acknowledgements

We acknowledge the gracious permission of Her Majesty the Queen to quote from material in the Royal Archives published in the correspondence of George III and George IV; and from Sir Henry Halford's clinical journal covering the period October 1811 to January 1812.

We are deeply indebted to His Royal Highness Prince Ernst August of Hanover, Duke of Brunswick, present head of the House of Hanover, for his personal interest and for allowing us to study and quote from family papers in the Niedersächsische Staatsarchiv.

His Grace the Archbishop of Canterbury and the Trustees of Lambeth Palace Library kindly gave us access to, and permission to quote from, the Queen's Council Papers.

The diary and papers of Sir George Baker were generously made available to us by Sir Randle Baker Wilbraham of Rode Hall, Cheshire; and those of Sir Henry Halford by the Honourable Mrs Timothy Brooks of Wistow Hall, Leicestershire. To both we are most grateful. Our thanks are also due to the directors of Messrs Coutts & Company, Bankers, for allowing us to see and quote from correspondence of the Royal Dukes.

We thank the following for kind permission to quote from manuscripts in their possession: the Trustees of the British Museum (also for figures 4, 8, 12, 13); Lord Sidmouth and the Devon Record Office; the Governors of King Edward School, Witley, Surrey; the Board of Management, Leicester Royal Infirmary and the Librarian, Leicester City Library; the Public Records Office; the Registrars of the Royal College of Physicians of Edinburgh, and of London; the President and Council of the Royal Society of Medicine.

We acknowledge permission to quote from their books to the following editors and publishers: Cambridge University Press for *The Later Correspondence of George III* (volumes 1 to 4, 1962–8); and for *The Letters of George IV* (3 volumes, 1938), both edited by A. Aspinall; Messrs Cassell,

B

London, for *The Correspondence of George Prince of Wales* (volumes 1 to 5, 1963–8), edited by A. Aspinall; Home and van Thal, London, for *Letters of the Princess Charlotte*, 1949, edited by A. Aspinall; John Lane The Bodley Head, London, for *The Diaries of . . . Robert Fulke Greville*, 1930, edited by F. M. Bladon.

The results of our researches into the medical history of George III and the royal houses were first reported in two articles in the *British Medical Journal*, 1966 and 1968 (the latter in collaboration with Professor C. Rimington) and reprinted in *Porphyria – A Royal Malady*, published by the British Medical Association, 1968. For permission to use this material we are indebted to the editor, Dr Martin Ware. Additional historical and psychiatric implications were discussed in the *Bulletin of the Institute of Historical Research*, 1967, and in the *Proceedings of the Royal Society of Medicine*, 1968.

We thank Sir Iain Moncreiffe of that Ilk, Albany Herald, for his encouragement and advice about the Tudors and Stuarts. We are particularly grateful for much help to R. Mackworth-Young, Librarian, Windsor Castle to E. G. Bill, Librarian, Lambeth Palace Library and to Professor Ohnesorge and the staff, Niedersächsisches Staatsarchiv, Hanover; and for many kindnesses to Hugh Murray Baillie of the Historical Manuscripts Commission; John Brooke; Professor Ian R. Christie, University College, London; and Professor T. J. B. Spencer, University of Birmingham. David Duguid gave us much valuable editorial help in the preparation of the manuscript.

Introduction

George III's illness is probably the most famous and most momentous in English history. Mad King George – this is the picture every schoolboy learns, which every textbook teaches, and which pervades, more or less subtly, every study of his long and complex reign. From 1760 to 1820 his sixty crowded years upon the throne saw the consolidation of the conquest of Canada, the discovery of Australia and New Zealand, the annexation of the West Indies, the final triumph in India – to name only some of the foundations of the Empire laid during the time. It was also the reign which was humiliated by the loss of the American colonies, shaken by the French Revolution, threatened by Napoleon and delivered by Nelson and Wellington. At home great constitutional battles led to the ascendency of parliamentary over monarchical power – a process speeded by the crises occasioned by the illness of the King.

The reign which 'began with a few islands, hardly visible on the face of the Globe' ended with 'an extent of territory unequalled in the history of Nations'. There had been a similar 'progress of the humane species in arts, in science and in civilization', not least in 'the most immediately interesting of all arts, the alleviation of human misery by the cure of disease'.[1] Conspicuous in this field were the advances made in psychiatry, and they were in large measure brought about by the royal malady, which dragged the mad-business, as it was affectionately called, out of obscurity and ill-repute into the limelight. When it was found to be 'of assistance in the treatment of a great personage' – as the phrase went – it became a respectable branch of medicine. Never again, after the King's illness of 1788–9, could doctors haughtily disdain acquaintance with the subject.

The fact that George III suffered from an illness which deranged his mind is therefore of particular medical interest and significance. But in glaring contrast to the increasing attention of historians to the period and the reign, remarkably little research has been done in almost two hundred years to find out what was really the matter with him. As recently as 1961 a psychiatrist was content to write that George III suffered from recurrent attacks of madness – an expression so vague that it would not be tolerated if a student applied it to a living patient. This absence of curiosity about the nature of the illness is all the more astonishing since during the King's lifetime its problematic nature was freely discussed in private, in public, in Parliament, in the press, by doctors, laymen and indeed by the King himself. The opinion of his physicians was that the trouble certainly lay in the body rather than in the mind – that it was part of a physical disorder and not psychological. As we shall see, they were right.

But after the King's death a conspiracy of silence seems to have descended, perhaps in deference to Queen Victoria, who is known to have been sensitive, to say the least, about her grandfather's derangement. It is remarkable that only two clinical studies have ever been made, both by psychiatrists, one in the middle of the last century and one in the middle of this, and both American. Not surprisingly, they concentrated on the mental symptoms. The lore of 'the mad King' gained currency, and by repetition this grotesque distortion became the generally accepted view. The fact is that the King was fifty years old when he first became deranged, and all periods of derangement added together up to his seventy-third year hardly amounted to six months in all. In his last illness from 1810 to 1820, when the Regency was established, it is said that permanent madness finally closed on him. But this is another convenient fable. What happened was that he suffered a series of accessions and remissions and certainly for the first twelve months his physicians confidently expected complete recovery. After that he was overtaken by senility, to which were added the isolation of blindness and ultimately deafness.

One of the reasons why the illness is difficult to study is that there are so many sources, and they are spread over almost sixty years. It was a period teeming with great men and great events. Never had there been so many diarists, correspondents and chroniclers who may have noted pertinent facts not recorded elsewhere. The journals of the Willises, who attended the King in 1788–9, 1801 and from 1811 to 1820, and which are now in the British Museum, were not available until 1959, and the diary of Sir George Baker, the first physician to be called in 1788, has only been known for a decade. Sir Henry Halford's papers and his journal covering the period 1810–11 have never been consulted before, nor have the twenty volumes of the records of the Queen's Council at Lambeth Palace Library.

The bulletins which were issued when the King was ill are of little value. They were intentionally non-committal and were framed in generalities out of respect for the invalid and to spare the feelings of the royal family. Their purpose was to allay alarm rather than record medical facts and to reveal no more than was 'sufficient for every good or loyal purpose'. A typical bulletin in 1788 reads: 'His Majesty has had a very restless night, and is this morning much indisposed.' Even when the doctors wanted to be informative, their reports were garbled, as, for example, that to the Prime Minister, Spencer Perceval, in December 1810: 'He is under a great degree of irritation, and the whole frame is so much disturbed as to make us consider Him in some danger'. One sympathizes with Lord Grenville, who complained that 'the report of the physicians is worded as foolishly as ever'.[2] Nor was what they said necessarily reliable or accurate, since many represented a compromise between dissenting opinions – or, more bluntly, between quarrelling colleagues, a point on which they were criticized in Parliament.

In order to understand what the King's doctors meant and did, one needs a background knowledge of eighteenth-century medical practice and the theory on which it was based. Medically they seem much further removed than the hundred and fifty or two hundred years which separate them from us. They attempted to think in terms of the new pathology of disease of organs and systems, but when their knowledge failed they still fell back on the almost two-thousand-year-old theory of the four humours – black bile, yellow bile, phlegm and choler. How the royal physicians pictured the King's illness is well illustrated in a letter by Lord Grenville in 1788, after the King had been ill five weeks:

> The cause to which they all agree to ascribe it, is the force of a humour which was beginning to show itself in the legs, when the King's imprudence [he failed to change out of wet stockings] drove it from thence into the bowels; and the medicines which they were then obliged to use for the preservation of his life, have repelled it upon the brain.[3]

However quaint their way of thinking may appear today, it reveals the manner in which the King's symptoms progressed from legs to abdomen and head, and that his illness rapidly became so serious that the doctors feared for his life.

What today is called a diagnosis, that is the identification of a disease and the parts of the body affected by it, could make little headway while there was as yet no science of physical signs by which the disease could be located. For this reason much of an eighteenth-century physician's consulting practice was carried on perfectly adequately across the table of a coffee-house or by correspondence, without his ever setting eyes on the patient. Doctors did not listen to the chest, for instance, for they would not have known what to make of what they heard. Next to nothing was known of the nervous system other than that the brain could be affected by injury, infection, strokes and fits, causing delirium, paralysis and 'fatuity'. It was not even known that nerves were either motor or sensory, that is, carried impulses away from or to the central nervous system – corresponding to the one-way traffic William Harvey had demonstrated in respect of the circulation of the blood, away from the heart in arteries and towards it in veins. The physicians had no stethoscope, no knee-jerk hammer, and even had to guess whether their patient had a fever, since the clinical thermometer had not come into use. Often they could not even agree on the King's pulse and bothered to feel it only at times of crisis.

Physical examination was therefore not practised, as it would have served little or no purpose. Treatment in any case was on general lines and followed a set routine of evacuation, counter-irritation and the administration of 'specifics', as for instance to subdue fever. It is difficult to believe that, with so many physicians about him, there is no indication that the King was ever examined at any time. Diagnosis was arrived at by what was called 'an estimate of symptoms and appearances': the doctor invited the patient to recite his complaints, inquired into his 'animal functions' and general health, looked at his tongue and felt the pulse.

Even within this limited range of fact-finding the royal physicians were peculiarly handicapped. When, for example, Dr Richard Warren was hurriedly called on 6 November 1788 because of the King's mounting delirium and the King refused him admission, he formed his judgement of the royal malady from what he could hear from the other side of the door and what his colleague Sir George Baker told him of the state of the pulse.[4] The physicians behaved to the end as though they were expected to observe protocol however ill or delirious the King was. If they were not addressed first, they asked no questions. Whole visits were therefore spent in fruitless silence, as they reported to the Queen's Council in January 1812: 'His Majesty appears to be very quiet this morning, but not having been addressed we know nothing more of His Majesty's condition of mind or body than what is obvious in His external appearances.' And in February: 'His Majesty appears tranquil, but some expressions lead us to believe His Majesty suffers something at present from Rheumatism, but His looks betray no character of fever attending.'

It was a different story when it came to the mental symptoms. No modern aids were necessary to assess whether the patient was excited or composed, elated or depressed, rational or deluded. The royal physicians had the same opportunity of forming a picture of their patient's mental state as any modern psychiatrist. They needed only to listen and observe. And so as soon as mental symptoms appeared they overshadowed the physical manifestations of the illness, which receded into the background, in emphasis if not in fact. Not only were the mental symptoms self-revealing and the loudest, but by their portent also the most dreaded for government and country alike, since it was the King's mental state which determined whether he was competent to rule. All eyes and ears and pens became fixed on it. The physical symptoms in contrast hurt no one other than the King.

They did not enter the social or political arena except when they were so severe that it was thought he was dying, and later they came to be regarded as unimportant or incidental. The mental symptoms gained added prominence in history, because whoever came in contact with the King could, and did, make his own observations and form his own conclusions and did not fail to record them.

The high point of this great drama of human, psychiatric and national history was reached in 1788 when for the first time the fifty-year-old King lost his reason. In the consternation which followed, the mental aberration naturally moved into the centre of the public stage in what became an intricate complex of medical and political controversy – the Regency Crisis – when confusion extended far beyond the mind of the patient, and so gave the illness its lasting stigma. The seal was set on this historic bias when early in December 1788 'Persons who make this Branch of Medicine their particular Study', as psychiatrists were delicately referred to in Parliament, were called in, installed themselves in the palace and took charge of the King's sickroom. This is how it came about that the King's physical sufferings were minimized and later disregarded, while his mental derangement was magnified as if it had been the whole illness – a hazard to which patients with mental symptoms of whatever kind are still exposed. So was created the false image of 'mad King George'. With it the door was shut to a proper understanding of the illness and the man, and their place in history and medicine.

All attacks followed the same pattern. None lasted longer than a few months except the last illness, and this also consisted of a series of accessions and remissions. But by then old age had overtaken him. All attacks left him wasted and weak, so that it took him months to regain normal health and strength.

It is generally stated that he had five attacks with derangement, the first in 1765, when he was twenty-six years old. But, as will be seen later, there is no evidence whatever that his mind was affected during that illness. He first became deranged during the illness of 1788–9, and again in 1801, 1804 and from 1810 to his death in 1820 in his eighty-second year.

The illness of 1788–9 is historically the most important, politically the most dramatic and hence also the most fully documented. To recount it in detail therefore gives a picture of the type and pattern of the disease from which the King suffered in all attacks. It shows unequivocally that mental symptoms developed as part and parcel of a widespread and severe physical disorder of a particular kind. The grievous illness which caused the Regency Crisis started in October 1788 but was preceded by a minor attack in the summer, which led to the Cheltenham episode.

PART ONE

The Illness of the Regency Crisis: 1788-9

I

The Cheltenham Episode

On 11 June 1788 'The King was seized with a bilious fever, attended with violent spasms in his stomach and bowels; the disorder lasted some days,' wrote Elizabeth Harcourt, Lady of the Bedchamber to the Queen, in her diary.[1] The first news from the King came in a letter he wrote to his Prime Minister, William Pitt, from Kew at midday on 12 June:

A pretty smart bilious attack prevents my coming this day to town. I am certainly better than yesterday, and if it goes on mending this day, I shall hope to see Mr. Pitt in town to-morrow. Sir George Baker approves of what I have done, and I trust his advice will remove the remains of this complaint. On returning from the review [of the Duke of York's Regiment of Foot Guards on Wimbledon Common] I was forced to take to my bed, as the only tolerable posture I could find. To be sure I am what one calls a cup too low, but when thoroughly cleared I hope to feel equal to any business that may occur.[2]

Pitt answered immediately:

Mr. Pitt is infinitely sensible of your Majesty's condescension in the note with which he has been honored. He earnestly hopes that your Majesty will find yourself free tomorrow from all remains of complaint. At the same time he trusts your Majesty will pardon him if he cannot help taking the liberty of expressing the anxiety he feels lest it should be renewed by your Majesty's coming to town tomorrow, and he requests your Majesty's permission to add that there is no business of any sort which materially presses.[3]

But before his letter reached Kew, another was on the way to him from the King, written at four o'clock the same afternoon:

Since writing this morning I have seen Sir George Baker, who, though he thinks everything goes on well, yet very fairly told me that quiet is essential to removing my complaint, and that I must neither go to London to-morrow nor return to Windsor. I therefore give this information to Mr. Pitt, that he may not think my not appearing to-morrow a sign of being worse. I certainly mend, but have been pretty well disciplined this day.[4]

Sir George Baker, President of the Royal College of Physicians of London, Fellow of the Royal Society, physician to their Majesties, created baronet in 1776, was renowned for his classical learning and his address to the University of Cambridge in 1755 'On the affections of the mind and the disorders that spring from them', and had shown by elegant reasoning and experiment that contamination of cider by lead was the cause of the endemic colic of his native Devonshire. By applying chemical advances to tracing the cause and prevention of disease, he made a classic contribution to the nation's health. By saying that he had been 'pretty well disciplined,' George III meant that Baker had given him what was called 'a pretty smart purge' in the language of the day. 'His complaint was very disagreeable and indeed alarming for the time that it lasted,' wrote the Princess Royal to her brother Augustus, later Duke of Sussex, who himself was very ill at Hanover at this time, 'the spasm beginning at three in the morning, and continuing till eight o'clock in the evening.'[5]

It affected the King more than was anticipated. 'We have passed a full fortnight at Kew owing to the King's bilious attack,' wrote Queen Charlotte to her son Augustus on 4 July. 'He did submit to see Sir George Baker & feels himself greatly relieved for his priscription. It is supposed that the dryness & heat of the season has occasioned these violent attacks.'[6] 'The King,' wrote W. W. Grenville* in the fourth week of June, 'has been a good deal out of order, but is recovered.'[7] In gossipy circles it was rumoured that his physicians pronounced his symptoms

to be gouty. Probably, the humour might have exhausted its force in the extremities, in the shape of gout, if his majesty had eat and drunk like almost any other gentleman. But his natural disposition to temperance . . . impelled him to adopt the habits of an ascetic. The most simple food, taken in very moderate quantity, constituted his repasts. Yet his German origin shewed itself in his predilections: for sour crout was one of his favourite dishes; as Handel's or Mozart's music charmed him more than that of Pergolesi, or of Paesiello. His ordinary beverage at table was only composed of a sort of lemonade, which he dignified with the name of *cup*; though a monk of La Trappe might have drunk it without any infraction of his monastic vow.[8]

Earl Fauconberg, Lord of the Bedchamber, offered his house, Bays Hill Lodge at Cheltenham, to the King to recuperate: 'His warm encomiums on the virtues of the mineral water, as on the beauty of the surrounding country, inspired his majesty with a wish to visit the place. Its privacy and simplicity formed additional recommendations.'[9] Sir George Baker warmly approved of drinking 'the Cheltenham Waters which are particularly good

* William Wyndham Grenville (1759–1834), Pitt's cousin and a member of his Administration, later Lord Grenville and Prime Minister in the Ministry of All Talents of 1806–7. He was the son of George Grenville (1712–70), George III's Prime Minister in 1763–5.

for all bilious complaints'[5] and it was arranged that the visit should take place as soon as Parliament was prorogued, which was delayed until Friday, 11 July, by the 'Slave Regulation Bill'.

Cheltenham was then 'a small, obscure provincial town of the county of Glocester. Its spring, though unquestionably endowed with powerful and salubrious qualities, yet during many years had fallen into neglect.'[9] It was becoming more popular as a resort for invalids and an alternative to Bath, in consequence of two medical accounts in praise of its waters published in the preceding three years.[10] Dr Anthony Fothergill wrote:

It is recorded, that the medicinal virtues of this spring first began to be noticed about the year 1715, since which it has been more or less frequented. The company have increased of late years, and the Spa is now become a place of very genteel resort during the summer months, insomuch that a Master of the Ceremonies has lately been appointed to preside over its amusements. Already Cheltenham exhibits a handsome Pump-room, two Ball-rooms, and a Theatre . . . The spring issues very slowly from a sandy soil intermixed with loam and clay; and though it has been calculated to yield only about 35 pints in an hour, it will be found fully sufficient to supply upwards of 350 persons . . . It has a smart, brackish irony taste; and emits a slight fetid odour . . . the purging salt of this water consists chiefly of a native Glauber salt, with an admixture of Epsom salt.[11]

The most suitable season was considered to be the summer, a course of three to five weeks was advised and because of its cathartic qualities 'the water itself supplies its own proper preparative, and, if properly managed supersedes the use of other evacuants'. It was particularly recommended to be drunk at the fountain head in amounts measured in quarters of a pint and was 'principally indicated in . . . morbid affections of the first passages, proceeding from costiveness, indigestion, acidity, vitiated bile . . . &c'.

On Tuesday, 8 July, while making preparations for his departure, the King wrote to his good friend Richard Hurd, Bishop of Worcester, announcing his visit and asking that the Three Choirs Festival proposed for the end of August be advanced to the first week so that he would be able to attend it from Cheltenham before his return to Windsor:

Having had rather a smart bilious attack, which, by the goodness of Divine Providence, is quite removed, Sir George Baker has strongly recommended to me the going for a month to Cheltenham . . . and that an absence from London will keep me free from certain fatigues that attend long audiences. I shall therefore go there on Saturday. I am certain you know the regard that both the Queen and I have for you, and that it will be peculiarly agreeable to us to see you at Hartlebury. I shall certainly omit the waters some morning to undertake so charming a party . . . I shall also come to the performance of the Messiah.[12]

Wraxall* recorded:

Such was the king's impatience to begin his journey, that after proroguing the two houses in person, and pronouncing a speech from the throne at three on Friday afternoon, he returned to St. James's, and drove down to Windsor. On the ensuing morning, before seven, their majesties, accompanied by the three eldest princesses, had already quitted the castle on their way to Cheltenham. They only stopped to take breakfast at Lord Harcourt's seat of Nuneham, and reached Bays Hill Lodge on the same afternoon at an early hour.[13]

Fanny Burney,† who lived at Court, left a lively account of the day:

We were all up at five o'clock; and the noise and confusion reigning through the house, and resounding all around it, from the quantities of people stirring, boxes nailing, horses neighing, and dogs barking, was tremendous.

I must now tell you the party; Their Majesties; the Princesses Royal, Augusta, and Elizabeth; Lady Weymouth, Mr. Fairly, Colonel Gwynn, Miss Planta, and a person you have sometimes met. Pages for King, Queen, and Princesses, Wardrobe-women for ditto, and footmen for all. A smaller party for a royal excursion cannot well be imagined. How we shall all manage Heaven knows, Miss Planta and myself are allowed no maid; the house would not hold one . . . Their Majesties travelled wholly without guards or state; and I am convinced, from the time we advanced beyond Oxford, they were taken only for their own attendance . . . All the towns through which we passed were filled with people, as closely fastened one to another as they appear in the pit of the playhouse . . . Every town seemed all face; and all the way upon the road we rarely proceeded five miles without encountering a band of most horrid fiddlers, scraping 'God save the King' with all their might, out of tune, out of time, and all in the rain; for, most unfortunately, there were continual showers all the day.[14]

On arrival, she was greeted by the King, who had reached Cheltenham before them, and the Queen showed Fanny Burney her room: ' "*This*, ma'am!", cried I, as I entered it – "is *this* little room for your Majesty?" "O stay," cried she, laughing, "till you see your own before you call it little!" '

The King had high hopes that the visit would restore him to full health. The very day after his arrival, he wrote to his son Augustus in Hanover:

I am much recovered and doubt that the efficacy of the waters, which are not unlike those of Pyrmont, the salubrity of the air, the change of scene,

* Sir Nathaniel William Wraxall (1751–1831), author of historical memoirs of his own time and a Member of Parliament.

† Frances Burney (1752–1840), later Madame D'Arblay, novelist, second keeper of the Robes to Queen Charlotte (1786–91), who began her diary at the time of publication of *Evelina* in 1778.

privation of long conversations at St. James, and above all the exercise of riding and good mutton will do what may be at present wanting.[15]

Wraxall mentions that here for the first time since his grandfather's death the King found himself 'transformed in some degree from a sovereign into a country gentleman', and continues:

No minister or secretary of state attended him. During near eight-and-twenty years of a stormy and calamitous reign, marked with the greatest national disasters, though set off by some days of glory, he had scarcely seen any part of his dominions. The Nore, Coxe Heath, Portsmouth, and Oxford, formed almost the extent of his travels . . . He visited the spring at so early an hour, that few of his subjects were found there to meet him. Constantly on horseback, when the weather permitted, from eleven to three, he sat down at four to dinner; strolled out, like a citizen, with his wife and daughters, on the public walk soon after seven; and by eleven at night, everything was as completely hushed at Bays Hill Lodge as in a farm-house. The king was not even accompanied on this excursion by any of his usual attendants; neither by a lord of the bedchamber, nor by an equerry . . . He delighted to emancipate himself from all restraint, to walk out alone in the fields, and to enter into conversation with persons who accidentally fell in his way.[16]

Once he had settled in and experienced the effect of the waters, he reported back to his physician, writing, as he often did, in the third person:

Sir George Baker must not impute it to negligence that He has not yet heard from hence; but that all having arrived perfectly well and not in the least heated, it was necessary that the Water should be drank a few days previous to giving any Account of them.

The King took the Rhubarb Pills the Night He came and having omitted to bring a Saline Draught with Soluble Tartar, added a glass of the Cheltenham Water, these had no effect on Sunday; as no heat appeared He began the Waters on Monday Morning at Six . . . The Waters certainly agree they only give good Spirits and Appetite; the Diet has been regularly Mutton and Potatoes.[17]

Sir George responded with more advice:

The influence of St. Swithin in the weather is now interrupted, and in consequence your Majesty will be more at liberty to extend your airings and persue your favourite system of exercise. On this occasion may I be allowed to give your Majesty a caution ? During the use of Cheltenham-water (which in part is chalybeate) strong exercise ought to be avoided, for whatever brings fatigue will at the same time heat the constitution, so that the water will become rather injurious than salutary.[18]

In reply, he received a further progress report from his patient:

The King cannot sufficiently express the benefit he finds from this Salutary Spring, He has never been in the least heated, He finds a Pint and half the proper quantity to give him two openings, these only clear him without any sinking on the contrary He finds himself in better Spirits and has never been obliged to take the Rhubarb Pills.[18]

In the meantime the newspapers were full of every detail of the royal visit – the excursions made by the royal party, the visits they paid and the sights they saw.[19] 'There is nothing, however minute and unimportant it may be, which his Majesty does at Cheltenham, but what the newspapers report to us daily, so that we know now more how he passes his time than if he were living at Buckingham-house. He eats cherries, it is found out, like other men, but walks further than most.'[20]

In order to keep the servants happy and fit, the King sent to London for cricket 'batts and balls, lest, having little to do, they should sicken for lack of exercise'.[21] On 24 July the royal party paid one of several calls on Sir George O. Paul, High Sheriff of Gloucestershire, who later played an important part in improving the lot of the insane, as he had done that of the convicted. In his company they visited Gloucester Infirmary 'and the gaol now building agreeable to a plan of Sir George Paul and Mr. Howard'.[21] The old County Gaol, Gloucester Castle, 'is taken down,' wrote the great John Howard,* reformer of prisons and hospitals, 'and a new one, with a house of correction is now building near the river, under the inspection of Sir *Onesiphorus Paul*, who has bestowed the most zealous and unremitting attention on this object; and will render it a lasting monument of his skill and humanity.' And he added in a footnote that the Act of Parliament for building and regulating it which had received the royal assent in 1785 and had been drawn up by Sir George '*well* deserves to be consulted by gentlemen who have any intention of building a small *county gaol* or *prison*'.[22]

'Next they carried us to the Jail,' as yet unfinished, recounted an unenthusiastic Fanny Burney,

to show in how small a space, I suppose, human beings can live, as well as die or be dead. This jail is admirably constructed for its proper purposes – confinement and punishment. Every culprit is to have a separate cell; every cell is clean, neat, and small, looking upwards to a wide expanse of country, and, far more fitted to his speculation, a wide expanse of the heavens. Air, cleanliness, and health seem all considered, but no other indulgence.

She was happier seeing over the Infirmary, 'for the sick and the destitute awaken an interest far less painful than the wicked and contemned'.[23]

On one of his rides the King observed on the outskirts of Cheltenham 'a neat-built timber-house' and 'being streightened for room at the lodge [in fact he was the only man sleeping at Bays Hill], and expecting a visit from the Duke of York [his favourite son], he conceived an idea that the build-

---

* 'Howard wants no statue,' said George III after a private interview with him. 'His virtues will live when every statue has crumbled into dust.'

ing, compleat as it was, might in a few days be easily removed, and placed on an elevated spot, at no great distance from the royal residence.'[19] By this means he hoped to 'accomodate his son immediately next to himself' at 'Falconberg Hall', as Fanny Burney rather snobbishly insisted on calling the little lodge.[24] 'On this romantic prospect, as it was then termed, getting air, it was treated ludicrously,' wrote the *Gentleman's Magazine*'s correspondent who followed the royal party to Cheltenham. He little realized that what was being witnessed was the erection of perhaps the first authentic 'pre-fab'. The King, who was 'no stranger to the mechanical powers', engaged a local surveyor, and with a task force of some twenty men the incredible was accomplished within five days, to everyone's admiration.

George III showed his practical bent in another way. Lord Fauconberg had thoughtfully installed a pump on the well in his own grounds.[25] But no water could be drawn from it. He therefore had another well sunk a short distance away and from it came 'the same mineral water as at the Well. Mr Clarke . . . has annalised the water, and produced salt as good as the former,' the King wrote to his host, 'it is now enclosing under the direction of that gentleman, and a padlock is to be put on it and the key kept by him till he shall receive directions from Lord Fauconberg on the subject.'[26] It became known as the King's Well and was opened to the public after 'some necessary accomodations' had been installed.[27]

Mr Clarke, surgeon and apothecary of Cheltenham,[28] was called to the members of the royal family who caught the influenza then prevalent. Among those affected was Fanny Burney, who left an amusing account of her encounter with the local doctor which also exemplifies vividly what a medical 'examination' – or rather its absence – consisted of in those days.

Sunday, August 3rd. – This morning I was so violently oppressed by a cold, which turns out to be the influenza, it was with the utmost difficulty I could dress myself. I did indeed now want some assistant most wofully.

The Princess Royal has already been some days disturbed with this influenza. When the Queen perceived it in me she told his Majesty, who came into the room just as she was going to breakfast. Without making any answer, he himself went immediately to call Mr. Clerk, the apothecary, who was then with the Princess Royal.

'Now, Mr. Clerk,' cried he, 'here's another patient for you.' Mr. Clerk, a modest, sensible man, concluded, by the King himself having called him, that it was the Queen he had now to attend, and he stood bowing profoundly before her; but soon observing she did not notice him, he turned in some confusion to the Princess Augusta, who was now in the group.

'No, no! it's not me, Mr. Clerk, thank God!' cried the gay Princess Augusta.

Still more confused, the poor man advanced to Princess Elizabeth. 'No, no; it's not her!' cried the King.

I held back, having scarce power to open my eyes, from a vehement

c

head-ach, and not, indeed, wishing to go through my examination till there were fewer witnesses. But his Majesty now drew me out: 'Here, Mr. Clerk,' he cried, 'this is your new patient!' He then came bowing up to me, the King standing close by, and the rest pretty near.

'You – you are not well, ma'am?' he cried in the greatest embarrassment.

'No, sir, not quite,' I answered in ditto.

'O, Mr. Clerk will cure you!' cried the King.

'Are – are you feverish, ma'am?' 'Yes, sir, a little.'

'I – I will send you a saline draught, ma'am.' 'If you please.'

And then he bowed and decamped. Did you ever hear a more perfectly satisfactory examination? The poor modest man was overpowered by such Royal listeners and spectators, and I could not possibly relieve him, for I was little better myself.[29]

There were gala evenings for the royal visitors at the local playhouse, which was granted the style of The Theatre Royal. Mrs Jordan, the celebrated actress, was specially invited to perform.* On 1 August, for instance,

The entertainment, by desire of their Majesties, was 'The Sultan'; the part of Roxalana by Mrs. Jordan . . . On the entrance of the Royal Family, the loudest acclamations continued for the space of seven minutes . . . A passage (somewhat allusive) in Mrs. Jordan's part was highly relished – 'The land where Liberty smiles upon every brow, from the king to the peasant – where every citizen is a king, and the king is a citizen,' were received with reiterated bursts of applause.[19]

Never had the crown been so popular or the King so carefree.

He declared more than once, at moments when the heart speaks its undisguised sentiments, that the hours he had passed at Cheltenham and in other parts of the country unguarded, and in the midst of his people had more than repaid him for all the hours of solicitude he had experienced during his reign. His Majesty would not allow any soldiers to do duty or reside within ten miles of the Royal Spa. The band of Lord Harrington's regiment, only, were permitted to attend his Majesty.[30]

At Worcester he walked through the streets with only one attendant:

The crowd voluntarily opened an avenue for His Majesty, forming a phalanx on each side, to prevent any rude intruder, if there had been one, from breaking in upon the passage. The scene was affecting; and, when taken in a political point of view, forms an interesting epoch in the history of the country. After so many centuries had passed in repeated struggles for and against liberty, and for the several successions which had taken place to the throne; after the crown had been obliged to resort to the unconstitutional expedient of a standing army for its support – to behold the King of the country walking the streets as a private gentleman, with only two or three

* Two years later started Mrs Jordan's liaison with Prince William, later William IV, and George III was presented by them with ten grandchildren who took the name FitzClarence.

attendants, amid thousands and tens of thousands of his subjects, without a single guard or peace officer, happy in the love, and rejoicing in the liberty of his people, was an event such as the oldest man then living had never seen, and such as the youngest, but a few years before, scarcely ever expected to see.[30]

Stories of his free and unguarded manner and conversations with 'persons of all ranks' abounded. On one of his rides

he overtook a farmer with a drove of sheep. His Majesty rode with him a quarter of an hour, conversing upon the value and properties of the land, the prices of sheep and of cattle . . . the farmer grown familiar asked the gentleman, as he thought, if he had seen the King; and being answered in the affirmative, the farmer said 'Our neighbours say, he's a good sort of man, but dresses very plain.' 'Aye,' said His Majesty, 'as *plain* as you see me now'; and rode on.[19]

Naturally the King enjoyed his freedom and his popularity, as he wrote to Pitt:

I am this instant returned from seeing the most beautiful sight I ever beheld, namely, the clothing country near Stroud: above forty thousand people were assembled, and they all confess the trade is now brisker than the oldest person ever remembers.[31]

At the same time he felt considerable benefit from taking the waters regularly: to Fanny Burney he declared they 'were admirable friends to the constitution, by bringing disorders out of the habit'.[32] To Pitt he was more specific: 'The waters are more efficacious than I possibly could have expected, for while they remove byle in a very gentle manner they strengthen the stomach and are a general bracer to the constitution.'[33] No wonder his spirits were high and his mood affable. 'The King . . . has a flow of spirits at this time quite unequalled,' wrote Fanny Burney[34] of one occasion when he was indulging in banter with Mr Fairly, who had an attack of the gout and whom he teased with being 'only fanciful'.

On Sunday, 16 August, the party left Cheltenham early in the morning to return to Windsor. The whole town turned out in the High Street, 'the gentles on one side, and the commons on the other, and a band, and "God save the King", playing and singing,' wrote Fanny Burney. 'And thus ends the Cheltenham episode.'[35] On their return it was observed that 'His Majesty appeared to have benefited by the journey, but the Queen seemed somewhat fatigued. The Princesses were all in high health.'[19]

'The King would not do justice to his consciousness of the attention of Lord Fauconberg in having offered the use of his charming house on Bays Hill, Cheltenham, if he omitted the first opportunity on his return to Windsor to thank him for it, and to assure him that the waters have been most efficacious,' wrote the King in appreciation.[36] And the Queen to her son Augustus:

1. The royal visit to Cheltenham in July–August 1788 gave a boost to the town: 'All the fashions are completely Cheltenhamised,' said the papers. Simon Moreau, self-appointed Master of Ceremonies, had a commemorative medal struck, but unfortunately before it was ready the King fell seriously ill. On his recovery Moreau decided to make the same medal serve both occasions. This is why it bears two dates, 1788 and 1789. On the face is Hygeia, Goddess of Health, with her serpent and holding a patera to nourish it. On the pillar is a medallion of the King which contemporaries considered a striking likeness, encircled by a young oak, another emblem of longevity. It is inscribed 'to the most excellent Prince George'. On the reverse is Cheltenham Well, inscribed 'S. Moreau, arbiter elegantiarum – master of ceremonies, caused this die to be sunk 1788'. The medal was 'worked off on St. George's Day 1789 . . . and presented to their Majesties . . . in gold and silver, on Monday, April 27' (H. Ruff, The History of Cheltenham, 1803).

We are now returned from Cheltenham after a stay of very near five weeks, & never did schoolboys enjoy their holydays equal to what we have done our little excursion. The situation of the place is beautifull & the people good & kind. The King went there without any guards, which appears to have pleased them, for at various times have they thrown out that he was better guarded without troops walking among his subjects whose hearts were ready to defend him, & that the people in general looked upon it as a proof of the King's affection towards them . . . The crouds of people were immense, & to give you a small idea of it, at Rodbury the Magistrates computed the number of people for that day only to have been between fifty & sixty thousand people.[37]

In the ensuing weeks the King had the pleasure of hearing how his contributions to the various charities encountered during his Cheltenham visit were bearing fruit. At Gloucester he gave £50 to the Infirmary and a similar sum to the poor of that city. Also 'His Majesty . . . very humanely left £300 for the relief of the debtors,' in Gloucester Gaol, wrote John Howard.[22] The King was informed that the Bishop of Gloucester and Sir George Paul had examined in detail the affairs of everyone of the seventeen debtors out of a total of some sixty prisoners confined there, and owing to the royal bounty had been able to discharge three, with a further three ready to go.[38]

His health remained good, apart from an attack of pain in the face in the third week of September which lasted a few days and prevented sleep.[39] When in the following month he had a recurrence of the colic which originally caused him to visit Cheltenham, there was no suspicion of the grave turn his illness was about to take.

2

Crisis at Windsor

On Friday, 17 October 1788, at twenty-five past seven in the morning, George III sent his physician an urgent summons:

The King has had this night a spasmodic byleous attack though much slighter than in the month of June. He therefore wishes to see Sir George Baker as soon as convenient, and desires He will bring one of the Opium pills in case the pain should not have entirely subsided before Sir George can arrive; He has as yet taken nothing but a pint and half of warm water from thinking there was an inclination to vomit; this has had no effect, and the inclination proved nothing but wind in the stomach.[1]

Sir George recorded in his diary:

Early this morning I received the King's commands to attend him immediately at Kew House. I found his Majesty sitting up in his bed, his body being bent forward. He complained of a very acute pain in the pit of the stomach shooting to the back & sides, and making respiration difficult & uneasy. This pain continued all the day, though in a less degree of acuteness towards the evening; but it did not cease intirely until the bowels had been emptied. It was observable that, during the extreme severity of pain the pulse was only at sixty strokes in a minute, and that the pulse became quicker in proportion as the pain abated. At night it was at ninety.

His Majesty informed me, in the course of this day, that of late he had been much tormented in the night by a cramp in the muscles of his legs, and that he had suffered much from the rheumatism, which affected all his limbs, & made him lame, especially on his first going out in the morning. It was likewise mentioned, that he had had a rash; but the skin being examined, I found only some very slight marks shewing that there had been an eruption on it, which evidently had spent itself.[2]

He attributed the cause of the disorder to the fact that on the preceding day 'His Majesty rose early, as usual, walked on the grass several hours, and without having changed his stockings which were very wet, went to

St. James's; and that at night he eat four large pears for supper.' Sir George 'gave him physic', castor oil and senna, purgatives which were so much medical stock-in-trade that he did not even bother to record the fact. 'The effect of this being too much,' observed the Countess of Harcourt, Lady of the Bedchamber to Queen Charlotte, if anything aggravated his already 'most excruciating pain'. Baker therefore 'gave him laudanum [tincture of opium] to counteract it'. This however cancelled the effect of the previous medicine, the King's bowels were not moved, and 'It became necessary to repeat the physic; the laudanum, too, was again repeated and within 24 hours he took three doses of each.' He was 'very lame, and those about him hoped he was going to have the gout'.[3]

Fanny Burney noted: 'The King is not well; he has not been quite well some time, yet nothing I hope alarming ... Our return to Windsor is postponed till to-morrow.'[4] Princess Elizabeth told Lady Harcourt that a week before, on 12 October, the King had 'complained of a rash' which almost disappeared in a couple of days but for 'some remains of it upon his arms, which he shewed her later. She told me it looked very red, and in great weals, as if it had been scourged with cords.'[3]

The following day Sir George recorded 'a slight degree of fever; but he had passed the night quietly except when interrupted by the effect of his medicine'. The King complained of pain in his left foot and Baker also observed 'some yellowness in the eyes & urine bilious', that is dark. On Sunday, 19 October, 'the King is but very indifferent,' noted Fanny Burney. Both feet were now swollen and painful, but 'the yellowness of the eyes [had] disappeared & the urine [was] of natural colour'.[2]

To his Prime Minister the King wrote:

I had flattered myself to have been able to write my opinion fully to Mr. Pitt on the volumenous dispatches arrived from Berlin and the lights that may be drawn from others arrived from the north, but I must owne I have been so thoroughly fatigued by the medicines that continued active all yesterday that it has required several hours for my reading the papers.[5]

On Monday, 20 October, Fanny Burney recorded: 'The King was taken very ill in the night, and we have all been cruelly frightened; but it went off, and, and, thank Heaven! he is now better.'[6] 'Between the hours of one & two this morning His Majesty had a return of the pain in the pit of the stomach ... at eight o'clock, when I arrived,' Baker noted, 'he complained only of soreness of the whole belly whenever he attempted an erect posture. His pulse was this day at ninety.' That evening the King wrote to Pitt:

I have not been able to answer Mr. Pitt's letter sooner this day having had a very indifferent night but the Medicine which Sir George Baker found necessary to be taken to remove the spasms has now greatly relieved me, indeed I think myself nearer getting rid of my complaint that [than] since the attack; if I should have a good night I will write and desire Mr. Pitt to come here previous to the meeting of the Cabinet.[7]

Despite feeling 'considerably weakened by illness' he tried to comment on the dispatches Pitt had sent, but his concentration failed. He could not keep to the point and began to ramble, as he himself realized. His corrections and insertions and the unusual repetition of letters clearly show the great effort he made. His handwriting becomes heavier, larger and tremulous as the letter proceeds and shows that his mental difficulty was matched by physical weakness. 'I am affraid Mr. Pitt will perceive I am not quite in a situation to write at present,' he ended, 'but I thought it better even to write as loosely as I have here than to lett the box return without an answer to his letter.'

On Tuesday 'The good and excellent King is again better,' joyfully observed Fanny Burney.[6] He had 'had a return of the pain in the stomach; but it was slight, and ceased without the assistance of medicine,' noted Baker. The swelling of the feet had subsided and his pulse fallen to eighty. To Pitt the King wrote:

I cannot boast much to Mr. Pitt of my Night's rest, but since I have dressed myself and eat a very comfortable breakfast, I certainly trust it was the state of one not quite recovered, but certainly not still oppressed with illness; I therefore take up my pen to assure him I think myself fully able and shall with pleasure see him as early this day as he can come here; indeed the talking over the present complicated Scene will rather amuse me, and perhaps the thinking I meant to do if possible last night in a reduced state a little contributed to disturb me; the contributing towards saving the present State of Europe and Defensive Measures I thoroughly feel myself bound to, and the preserving the present peaceable and flourishing State of my Dominions but few objects I can think worthy of endangering. An invalid cannot keep London hours I hope therefore if possible that Mr. Pitt will be here by one.[8]

Mr Pitt came as requested and 'was with His Majesty several hours; & His Majesty complained of great fatigue afterwards,' wrote Baker.[2]

On Wednesday, 22 October, signs of developing delirium appeared. He had slept well, but his spirits were low, his bowels costive and his pulse fast. In the morning Baker ordered him another dose of 'a gentle purgative'. But

In the afternoon I was received by His Majesty in a very unusual manner, of which I had not the least expectation. The look of his eyes, the tone of his voice, every gesture and his whole deportment represented a person in a most furious passion of anger. 'One medicine had been too powerful; another had only teazed him without effect. The importation of Senna ought to be prohibited, and he would give orders that in future it shall never be given to any of the royal family.' With a frequent repetition of this and similar language he detained me three hours. His pulse was much quickened; but I did not number the strokes. Having had no opportunity of speaking to the Queen, I wrote a note to Mr. Pitt immediately on my return to London, and informed him that I had just left the King in an agitation of spirits nearly bordering on delirium. Mr. Pitt called on me that evening; and I had an opportunity of giving him a full description of his Majesty's condition.[2]

The onset of delirium showed that the underlying illness, whatever it was, was more serious than Baker had allowed for, and Pitt informed senior ministers of it. Mr W. W. Grenville wrote to his brother the Marquis of Buckingham, Lord Lieutenant of Ireland, a letter marked 'Most Secret', dated Whitehall, 22 October. He spoke of a 'no small degree of uneasiness' which was felt at the King's illness. It had

begun with a violent spasmodic attack in his stomach; and has continued with more or less violence, and with different symptoms ever since. We put as good a face as we can upon it; and, indeed, I hope the danger is now over, but I cannot but own to you that I think there is still ground for a good deal of alarm. He brought on this particular attack by the great imprudence of remaining a whole day in wet stockings; but, on the whole, I am afraid that his health is evidently much worse than it has been, and that there is some lurking disorder in his constitution . . . part of the King's disorder is an agitation and flurry of spirits, which hardly gives him any rest. I need not mention to you, that I should not allow myself to say all this, but in the strictest confidence, and that, independently of the King's great dislike of its being known that he is ill, we have the strongest reasons of policy, both foreign and domestic, in the present moment particularly, to wish that idea not to prevail.[9]

The next morning, Thursday, 23 October, 'His Majesty' relieved Sir George 'from great uneasiness. He had passed the night quiet; and I found him calm, composed, and free from fever.' His family, however, remained alarmed by the events of the preceding day and Princess Augusta Sophia was deputed to write to Baker in confidence:

I am ordered by Mama to desire if You find it necessary to prevent the Kings going to Town to morrow, that You would advise His Majesty to remain at Kew till he is better [that is, not to return to Windsor]. T'is not her partiality for this place that makes her wish for it, but Your being nearer to us in case any thing should happen again that We might have Your advice immediately. Mama desires You would express it *not* as hers, but as a wish of Your own.[10]

But the King was not to be diverted from his purpose. 'He had not slept well,' recorded Sir George on Friday, 24 October, 'He seemed languid, and uneasy at the thoughts of going to the levée. He went however contrary to my opinion & advice. He was weak, & somewhat lame.'

His appearance in public was greeted with relief, as he hoped it would be. 'His Majesty was so well recovered of his late indisposition,' reported the *Gentleman's Magazine*, 'as to be able to show himself at the levée, with his legs wrapped in flannel. His Majesty's disorder originated from a cold . . . This produced a rheumatic pain in his stomach, which two or three glasses of Madeira wine threw into his extremities.'[11] But the effort proved too much for him, as Grenville told his brother:

His appearance at the levée on Friday was an effort beyond his strength, but made with a view of putting an end to the stories [that he was seriously ill] that were circulated with much industry. He has, however, considerably weakened himself by it, and his physician now declares that rest, and an absolute cessation from all business, are of indispensable necessity to him.[12]

The same day the Duke of York told his brother:

I am exceedingly happy to have the pleasure of acquainting you that I saw the King this morning and that I think him getting well very fast. Dr. Baker has confessed to him that this was no return of the spasms which he had in the beginning of the summer, but a rheumatick attack in his stomach owing to his having remained the whole day with feet wet, and that with a common degree of precaution he will not be liable to it again.[13]

To the public it was given out that he had 'a regular fit of the gout'[11] from which he was recovering. On Saturday, 25 October, Fanny Burney observed that the King 'was so much better that our Windsor journey at length took place, with permission of Sir George Baker, the only physician His Majesty will admit'.[14] To assuage the anxiety Pitt had shown for him at the levée, before leaving Kew the King wrote:

Mr. Pitt really seemed distressed at seeing my bodily stiffness yesterday which I alone exhibited to stop further lies and any fall of the Stocks; for this kindness I shall desire Sir George Baker (who is to call here previous to my setting out for Windsor this morning) on his return to Town to call in Downing Street that if Mr. Pitt is at leisure he may know exactly how Sir George found Me. I am certainly weak and stiff but no wonder, I am certain air and relaxation are the quickest restoratives . . . Mr. Pitt is desired by me to acknowledge the receipt of this, and to prevent all Political Papers being sent to Me till I meet him on Wednesday at St. James's.[15]

In the evening at Windsor Fanny Burney ran into him:

He spoke, with a manner so uncommon, that a high fever alone could account for it; a rapidity, a hoarseness of voice, a volubility, an earnestness – a vehemence, rather – it startled me inexpressibly . . . The Queen grows more and more uneasy. She alarms me sometimes for herself, at other times she has a sedateness that wonders me still more.[14]

Sir George Baker saw the King before he left Kew:

He had slept well, breakfasted with a good appetite, but complained of weakness. His pulse very quiet. I now received his Majesty's commands not to attend him at Windsor until I should be called. I am informed that he was much agitated when he first saw the Princesses on his arrival at Windsor; but that afterwards he persued his usual habits, visited his horses, dined with the royal family, and afterwards attended the concert in the evening.[2]

On the following day, Sunday, 26 October, Sir George learnt only 'that his spirits were uncommonly agitated, and that he talked with more than usual rapidity & vehemence.' Fanny Burney described another encounter in which the King

conversed upon his health near half-an-hour, still with that extreme quickness of speech and manner that belongs to fever; and he hardly sleeps, he tells me, one minute all night; indeed, if he recovers not his rest, a most delirious fever seems to threaten him. He is all agitation, all emotion, yet all benevolence and goodness, even to a degree that makes it touching to hear him speak. He assures everybody of his health; he seems only fearful to give uneasiness to others, yet certainly he is better than last night.[16]

The next day, Monday, 27 October, Sir George was summoned by the Queen to Windsor:

This morning he took an airing in the chaise. His great hurry of spirits, and incessant loquaciousness continuing gave great uneasiness to the Queen; and Her Majesty sent me a private order to go to Windsor this evening; to say nothing to the King on the subject of physic, but to inform Col. Goldsworthy [his equerry] of my opinion. When I arrived the King was at the concert. He at first seemed much disconcerted at my attending him without his orders, but was very soon satisfied, having himself conjectured that I had acted under the Queen's direction. During the whole music he talked continually, making frequent & sudden transitions from one subject to another; but I observed no incoherence in what he said, nor any mark of false perception . . . His sleep and appetite had been natural. His pulse in a room much heated with company, fires and candles was only at 84. He was lame; complained of rheumatic pain, & weakness in the knees, & was continually sitting & rising.[2]

The next day Sir George learnt that the King 'had slept quietly. His pulse at 72. The agitation of his spirits, & inordinate flow of words continued nearly as yesterday; and it was not without some difficulty that I could prevail on him not to go to the levée the next day, but to be contented with seeing the Ministers at Windsor.'

On Wednesday, 29 October, 'The dear and good King again gains ground, and the Queen becomes easier,'[16] observed Fanny Burney; and the Duke of York, who again visited his father that day, wrote to the Prince of Wales:

I found him with respect to his rheumatic complaint certainly better, though still very weak, but it appears now as if everything has thrown itself upon his nerves, which has given him a very violent degree of agitation which nothing but rest and quiet will remove. I cannot help adding that he spoke with tears in his eyes and with the greatest affection concerning you and said how happy you had made him by coming to see him.[17]

That evening Sir George Baker saw him:

It was reported to me, that he slept well the preceding night, that he had taken an airing in the morning, that he had received Mr. Pitt, and that he had eaten his breakfast & dinner with good appetite. My medical advice had not been followed. I found His Majesty at his concert, not seeming to attend the music, but talking incessantly. His pulse was 84. He now complained, that [he] was of late become near-sighted; that his vision was confused, and that whenever he attempted to read a mist floated before his eyes, & intercepted the objects. He likewise mentioned to me, as a cause of great distress, that having in the morning selected a certain prayer, he has found himself repeating a prayer which he had not proposed to make use of.[2]

Not only were his memory and eye-sight affected, but also his hearing. From this time dates the story of the King after one of his private concerts going up to Dr Edmund Ayrton, Master of the Children of the Royal Chapel, 'and, laying his hand on the doctor's shoulder, with his usual benignity – "I fear, Sir," said His Majesty, "I shall not be able long to hear music: it seems to affect my head; and it is with some difficulty I hear it." '[18]

The King's continued illness now became a talking point, the more so because no one knew what was the matter with him. 'The King is certainly in a bad state of health, but I fancy nothing material,' wrote Sir Gilbert Elliot, who was a supporter of the Prince of Wales during the Regency Crisis and later first Earl of Minto and Governor-General of India, to his wife on 27 October. 'They make a great mystery about it, so that nobody knows much of the truth; but the best opinion seems to be that it is an unformed gout.'[19] 'Unformed gout' to Elliot meant aches and pains in different parts of the body, with digestive disturbances and marked malaise. He, like others, could not believe that the source of the mystery was that the King's doctor himself was mystified. But even now, in the third week of the illness, there was not a suspicion of the legend which history made of that period. What that fiery Opposition spokesman Edmund Burke, who would have made capital out of it had he but the slightest suspicion that the King was deranged, told Elliot on 28 October, when the first wave of physical symptoms was subsiding, demonstrates this clearly:

Burke told me yesterday that the King had been in extreme danger during his late illness; that he had been seized with violent spasms in his stomach, which were so serious and so severe as to render him speechless for an hour and a half; that the immediate cause of that attack appeared to be a cold, but that in fact he was in a bad state of health before, and that the cold produced this effect because it met with a disordered constitution. The severity of this attack did not last long, but he is still ill. The spasms have affected him downwards in his limbs and feet, which has given occasion to the report of the complaint being gout, which he told me was not the case. Burke had never heard distinctly what the complaint was for which he had gone to Cheltenham, a great deal of mystery and secrecy having been observed on the subject of this illness, which of itself shows it to have been somewhat serious, though it has concealed the particular nature of the disorder. I do not know what Mr. Burke's authority is for this account, but he considered it as authentic.[19]

It is a touching fact that the King realized earlier than those around him that he was losing control over his body and his mind. He knew it from the 'degree of bodily agitation' he felt. He himself said: 'They would make me believe I have the gout, but if it was gout, how could I kick the part without any pain?' and demonstrated that the pain was of a different kind by 'kicking one heel against the other foot'.[20] He was also painfully aware of 'a desire of talking he was scarcely able to control' and when the following week

his physicians told him of it, it increased the irritation, and hurt him essentially; at times he would desire those about him to check him, and propose that some one should read aloud to keep him quiet, but these means seldom obtained the desired effect.[21]

To the Queen it appeared in retrospect that he felt iller than even his doctor allowed him to be, for when she tried to cheer him by saying 'everybody ought to endeavour to bear up under afflictions' he had put his arm round her waist and replied, 'Then you are prepared for worst.'[22]

The next two days' developments are recorded by Baker:

Thursday 30 October. He had slept quietly, and his pulse in the morning was at 76. He had slightly mentioned that he had been giddy, & that he had a sensation in the back of the head, which he would not allow to be pain [a throbbing, he called it to his son[23]]. During the operation of cupping he talked continually; and his whole behaviour at this time was observed to be childish & trifling in the extreme. He afterwards went out on horseback, then dined with a good appetite. In the evening, at the concert, I found his pulse much quickened; but I had no opportunity of numbering the strokes.

Friday 31 October. He had slept, as he told me, all the night like a Child, but, as I was informed afterwards, his sleep though continual had been unquiet. This morning his pulse was at 76. The same agitation of spirits continued without abatement. He again rode out, & spent the remainder of the day as usual. His appetite had been very good at dinner. His pulse at night was quicker; and his eagerness in talking could not escape the observation of any one present at the concert.[2]

On Saturday, 1 November, Sir George was informed that the King had 'slept in the same disturbed manner as in the preceding night'. That evening 'his spirits were greatly agitated. He talked much and with great eagerness & anxiety on things respecting his health not of the smallest importance in themselves. The pulse at 88.' But Baker was by now right out of his depth. He still gave no serious thought to what was really the matter with his patient; he still only counted the pulse – and not always that. He did not even look at the tongue or inspect the excreta again. For this reason the observations of a layman in close proximity to the King, like Fanny Burney, become at this stage paradoxically more informative than those of the royal physician. The King was now chiefly troubled by painful weakness of his arms and legs, hoarseness, inability to focus his vision, difficulty in concentrating, mounting excitement and confusion most marked in the evening and at night and sleeplessness. On 1 November she recorded:

Our King does not advance in amendment; he grows so weak that he walks like a gouty man, yet has such spirits that he has talked away his voice, and is so hoarse it is painful to hear him. The Queen is evidently in great uneasiness. God send him better! . . . The King is very sensible of the great change there is in himself, and of her disturbance at it. It seems, but Heaven, avert it! a threat of a total breaking up of the constitution. This, too, seems his own idea. I was present at his first seeing Lady Effingham on his return to Windsor this last time. 'My dear Effy,' he cried, 'you see me, all at once, an old man' . . . He then produced a walking-stick which he had just ordered. 'He could not', he said, 'get on without it; his strength seemed diminishing hourly' . . . How the Queen commanded herself I cannot conceive; but there was something so touching in this speech, from the hoarse voice and altered countenance, that it overset me very much.[24]

Characteristic of a delirium was his deterioration in the evening, when he became voluble and repetitive in his talk. To the Queen he repeated 'At least a hundred times' that she might not 'speak to him when he got to his room, that he might fall asleep as he felt great want of that refreshment . . . though, far enough from needing it, the poor Queen never uttered one syllable!' His nights were disturbed and sleepless. To Fanny Burney he said he was well 'except in that one particular, that he could not sleep', and 'there was a hurry in his manner and voice that indicated sleep to be indeed wanted. Nor could I, all night, forbear foreseeing "He sleeps now, or to-morrow he will surely be delirious!" '[24]

On Sunday, 2 November, Fanny Burney thought he was better. In the evening he talked to Sir George Baker 'on various subjects . . . in a very desultory manner; but afterwards conversed with [General] Sir W. Fawcett on military arrangements with great acuteness & precision.' During the night the pages heard him talking 'in a very incoherent manner'[2] and the next day everyone at Windsor was most uneasy:

The King is better and worse so frequently, and changes so, daily, back-wards and forwards, that everything is to be apprehended, if his nerves are not some way quieted. I dreadfully fear he is on the eve of some severe fever. The Queen is almost overpowered with some secret terror. I am affected beyond all expression in her presence, to see what struggles she makes to support serenity. Today she gave up the conflict when I was alone with her, and burst into a violent fit of tears . . . To-night, indeed, at tea-time, I felt a great shock, in hearing . . . that Dr. Heberden had been called in. It is true more assistance seemed much wanting, yet the King's rooted aversion to physicians makes any new-comer tremendous. They said, too, it was merely for counsel, not that his Majesty was worse.[24]

The King 'at last consented to my calling further assistance', wrote Baker in his diary on 3 November, 'which I had in the course of the last week often in vain solicited'. That evening at nine o'clock

I waited on His Majesty with Dr. Heberden. The report to us was that His Majesty had been in the morning on horseback, but that he had given great pain to His Attendants by his very incautious manner of riding. It was now too evident that his mind was greatly disturbed. All the marks of it, before mentioned, appeared with aggravation. The pulse was 84.

Dr William Heberden senior, then aged seventy-eight and some twelve years older than Baker, was living in retirement near the castle at Windsor. Doyen of English physicians, author of an important textbook on medicine,[25] he had in 1761 declined the King's offer of the post of physician to Queen Charlotte on account of his great business in practice.[26] It was to him that Baker owed his position at court.[27] He saw the King only a few times, and left no record of his impressions.

The public now learnt that the King was 'dropsical', that the disease was a complicated one and that he was recovering but his strength was return-ing rather slowly; the levées for Wednesday and Friday were therefore cancelled.[28]

On this day, 3 November, the King wrote to his Prime Minister:

The King thinks it must give Mr. Pitt pleasure to receive a line from him. This will convince him the King can sign warrants without inconvenience: therefore he desires any that are ready may be sent, and he has no objection to receive any large number, for he shall order the messenger to return to town and shall sign them at leisure. He attempts reading the despatches daily, but as yet without success; but he eats well, sleeps well, and is not in the least now fatigued with riding, though he cannot yet stand long, and is fatigued if he walks. Having gained so much, the rest will soon follow. Mr. Pitt is desired to be at Kew at two or three o'clock, whichever suits him best.[29]

It was the King's last letter to his Prime Minister for almost four months.

By the time he was in a position to write again, on 23 February 1789, he had been on the brink of death and passed through many weeks of oblivion and alienation, and the country had suffered the agonies of the Regency Crisis.

On Tuesday, 4 November, his 'conversation' with Baker was 'very unconnected & desultory. He complained . . . of a giddiness, & of confused vision. It appeared likewise that he had not always the power of distinguishing colours.'² But Baker remained sanguine when he saw the Duke of Gloucester, George III's youngest and favourite brother. 'I am much better satisfyed than I expected with his account,' wrote the Duke to the Prince of Wales. Baker 'says at present there is no danger . . . He was cupped again this morning; afterwards, he went out as usual, riding.'³⁰

'The great subject of inquiry and speculation at present is the King's health,' Sir Gilbert Elliot told his wife, 'and he is certainly very ill, though perhaps not in immediate danger of his life.'³¹ He had heard that on the night of 16 October when the illness started, the King

was unwell all the evening, and went to bed at his usual hour. About one in the morning he was seized violently with a cramp or some other violent thing in the stomach, which rendered him speechless, and in a word was *all but*. The Queen ran out in great alarm, in her *shift*, or with very little clothes, among the pages, who, seeing her in that situation, were at first retiring out of respect, but the Queen stopped them and sent them instantly for the apothecary at Richmond, who arrived in about forty minutes, during which time the King had continued in the fit and speechless. The apothecary tried to make him swallow something strong, but the King, who appeared not to have lost his senses, still liked a bit of his own way, and rejected by signs everything of that sort. They contrived, however, to cheat him, and got some cordial down in the shape of medicine, and the fit went off. He has been ill ever since, although he has been out and at Court.

The next morning, Wednesday, 5 November, he had had 'some quiet sleep' and in the morning Baker found him 'more composed. His appetite was perfectly good at breakfast; and he conversed with his family cheerfully, and with very little inconsistence.' The Queen was that morning 'greatly offended by some anecdote in a newspaper . . . relative to the King's indisposition,' which revealed that he had been delirious.³² 'O dreadful day!' exclaimed Fanny Burney. At midday she watched the King set out for an airing in his chaise – he was no longer judged capable of riding a horse:

I looked from my window to see him; he was all smiling benignity, but gave so many orders to the postillions, and got in and out of the carriage twice, with such agitation, that again my fear of a great fever hanging over him grew more and more powerful. Alas! how little did I imagine I should see him no more for so long – so black a period!

That evening 'a stillness the most uncommon reigned over the whole house. Nobody stirred; not a voice was heard; not a step, not a motion.' Music was now forbidden, and the regular evening concerts were cancelled and not heard again until the following spring. 'All seemed stranger and stranger.' Fanny Burney was given the reason later in the evening:

O my dear friends, what a history! The King, at dinner, had broken forth into positive delirium, which has long been menacing all who saw him most closely; and the Queen was so overpowered as to fall into violent hysterics. All the Princesses were in misery, and the Prince of Wales had burst into tears. No one knew what was to follow – no one could conjecture the event.

Afterwards, in contrast to what he had seen in the morning and to his great consternation, Sir George found the King 'under an intire alienation of mind, and much more agitated than he had ever been. The pulse was very quick; but he never was so quiet as to allow me to number the strokes.' Lady Harcourt confided to her diary:

Every alarming symptom seemed increased; the bodily agitation was extreme, and the talking incessant, indeed it was too evident that his Majesty had no longer the least command over himself. His eyes, the Queen has since told me, she could compare to nothing but black currant jelly, the veins in his face were swelled, the sound of his voice was dreadful; he often spoke till he was exhausted . . . while the foam ran out of his mouth.[33]

On the pretence of the Queen not being well, the King was persuaded to sleep in the second dressing-room, adjoining her bedroom. 'He would not be further removed.' Fanny Burney learnt next morning that Colonel Goldsworthy and Mr Battiscombe, the royal apothecary, had sat up all night. Yet

The King, in the middle of the night, had insisted upon seeing if his Queen was not removed from the house; and he had come into her room, with a candle in his hand, opened the bed-curtains, and satisfied himself she was there, and Miss Goldsworthy by her side. This observance of his directions had much soothed him; but he stayed a full half hour, and the depth of terror during that time no words can paint. The fear of such another entrance was now so strongly upon the nerves of the poor Queen, that she could hardly support herself.[34]

Sir George entered in his diary on Thursday, 6 November: 'The delirium had continued through the night without sleep. The pulse this morning was at least 120; but after bleeding it fell to 100.' When Fanny Burney went to the Queen, he and Heberden were still with the patient and she could hear him next door 'talking unceasingly', his voice hoarse, weak and almost inarticulate. But to her astonishment there was no fury in it, 'its tone was still all benevolence – all kindness – all touching graciousness'. She heard him say

D

'I am nervous . . . I am not ill, but I am nervous: if you would know what is the matter with me, I am nervous. But I love you both very well; if you would tell me truth: I love Dr. Heberden best, for he has not told me a lie: Sir George has told me a lie – a white lie, he says, but I hate a white lie! If you will tell me a lie, let it be a black lie!'[34]

In the meantime Dr Richard Warren* had arrived. He 'had been sent for express, in the middle of the night, at the desire of Sir George Baker, because he had been taken ill himself, and felt unequal to the whole toil.'[34] The order had come from the Prince of Wales 'unknown to the Queen, who would never have consented to the calling in a physician to whom the King had a particular objection,' wrote Lady Harcourt:

From this fatal step many of the evils that followed resulted; and I have ever been of opinion that Sir George Baker's natural timidity, increased by the danger he saw coming on, made him act as he did, that some other of the faculty might be sent for to share with him the responsibility of the situation. Warren was a man of very different character; he was at that time considered, at least by the fashionable world, as being at the head of his profession . . . he was constantly received in the houses of the Dukes of Devonshire and Portland, as well as in Lord Fitzwilliam's, Lord Spencer's, Mr. Fox's, and many others of the leading men in opposition. Through their protection he became known to the Prince of Wales . . . His being sent for to Windsor gave dissatisfaction to many of the King's most attached friends, and his Majesty said to him, the first time he went into his room, 'You may come here as an acquaintance but not as *my* physician; no man can serve two masters; you are the Prince of Wales's physician, you cannot be mine.' Similar marks of dislike were shewn him by the King throughout the whole course of his illness.[35]

Unlike the patient, Warren's colleagues welcomed him with open arms. He was 'grievously awaited, for Dr. Heberden and Sir George would now decide upon nothing till Dr. Warren came,' wrote Fanny Burney:

With what cruel impatience did we then wait to hear his sentence! An impatience how fruitless! It ended in information that he had not seen the King, who refused him admittance. This was terrible . . . Dr. Warren was then planted where he could hear his voice, and all that passed, and receive intelligence concerning his pulse, &c., from Sir George.[36]

The Queen 'expected every moment Dr. Warren would bring her Majesty his opinion; but he neither came nor sent. She waited in dread incessant. She sent for Sir George – he would not speak alone: she sent for Mr. Hawkins, the household surgeon; but all referred to Dr. Warren.'

* Richard Warren (1731–97), physician to the King (1763) and to the Prince of Wales (1787), the most sought-after society doctor of his time. It was said of him that when he looked at his own tongue in the morning he automatically transferred a guinea piece from one pocket to the other.

A lady-in-waiting was dispatched after him, but 'Dr. Warren was gone'. He had left his vantage point outside the royal bedchamber, slipped from the Queen's house and gone directly 'over to the castle, to the Prince of Wales' – first rumblings of the Regency Crisis. To him 'he immediately announced the King's life to be in the utmost danger, and declared that the seizure upon the brain was so violent, that, if he did live, there was little reason to hope that his intellects would be restored'.[35]

For the Queen, wrote Fanny Burney, 'I think a deeper blow I have never witnessed. Already to become but second, even for the King! The tears were now wiped; indignation arose, with pain, the severest pain, of every species.' And the Queen never forgave Warren. Shortly afterwards Colonel Goldsworthy came to inform her that it was 'the opinion of all the physicians in consultation, "That her Majesty would remove to a more distant apartment, since the King would undoubtedly be worse from the agitation of seeing her, and there could be no possibility to prevent it while she remained so near." '[36] Five months were to pass before they were allowed to share a bed again.

Backed by the consultation, Baker reported officially to Pitt that the King was now frankly delirious even by day:

Sir George Baker presents his compliments to Mr. Pitt. He is very sorry to inform Mr. Pitt that the King's delirium has continued through the whole day. There seems to be no prospect at present of a change either for the better or worse. H.M. is now rather in a quiet state.[37]

And Pitt wrote posthaste to the Lord Privy Seal:

I write from Lord Carmarthen's, having just had an account from Windsor, by which I learn that the King's disorder, which has for some days given us much uneasiness, has within a few hours taken so serious a turn that I think myself obliged to lose no time in apprising your Lordship of it.

The accounts are sent under considerable alarm, and therefore do not state the symptoms very precisely; but from what I learn, there is too much reason to fear that they proceed from a fever which has settled on the brain, and which may produce immediate danger to His Majesty's life . . . I thought no time should be lost in letting you know the situation.[38]

On Friday, 7 November, Baker made the last entry in his diary: 'Pulse 86. The same alienation of mind.' His period of sole responsibility for the King was over and he closed his book. It seems that he did not keep it day by day but wrote it to jog his memory when at the end of November he was warned by a friend of his forthcoming examination by the Privy Council. Its great value lies in the fact that it documents the vital evidence of the beginning of the royal malady, although one could have wished for more clinical observations.

For what really happened behind the scenes on this black Friday one must again consult Fanny Burney's diary:

While I was yet with my poor Royal sufferer this morning the Prince of Wales came hastily into the room. He apologised for his intrusion, and then gave a very energetic history of the preceding night. It had been indeed most affectingly dreadful! The King had risen in the middle of the night, and would take no denial to walking into the next room. There he saw the large congress I have mentioned [the Princes of the Blood, the physicians, equerries and pages]: amazed and in consternation, he demanded what they did there? Much followed that I have heard since, particularly the warmest elogé on his dear son Frederick, his favourite, his friend. 'Yes,' he cried, 'Frederick is my friend!' – and his son was then present amongst the rest, but not seen!

Sir George Baker was there, and was privately exhorted by the gentlemen to lead the King back to his room; but he had not courage: he attempted only to speak, and the King penned him in a corner, told him he was a mere old woman – that he wondered he had ever followed his advice, for he knew nothing of his complaint, which was only nervous!

The Prince of Wales, by signs and whispers, would have urged others to have drawn him away, but no one dared approach him, and he remained there a considerable time, 'Nor do I know when he would have been got back', continued the Prince, 'if at last Mr. Fairly had not undertaken him . . . He came boldly up to him, and took him by the arm . . . and said he must go . . . "your Majesty has been very good to me often, and now I am going to be very good to you, for you must come to bed, sir: it is necessary to your life" . . . and they got him to bed.'[39]

On this painful scene, Earl Stanhope commented:

Here, then, was the turning point. This was the precise moment when ceased the dominion of a Sovereign over his subjects, and when began, on the contrary, the dominion of sound minds over an unsound one. Here, then, let History pause.[40]

On the same day, Friday, 7 November, Mr Grenville wrote to his brother:

The King has now been two days entirely delirious, and during part of the time has been thought to be in the most imminent danger. It now appears that Warren, Heberden and Sir G. Baker, who are the three physicians who attend him, profess themselves unable to decide whether the disorder is or is not of such a nature as may soon produce a crisis which may lead either to health or death. The other alternative is one to which one cannot look without horror – that of a continuance of the present derangement of his faculties . . . I believe the general idea of his danger is now very prevalent; but we endeavour (I know not with what success) to keep these particulars as much as we can from the public.[41]

Later the same day he wrote again and his news was even worse:

I am afraid that it would be very sanguine indeed to say that there is even *any* hope that the King will recover both his health and his understanding,

though the physicians do not say that it is absolutely impossible for his disorder to have a crisis which may produce such an effect. His disease is now
almost entirely confined to his brain . . . It is apprehended that this is the
effect either of water on the brain, or of an ossification of the membrane . . .
If his indisposition of mind continues, without some more material bodily
illness, he may live years in this melancholy state; and this, of all events
that can happen, is perhaps the most to be feared. He was, however, thought
yesterday to be in imminent danger of death. Should this not happen, but
the other, it seems generally agreed that the Prince of Wales must be
appointed Regent, with kingly power.[41]

With this political prize in view Mr John Crawford, a staunch Whig,
wrote to the Duchess of Devonshire: 'I can give you no just account of the
King's disorder . . . he is certainly very ill and dangerously ill . . . The
humour to which his whole family is subject has fallen upon the brain.'[42]
Because the King's condition deteriorated so rapidly and they thought he
was about to die, another physician, Dr Henry Revell Reynolds, was hastily
summoned, the third in as many days.[43]

On 8 November Sir George Baker sent the following evening report to
Pitt:

> The dose of James's powder which the King had taken before Mr. Pitt
> left Windsor produced a gentle perspiration but no diminution of the
> delirium; a second dose taken six hours after the first, is now operating in
> the same manner but with as little effect upon the delirium.[37]

James's powder was the standard febrifuge of the day, the aspirin of the
eighteenth century and the patent of Dr Robert James, friend of Samuel
Johnson. A week or two earlier Baker had given the King a course of the
'bark' (quinine) with equally little effect.[24]

Grenville learnt 'from a variety of different reports that the King's fever
was considerably increased afterwards, and that between two and four this
morning he was in the utmost danger'. And he foresaw correctly that

> In the event which Sir George Baker's note gives reason to apprehend,
> there will be the greatest embarrassment as to the mode in which it is possible
> to proceed to any appointment of a Regent. The Parliament is now prorogued
> only till 23rd instant [correctly 20th], and must meet at that time, because
> no person but the King has authority to prorogue it further . . . Parliament
> cannot proceed to business without the session being opened by the King,
> or by some Commission authorized by him. No Regent can be appointed
> or authorized to exercise acts of royal authority but by Act of Parliament;
> nor can any such Act be valid and binding in law without the King's consent
> . . . It is a heavy calamity that is inflicted upon us in any case except that
> of his perfect recovery; but in the event which there seems most ground to
> fear, it may give rise to serious and difficult questions, such as cannot even
> be discussed without shaking the security and tranquillity of the country.[44]

That day the Prince of Wales had a conference with Pitt at Windsor and the following is Pitt's memorandum of the conversation:

Began his conversation by saying that he had sent to me in consequence of the present distressing situation of the King. The Prince of Wales then communicated a particular account of the progress and circumstances of the King's disorder, and many instances of conversation and conduct which shewed the derangement of his mind. He then sent for Drs. Baker, Warren and Reynolds, who stated their opinion of the present situation; which was that his Majesty's understanding is at present so affected, that there does not appear to them any interval, in which any act that he could do, could properly be considered as done with a consciousness and understanding of what it was about – that the disorder might either be one locally fixed on the brain, or be a translation of a disorder from one part to another, that if it proved to be the latter, there might be a hope of removing it, but there would then be a possibility that it might attack some part where it might be dangerous to life – that if it was the former there was more reason to think the disorder would be permanent, without affecting life; but that it was also possible it might proceed from local causes, which might come to affect the life. That on the whole there was more ground to fear than to hope, and more reason to apprehend durable insanity than death.[45]

To the Lord Chancellor, Thurlow, the Prince of Wales wrote: 'I am sorry to acquaint you, that H.My. is in infinitely a more dangerous state than he has hitherto been, having no recollection whatever.'[46] And Mr Grenville sent his brother a long account of the opinions of the physicians and the political portents:

Pitt came back to town last night about nine [from Windsor], and afterwards called here. He had seen all the physicians, and had much conversation with them. They seemed still unwilling, or unable, to decide as to the nature of his disorder; but Warren appeared to incline to the opinion of an ossification. They told him that they had determined, as an experiment, to give the King medicines to remove his fever, in order to observe whether this produced any effect on the state of his mind, and to draw an inference from that whether the disorder on his brain was connected with the fever.

They accordingly gave him two doses of James's powder in the course of the day, but without any other effect than lowering his pulse; and this morning we have the severe mortification of hearing that a third dose has operated by a profuse perspiration, so as almost entirely to remove the fever, but that the state of his mind continues unaltered. The physicians, however, all agree that it must still be at least a fortnight before they can venture even to pronounce that it is a disorder of the brain. That even in that case they can give no further opinion; that disorders of that sort are of all others those that are least understood; and that this may continue for many years, or may suddenly leave him, or as suddenly kill him.

I need not tell you the effect which this dreadful calamity produces . . . I hope God, who has been pleased to afflict us with this severe and heavy trial, will enable us to go through it honestly, conscientiously, and in a manner not dishonourable to our characters.[47]

'From this time,' wrote Fanny Burney, 'as the poor King grew worse, general hope seemed universally to abate; and the Prince of Wales now took the government of the house into his own hands. Nothing was done but by his orders, and he was applied to in every difficulty. The Queen interfered not in anything; she lived entirely in her two new rooms, and spent the whole day in patient sorrow and retirement with her daughters.'[48]

'His recovery is hopeless,' Sir Gilbert Elliot told his wife, but 'he may linger a few days . . . The Queen does not now see him; the state of his head probably rendering the scene too painful to her.'[49] That Saturday night of 8 to 9 November Captain J. W. Payne, Comptroller of the Household of the Prince of Wales, wrote in great excitement to Richard Brinsley Sheridan, playwright, Member of Parliament and with Fox and Burke the third of the Whig triumvirate, from Windsor:

I enclose you the copy of a letter the Prince [of Wales] has just written . . . which will give you the situation of the King's health . . . The Duke of York . . . is just come out of the King's room, bids me add that His Majesty's situation is every moment becoming worse. His pulse is weaker and weaker; and the Doctors say it is impossible to survive it long, if his situation does not take some *extraordinary* change in a few hours . . . His Royal Highness would write to you himself; – the agitation he is in will not permit it. Since this letter was begun, all articulation even seems to be at an end with the poor King . . . Cataplasms are on His Majesty's feet, and strong fomentations have been used without effect . . . The Archbishop has written a very handsome letter, expressive of his duty and offer of service; but he is not required to come down, it being thought too late.[50]

On Sunday, 9 November, it was widely rumoured that the King had died. 'On the ninth of that month, which was *Lord Mayor's Day*,' wrote the historiographer royal in his *History of the late important period . . . of his Majesty's illness* (1789), 'the belief was universal throughout the metropolis, that his Majesty was no more, and that the awful event was with-held from publication, till the Mayor of London was sworn into office.'[51]

Meanwhile Captain Payne, who 'had much influence over the mind of his Royal Master [the Prince of Wales], and was actuated by a keen love of intrigue . . . opened separate negotiations with the two rivals and enemies, – Lord Loughborough and Lord Thurlow, holding out to each the certain prospect of favour under the new regime, which might be expected speedily to commence.'[52] That night he wrote to Loughborough:

I took the liberty of mentioning to the Prince the very liberal accomodation of your conduct in promotion of his service. He said, 'Well, if the C[hancellor Thurlow] chooses to remain where he is, Lord L[oughborough] can have the Privy Seal or President for the present, and settle the other arrangements afterwards, if it is more to his mind.'[52]

The party of the Prince of Wales were already allotting ministries – but the King survived the night. The next day 'after long and violent efforts nature seemed exhausted, and he remained two hours senseless and motionless, with a pulsation hardly perceptible'.[53] This was the physician's way of describing convulsions followed by coma. At night he slept only two hours, 'but there was no amendment in brain,' noted the Marquis of Ailesbury, who had it from Warren.[54]

Monday, 10 November, 'was a most dismal day. The dear and most suffering King was extremely ill,' wrote Fanny Burney.[55] And Baker reported to Pitt: 'H.M. has but little fever, is very incoherent, but without vehemence of bodily efforts.'[37] It appears that he was still only semiconscious, but had no return of convulsions. At Windsor the physicians said 'that the medicines they had given him had lowered the pulse and lessened the fever without in the least relieving the head, so that the delirium continued as strong as ever, tho' the life does not seem in such immediate danger.'[56]

Throughout Monday 'the same disturbed rambling continued and all the late unfavourable Symptoms remain'd the same and unabated'.[57] 'He was still extremely ill,' Baker told the Duke of Portland.[58]

On Tuesday, 11 November, there was 'for the first time a Lord-in-waiting at St. James's to answer inquiries,' wrote Sir Gilbert Elliot. 'I have been there, and a paper written by Dr. Warren lay on the table, dated ten o'clock this forenoon at Windsor. The words are – "His Majesty has passed a quiet night, but without any abatement in his complaints".'[58] The *Morning Chronicle* corrected persistent rumours that the King had died:

An universal consternation prevailed throughout the metropolis, in consequence of a report that was extremely current, and that shocked all who heard it, but which we have the happiness to have it in our power to pronounce wholly unfounded.[59]

Lord Bulkeley wrote to the Marquis of Buckingham direct from Windsor that he believed the crisis of the weekend had left the brain permanently impaired and the King senseless:

We have been at Windsor the last three mornings, and sorry am I to tell you that poor Rex's state seems worse than a thousand deaths; for unless God interposes by some miracle, there is every appearance of his living with the loss of his intellects. Yesterday the fever, which had raged the day before, was abated; but the lucid intervals were few, and lasted a very short time. I saw the General [Harcourt], who was exceedingly guarded, as they all are who really love poor Rex; the real state, however, of his melancholy condition seems now to have transpired, and my letters from London are full of the greatest consternation. The Queen sees nobody but Lady Constance,

2. *No piece of political gossip had greater circulation during the beginnings of the Regency Crisis in the second half of November 1788 than that Lord Chancellor Thurlow 'secretely from the rest of the King's friends, was carrying on a negotiation with the Prince's party for the purpose of continuing himself in office under their expected ministry' (Twiss,* Life of Eldon, *1844, vol. 1, p. 197). In the debate on the regency in the upper chamber on 15 December he became so overwrought at the conclusion of his own peroration declaring his grief and his gratitude to his sovereign that he ended with these celebrated words: 'And when I forget my King, may my God forget me.' Some of the members thought they heard him say at first 'may my God forgive me' and then correct himself (Massey,* History of England, *1865, vol. 3, pp. 195–6). Burke, who was present, was heard to mutter 'The best thing that could happen to you', and Pitt rushed out of the chamber exclaiming 'Rascal, rascal' (Stanhope:* Pitt, *1867, vol. 2, pp. 9–10). When the King recovered Thurlow celebrated the event with this token of his loyalty.*

Lady Charlotte Finch, Miss Burney, and her two sons, who, I am afraid, do not announce the state of the King's health with that caution and delicacy which should be observed to the wife and the mother, and it is to them only that she looks up. I understand her behaviour is very feeling, decent and proper. The Prince has taken the command at Windsor, in consequence of which there is *no command whatsoever*; and it was not till yesterday that orders were given to two grooms of the bedchamber to wait for the future and receive the inquiries of the numbers who inquire; nor would this have been done, if Pitt and Lord Sydney had not come down in person to beg that such orders might be given. Unless it was done yesterday, no orders have been given for prayers in the churches, nor for the observance of other forms, such as stopping the playhouses, &c., highly proper at such a juncture. What the consequences of this heavy misfortune will be to Government, you are more likely to know than I am; but I cannot help thinking that the Prince will find a greater difficulty in making a sweep of the present Ministry, in his quality of Fiduciary Regent, than in that of King. The Stocks are already fallen 2 per cent, and the alarms of the people of London are very little flattering to the Prince.[60]

It seemed 'that we have little hope from the effect of the medicines with respect to the state of his mind,' wrote Mr Grenville in distress to his brother. 'The consequence must be such as I mentioned to you in my last.'[61] And Mr Neville added: 'I fear there is very little hope of amendment . . . The King had some lucid intervals this morning, conversing with great composure with a page . . . He soon, however, returned to his unfortunate agitation and delirium, in which he still continues. Sad state!'[62]

The Queen sent to the Archbishop of Canterbury 'to issue out public prayers for the poor King, for all the churches'[63] and the Privy Council sent a similar request.[64]

For clinical details of what happened in the sickroom one must now turn to the diary of the King's equerry, Robert Fulke Greville, who had hurried to Windsor on hearing that the King was ill 'in order that every possible Aid within my reach might be called upon on the spot'. His observations are of the greatest value. But for his attachment to the King he had no axe to grind, no interests to further, nor any medical theory to defend. He simply and naïvely noted the daily events. His diary opens on 5 November, when he recorded 'the ramblings continued, and were more wild than before, amounting alas to an almost total suspension of reason – No sleep this Night – The Talking incessant throughout'.[65] And he described the events of 12 November:

In the morning constant rambling of thought continued, yet still at times recollecting Persons around Him by Name – H.M. was quiet until 11 o'Clock this day – after that time to 1 o'Clock He became more loud, and his Voice more Exerted than I had ever heard it, and He became much agitated, and the subjects changed . . . At length this Extreme agitation, continued through the two last hours, caused a Violent perspiration – He called to have the Windows opened, and complained of burning . . . About 3 o'Clock this day He became more violent & his talking was hurried & agitated to a great degree, & in consequence He put Himself in a violent perspiration. At this time his pulse rose to 130 . . . but at five o'Clock this Evening H.M. became exceedingly turbulent, & made strong efforts to get out of bed – His exertions with great agitation of Words, continued about an hour. He afterwards became more composed, but the ramblings remained.

Greville's description is that of a severe and mounting toxic-confusional state. That night, at its height it culminated in another series of convulsions:

This night I sat up with H.M. during the first part of which the ramblings were great . . . About five hours after, viz. about three o'Clock, H.M. had a violent struggle, jerking very strongly with his Arms & legs, but made no attempt to rise – Three quarters of an hour after this, He became quite recollected, during which time the opportunity was taken of making Him more comfortable, by changing the Sheets & Blankets, & at which He expressed much satisfaction. Immediately after He was put to bed, & sitting up in it, He talked of being shaved, & proposed to clean his mouth. Water being brought to Him for this purpose He did it as well as could be, washing his Mouth & gargelling his throat as well Ever in his usual habits.

At this time He appeared to Me more collected than I had seen Him since his illness begun – He asked how many days He had been confined to his bed, looked round at his Attendants with attention, & smiled, & nodded to Them frequently – He then laid down & said it was most comfortable to get clean things, & then recollecting Himself He desired He might change his linnen – All this He did as well as could be, & on one of his Pages offering to assist Him in putting on his flannel Waistcoat He said, 'No sir, I can do that for Myself, when I have the use of My own hands'. On laying down He promised to endeavour to compose Himself, & said He would sleep if He could; & indeed it was now particularly desireable He should have some rest, as He had been without sleep for above twenty-nine Hours . . . During the rest of this Night H.M. seem'd composing . . . slept however but one hour, & awoke more composed.[66]

The official 'Notice of the state of his Majesty's health sent . . . from Windsor to the Lord-in-waiting at St. James's, and thence to Lloyd's Coffee-House, gave information "that his Majesty had an Access of fever on Wednesday afternoon, that it abated in the night, but had not left him when the express left Windsor" ' the following morning.[67] Clearly degree of fever was now measured by severity of delirium. It is not to be wondered at that the air was full of rumours and contradictions, seeing that not even now, after four weeks of grave illness, had medical bulletins signed by the physicians been issued.

From Windsor, Warren communicated his opinion of the King's illness based on this day's events to Lady Spencer, mother of the Duchess of

Devonshire, confidentially in one Latin sentence: 'Rex noster insanit; nulla adsunt febris signa; nulla mortis venturae indicia' ('Our king is mad; there are no signs of fever; no danger to life').[68]

The Marquis of Buckingham commented from Dublin on the information which his brother had sent him:

> I collect from it the probability, amounting almost to certainty, that the insanity is fixed. I can hardly expect any thing from the miraculous idea of a sudden restoration of the reason; and the little observation which occurs to everyone in private life, hardly gives an instance of a recovery from water on the brain . . . several letters have been . . . put into my hands with details . . . of the perfect insanity, and the probable restoration of the bodily faculties without those of the mind.[69]

Nevertheless, his brother in Whitehall still continued 'to hope for such a crisis as may end this scene, either by his death or by his total recovery'.[70]

At this stage of rapid changes in the King's physical and mental state began the clash of opinion between the royal physicians which did so much to prolong the suspense and uncertainty of the political crisis which was looming. When the crisis came it was aggravated by the discrepancy between the public bulletins and what each physician in private conversation or in correspondence expressed as his own and real opinion. However, while his pulse continued fast and his nights disturbed and almost sleepless, it was reasonable for them to hope that the mental derangement would still subside as his physical health improved. 'When there is sleep, where before there was none, & when less restlessness exists, & less agitation of ideas prevails, I think it may be inferr'd, that some amendment has taken place . . . Now every succeeding day comes on with the most anxious Expectations.'[71] So reflected Greville on Saturday, 15 November, after the King had had six hours' sleep at night and was a little quieter, although he talked incessantly on a variety of subjects. That evening he suddenly became 'sensible (without prompting) that He was talking very fast, He altered & spoke in the third Person – "The King did so – The King thinks so" &c. This correction He thus explained, "I speak in the third person, as I am getting into Mr. Burke's Eloquence, saying too much on little things".'[72] On Wednesday, 19 November, Greville noted that after only two hours' sleep the previous night, the King 'talked for nineteen hours without scarce any intermission'.[73] When Dr Warren 'told him that he ought not to do so, he said "I know that as well as you, it is my complaint; cure me of that, and I shall be well".'[74]

On Sunday, 16 November, it was noticed that 'He has no longer that convulsive motion in his hands, which the physicians thought so bad a symptom'.* However, at times 'he gives orders and makes arrangements,

---

* This is one of the many instances in the records of the royal malady where, tantalizingly, a clinical phenomenon is heard of for the first and only time when it had ceased.

that would be admirable if they were not all founded in error, for often the persons concerned in them do not exist'.[75] Greville recorded that although

Wild incoherences have increased rather than diminished since yesterday, & the hopes of this day have become less flattering – H.M. from having some-what recover'd bodily Strength, believes Himself to be almost well, & in consequence now trys to command, & struggles hard for Obedience.[76]

And he confided a little prophecy to his diary: 'H.M. will e'er long give more trouble to his Attendants than hitherto – Already He talks of the many plans He has in view, when He gets up.' Indeed, the first battle of wills came about the following day: 'A warm bath having been order'd H.M. proposed terms if He took it, but his consent was at last obtained by Management'[76] – Greville's respectful euphemism for force, a premonition of what was in store for the King in the ensuing months. Another incident of the King's growing opposition to the physicians' rule happened later the same day. Two of them had gone into his room and told him they

hoped that if He called for any particular Person or for any particular thing, that He would not be angry if He was not obey'd, as that would be done by the Physicians orders from an Attention to his Health & which they owed to God, to Himself, & to the whole World – Upon this without assenting He was at first silent, & then He told the Physician who had thus addressed Him, 'That He should follow His prescription when He stood in need of it, but desired He would retire a little at present, as he must see He was nervous' & then turning to another He artfully said 'You shall talk to Me, for our poor Friend there (meaning the one had last spoke to Him) is too nervous at present'.[77]

Another disturbance two days later, on 19 November, followed after the physicians ordered that two pages should always remain with him in the two rooms to which he was confined:

These Arrangements being made, the King got up, & came into the next room – He was ill pleased that the Pages should remain in it while He was there – He battled this long & strenuously, but necessity & prudence carried the point against his Wishes – He became out of humour at the disappoint-ment – He would not be shaved – He would not eat his dinner, this at last was overcome tho' He stood out against being shaved – This operation He had all along much opposed, unless He might be permitted to perform it Himself – At length on this occasion He consented after much difficulty, but when half shaved He refused to let the other half be finished, unless certain indulgencies were granted – After continuing some time half shaved (a singu-lar appearance as He had not been shaved for upwards of a fortnight) He at length gave up the point.[78]

On another occasion he went for Warren. He wanted the keys to his drawers returned and sent Colonel Goldsworthy to the Duke of York with a note for them:

The request was submitted to The Physicians & Col. Goldsworthy was sent by Them to The King to acquaint Him that they did not think it right at present to comply with it – The King received this Message, but certainly not with satisfaction – Sir George Baker & Dr. Warren in consequence were sent in to speak to Him. On seeing Them H.M. was angry & agitated, on which Col. Goldsworthy looking out of his Apartment, called for Two Equerries to Come in – Col. Manners & Myself immediately went in – We found the King violently agitated, & very Angry, but more particularly with Dr. Warren – Shortly after some other Gentlemen in Attendance & Pages came into the room – Dr. Warren spoke to the King and endeavor'd to pacify Him – He requested at the same time that He might feel his Pulse – This the King refused & then getting up briskly He desired Dr. Warren to leave the room, telling Him He had sent Him a harsh order that day, & which Sir George Baker had got altered – Dr. Warren still tried to pacify H.M. upon which the King advanced up to Him & pushed him – Col. Manners & Myself being at this time close behind Dr. Warren, interfered, & stopped His Majesty, who on this, & seeing others coming up, He retired from Dr. Warren pale with Anger, & foaming with rage. The King now desired Dr. Warren to go for the present & to leave Sir George Baker with Him promising to see Dr. Warren at another time – This was complied with – & thus has this Turmoil ended tho' there are those who have queried whether future trouble may not arise from this concession at such a moment, when the Physicians should have Established their Authority.[79]

It was this failure in their management which led to more and more difficulties, as the King's physical health improved and his energies returned while excitement and irrationality remained. Ultimately, chaos within the sickroom and the confusion and uncertainty it created outside were responsible for the King's closer confinement at Kew a fortnight later and for a person accustomed to managing the irrational being called to take charge. Greville was quite right when he criticized the physicians for being too indecisive and not as

firm as the occasion of their Attendance has required – They appear to shrink from responsibility & to this time they have not Established their authority tho' pressed by Every Attendant . . . Our situation as Attendants on His Majestys Person, struggling under the Severest Affliction, is a most anxious & most responsible one – All of Us are most desireous to do our best for the good & comfort of our Dear King, but We must be plainly & properly directed in our course.[80]

The situation in which the royal physicians found themselves was not an enviable one. They were frightened by and of their unmanageable sovereign and his unpredictable behaviour. They had to account for his condition and their measures to the ministers of the crown. They had to consider the feelings of the Queen and her family and to bear in mind that the King himself was likely to see their reports in the papers – if not at the time then surely if he recovered. They were also apprehensive that the future of the Government hung on what they said. They were shadowed by the Prince of Wales and the Chancellor, harassed by public opinion and had newsmongers breathing down their necks. They had to think of their professional reputation, and above all else loomed the remorseless fact that they did not, as indeed they could not, know what was the matter with their patient.

Ill or well, sinking or convalescent, quiet or disturbed, restful or sleepless, rational or deluded – the greatest public interest attached

to the slightest item of intelligence . . . All other subjects were of inferior consideration. Even the serious inconvenience occasioned to the public service by the suspension of business in Parliament was forgotten in the absorbing topic. The uncertainty which hung over the issue, the responsibility that attended the treatment of the case, and the extreme caution observed by the physicians in the opinions they were called upon to pronounce, kept all classes of the people in a state of constant agitation.[81]

Meanwhile, Baker continued his laconic reports to Pitt:

Nov. 16. This morning his discourse was consistent, but the principle upon which it went for the most part founded in error. Nov. 18. H.M. had a good night, but the disorder remains unabated. Nov. 21. H.M. has been . . . more than once under the influence of considerable irritation. Nov. 22. 10 a.m. H.M. is entirely deranged this morning in a quiet good humoured way. Nov. 22. He showed many marks of a deluded imagination in the course of the day. In the evening he was more consistent.[82]

The public bulletins spoke of 'fever', by which they meant delirious rambling, intermittent irritability and excitement, uncontrolled behaviour, sleeplessness, fast pulse, sweating and hoarseness. The first bulletin was issued Tuesday, 18 November, and read 'His Majesty has had a good night, but as yet is not perfectly free from fever.' The next day: 'His Majesty has had a rather restless night, and his fever is increased.' On 20 November: 'His Majesty has had a more undisturbed night than the former, but the fever has not quite left him,' and so on.

Mr Grenville wrote complainingly:

You can . . . hardly conceive the difficulty which we have, even at this small distance [from Whitehall], to procure such information as can be in any degree depended on. All the private accounts are so strongly tinctured by the wishes of those who send them, that no reliance can be placed upon them; and the private letters of the physicians are frequently inconsistent with each other, and even with the public account which they send to St. James's. In general, that account has been uniformly found to be the least favourable; and seems as if it was drawn for the purpose of discouraging the hopes which their own letters and conversation excite. The letters which they read to Pitt, though frequently varying in their general tenor from the public account, are not at all more detailed than that is, and take no sort of notice of the most material circumstances. I imagine all this is to be imputed to a difference of opinion which is supposed to prevail amongst them, it being believed that Warren is strongly inclined to think the disorder permanent, and that Reynolds is sanguine in the contrary opinion.[83]

The publication of contradictions, half-truths and unchecked rumours inflamed public feeling still more. In the last week of November it ran so high that Sir Lucas Pepys, who had joined the attending physicians on 18 November, told Fanny Burney

that none of their own lives would be safe if the King did not recover, so prodigiously high ran the tide of affection and loyalty. All the physicians received threatening letters daily, to answer for the safety of their monarch with their lives! Sir George Baker had already been stopped in his carriage by the mob, to give an account of the King; and when he said it was a bad one, they had furiously exclaimed 'the more shame for you!'[84]

Unlike Warren, who had refused to talk to Fanny Burney about the illness when she met him in the Windsor corridors, 'Sir Lucas opened upon the subject in the most comfortable manner. He assured me there was nothing desponding in the case, and that his royal patient would certainly recover, though not immediately ... the moment he left me I flew to demand a private audience of the Queen, that I might relate such delightful prognostics.'[85]

Once the news got round that the derangement was likely to persist after 'fever' had subsided, some of the King's old friends came out with remarkable displays of loyalty. 'The Courtiers all affect to have been mad – Lord Fauconberg declares all the world saw him in a strait waistcoat,' recorded the Duchess of Devonshire in her diary of the events as seen from the view of the Prince of Wales's supporters, 'and Lord Salisbury says the King has as much sence as he has.'[86]

Lady Harcourt off her own bat now consulted Sir William Fordyce, hoping that he would be called in to treat the King. Sir William was well known for his treatise, 'Cultivating and Curing Rhubarb in Britain for Medical Uses', and for a section on insanity in a book on medical observations in which he gave an account of his teacher, Dr William Battie's treatment with tartarized antimony.[87] Lady Fordyce answered for her husband:

He says, that, from all he has heard or read of the case, he sees no reason for despondency if it be properly treated; that, in the early part of his life, he was the intimate friend of Dr. Battie, who, besides his skill in other branches of his profession, was the Dr. Monro of his time, and to whose practice and experience he had access. Since that period he has made this dreadful malady his study; he has seen many, who, from over-fatigue and low diet, have been in situations similar to the King's and who have perfectly recovered their faculties without ever experiencing a relapse. He has written upon the subject, and explained the method of cure, and he thinks that the physicians now about the King are not pursuing the means most likely to effect a cure; they appear to him to consider that to be the cause which is only the effect, and by so doing the root of the malady is suffered to remain . . . Sir William speaks with confidence; get him called in.[88]

On 20 November the King said to Greville that he knew how ill and disturbed he had been:

He was sensible of having been very much out of Order, & that still He stood in need of Attention & care – Sometimes He doubted his own Accuracy in what He was saying, & would ask Me if such & such things had been so, as said He 'I have certainly been very much out of Order' – He added that his recollections had been very imperfect & confused, until last Sunday (Nov. 16th) when all had become more arranged day after day from that period.[89]

To General Budé, another equerry, the King confided 'some phantoms of his delusion during his delirium – Said He had thought there had been a deluge – That He had seen Hanover through Herschel's Telescope – That He had thought Himself inspired &c.'[90] 'He fancies London is drowned and orders his yacht to go there,' wrote Lord Sheffield to Mr Eden. 'To divert him . . . they endeavoured to turn him to writing: at length he began to compose notes on Don Quixote.'[91] He composed despatches to foreign courts 'founded upon imaginary causes' and 'lavished honours upon all who approached him; elevating to the highest dignities, pages, gentlemen of the bed-chamber, or any occasional attendant'.[92] When in his confusion he saw London being flooded he

expressed great unwillingness that a valuable manuscript the precise situation which he described should suffer; and declared an intention of going . . . to rescue it from the approaching evil . . . To these gentler workings of a disordered mind, [there] often succeeded sad transports of vehemence and agitation, which were expressed in tones so ungoverned as sometimes to reach beyond the walls of the royal apartment. Exhausted nature would then feel a pause; during which, it was not uncommon for His Majesty to express consciousness of his unhappy state, and a despair of ever being relieved from it.[92]

Such rapid fluctuations between great excitement and comparative calm, between insight that his mind was playing him tricks and a conviction that his hallucinations were reality and building false beliefs on them, between rational behaviour and impulsive inappropriate actions, showed that the worst phase of continuous aberration was passing and that his delirium was becoming subacute. But his semi-purposeful activities made his management that much more difficult and his partial or momentary insight made his sufferings all the greater for him, while to the uninformed they suggested that he was not temporarily confused but permanently insane. It was now

E

the fourth week of November and the sixth week of his illness. On the physical side also the serious illness through which he had passed had left another mark besides weakness: 'His malady . . . had so emaciated him, that it was judged expedient to remove every mirror, lest the reflection of his own figure should affect him too sensibly.'[93]

His Majesty's Hanoverian government were greatly alarmed when they heard of the grave turn the illness had taken. The *London Chronicle* of 5 December learned from a letter dated 25 November that on the order of the authorities 'Dr. Zimmermann, the King's physician, set off this morning for The Hague ,intending, if he receive orders, to go from thence to England.'

From this time 'The controul which the Physicians were obliged to maintain agitated Him'[94] and he complained to Greville about the physicians

who had been forced upon Him, & He then dwelt on the treatment He had received from the Doctors, with much sensibility – I took this occasion to hint to H.M. that nothing was worse for Him just now than Agitation, & that an unremitting object of His Physicians was, by every means in their power to keep Him quiet, as a measure absolutely necessary to his recovery; & that the trifles He complained as having been withheld from Him, & the occasional restraints He had experienced, had been measures which had been adopted solely to this point, & that they would all cease in a very short time.[95]

The 'restraints' to which Greville referred so discreetly revealed the fact that at times of his most ebullient opposition to his doctors' treatment he had been 'sheeted', that is 'swaddled in fine Linen' and 'pinioned with an envelopement of Lawn'.[96] Yet 20 November, the day when he first rebelled against this regime, was the very day, as George Selwyn, Surveyor-General of the Works, wrote, which had been

fixed upon to speak reason to One who has none. Dr. Warren, in some set of fine phrases, is to tell his Majesty that he is stark mad, and must have a strait waistcoat. I am glad that I am not chosen to be that Rat who is to put the bell about the Cat's neck. For if it should please God to . . . restore his Majesty to his senses . . . I should not like to stand in the place of that man who has moved such an Address to the Crown.[97]

The strait-waistcoat may indeed have been used a few days later. The King had continued as turbulent as ever at times, 'very hurrying in Conversation & giving all a variety of Orders . . . [and] Commissions' and 'talking much unlike Himself, I mean indecently,' wrote Greville.[98] All efforts to sedate him with opiates had failed.[99] On 24 November after a short sleep in the evening he awoke 'particularly confused and remained so most of the night'.[100] Baker told Pitt that the King was 'in a perfectly maniacal state' and that the next evening they had been obliged to put him under 'a strict regimen'.[101] Mr Grenville informed his brother of developments at Windsor and how the physicians now regarded the illness:

The account, as far as relates to the King's actual situation for these two or three last days, is much less favourable than it has been. The disorder of his intellects has continued almost, if not entirely, without intermission for the whole of that time. He talks incessantly for many hours together, and without any appearance of sense or reason, sometimes knowing the persons who are about him, at other times mistaking them, or fancying himself employed in different occupations, such as taking notes on books, or giving different orders. He has appeared several times to have that sort of consciousness of his situation which lunatics are observed to possess, and to use the same sort of methods for concealing it. All this constitutes the gloomy side of the picture; and Warren is so much impressed with this, that he told Pitt there was now every reason to believe that the disorder was no other than direct lunacy.

On the other hand, I understand that he, as well as the other physicians, are now agreed as to the cause of the disorder. You may remember that, at the beginning of this unhappy situation, I mentioned to you that an idea had been entertained of its proceeding from some local cause, such as water on the brain, or some change in the texture of the brain itself, by induration or ossification. Warren has decidedly said, that he is satisfied this is entirely out of the question; this he told Pitt in express terms. The cause to which they all agree to ascribe it, is the force of a humour which was beginning to show itself in the legs, when the King's imprudence drove it from thence into the bowels; and the medicines which they were obliged to use for the preservation of his life, have repelled it upon the brain. The consequence of this opinion is so plain, that there certainly requires no professional skill to know that his recovery must depend upon this single circumstance, whether there is, or is not strength enough in his constitution to throw off this humour by any other channel. The physicians are now endeavouring by warm baths, and by great warmth of covering, to bring it down again into the legs, which nature had originally pointed out as the best mode of discharge.[102]

The great John Hunter, Surgeon Extraordinary to the King, also hoped the illness would 'come to some sort of crisis, by which it would appear whether there was strength enough in the constitution to prevail' and maintained 'that it would be very bad luck indeed if he did not recover, and that the chances were nine to one in his favour'. On such authority, concluded Grenville, 'one certainly may be allowed to indulge some degree of hope'.

Most, however, found the profusion of medical opinions and theories confusing. 'You may easily conceive all this while how various, how contradictory, and how unintelligible the reports are,' wrote Mr Anthony Storer on 28 November to his friend William Eden, Ambassador Extraordinary at Madrid. 'When his disorder began, what contributed to it? Did Cheltenham do him harm? All these questions are perpetually discussed and very little satisfaction and no knowledge gained.'[103] Even the statesman-like

Lord Sheffield, writing from Downing St, was perplexed: 'There is a difference of opinion . . . and one part of the public believes his constitution is broken up, while another part flatters itself that the illness is the effect of fever.'[104]

On 24 November, Pitt went to Windsor 'to propose that Dr. Addington . . . should be added to consultation'.[105] Dr Anthony Addington, aged seventy-five, had some forty years earlier for a space of seven years kept a private madhouse at Reading before he moved to London as a general physician in 1754. He was the Pitt's family doctor and had gained celebrity for looking after Pitt's father, first Earl of Chatham, whose affliction was as mysterious as the King's. He was unaware of the restrictions which the physicians at Windsor had placed on the King's contact with his family and 'made a sad blunder at his first Interview with H.M. [on 27 November] by inconsiderately telling Him there would be no impropriety in his seeing the Queen. This slip occasioned much confusion, as the King immediately begun to prepare His room for Her reception.'[106]

To the King's friend, the Marquis of Ailesbury, 'he declared that he thought rash, getting wet in bed, and gallstones to do with disorder in mind which was a simple thing and not complex'.[105] He was 'favourable as to a possibility, and even a prospect of recovery' and explained to Pitt 'that the symptoms as they at present appeared, were those of a morbid humour, flying about and irritating the nerves.'[107] Whatever one may make of 'Addington's opinion,' commented Grenville, it at least 'seems to have encouraged the rest to speak out'.

On 28 November, Mr Storer wrote to his friend, William Eden: 'The physicians vary their phrases every day in the newspapers, meaning to say as little as they can . . . The bulletin daily talks of a fever; but fever he [now] has not . . . The word fever is probably substituted for insanity.'[108] After 25 November the words 'disorder', 'indisposition' and 'restlessness' began to appear linked with an account of the night's sleep. On 26 November it was announced: 'His Majesty has had sufficient sleep in the night, but does not appear to have been relieved by it.' These ominous words marked the transition from the stage of severe physical disease, of which delirium was but one aspect, to apparent recovery of health while the mind and conduct continued to be disturbed. This meant the King had now delirium without fever, a very different matter. By definition it meant insanity, that is a derangement of the mind not dependent on systemic disease, but due directly to disease of the brain, the other bodily functions remaining healthy. It was much less likely to be amenable to medicines or to end in complete recovery.

The *Morning Chronicle* valiantly assured its readers that despite this development the King's disorder may yet 'be attended with a cure as sudden as the approach of his malady, and as effectual as if he had never been afflicted. Such a possible event (which God grant) shows that although the disorder has deranged the head, it is not, as was once dreaded, a mental incapacity, called Insanity, for that calamity will not admit of a sudden and effectual cure.'[109] Nevertheless, the fact was that delirium was continuing, although his physical health had improved.

Politically inspired rumour now started that the King had been insane from the beginning of the illness, because the case for a regency was strengthened by everything which made the King's incapacity appear hopeless. What became the Whig interpretation of the illness was stated by Sir Gilbert Elliot in a letter to his wife:

The physicians . . . talk of fever, but I am inclined to believe he has never yet had any fever, in the common acceptation of that word, and that they avail themselves of some occasional quickness of pulse to avoid the true name of his disorder, and also to avoid the declaration of a circumstance which would make his case much more hopeless – I mean that of delirium without fever.[110]

Warren, the medical Whig, whom contemporaries accused of allowing political allegiance and intrigue to bias his judgement, and who was not called in until the fourth week of the illness, bluntly told Pitt at this time 'that the physicians could now have no hesitation in pronouncing that the actual disorder was that of lunacy' and 'that the King might never recover'.[111] 'With this sort of information,' wrote a grim-faced Grenville, 'we shall probably have to meet Parliament.'

This campaign was carried so far that it was even said that the King was mentally deranged in the summer. 'Several strange instances are now told of what happened at Cheltenham,' wrote Lord Sheffield.[104] They were embellished as they spread, although eye-witnesses who knew they were false strove to give them the lie. Lady Harcourt, for one, wrote:

I have been the more particular in what I have related, because it was afterwards said by some ill-disposed persons, that even at the period of which I have given an account [the Cheltenham visit], his Majesty shewed signs of the unhappy malady with which he has since been afflicted. Living with him, as I did, in the most unreserved intimacy from six in the morning till eleven at night, it is impossible but that if this had been true I must have observed it. I can most solemnly affirm that I never saw the least symptom of mental derangement.[112]

Such tendentious rumour-mongering, however unfounded, left its mark on history. It added verisimilitude to the Opposition's view of the King's illness and led to a historical distortion which further obscured the true nature of the royal malady.

Even the Cheltenham waters were implicated. The *London Chronicle* of 24 February 1789 informed its readers that 'It is now authenticated from the best authority that the King's late disorder was owing solely to his drinking the waters at Cheltenham.' As late as 1826 the author of a medical history of Cheltenham still felt obliged to apologize to the nation for the events of 1788:

In mania, or in those predisposed to this most melancholy of human diseases, the waters have been charged with having done mischief. The recurrence of his late Majesty's indisposition after visiting Cheltenham, and drinking the waters, brought a temporary cloud over the popularity of the place. As one, who is by his conscience bound to speak with honest fearlessness . . . I do conceive that it were prudent in these cases to avoid the waters.[113]

To the six physicians now in attendance there was added a seventh, Dr Thomas Gisborne, retired physician to St George's Hospital, whom the King came to like better than the rest. But even the loyal Greville felt 'wholly destitute of all hope, and persuaded the malady was a seizure for life . . . Universal despondence now pervaded the whole house. Sir Lucas [Pepys], indeed, sustained his original good opinion, but he was nearly overpowered by standing alone, and was forced to let the stream take its course with but little opposition.'[114] Mr Charles Hawkins, one of the apothecaries to the household, gave Fanny Burney on 27 November such a 'determined decision of incurability' that it left her 'quite in horror'.[114]

3

Confinement at Kew

As early as 24 November it was mooted that the physicians wanted the King moved from Windsor to Kew.[1] Their ostensible reason was that Kew had a private garden where he might take exercise and air 'without being overlooked or observed'.[2] Others said they found the distance to Windsor from London 'extremely inconvenient'[3] for keeping up their practice in town. But when the plan was mentioned to him 'the King showed the most extreme repugnance to leave Windsor'.[2] It was therefore decided that the moment of departure should be 'kept profoundly secret . . . and to allure him away by some stratagem occupied all the physicians,' as Fanny Burney wrote on Wednesday, 26 November.[4] Two days later, she heard in confidence from Sir Lucas Pepys that

we were to go to Kew tomorrow . . . The difficulty how to get the King away from his favourite abode was all that rested. If they even attempted force, they [the physicians] had not a doubt but his smallest resistance would call out the whole country to his fancied rescue . . . The Queen's knowledge of the King's aversion to Kew [or rather his love for Windsor] made her consent to this measure with the extremest reluctance; yet it was not to be opposed: it was stated as much the best for him, on account of the garden; as here there is none but what is public to spectators from the terrace, or tops of houses. I believe they were perfectly right, though the removal was so tremendous.[5]

The Queen only insisted that she should go too.

Before such a serious step against the King's expressed wish was taken, the Prince of Wales wrote on 26 November to the Lord Chancellor to 'convene the King's confidential servants', that is the members of the Cabinet, 'in order that his Majesty's situation may be fully & formally examined into by them previous to any new arrangement whatever being adopted'.[6] Accordingly the next day, Thursday, 27 November, they assembled at Windsor. Among them was the Duke of Leeds, Secretary of

State for the Foreign Department, who left a memorandum of the meeting. They took statements from the royal physicians. Addington was the most optimistic and his opinion was backed by Pepys and Reynolds. Warren and Baker 'did not seem to entertain so much favourable expectation'. All concurred 'in Restraint being necessary, and that the degree in which they thought it expedient could be much better observed at Kew'. In addition, it would afford a desirable 'change of air and objects'. They declared no force would be employed 'however necessary they thought the removal to be'.[7] The ministers having these assurances and having 'heard the sentiments of the King's physicians . . . and being of opinion that their advice ought to be followed in all points material for his Majesty's recovery', declared themselves 'satisfied in our judgments, that it is desireable that his Majesty should be removed to Kew'.[8]

The move was planned for Saturday, 29 November, and despite 'considerable difficulty in persuading him to agree . . . was at last accomplished without violence'.[9]

Inexpressible was the alarm of every one, lest the King if he recovered should bear a lasting resentment against the authors and promoters of this journey. To give it, therefore, every possible sanction, it was decreed that he should be seen by the Chancellor and Mr. Pitt. The Chancellor went into his presence with a tremor such as, before, he had been only accustomed to inspire; and when he came out he was so extremely affected . . . that the tears ran down his cheeks, and his feet had difficulty to support him. Mr. Pitt was more composed, but expressed his grief with so much respect and attachment, that it added new weight to the universal admiration with which he is here beheld.[10]

On the very day the

poor Queen was to get off in private: the plan settled between the Princes and the physicians was, that her Majesty and the Princesses should go away quietly and then that the King should be told that they were gone, which was the sole method they could devise to prevail with him to follow. He was then to be allured by a promise of seeing them at Kew . . . Terrible was the morning . . . all spent in hasty packing up, preparing for we knew not what, nor for how long . . . nor scarcely with what view! We seemed to be preparing for captivity, without having committed any offence; and for banishment, without the least conjecture when we might be recalled from it . . . [the Queen's] mind . . . quite misgave her about Kew: the King's dislike was terrible to think of, and she could not foresee in what it might end.[11]

The transfer to Kew became an epic struggle between the patient and those who meant to rule him, and against all odds he very nearly won the day. 'All preparations for H.M.'s removal being made The intentions were gradually & cautiously mentioned to Him – but the King most stoutly objected to Every hint for his removal, & he would not get up.' Pitt, whether motivated by compassion for the King or mistrust of the competence of the doctors and the princes, had returned to Windsor that morning to ensure that all went well. On the King's refusing to leave his bed, the physicians suggested he go in and tell the King that the Queen had preceded him to Kew and ask whether he would not like to join her there. But 'the King objected, & said that the Queen had gone without leave, & that She should return to supplicate his pardon . . . Mr. Pitt baffled in his Endeavors left his Apartment & the King continued in bed – The day was advancing, being now one o'Clock.' The Prince of Wales conferred with the physicians and it was decided that the two equerries, Greville and General Harcourt, should go in next: 'We urged Him to get up & prepare Himself to go to Kew, on which He became very angry & hastily closed the Bed Curtains, & hid Himself from us.'[12] After an interval the King emerged and showed them two letters, one to the Master of the Horse and the other to the Colonel of the Welsh Fusiliers then on Windsor duty, and the urgency with which he asked them to forward them induced the equerries 'to suspect that its purpose was, that He should be assisted by a Military force' to defend him. The equerries, like Pitt, retired defeated. The physicians now decided to ask Pitt to write an official letter from the ante-room:

Mr. Pitt humbly begs leave to acquaint your Majesty that he finds the physicians think it of the greatest consequence for your Majesty's recovery to change the air; and they have informed Mr. Pitt that they think themselves obliged not to permit Mr. Pitt to pay his duty personally to your Majesty again till after your Majesty's arrival at Kew.[13]

The bait was countersigned by Warren, Baker, Pepys, Addington and Reynolds. The King became 'much agitated' at this letter and tried to write an answer but could not and again withdrew behind his bed curtains. It was then agreed that all the physicians except Addington, who was too old, should enter his room and 'bring the question to a point . . . On seeing Them his agitation increased, & perceiving Dr. Warren He instantly desired He would get out of the Room & on his not retiring He jumped out of bed to go to Him. I laid hold of H.M.'s Arm, & with some of the Attendant Pages stopped Him – On this he returned to his bed,' wrote Greville. All attempts at persuasion having failed, 'He was told if He continued his refusal longer, He would be forced.' Finally, after the three equerries promised to escort him, they managed to get him dressed and conveyed to his carriage. With General Harcourt by his side and Colonels Greville and Goldsworthy opposite, he finally drove off 'about a Quarter before four o'Clock, attended by an Escort of Cavalry.'

But their troubles were by no means over. On arrival at Kew the King was hustled into the apartments allotted to him, the remaining doors being bolted. Despite the promises held out to him, he was after all not to see the

A View of the Palace at Kew, from the Lawn.

3. The old Palace at Kew where the King was confined in 1788–9. It was demolished in the early nineteenth century and stood near the sun dial on the lawn in front of the present red-brick building.

Queen or his family. He protested that he had been deceived, which indeed he had – and, of course, to mislead a patient in such circumstances is an irreparable mistake. He tried to escape. When his attempt was foiled, he determined to stay awake until everybody was asleep and effect it then.

This Night as We Expected was an Unpleasant one – The King refused to go to bed & kept up until near 4 o'Clock, when becoming turbulent & violent towards one of his Pages He was forced to his bed. This put Him in great agitation He pulled one of his Pages by the Hair & attempted to kick another. This day [Sunday, 30 November] his violence did not much subside, & when controuled, violent symptoms of resistance appeared. At times He became sullen ... He eat very little during the day & refused all Medicine, & threw what He could away.[14]

That day the first bulletin from Kew merely announced that 'His Majesty arrived at this palace from Windsor and bore the journey extremely well'. Now all 'the unfavorable Symptoms of his disorder' greatly increased: 'Oaths, which had never yet been heard from his lips, were now for the first time blended not unfrequently, with indecencies.' He was so much depressed in the situation in which he found himself a prisoner 'that He even gave hints of being tired of his Existence & actually entreated his Pages to dispatch Him. Nothing could mark in a stronger degree the confirmed & desperate derangement of his Mind in these moments, or more fully point the necessity of unremitting & watchful care to those to whom the security of his Person was now confided.'[15] The days were turbulent and at night he was 'almost unmanageable' and had to be tied to his bed. Wednesday, 3 December, was according to Greville 'Altogether ... the worst day H.M. has experienced'.[16] The Queen, wrote the Marquis of Ailesbury, was 'much displeased with physicians, which she could never forget or forgive, for moving King from Windsor for their own convenience and leaving His Majesty first night without any physicians.'[17]

It was now too painfully obvious that the regular physicians were not equal to the task of managing him, either by personality, inclination or experience. To add to the royal family's unhappiness, Kew Palace had 'never been a winter residence, and there was nothing prepared for its becoming one'. In consequence, it was 'in a state of cold and discomfort passed all imagination,' wrote Fanny Burney. The rooms had no carpets or rugs on their bare boards, and sandbags had to be placed against the windows and doors to keep out the draughts. What little room there was was further reduced by the locking-up of all the rooms immediately above the King's on the ground floor, so that 'he may never be tantalized by footsteps overhead' reminding him of the Queen's presence.

Mournful was the opening of the month! My account of the night ... was very alarming, and my poor Royal Mistress began to sink more than I had ever yet seen. No wonder; the length of the malady so uncertain, the steps which seemed now requisite so shocking: for new advice, and such as suited only disorders that physicians in general relinquish, was now proposed, and compliance or refusal were almost equally tremendous . . . Dr. Willis, a physician of Lincoln, of peculiar skill and practice in intellectual maladies, [was to be] sent for. The poor Queen had most painfully concurred in a measure which seemed to fix the nature of the King's attack in the face of the world.[18]

And so it did. The name of Dr Willis was first suggested on Sunday, 30 November, the King's first day at Kew, on which day a council was held there, attended by 'The Prince, the Duke of York, the Chancellor and all the medical tribe . . . in order to arrange the future system of management, the necessity of which is, indeed, but too apparent'. The consultation over, General Harcourt, one of the equerries who had escorted the King to his confinement, wrote to his wife: 'I am happy to tell you that the Chancellor alone is to have the direction of everything; and that Dr. Willis . . . who has great skill and experience in treating this unhappy malady, is sent for.'[19] It was supposed that his name had first been brought forward by Lady Harcourt, who had drawn up a paper 'stating her knowledge of his merits from his successful treatment of her mother'.[20] At Lord Thurlow's request, the Queen asked that the ministers 'might approve of Dr. Willis being sent for'.[21] A King's messenger was accordingly dispatched for him.

'Dr. Willis . . . is a clergyman, and keeper of a mad-house in Lincoln-shire,' wrote Lord Sheffield to Mr Eden. 'He is considered by some not much better than a mountebank . . . That such a man and Dr. Addington should be called in the manner they have been, has caused some jealousy; but the opinions of all the physicians are not much respected.'[22]

After meeting all the physicians in consultation at Warren's house, Dr Willis was introduced to the King on Friday, 5 December, and the King knew very well what it meant.

The Appearance of Dr. Willis seemed to Engage much of His Majesty's Attention throughout this day – He was at no time Violent but often seem'd distressed – He felt much on his arrival to be placed about Him – He told one of his Pages, that as Dr. Willis was now come He could never more shew his face again in this Country that He would leave it for Ever, & retire to Hanover.[23]

Despite his distress and this further affliction, the King made a great effort to control his feelings;

His Majesty received Dr. Willis with composure & began immediately to talk to Him & seem'd very anxious to state to Him that He had been very ill, but that He was now quite well again . . . He told Dr. Willis that He knew where He lived, & He asked Him how many patients He then had with Him under his Care – He then thus address'd Dr. Willis 'Sir Your dress &

appearance bespeaks You of the Church, do You belong to it.' Dr. Willis replied 'I did formerly, but lately I have attended chiefly to physick'. 'I am sorry for it' answered the King with Emotion & Agitation, 'You have quitted a profession I have always loved, & You have Embraced one I most heartily detest.'[23]

Willis, no whit abashed, is said to have replied: 'Sir, our Saviour himself went about healing the sick.' 'Yes, yes,' replied the King testily, 'but he had not 700*l*. a year for it.'[24] The Marquis of Ailesbury heard also that the King had demanded of Willis 'by what authority he came', and when Willis answered 'by that of the Privy Council and the wishes of his subjects' the King said 'that the game was up for he had received not a check but a checkmate'.[25]

The vexed question who was responsible for decisions affecting the King's person gave rise to much heart-searching. During the early chaotic days of November the Prince of Wales had taken charge, but because of the conflict of political interest the task had devolved upon the Queen, much against her inclination. When the Chancellor had wanted her 'to take charge of King's person she desired to decline it, which he said it would be cruelty to do, but she answered if the Prince of Wales had declined acting and leaving everything to Council, why might not she.'[25] The consequence was that she had to give her approval to measures which she did not like but was not in a position to oppose, and for which she was blamed by the King before he had recovered and realized her position. Among these decisions were his confinement, his removal to Kew and above all the calling-in of Willis. In later attacks, particularly during the Regency, she was manoeuvred into the same unenviable position of having to decide between the urgent advice of the officers of her Council and what she knew to be the King's own feelings.

'Thus begun the first acquaintance' with Willis, wrote the faithful Greville. 'In progress H.M. . . . launched out in strong invective against His Physicians, & abused the profession . . . his displeasure pointed principally against Dr. Warren & Sir Lucas Pepys – and He most earnestly begged that Dr. Willis would take the former under his care as one of his Patients & remove Him to Lincolnshire.'[26]

Dr Willis brought with him a strait-waistcoat and was followed by his son and assistant Dr John and three of his keepers, or 'physical assistants' as they were called.[27] He told Greville his method was that he ' "broke in" ' patients like ' "Horses in a manège" – as his expression was,' added Greville in horror.[28] That very evening the battle for ascendancy and control was joined. Willis told the King 'that his ideas were now deranged, & that He required attention & Management'. At this, 'The King became violently Enraged' and attempted to rush against Willis. He, however, remained firm and told him 'He must controul Himself otherwise He would put Him in a strait Waistcoat,' and immediately fetched one from the next room. From that time recourse was frequently had to it. After his first night in 'the Strait waistcoat . . . the King repeatedly said, that He would never more wear the Crown, & desired his Eldest Son might be sent for.'[29]

So began the new system of government of the King by intimidation, coercion and restraint. No account of the illness from this point on can disregard the King's treatment, and to what extent the turbulence he displayed was provoked by the repressive and punitive methods by which he was ruled. For every non-compliance – refusing food when he had difficulty in swallowing, no appetite or a return of colic, resisting going to bed when he was too agitated and restless to lie down, throwing off his bedclothes during sweating attacks – he was clapped into the strait-waistcoat, often with a band across his chest and his legs tied to the bed. Knowledge of how he was treated leaves little room for the statement often made that the King took an unwarranted dislike to the Willises, or, as was later said, that his hatred of them was delusional. How reassuring if it had been so.

Meanwhile, Parliament had reassembled on 20 November. Pitt moved that the Commons adjourn for two weeks, when, should the King's disorder continue, they could consider what measures ought to be adopted to ensure the continuation of executive government. Lord Camden, Lord President of the Council, made a similar proposition in the Lords and the motions passed both Houses without a single observation from any side. On 3 December, the day before Parliament reassembled, a Privy Council was held at which the physicians were examined on oath, 'the object being to impart in the most authentic form accurate intelligence on the situation of the king' to guide Parliament in its deliberations.

It was agreed before the meeting that only general questions should be asked: whether the King was capable or incapable of coming to Parliament or attending to business, what hopes were there of his recovery, how long might it take, and what experience the physicians had of such cases. All except Warren 'were clear and distinct in their answers, all five agreeing That the King was at present totally incapable of attending to business; that there certainly from their experience of similar cases appeared a probability of his recovery, but the time which would be necessary to effect his cure was not possibly to be ascertained.'[30] Warren, on the other hand, 'appeared under much confusion and his answers both in respect to matter and language were very unlike what one naturally expected from him'. For instance, to the question 'What are the hopes you entertain of His Majesty's recovery?' he answered: 'The probability of Cure can only be determined by past Experience, by which I learn that the greater number of Persons who have fallen into the same state in which His Majesty now is, including all the species of the Disorder, have been cured . . . It is not in my Power to ascertain the Species, because no known Distemper has preceeded, that can account for it.'[31] 'An explanatory question was put to him which it took about an hour and a half to settle; whether, as far as experiences enabled him to judge, he thought it more probable that the King would or would not recover. To this he said that he had not and he believed no one else had sufficient data to answer that question.' So reported Grenville, who was present.[32] Lord Ailesbury confided to his diary:

> Dr. Warren was first, and I was struck at his answer, particularly at his mentioning the word insane; and when he was advised not to, and another expression was dictated to him, he answered it was the same thing, and he described particular causes, such as a fall from a horse and disturbed mind from disappointment, as causes of such a state as the King was in; but he insinuated that King's was from unknown distemper, and he mentioned bilious complaint as nothing.[33]

As the meeting broke up, after four hours, Lord Camden approached the Duke of Leeds and said 'he had a word for my private ear, and then whisper'd me *Dr. Warren is a damn'd scoundrel, tho' I believe him to be a very able Physician, and I dare say you will agree with me in both*,'[30] implying that Warren's political affiliation had got the better of the doctor in him.

Lord Ailesbury took the trouble to drive to Kew after the meeting to tell the Queen in person what had passed. From her he heard that the King's pulse remained 'at above 130 [and that] She thought King's languor and pain in his legs and arms were from his head, and that [as early as 4 November] he was aware of that attack coming on him'.[33] She also told him that 'a Doctor Willis' was to be sent for, because she 'wished a person to be constantly with King'. What the Prince of Wales and the Duke of York made of their father's condition on that same day is contained in a letter they wrote to their brother Augustus: 'His complaint, which is a total loss of all rationality, has apparently been coming upon him for some time but now is grown to such a pitch that he is a compleat lunatick.'[34]

When Parliament reassembled on 4 December, the report of the examination of the physicians by the Privy Council was laid before both Houses. At their adjourned meeting four days later, it was agreed that each House should appoint its own committee to examine the physicians for themselves. The Commons' committee sat on Tuesday, 9 December, and the Lords' on Wednesday. They reported to their respective chambers on 10 and 11 December. The physicians were summoned by George Rose, then clerk of the Parliaments, who became a good friend of the King and – appropriately – later, as will be seen, played a great part in reforming the treatment of the insane. They were now also asked what they thought was the cause of the illness, and Dr Willis was examined for the first time.[35]

Baker appeared to have lost heart. He said, 'There had been fever, and other Complaints' at the beginning, but hesitated to assign them as the cause of the persistent derangement. Before the House of Lords' committee he was more explicit. He detailed how he had first been called on 17 October, when the King had symptoms of 'biliary Concretions in the Gall Duct', his legs swelled for a couple of days, he was lame and had rheumatic pains in his feet and thighs which had continued all along. But in his opinion none of these could account for the King's present complaint. In short, he now shared Warren's view, who stated with 'Certainty' that the disorder was not 'the Effect of Fever'. Warren said 'I cannot assign His Majesty's Malady to any Cause whatever,' and so implied that the King was not delirious but insane, just as he had told the Privy Council.

Baker and Warren became accordingly known as 'the "opposition" physicians about his Majesty . . . however odd it may sound'.[36] Their colleagues were optimistic. Sir Lucas Pepys was satisfied from his own experience 'and from the Assurance of a Person who has most Experience in Cases of this Sort . . . that the Majority labouring under it did recover'. His authority was Dr John Monro of Bethlem Hospital, of whom it was wrongly rumoured that he had been called to the King. Although Sir Lucas knew 'no evident, or assignable Cause', he was inclined to think that the 'Amendment . . . in His Majesty's general State of Health' occurring at the same time as an 'Abatement of His particular Disorder' suggested that it arose from underlying bodily disease. Old Dr Addington saw 'very good Grounds of Hope' for the King's recovery from his experience of his madhouse at Reading, because of 'this Circumstance – that it had not for its Forerunner that Melancholy which usually precedes a tedious Illness of that Sort', meaning persistent insanity without obvious disturbance of physical health. Willis was both the most specific and sanguine in his answers. The King, he said, would recover:

I have great Hopes of His Majesty's Recovery. If it were any other Person but His Majesty, I should scarce entertain a Doubt: When His Majesty reflects upon an Illness of this Kind, it may depress his Spirits, and retard his Cure more than a common Person.

He told the committee he had had twenty-eight years' experience 'of the particular Species of Disorder with which His Majesty is afflicted' and 'never had less than 30 Patients every Year of the Time'. Nine out of ten of these had recovered, the majority within six months. Being asked whether he could name a cause to which 'His Majesty's Disorder is referrible', he answered:

From my own Experience with Regard to His Majesty, I cannot say any Thing; but from a very particular Detail of His Mode and Manner of Life for Twenty-seven Years, I do imagine, that weighty Business, severe Exercise, and too great Abstemiousness, and little Rest, has been too much for His Constitution . . . I may be mistaken, but I am more inclined to think myself right, because the Medicine that has been given His Majesty ever since Sunday Morning, and was intended to meet and counteract those

Causes, has had as much Effect as I could wish; and His Majesty has certainly been gradually better from the First Six Hours of His taking it.

They were asked about the diagnosis, not as an academic exercise or as a guide to their treatment, but as the clue to prognosis. 'Original Madness', otherwise mania or insanity, was considered not amenable to art, spontaneous recovery from it was uncommon and its course was therefore prolonged; whereas 'Consequential Madness', delirium and derangement, could be expected to subside with the underlying condition, whether it was a fever or not, rarely leaving an intellectual defect called fatuity or dementia.[37] Willis and Warren, therefore, represented the opposite poles of hopefulness and despair. If Willis was right, then recovery was in sight and a regency might be avoided; if Warren was right, a regency was inevitable and possibly permanent.

The report of the physicians, wrote Burke to Fox, 'is to settle the State' and they 'are now therefore the men in power'.[38] A jubilant Grenville wrote:

Willis's examination before the Committee . . . was all but decisive as to the certainty of his recovery in a short time . . . it is not very sanguine to hope that the King's actual recovery may take place before the measure [a regency] can pass here; or, at least, such a prospect of it as may make it absolutely *impossible* for the Prince . . . to change the Government.[39]

The Queen, too, was overjoyed. Willis told her that he believed that his evidence had 'knocked up all their [the Opposition's] hopes'.[40] She expressed herself 'very much dissatisfied with Sir G. Baker and Dr. Warren, and very well satisfied with . . . Dr. Willis'[36] and wished to have the care of the King left to him and his son 'without interference of the other physicians'. Willis confidently told Lord Ailesbury that the cause of the illness was that the King's nerves were 'exceedingly shaken . . . from over-exertion' and that he would not only cure him but leave him even better than he was before he fell ill: 'if he can bring them to a proper tone he thinks the King may enjoy himself more than he has done for years.'[40]

In the debates which followed in the House, tempers ran high. The Opposition demanded an immediate and absolute regency for the Prince of Wales as of right, while the King's ministers argued that if there had to be a regent he must be appointed by both Houses, with such limitations of his powers as they might think fit during the emergency. Fox declared that 'the Prince of Wales had as clear, as express a right to assume the reins of government, and exercise the power of sovereignty, during the continuance of the illness and incapacity, with which it has pleased God to afflict his Majesty, as in the case of his Majesty's having undergone a natural and perfect demise.'[41] Pitt on the other hand maintained 'that in the case of the interruption of the personal exercise of the Royal Authority . . . it belonged to the other branches of the legislature, on the part of the nation at large to

F

provide according to their discretion for the temporary exercise of the Royal Authority . . . in such manner as they should think requisite.'[42]
Each party rallied behind a medical flag-bearer, as it were:

Mr. Pitt constantly and warmly maintained the probability of its happy termination; and . . . made the resumption of the Royal power by the Sovereign . . . as soon as he should be enabled to wield the sceptre, the first and leading principle of all his measures and propositions. The adherents of the Prince of Wales saw the prospect of his father's recovery through a very different medium, and conceived of it not only as improbable, but as hourly augmenting in that improbability. They were sustained in this opinion by Warren, as the Minister was confirmed in his opposite sentiment by Willis; two physicians, on whose contradictory prognostics and apprehensions each party implicitly relied. The former, at the summit of his profession, and unquestionably possessed of great medical skill, was yet accused by the public voice of leaning in his inclination towards the party of the Prince. The latter, brought from a distant province to attend the Sovereign under his severe disorder, and having been peculiarly conversant in that species of disease, boldly and early asserted that he entertained scarcely any doubts of the King's perfect re-establishment at no remote period.[43]

In the House, Pitt contrasted the skill and experience of Willis with that of Warren.

He did not rise, he said, to speak of the character or skill of Dr. Warren, his general skill as a Physician was generally known and acknowledged; but with respect to the particular disorder with which his Majesty was afflicted, his skill was comparatively little, considered or compared to that of those physicians who had made that disorder their peculiar object of attention; and in saying this, he begged the House to know that he spoke from . . . the authority of Dr. Warren himself, who in his examination told them, that he always thought it necessary to call in and consult others more experienced in this species of practice than himself . . . He spoke of the skill, integrity, and good sense of Dr. Willis, which were evinced under a severe cross examination, calculated to puzzle simplicity . . . and declared that if he wished to draw a true conclusion of his Majesty's State of Health, and prospect of Recovery, he would wish to draw it from Dr. Willis, more than from any other Physician.[44]

Burke 'immediately took fire . . . Were they going to rob the first physician in this country of his character? He called upon them to shew how Dr. Warren was likely to have given a false, precipitate and ill-grounded account of his Majesty on oath? By their clamour they had furnished an unanswerable argument for fresh enquiry.' Besides, he declared,

If there was a difference of opinion among his Majesty's Physicians, why was not Dr. Monro called in? The keeper of one mad-house ought to be set against the keeper of another, and by the opposition they would come at the truth . . . Let Dr. Warren be placed against another eminent physician, and the keeper of a mad-house, with thirty patients against the keeper of a mad-house with three hundred, and by that means the House would obtain real information.[45]

Sheridan regretted 'the competition that had been set up between the skill of Dr. Warren and Dr. Willis'. On an occasion like the present one, he said:

it was ridiculous to stand upon idle ceremonies and trifling etiquettes; he would speak out and say, that if there was a witness who appeared to give prevaricating and evasive answers, that witness was Dr. Willis . . . When he heard Dr. Willis attribute his Majesty's illness to seven-and-twenty years of extreme study, abstinence, and labour, and declare that his Majesty was recovering, assigning as a reason, that the physic he had that day given him, had produced the desired effect; what must he think of Dr. Willis, when he heard him assert that his physic could in one day overcome the effects of seven-and-twenty years hard exercise, seven-and-twenty years study, and seven-and-twenty years abstinence, it was impossible for him to keep the gravity fit for the subject. Such assertions put him in mind of those nostrums that were to cure this and that; *and also disappointments in love and long sea voyages*. He did not . . . impute Dr. Willis's answers to any intention to deceive, but when he heard him roundly declare what every other of his Majesty's Physicians pronounced it impossible to speak to, he must assert, that Dr. Willis was a very hasty decider, and a random speaker.[46]

At Kew, the patient 'went on now better, now worse, in a most fearful manner,' wrote Fanny Burney,[47] but as Dr John Willis explained to her it was 'amendment' even if not progressive: 'it fails and goes back and disappoints most grievously; yet it would be nothing were the case and its circumstance less discussed, and were expectation more reasonable.'[48] Pepys, Gisborne and Reynolds in rotation stayed at the palace from four in the afternoon till eleven next morning; at ten o'clock Baker or Warren came to consult with the night physician and Willis. Willis and his son were constantly in attendance, as were the Windsor surgeons and apothecaries Messrs Hawkins, Keate, Dundas and Battiscombe, and there was always one of Willis's men and a page in the King's bedchamber and in the antechamber. 'H.M.'s Physicians still come,' wrote Greville, 'but Dr. Willis on the Spot, & He only, in constant attendance, now regulates principally in Every direction.'[49]

Willis's optimism seemed confirmed by the King's improvement in the second week of December. The bulletin of the eighth announced: 'His Majesty has had some hours quiet sleep; and is this morning much more composed than yesterday.' And on the ninth, 'His Majesty has had more than seven hours undisturbed sleep last night, and is better this morning.' 'Since Dr. Willis . . . has been called in, our hope has been more firm and constant, and at this moment stands very high,' wrote the Archbishop of Canterbury. 'A sense of the necessity of acquiescing in the advice he gives now induces the patient to submit to that advice, to eat what is ordered, to be more silent, to go to rest early and court sleep. Sleep is obtained without opiates, and the refreshment very considerable both in mind and body.'[50]

The King took his first walk in the garden[51] and on 13 December was permitted to see the Queen for the first time since the beginning of November.[52]

All seemed to be going well for Willis and his patient, when that very evening a fresh accession of his malady began. It had reached its first crisis in the second week of November and was to progress in fits and starts to its second in the last week of December. Again, they tried to divert the morbid humours from the King's head by at once applying blisters to his legs* as they had done early in November, but now, as then, he continued to get worse. At four o'clock the next morning he was as delirious as ever he had been and for the first time, officially at any rate, he had 'the strait waistcoat . . . put on him till 9'.[52]

Now also began that perpetual dissension among the attending physicians which disfigured so much of the medical management of the King. When the next parliamentary committee sat on 7 January 1789 to consider the King's progress and present state, it took them six days – as against six hours in the previous inquiry – to disentangle fact from faction. In fact, it was chiefly a record of the physicians' quarrels. Warren blamed the aggravation of the illness on Willis for having allowed the King to go for a walk on which he saw his daughters and the next day to become even more excited by seeing the Queen. Willis in turn blamed the blisters. But Warren said it was Willis who had recommended them because 'he never knew Blisters applied to the Legs of such a Patient without Benefit'.[53] Willis threw the responsibility on Pepys and protested that he had agreed only when he was told they had had a good effect before. To the blisters 'he imputed much of the Excessive uneasiness . . . & much of his later Violence,' wrote Greville on 18 December.[54] Willis even coolly told the parliamentary committee that he might never have had to put the King in a strait-waistcoat had it not been for the unfortunate blisters:

Perhaps, had there been no Blisters applied to His Majesty's Legs, which had an Effect upon his nervous System, which I was not aware of, from

---

* To draw ill humours out of the body various kinds of irritants, sometimes called counter-irritants, were applied to the skin. The most popular blister-raising substances, vesicatories, were cantharides or powdered Spanish fly and mustard plasters. The humours were thought to be eliminated through the serum of the blisters and through the pus which inevitably formed as they became infected. George III had blisters 'put on' his legs which discharged 'well' and for weeks, and in his last illness also on his back. He was cupped and had leeches placed on his temples with the same intention.

being told that His Majesty was scarce sensible of the Blisters that had been applied at Windsor, there never would have been any Occasion for such Coercion; but His Majesty's Blisters not operating kindly, had a very extra-ordinary Effect, as I thought, upon His whole System, and made me sensible that we were wrong in applying Blisters – though perhaps in the End they may not have retarded a Cure.[55]

The physicians' original intention when Willis came was to pursue the 'tonic' plan of treatment, Warren explained to the same committee, namely

that of endeavouring to restore His Majesty to the best bodily Health we could; to make His Constitution, if we possibly could, such a one as a healthy Man has at Fifty . . . I carried Dr. Willis to Kew in my Chaise, and gave him an Account of His Majesty's Mode of Living, former Habits, and present Disease. He agreed with me, that an Endeavour to restore the Constitution by the Bark, and occasionally adding some other Medicines, which we dis-coursed about, was the most likely Way to restore His Majesty's Health again.[56]

The King had already had a short course of the bark early in November, Warren said, but it had to be interrupted because of a return of his 'fever'.[57] Warren having previously denied that the King had ever had a fever, this was a strange inconsistency and one of the many contradictions in what he said at various times and to different persons and committees about the King's illness which make it difficult to sort out what his real opinion was and why he behaved as he did. It also laid him open, more than his col-leagues, to the charge of political bias in his medical pronouncements.

Willis had spent his first evening at Kew making up pills of calomel and 'a Cathartic' or 'Saline Draught' – a manual task which the royal physicians would always delegate to the artisan, the apothecary – to give the King the next morning 'to prepare Him for the Bark'.[58] He was referring to these when he told the parliamentary committee that he was confirmed in his hopeful judgement of the royal malady because within six hours his medi-cine had had the desired effect,[59] the claim Sheridan had rightly ridiculed. Had all gone well with the King, the physicians' rivalries would probably not have come to the fore as they did. But it did not, and 'The Change which has now taken place [in the King's state] produced early jealousies among some of the Faculty,' wrote the guileless equerry Greville, '& now from some cause or other, usual Transactions were not so smoothly carried on as before; interrupting that Harmony & general cooperation which had hitherto prevailed, & various reports of the same Case now spread abroad. These did not become less intricate from Party, & which jarring politics influenced.'[60]

'Jarring politics' or party allegiances apart, the royal physicians found it hard to accept Willis on an equal footing socially or medically. Like many physicians before and since, they regarded 'maniacal practice' beneath their dignity and 'so forlorn a study' as to be fit only for 'the coercive attendant'.[61] Furthermore, though Willis was medically qualified he was not in their eyes a physician, not being a member of the Royal College of Physicians, and was therefore outclassed. Indeed, it was not until after he had been at Kew one week, after much acrimony and the direct intervention of the Chancellor,[62] that he was suffered to append his name to the bulletins, and to the last day his name appeared last. The name of his son John, an Edinburgh graduate, who was constantly with the King and had the largest share in his immediate management, was never allowed to appear. Warren did not consider him 'in the Light of a Physician' any more than he did such inferior orders of the medical hierarchy as the Windsor surgeons and apothecaries who were also in attendance. 'We enquire of him how the King has passed His Time,' acknowledged Warren, but allowed him no responsibility 'in the Prescriptions and Physical Treatment'.[63] Besides, he added, 'Degrees in Physic give no Authority to practise in London, or within Seven Miles of London – there is no other Qualification than that of being a Fellow or Licentiate of the College of Physicians.'

Warren was not only a stickler for professional dignity, as befitted a successful society doctor, but also, because he was the first to be called in to help when Baker could do no more, regarded himself as the senior among the King's physicians. 'I was always considered, by the Highest Authority [meaning the Prince of Wales], as the first Physician,' he told the parliamentary committee in January 1789, 'and therefore thought myself particularly responsible: I thought myself obliged to look into, and to enquire after every Thing that related to His Majesty: I did not suppose myself in a different Situation upon the Arrival of Dr. Willis, and therefore took the Liberty of speaking to him with some Degree of Authority.'[64] He had informed Willis 'that he was there in a double Capacity, as Physician, and Attendant on His Majesty in the interior Room' and that he, Warren, must direct him in 'whatever related to him [Willis] in the Capacity of Physician', that 'whatever could be done by Deliberation, should be referred to Consultation', but that 'the Conduct of His Majesty, in the interior Room, should be left to Dr. Willis's Discretion, because it did not admit of Deliberation'. In short, Warren regarded Willis as the head keeper, and for this reason had spoken to him 'with some Degree of Sharpness' for having off his own bat allowed the King to take a walk and see the Queen – indiscretions which he blamed for the present exacerbation of the illness.

But Willis was not to be browbeaten into accepting an inferior role, either by temperament or by respect for etiquette, social or medical. Besides, he was accustomed to rule patients in his own house with that absolute power over body and mind such as psychiatrists alone ever possessed. He knew, too, that everything depended on controlling the King, and this was the function he had, as the expert, been called to perform.

Above all, he realized that, come what may, the Government would support him just as his optimism supported the Government by staving off a regency. He had also obtained the confidence of the Queen by taking charge of the sickroom and bringing order where the royal physicians left turmoil. He therefore soon turned the tables on Warren, and it was not long before he was able to exclude Warren and the other physicians from the sickroom altogether on the pretext that their visits agitated the patient – as, indeed, they did.

Their differing viewpoints and lack of objective standards by which to judge how the King really was, other than his degree of confusion, led to repeated quarrels about the phrasing of the public bulletins. Each in private made the King out to be better or worse than he was and than the bulletins announced, so that before long no one knew what or whom to believe and what the King's actual state or chances of recovery were. The physicians 'say everything they can to invalidate the daily testimonies of the others, so between both, the public are strangely divided in doubts, hopes and fears'.[65] The resulting uncertainty naturally heightened the political fever, particularly as discussion in Parliament centred on whether the Regency – which seemed more likely with every day derangement persisted – was to be a restricted one with limited powers for the Prince of Wales or whether the King was so ill and recovery so far off and uncertain as to justify giving him unlimited powers. Such a step would certainly have brought with it dismissal of the King's ministers and a government by the Whigs of the Prince of Wales's own choosing. In consequence, 'the demands of the Opposition rose and fell with the bulletins and according to whether the King was made out better or worse their resistance to any limitations on the Regent were faint or violent'.[66]

I am so tired with perpetual conversations about insanity, that I wish for any new event to think or talk of [wrote Mr Storer]. There is no circle into which one goes, where one person does not tell you that the King is now so near the re-establishment both of his bodily and mental health, that he will meet his Parliament in a fortnight; and some other contradicts him flatly by asserting that both his mind and his body are in the most desperate situation. One cannot say that doctors disagree. They are all on the same side, but Willis.[67]

How the physicians quarrelled about the wording of the bulletins and how little reliance could be placed on them is clear from the consultation of the morning of 16 December, when it was Baker's turn to make the morning visit. It is only one of many similar instances. The King had had six hours' sleep and Willis proposed that they should announce a very good night. Baker heard from the page Ernst that:

The 6 hours sleep was composed of 3 different sleeps. Upon which Sir L.

Pepys said, 'you see Dr. Willis, do what you will, you cannot make it a good night without splicing'. Dr. Willis would only sign to very good night. Sir G. Baker would not sign to the word *very*. Sir G. Baker said that in 30 Years Practice he never before met with the instance, where, when 3 Physicians disputed, and 2 agree in one opinion, the third did not comply.[68]

Willis, however, remained adamant and the bulletin read: 'His Majesty had a very good night having had six hours sleep', and was signed by Baker, Pepys and Willis.

This incident came up before the parliamentary committee. They found it incredible that a bulletin to which the President of the Royal College of Physicians signed his name did not represent the real state of the patient as he knew it. 'Do you not hold yourself responsible in your Character to the Public for the Truth of the Reports sent to St. James's, to which you sign your name?' they asked him, and he answered, 'I have never signed my Name to any thing that I have not thought true, or very near true,'[69] and went on to excuse himself by saying he had done it not to deceive but only 'for the Sake of Agreement'.

On 16 December, the day when the patient 'made great complaint of his legs hurting him exceedingly' and he 'was obliged to be wheeled' because they were so weak he could not walk,[68] he talked lucidly to John Willis. He said, 'It was always my duty to protect science . . . the interests of the People and mine are inseparable. I always hated an ambitious Man. I never made a friend of a Minister,' and so on – statements borne out by the catalogue of his patronage of the arts and sciences, and which the record of his relation to his ministers confirms. In the evening, however, he became 'incoherent' and continued in that state throughout the night, so that he had 'not a wink of sleep'.

Next morning he was still 'much disturbed, particularly at the Blisters, which burnt and tortured Him', and the Willises accordingly 'confined him'. While the King lay rambling in the strait-waistcoat, Warren arrived for the morning consultation and insisted upon seeing him. The Willises advised not. 'See him he must,' said Warren as he was 'responsible to the Public' and burnt his fingers in the process. He 'went into his Majesty's Room: at a time, when He was muttering in a low tone of voice.' His pulse was 112 and he was perspiring. Warren's entry brought him to awareness and 'He abused those who had confined Him and desired to be released'. Warren released him, 'when He instantly jumped up and down in Bed, grew more and more irritated till, in short, he tore off his Blisters and became so high and ungovernable as to make it necessary to confine him again'. The physicians withdrew discomfited and never again interfered with this aspect of the Willis regime. When later in the day he was allowed up, he was unable 'to bear his legs upon the ground', so weak and painful were they.

The physicians now gave him six-hourly doses of digitalis, the foxglove which Dr Withering had introduced into therapeutics three years earlier, in the hope of inducing calmness by lowering the pulse.[70] He slept five and three-quarter hours (so persistent was his insomnia that his sleep throughout was measured in quarters of an hour) and spent 18 December in 'high spirits, good humoured and sociable, inclining to mimickry'. To nullify any bad tidings which Warren may have spread in town, John Willis wrote a note to Pitt saying that the King had had the best night yet and that his father and he were 'more and more confirmed in the opinion' that 'His Majesty's compleat recovery' was in sight. And to put the other physicians in their place, he added 'the Blisters [that is their treatment] continue to give the King so much pain that his legs are constantly upon a chair, while sitting. And when His Majesty moves from one room to another, it is with greatest difficulty.'

To give heart to his supporters Pitt proudly showed this letter around.[71] Warren countered by telling Sheridan that, whatever the Willises claimed, the King remained 'quite mad'.[72] At the consultation the following morning, Warren reinforced this by declaring 'that he was "Shocked, agitated, rendered nervous, by seeing the poor King more mad than ever he had seen him before" '.[68] Turning to John Willis, he said, 'in a pshaw kind of dictatorial style' in reference to this unilateral declaration of the Willis faith, 'no more of it. You never can set it right as long as you live, adding at the same time that this *Political Letter* arrived too late at the House.' It is not surprising that Willis came to be regarded as Pitt's poodle and his opinion was discredited by the Opposition, as Warren's was by the ministers. 'I begin to think Dr. Willis is rather incautious a Man for his present conspicuous & responsible situation,' pondered Greville,[73] adding: 'By what I have lately observed I expect an Explosion soon among the Faculty, who are Evidently already shy of each other.'

Another restless night with only two and a half hours' sleep followed, and early in the morning of 20 December 'recourse was had to the strait Waistcoat: His legs were tied, & He was secured down across his Breast, & in this melancholy situation'[74] the Willises left him till lunch time.[68] As he lay he muttered, 'Oh Emily [his pet name for his favourite and youngest daughter Amelia, then aged five years] why won't you save your Father? Why must a King lay in this Damned confined condition? I hate all Physicians but most the Willises they treat me like a Madman. Digby, Greville, you are honest fellows, come and relieve me, take off this cursed &c' – the discreet symbol which signifies the strait-waistcoat in the Willis journal. But his pitiful entreaties were in vain. John Willis, who recorded this supplication, concluded only that he was becoming 'too low and that he might soon require the Bark'.

Greville was horrified. 'However persuaded I had been of the necessity of obtaining positive submission from H.M. under his Afflicting Malady, as the best means whereby His recovery might be ultimately expected, I have not been prepared for those harsher processes, which have followed . . . I can but grieve, & hope the best.'[74] Sir George Baker told him, 'this derangement was called Delirium rather than Insanity' and hoped the King's 'profuse Sweat' and pulse-rate of 'not less than 140' would prove to be the crisis by which the King would throw off his disease. Throughout the day 'He lay with a Pulse of 120, very irritable and easily offended'.[68]

'His Majesty was rather unquiet yesterday,' stated the bulletin on 21 December, 'but has passed a quiet night, and is better this morning.' Camphor emulsion was now given for 'the pain from the Blisters' and Warren suggested they make an occasional item of the state of the King's mind in the bulletins, since no official note had been made of it since 7 November.

On that day, after five hours' sleep, the King woke 'in good humour, and forgiving as to what had passed the day before. . . He got up and said, my legs are so well this Morning I could dance.' But neither the mood nor the ease lasted long. As the day went on, he became irritable again and his legs weaker and more painful, so that 'he could not bear to stand upon them more than a few minutes at a time'.[68] In the evening he 'was inclined to be a little unruly. He was checked this time by holding him down in his Chair, & by the interference of Dr. Willis, who recommended Him to be more calm, or that He would certainly talk Himself into a strait Waistcoat.'[75] 'H.M.,' however, 'continued Angry and abusive.'

After another night with only a few hours' sleep, on 22 December, the blisters were found to be discharging more than usual and 'thick matter'.[68] But the surgeons rightly maintained that they could not account for either the pain or the weakness in his legs. In fact, they took another fortnight to heal. The day was spent in 'good humour' and 'high spirits'; the King ate well and played backgammon with Willis. He felt his legs were stronger and Greville noted that he 'was now obliged to be managed at times with great caution to prevent his flying out',[75] that is escaping. In Whitehall, in contrast, spirits were drooping. 'The accounts . . . for the last week, though they have varied, are yet, on the whole, less favourable than before,' wrote Grenville. 'Willis ascribes this entirely to the effect of the blisters, which give him great pain; and Willis says that is, on the whole, by no means an unfavourable symptom. The effect, however, which these accounts produce here, is injurious to us.'[76]

The Government remained confident that the King would eventually recover, although 'almost all the physicians' now indicated that it might take 'a year or a year and a half',[76] if he recovered at all, and counted on it to make Parliament agree to a restricted regency. 'As His Majesty never showed any symptom or tendency to this disease before,' wrote the loyal

Lord Hawkesbury reassuringly to Earl Cornwallis, Governor-General of India, 'and as his mind evidently appears not to be enfeebled or broken, but only deranged, I look forward with confidence to his recovery.' [77]

Warren was said to be pressing for a further parliamentary inquiry to impose his bleak view of the illness on the politicians and to silence Willis by reducing him officially to a place subordinate to the physicians. Many details of the King's parlous state filtered out: 'accounts from ladies about the Queen, and from the physicians themselves' told of 'violent intermitting fevers, and profuse ... perspirations'.[78] Again public opinion was divided, as it had been early in November: 'According to wishes or fears, men construe this crisis to portend health or decease.' [79]

A change of administration now seemed so inevitable that a meeting of the Association of Bankers of London was 'understood to be for the purpose of tendering W. Pitt, on his going out of office, a transfer of £3000 per annum, Bank Stock, or a principal of £50,000 in the name of the commercial world'.[80]

In the sickroom the crisis was reaching its height. In the night of 22 to 23 December the King had only one hour's sleep, was 'restless and ungovernable' and had to have the strait-waistcoat. In the morning his pulse was 108 and he was considered so 'low' that another course of bark was started. He was through the day 'riotously inclined' and 'troublesome'[81] and had to be confined on his couch most of the time, although there were rational intervals of short duration. Greville vividly and movingly described the scene:

> About 7 o'Clock it was proposed that He should go to bed. He objected & resisted much but was undressed & bound down in bed in a strait Waistcoat. His spirits were at this time very extraordinary. He was not violent, Neither did his Situation, and his restraint seem to press uncomfortably on Him, and now as He lay stretch'd out on his Bed, He sang.[81]

That morning, Warren had returned to the attack and persuaded all his colleagues except Willis that, however discreet their official bulletins, they should report the true state of the King's mind to the Prince of Wales. Willis sensed danger and refused, on the grounds that it would be hurtful to the family, and for the record wrote an official letter to Warren:

> I cannot refrain from explaining myself particularly upon what has passed this Morning: It has ever been my practice not to publish to the relations and of any Patients, circumstances of their cases, which can only serve to wound and afflict their minds. I must therefore beg to be excused putting my name to such particulars, as are at once humiliating to his Majesty, and distressing to His Family.[68]

Warren took Willis's letter to the Prince of Wales, who commanded him to tell Willis 'that he does not desire you should sign any paper with the other

Physicians to be sent to him unless you chuse it, but that he desires he may have an account from you of His Majesty's health every day in general terms, without specifying any word or action . . . that you think should not be mentioned'.[68]

That night the King's condition deteriorated further. 'He slept not above an hour' and lay 'near two hours without speaking, yet at this time He was thought not to be asleep.'[82] This suggests he had another lapse of consciousness and perhaps another convulsion, which was not observed because he was tied to his bed and pinioned in a strait-waistcoat.

As happened after the similar crisis in November, he was quieter the following day, and the day after, being Christmas Day, more obviously confused than excited, as Greville described:

He was as deranged as possible . . . Among his extravagancies of the Moment He had at this time hid part of the Bed Clothes under his bed, had taken off his Night Cap, & got a Pillow Case round his head, & the Pillow in the bed with Him, which he called Prince Octavius [his youngest son, who died at the age of four in 1783], who He said was to be new born this day.[83]

His pulse was mostly 120 throughout the day and he sweated profusely. His voice was again very hoarse and he was severely constipated. Castor oil three times a day had no effect. In the evening, while the blisters, which still discharged a good deal of pus, were dressed, he 'talked wildly & in a very hoarse Voice. He was angry & much agitated. Dr. Willis was very anxious to pacify Him and to keep Him out of the Waistcoat, but to no purpose, & it was order'd to be put on – He became violently agitated & made great resistance.'[84]

'Violent & long have been the bewilder'd struggles of this day,' wrote Greville. 'He has been worse altogether this day than I have yet known Him to be & Dr. Willis's Men say they have not yet seen Him so bad.' However, he slept five hours that night and woke 'good-humoured but quite wrong', that is confused, and 'His hoarseness still continued',[84] but he was allowed up with the strait-waistcoat under his gown. His vision had troubled him for some weeks and he had difficulty in focusing, which made reading impossible, and 'a Parcel of Spectacles' was sent by George Adams, his optician. After trying them all, he 'selected two for mounting'.[85]

Meanwhile, the Queen had heard that reports were being sent direct to the Prince of Wales without her knowledge. Willis went to London to tell the Chancellor, who came to Kew and ordered that 'nothing should be sent from the House without Her Majesty's concurrence,'[68] and she was now shown the draft bulletins for approval. On 26 December she objected to the words 'much disturbed' as unnecessarily afflicting and on this occasion only was the bulletin altered. The version sent to St James's read 'His Majesty became less calm yesterday in the afternoon, an indifferent night, and calm this morning.'[68]

4. *Entry in Willis Journals for 24 December 1788 (British Museum Add. MSS 41690, folio 18) in the hand of Dr John Willis, showing the contrast between the official bulletin and what actually took place in the sickroom. Sir George Baker and Dr Reynolds attended. 'The waistcoat was taken off at nine – & blisters dress'd – discharg'd well – very sore – Pulse 96 – perspir'd through the night profusely – but little sleep'. The Prince of Wales was told that the King had been continuously in the strait-waistcoat from 2 o'clock the previous afternoon, had had 'not more than an hour's sleep' and was in the morning 'as incoherent as ever'. The public bulletin stated 'His Majesty pass'd the night quietly, but with little sleep – & is quiet this Morning'.*

In the evening the patient played backgammon with Dr Willis:

It was evident that playing did Him good, in as much as it stopped much conversation, & by occupying so much of his Attention, it gave a respite to his Mind from the continual hurries, brought on by inconsistent thoughts. He went to bed composed, & passed the Night quietly, but had not much above two hours sleep.[85]

On the morning of 27 December the pulse had for the second day running dropped to below one hundred, but still remained in the nineties. In the consulting room it was ordered that if necessary he should be given a larger dose of castor oil, as his prolonged constipation continued to be worrisome.

The crisis had passed and the Willises now rightly considered him 'considerably better', but Warren argued that 'tho' the King might speak 6 or 7 or more rational sentences than usual, yet, at the end of those he was again incoherent and gave proofs of insanity; he would not allow him better, for if He was insane He was insane'.[68] He denied 'that there were degrees . . . in maladies of this kind'. That day another of Dr Willis's sons arrived at Kew to help his father. This was the Reverend Thomas Willis, rector of St George's, Bloomsbury, whom the King liked and of whom he saw more after his illness. On hearing he had come, the King 'desired to see him that he might enquire of Mr. Fox's health', who since his return from the Continent had himself been ill – a remarkable example of how he tried to keep in touch in his clear moments.

As the worst phase of his delirium began to subside and his confusion sporadically lifted, the King again showed remarkable insight into how his mind had played him tricks. Greville recorded this welcome sign of returning awareness and reason:

In his more disturbed hours He has for some time past, spoke much of Lady Pembroke – This Evening He recollected, what He had at times said of Her, & a sense of shame accompanied his transient & deliberate moments – He very feelingly said to one of his Pages He hoped nobody knew what wrong ideas He had had, & what wrong things He had said respecting Her – This sense of his improprieties which now flashed with a gleam of returning reason, reminded Me of a similar Instance which occurr'd at Windsor on one of those days in which there had been symptoms more favourable than had yet appeared since his Attack – He observed at this time, that in his Delirium He must have said many very improper things, & that much must have scaped Him then which ought not, & that he must try & find out what had slipped from Him.[86]

For the first time in many nights he slept without a strait-waistcoat and it was thought reasonable to accede to his wish to see the Queen, but in the presence of Dr Willis. She had not seen him for a fortnight and found him looking 'thin and ill; he was tolerably composed, but very unwilling to part with her . . . and wanting her to promise to return to dinner'.[87] Willis gave out 'that the King received the Queen with much kindness. He sat down by her . . . & kissed Her hand, & He cry'd frequently.' As the conversation was cunningly conducted in German, which Willis did not understand, Greville wondered whether their meeting had been so peaceable, since the King afterwards 'continued for some time so violent' and from what he told his pages the conversation had been 'extravagant & wild'.[88]

Nevertheless, his physical health continued to improve; his pulse was now below ninety in the morning and his drenching sweats had also ceased. How much he had perspired is shown by the fact, recorded by Lady Harcourt but not by the Willises – 'they do not chose to have [it] known' – that he had developed an eruption 'at the bottom of his back . . . his skin is particularly tender, so that when he went to bed Willis was obliged to dress it with Turner's cerate'.[89]

On 30 December the Willises declared him to be 'more pettish than delirious' although still having little sleep. To their great relief he had three bowel motions that day, and the medicine was changed to calomel and camphor. He still lacked appetite and his refusal of food led to more altercation. But there were longer periods of rationality. For instance, in the evening of 31 December he asked Dr Willis about his house in Lincolnshire, his patients and his terms: 'The Doctor told Him that none gave less than four Guineas a Week . . . H.M. then asked who it was that kept another house like his at Leicester – He was told Dr. Arnold,'* wrote Greville, and added 'On the whole this has been a very remarkable day. One of Dr. Willis's men told Me He had never seen the King so bad as He had been during one part of this Morning, nor so well as during some parts of the Evening.'[90]

The New Year's Day bulletin stated: 'His Majesty passed yesterday in a good manner, had an extremely good night, and is in a better state than usual this morning.' That day, he asked John Willis 'to wait upon the Chancellor to tell him how he was, and wished me to find out what they thought of his illness in London'.[68] The Reverend Dr Francis Willis himself sent a New Year's message to the Prince of Wales and to Pitt, informing them that the King was 'in all respects better than . . . he has ever seen him'.

As before, the King's improvement aggravated the quarrel between the Willises and the other physicians about the extent of the amendment and how to convey it in the bulletins. Again, Warren insisted that he did not recognize degrees of insanity and he still regarded the King 'in a decided

* This is another example of how well informed George III was. Dr Thomas Arnold had distinguished himself by his scholarly and comprehensive *Observations on . . . insanity* (2 volumes, Leicester, 1782 and 1786).

state of insanity', irrespective of his lucid or rational intervals. 'On being pressed further, Doctor Warren said He had often in such cases heard many sensible remarks made by a Patient, but these did not prove that the Person was well, but improper remarks always were decisive & proved that the Person was still deranged.'[91]

The Willises took their quandary to the Chancellor, who was at Kew that morning. Evidently with a view to excluding the other physicians altogether from seeing the King, they told him that much mischief was done 'by the going in of so many People'. The Chancellor, caught off his guard, said, 'Why do you suffer it? Why don't you give an order to the contrary?' which they did. 'To comply with the wish of the Chancellor,' reads the Willis journal, compiled by Dr John, 'My Father stuck up a paper in the Pages Room containing the following words: "No one is to be suffered, except the Pages, to go into His Majesty's room unless introduced by, or with the leave of, the Dr. Willis's".'[68] The Chancellor reassured them further: 'Let them [the other physicians] sign to what they please in the Bulletin, if it be not your opinion say "This account Dr. Warren from 15 minutes conversation believes to be true, therefore he is right in signing it; from 24 hours conversation I believe it to be false, therefore I ought not to sign it".'

'Willis has been detected writing letters to Pitt,' wrote Sir Gilbert Elliot, 'who has read them . . . to the M.P.s and other people, giving assurances of the King's great amendment and of his immediate recovery, and this on the days when he had been in a strait waistcoat . . . Warren and the other physicians have remonstrated against this and it made some noise.'[92] The Prince

confiding in Warren's judgement, naturally considered the favourable reports as mere fabrications, to serve a sinister purpose, – and could not refrain from some expressions against the Queen – who, relying upon the infallibility of W[illis], considered the Prince's backwardness to credit her assurances as an argument for his discontent at the nature of them.[93]

Poor Queen – not only had she to endure the anguish of a desperately sick husband, but she was drawn into every concern of the sickroom and, of course, she had the responsibility of her family. Even so, she was not master of events, since all matters concerning the King also concerned the Government and in all decisions she was dependent on the ministers of the crown. The King's illness had brought their eldest son in active opposition to his administration and so also to her. However much she meant to keep above political strife, the Prince of Wales to her mortification reproached her now with political motives in trusting Willis. In despair, she appealed to the Lord Chancellor:

We have had another difference with the physicians about the Bulletin.

I saw Dr. Warren myself & got him to alter it, but I must own that, though he was careful not to say anything disrespectful to me, yet do I intend never to see him again, & told him, by what I understood below stairs, both parties have been warm, which I am sorry for, & do not intend to see Dr. Willis today; but this difference of opinion, arising so constantly amongst the physicians, makes me the more desirous of seeing some alteration made in the mode of their attendance; &, as your very kind & amicable advice has not succeeded, may I desire that you would . . . consider with the rest of the Cabinet some means to get rid of this physical & incomprehensible calamity? I see clearly by Dr. Warren's behaviour that his ambition & those who depend upon him, look upon the Willis's with a jealous eye . . .

I will only add, that if Dr. Guisborne was to come every evening, & make up the Bulletin the next morning, the world might depend upon hearing the exact truth of his Majesty; & any one of the other physicians coming every fortnight would be sufficient to disturb the whole house, & the world too. May I beg that my poor mind may soon be made easy upon this subject?, as the sight of that black spirit, Dr. Warren, has agitated it very much.[94]

There was no doubt that the King showed some improvement, but full recovery and resumption of his authority seemed as far off as ever, particularly as twice before amendment had been followed by relapse. Even Pitt conceded the necessity for a regency. In December he had persuaded the House that the Prince of Wales did not have a natural right to become Regent but that this was a matter for Parliament to determine. Now, in January, he proposed a limited regency, restricted with respect to its powers and duration. The Opposition, however, saw in the King's prolonged incapacity a second chance to gain full powers for the Prince. They reckoned that with another month having passed, the physicians would no longer be in a position to agree on the prospect of recovery.

On 6 January the House voted for another examination of the King's physicians before deciding on so grave and possibly irreversible an issue. Pitt, anxious to get government going as quickly as possible, thought this was unnecessary. He considered it

very unadvisable that the least delay should be interposed to the adoption of such measures as should restore the government and give it energy and effect . . . Any delay therefore, to the remedy which should be proposed, if something very particular was not advanced, he would deprecate and oppose . . . There was sufficient evidence for every one's conviction, that the actual state of his Majesty's health incapacitated him from business

and as he knew of no material alteration in his Majesty's health since the previous examination of the physicians, 'it was the duty of the two Houses forthwith to take measures for supplying the defect arising from that incapacity'.[95] Fox argued for a further inquiry in the hope that the physicians would be bound to regard his illness now as a chronic one and the House would move to an unrestricted regency:

G

He agreed that there was sufficient proof of his Majesty's actual incapacity to govern, and that the two Houses were proper in taking measures for supplying the deficiency; but if there were those who thought it neccessary to confer the exercise of the royal authority, with limitations, under the pretence that his Majesty was likely to be soon in a condition to resume it himself, these limitations must of course be influenced by the actual condition of his Majesty, and the probability of the malady either ceasing or continuing. If his Majesty's condition rendered it improbable that he should ever be relieved, the idea of restrictions, at all times improper, would then be done away; so that, on the whole, he thought the motion for further enquiry, extremely proper and necessary.[96]

Burke and Sheridan seconded the motion because of the contradictory reports and opposing medical opinions which had come from Kew.

Sir Lucas Pepys was examined first. He said that his hopes of the King's recovery were unaltered by the persistence of the illness. He had seen the King on 27 December so calm and rational that he expected signs of convalescence would soon appear. He also considered that it was a good sign that the King was 'more easily controuled now than He was a Fortnight ago, when under the same Care . . . As Controul is the principal Means used for Recovery, I consider Patients submitting to it more readily as a Mark of some Sort of Ground being got.'[97] Returning moments of insight were also a favourable sign. The King, he said, had shown marks of 'Consciousness of the Situation He then was . . . in . . . He spoke of His having been delirious at Windsor, and was surprized on my telling Him, that His Delirium had continued above Three Weeks.'

Willis had not 'the least Doubt of his recovery' but could not hazard any opinion as to how long the illness might last. The King's vision and concentration had improved, so that he was able to read several pages of a book where two weeks before he had not been able to read a single line. Because his evidence was crucial he was questioned about his difficulties with the other physicians, how the bulletins were made up, what alterations and why they had been made.

Warren, in contrast, saw no signs of amendment and much of his evidence was about the differences which had arisen between him and Willis. Baker spoke in the same vein as Warren, and so did Reynolds. Gisborne saw in the improvement which had taken place in the 'King's bodily Health . . . the Prelude to further Amendment'.[98]

In short, they said much the same as before, with the exception of Warren, who now admitted that the King had had periods of fever, and Baker, who expressed himself puzzled by the fact that 'His Majesty is grown extremely thin' and by the wide fluctuations – from 68 to 126 – in his pulse rate.[99]

When the report was debated in the House on 16 January, Pitt remarked:

With regard to the difference of opinion between the physicians, as to the prospect of a recovery, it appeared to him to depend on two circumstances, by which it could be decided on whose opinion the greatest reliance ought to be placed. The first circumstance was the knowledge of the malady in general; and the second, the knowledge of the particular case of the patient. Three of his Majesty's physicians [Drs Pepys, Gisborne and Reynolds] had been conversant with the malady. Two others, though not so conversant, are well acquainted with his Majesty's habits. These two [Sir George Baker and Dr Warren] attend his Majesty for two hours each day; the three others, from the evening until eleven in the forenoon. Surely it was natural for those who attended his Majesty most to be the best judges of his situation; and it was remarkable, that Dr. Warren and Sir George Baker were the least confident of a cure, and that the other Doctors possessed much greater hopes; but Dr. Willis, who attended his Majesty more than any of the others, was more sanguine than them all.[100]

Burke argued fiercely for an unrestricted regency. Not even

that bold Promiser, Dr. Willis, himself could . . . fix a probable time for the chance of his Majesty's being capable of recovering sufficiently well to be fit and able to resume the exercise of his Royal functions . . . The disorder with which the Sovereign was afflicted, was he said, like a vast sea which rolled in and at a low tide rolled back and left a bald and barren shore . . . He had taken pains to make himself master of the subject, he had turned over every book upon it, and had visited the dreadful mansions, where those unfortunate beings were confined . . . An author of great authority, he said, having mentioned the uncertainty of the symptoms of sanity, had declared, that after having been kept a month . . . after their recovery . . . they would sometimes dread the day of their departure, and relapse on the very last day . . . He had read enough to give the Committee a sense of the danger of an uncertain cure, arguing from the great disasters that had followed in private life, that it was the more necessary to take care that a sane sovereign was put in the possession of Government. He drew a picture of the King's supposed return, which he described as most happy, if really cured, but as horrible in the extreme, in its consequences, if a sudden relapse took place.[101]

So central to the political argument were the opinions of the physicians that the results of their examination were published not only in the Journals of the House of Commons and reprinted separately by order of Parliament but also fully reported in the daily press. They were also issued by a number of commercial publishers – for instance, in 'Bell's cheap edition', which was three times reprinted, so great was the demand. The Opposition went so far as to bring out their own version, entitled *Important facts and opinions relative to the King; faithfully collected from the examination of the royal physicians* (1789), in which the doctors' answers were cunningly 'arranged under general heads' so as to place Willis in the worst possible light. Different points of evidence were compared and contrasted to ridicule him as a doctor and discredit him as a man under such headings as 'Facts illustrative of Dr. Willis' Credibility' and 'Dr. Willis's Contradiction of himself'.

No parliamentary report had ever achieved such readership nor had any medical topic become so much a part of everyday conversation and debate. One fact stood out clearly: the fundamental difficulty of the political situation was how little was known about derangements of the mind. The doctors' differences, which in the last resort had their root in lack of knowledge, were however thought to be determined by their political allegiances. 'It is a strange subject for party to exist upon, and disgraceful to the country that it should be so,' wrote the Archbishop of Canterbury, 'but so it is, and many pronounce Warren a party man in his accounts of a deep dye, while Willis is supposed to delude himself by his ambition to recover the patient.'[102]

The bulletin on 5 January stated that he had become 'less tranquil last night, but has had three hours sleep'. There was, in fact, another short-lived setback in the King's condition which reached its climax on the 11th. The *London Chronicle* commented with justification: 'The variations in His Majesty's disorder, are considered as favourable symptoms: and the accounts for some days past have given great hopes ... The intervals of reason last week were many and long.'

Willis and the other physicians meanwhile continued at loggerheads. Warren said the King was feverish and Willis that he was not. They could not even agree on his pulse, which on 12 January Willis made 96, Warren 106, and 'more said Sir L. Pepys'. Baker also tried to harass the Willises. On 13 January the King had had six hours' sleep and John Willis wanted to put in the bulletin the words 'continued or uninterrupted sleep', but Baker objected because a page 'had told him that His Majesty had turned twice' during the night. When on 11 January Pepys ordered 'a quieting draught' of Tincture Thebaicum, an ancient preparation of opium, the Willises refused to give it as being unnecessary, and more trouble ensued, although a few days later the King was given opium pills again.[68]

As before when the patient was improving, his mental state was extremely variable, so that he was 'irascible in his manner & wild in his Conversation' at one moment and at another quiet and composed. When agitated, 'He talked much of Lady Pembroke ... much against the Queen & dwelt on varieties of subjects, with great inconsistency and incoherence,'[103] and spent many a long hour in the strait-waistcoat. When quiet, noted Greville, he was often 'sensible of his unhappy situation'. On 16 January, after an emetic, tartarized antimony, had for the first time been given but without his knowledge and he was violently sick, the King knelt on his chair and 'prayed that God would be pleased either to restore Him to his Senses, or permit that He might die directly'.[104]

On 17 January, after an entirely sleepless night, most of which he spent confined in the strait-waistcoat, he improved rapidly during the day and his pulse dropped from above 100 to 74. Greville commented:

Throughout this long & severe illness the suddenness of opposite changes have been frequent & most remarkable . . . Comparing the King's situation during last night, & the earlier part of this Morning, with what it was reported in the Evening, a more sudden contrast has not appeared.[105]

For the first time in many weeks the King had no abdominal discomfort, had an appetite and was allowed meat in his meagre diet. In the evening, at his own request, he saw the Queen and played piquet with Sir Lucas Pepys, and 'made not one observation that was not perfectly rational and collected'.[68] The night following he slept seven hours, but awoke 'never more disturbed in his life', on Willis's own admission. 'He continued in this state during the Morning and at times He became violent – He struck one of the Willis's Men, Took up a Chair to throw at another, &c., &c.'[106] The bulletin of the day read: 'His Majesty became calm yesterday before noon, and was remarkably composed during the rest of the day. His Majesty has slept seven hours, but is as usual this morning.'

He was certainly not an easy patient and his condition at that time perhaps the most trying a doctor can be called upon to deal with. That evening he demanded to see the Queen again and the three princesses, and the Willises, who apparently had lost some ground in controlling him, could not refuse. Nor could they refuse the next day, 19 January, when he insisted on going for a walk, because when they had a week before he had reacted violently. He had got as far as the Pagoda, but, not being allowed to go in, he lay down on the grass and either could or would not walk further and had to be carried back. The King's return, noted Greville with glee, gave 'full exertion to seven Persons who had attended Him in this walk – viz. Doctor Willis's Two sons, Two of H.M.'s Pages, & Three of Dr. Willis's Men'.[107] According to John Willis, the King had become weaker and weaker on the walk and had lain down when his legs would no longer carry him. However, when they reached home, 'he was put under coercion' as punishment for the rest of the evening, and taken to bed at eight, 'at which time He was in a more composed state, but not soften'd'.

The next evening Pepys 'found H.M. very deranged, his looks wild, & his conversation turned on the usual incoherent topics – He was full of Strategem & project, & among others He told Sir Lucas that He should contrive to escape from Doctor Willis'.[108] To further his plan, he tried to bribe the keepers with 'promisory Notes for various annuities'.

The most tricky time of his management followed in the next two weeks. As his active delirium subsided he had increasingly long periods of purposeful and consecutive reasoning, although much of it was still founded on irrational notions and beliefs. His physical strength also improved and a restraining device additional to the strait-waistcoat was procured for use in daytime. A great deal of the trouble and violence that ensued was in direct response to the control and coercion to which he was subjected and against which he rebelled. Unfortunately, the lesson that harsh treatment makes violent patients and that violence is often a reaction of fear was not learned until the nineteenth century. The Willises took it as a sign of irrationality and accordingly increased the sternness – not to say cruelty – of their measures and medicines, so creating a vicious circle of reciprocal violence between patient and keeper. In the evening of 22 January, for instance,

He became cross & untractable, And at length so unmanageable, that recourse was had to The Waistcoat. Before this extremity was resorted to He had struck one of the Pages & one of Dr. Willis's men. Under confinement H. My. became still more outrageous & abusive. Dr. Willis coming into the room He was particularly abusive to Him; order'd Him out of his Sight, & to get out of his House.[109]

On the same day, 22 January, 'a very great meeting' was held at Carlton House, where 'some of the principal arrangements that will take place immediately after passing of the Regency Bill' were made, reported the *London Chronicle*, and on the following day that 'It is believed the business of the Regency will be completed next week.' The long-drawn-out debates in the House were nearing their end. On 3 February the Prince of Wales pledged himself to accept the Regency under the proposed restrictions. On 13 February the Bill went from the Commons to the House of Lords. There it had its second reading on 16 February, the third reading was scheduled for 19 February and the Regency was to come into force forthwith.

At Kew the Willises used the newly installed restraining-chair for the first time on 24 January, when the King 'would do only what He chose' and upon being checked struck one of Willis's men:

The Chair in which He had now been confined was a new one made on purpose. It is a common chair placed upon a floor of its own, which prevents a Person from moving it, nor can it be thrown down as a common Chair might be. When it was first brought into the Room to be made use of, the Poor King is said to have eyed it with some degree of Awe.

And with bitter irony he dubbed it his 'Coronation Chair'.[110] It was the policy of Dr Willis, now more than ever, to maintain absolute control over his patient. He sent a memorandum to the Queen, stressing the particular need for it at this juncture of improvement 'to keep Him in a state of composure and . . . compliance with whatever is thought proper'.[68] This could be achieved only by surrounding the King with strangers who were not accustomed to receive the King's command as his pages were, and who would enforce 'that uniform Controul which is necessary' to avoid the 'great danger of the disorder becoming fixed'.[68]

The Queen, who had no choice but to give Willis, whom she trusted, full powers, accordingly instructed Greville to order the pages not to enter the King's apartment without specific directions from the Drs Willis. 'The Channels of obtaining regular & correct information of the real State of his Majesty's health, have thus become much narrowed, & possibly they may be much impeded,' feared Greville, who was himself now excluded from the sickroom, as the physicians had virtually already been for four weeks.[111] To implement the new order new keepers were brought in, of whom there were now nine at Kew, three constantly with the patient in daytime and two at night. The King, isolated from all familiar faces, 'has evidently shewn alarm at being attended by Keepers only' and took it 'into his bewilder'd Head, that Willis's Men meant to murder Him ... [which] much disturbed Him at times', noted his unhappy equerry.[112]

As confusion and incoherence further receded, there remained some phantoms of his delirium which he could not shake off. His mind, like his body, required time to find its previous balance. He believed 'that all marriages would soon be dissolved by Act of Parliament' and 'that his Hanoverian dominion was restored, and that he was shortly to go there'.[113] Involved in these phantoms was Elizabeth, Countess of Pembroke. She was a member of the Marlborough family, with which the King was very friendly, and at that time a grandmother of over fifty, Lady of the Bedchamber to the Queen, her husband Lord of the Bedchamber and their son Vice-Chamberlain of the Household. She therefore belonged to his everyday environment, had done so for years and continued to do so. It is well to remember this, because his pre-occupation with his relation to her came to play an unwholesome part in later studies of the illness.

Events experienced in delirious states, as in dreams, have a quality of reality far exceeding normal impressions and if remembered are for this reason all the harder to shake off. They are as a rule not relinquished from one moment to the next, but wear off gradually and recede again as vivid dreams do. At this moment of his illness they stood between him and his return. The Willises therefore took great pains to argue him out of them, as if the hammering home of reality could drive them out. Their method was little short of brainwashing, as Greville described in his diary on 30 January:

Dr. Willis had the King confined to his Chair this Morning for a short time, & gave Him a severe lecture on his improper conversation, Eliza, &c.; H. My. becoming more loud & impatient under this Lecture, Dr. Willis ordered a Handcherchief to be held before his Mouth, & He then continued & finished his Lecture.[114]

The King also had notions which to an observer might appear delusional, but were in fact adjusted to his situation. For instance, when he wished to institute two new orders, one was to have as its motto 'Rex Populo non separandus', which was patently inspired by his being kept against his will in close confinement.[115]

The Willises also plied him daily with tartar emetic,

a medicine on whose efficacy there is at present much dependance, & which it is thought has latterly done the King much good, & to be very quieting . . . whenever any irritation appears. It is curious, so often as H. My. has now taken it, how little he suspects the cause of his many sicknesses – but this medicine is so cunningly & so variously masked by Dr. Willis, that it is almost impossible to detect, or even to suspect the Vehicles. At one time it comes in Whey, at another in Asses Milk, Sometimes in Bread and sometimes . . . in bread and Butter &c., &c.[116]

Almost miraculously, despite all his trials, tribulations, treatments and low diet, the King steadily improved at a rate nobody could have foreseen. Not always can nature be trusted to triumph against such odds. The bulletin of 1 February had announced that he 'passed yesterday quietly, had a good night, and is quiet this morning'; and a week later that he 'continued in a composed state yesterday, had a very good night and is calm this morning'. Pain, sweating, irritability and fast pulse diminished, sleep improved and appetite returned. On 3 February he shaved himself for the first time in three months, and on 6 February was allowed to use a knife and fork again.[117] On 7 February the Willises noted with relief that even the stubborn constipation had ceased and the King was 'very open in his body'. He had spent the night 'in a composed manner' and was so in the morning when the physicians assembled to make up the bulletin.

The Willises now played a trick on the physicians. They encouraged the King to assert his royal authority and 'dismiss the Physicians as he would have done before his Illness' to show that he no longer needed the body doctors – and hoping secretly perhaps to get rid of them altogether. 'In consequence of this advice His Majesty after they had been in the room about a quarter of an hour said, he would not detain them any longer, and bowed. This was something so new and so proper in the King,' Dr John recorded with a chuckle, 'that, as if *Thunder struck*, they instantly retired, walking solemnly one after the other as at a funeral, thro' 2 rooms and a passage into the Consulting Room without uttering a word.' Warren was so impressed by the King's courtly behaviour that he told the Chancellor he was 'much better, that he finds the Character of his countenance much more promising than he has observed it before his Illness'. He also asked the Chancellor to convey to the Willises his 'earnest wishes' that they 'persist steadily in keeping him under that state of suppression to which he imputes the favorable appearance' and to continue to exclude all sources of irritation, that is visitors.[68] Warren's advice, no doubt, was as double-edged as Willis's, because he could argue that if the King were symptom-free under coercion and in isolation this was no proof that he was sufficiently recovered to take the decisions and buffetings inseparable from the performance of his regal authority.

Now came the crucial period, from 10 to 14 February. The bulletin on 10 February stated that he passed 'the day before in a state of composure, had four hours sleep, and has more recollection than usual this morning' and was signed by Baker, Reynolds and Willis. On that day, the King 'told Willis he wished to see the Chancellor; Willis replied he must desire that might not yet be, it would lead to conversations of length beyond his present strength. His answer was: "I will not do it till you think fit; but I have been ill seventeen weeks and have much to inquire about. I must have lost some friends in that time." '[118]

Willis attributed the improvement 'to a more generous regimen . . . part of which is a reasonable allowance of animal food once a day'.[119] The following day he was declared 'better this morning than he was yesterday' by Warren, Pepys and Willis. And on 12 February 'a progressive state of amendment' was announced. The King saw 'Vulliamy, a very sensible man, his old watchmaker . . . [who] protests he never saw him better. The astronomer [Rigaud], who keeps the observatory, saw him an hour . . . and received orders from him intelligible and perfectly collected.'[120] 'He compared his time-pieces with observations of the sun, and computed how much each had lost or gained time.'[121]

He took a walk

in the Exotic Garden where He saw Mr. Eaton his Botanic Gardiner – who talking to Dr. Willis, the King overheard his promise to make up a Basket of Exotic Plants for the Doctor some of these days; & on hearing this, he added 'Get another Basket Eaton at the same time, & pack up the Doctor in it, and send Him off at the same time'. [122]

He had already ordered a gold watch from Vulliamy as a parting present for the doctor.

The Opposition, too, had now to face the fact that the King was mending, as Sir Gilbert Elliot wrote on 12 February:

The King has been really considerably better the last two days. Sir G. Baker . . . says that he conversed rationally and coherently, with a great deal of recollection, for twenty-five minutes . . . he does not consider this amendment as actual convalescence (or as proving anything with regard to a final cure of the disorder), but it is certainly an amendment, and as he could not recover without passing through this state, it is a circumstance of encouragement . . . Warren also . . . found him considerably better, but does not seem to think the hope of perfect recovery even now a probable one. You can hardly conceive the effect this had in the town. The appointment of the Regency goes on just the same . . . There certainly never was a greater combination of embarrassing circumstances for a government or a country than at present.[123]

On 14 February an elated Grenville wrote to his brother:

I could not refuse myself the pleasure of letting you know that I have been at Kew to-day with Pitt, and that the account which he received from Willis is such as to confirm and strengthen all our hopes . . . His account is confirmed by . . . the other physicians . . . Sir G. Baker told him today, that if it was the case of a common patient whom he was attending, he should not think it necessary to give him any more medicines. The most favourable circumstance of all is, the great abatement of the pulse, which, till now, had always been much too high.[124]

On the same day, records the Willis journal, Baker 'was for leaving off the medicines, by way of trial . . . We objected to it. We could not be doing better than we were, and we might do worse. For the first time I ever heard Sr G. Baker spoke in favour of the case. He exclaimed, "of my heart, I believe the King will get quite well".'[68] On 15 February 'a state of improvement' was officially announced, and even 'Dr. Warren said that if his Majesty continued through the day in the same state in which he has seen him this morning, He might be said to be well.'[68]

The Willises were rightly concerned that the patient should avoid affecting or trying interviews. The Prince of Wales and the Duke of York had appeared at Kew on 13 February, and the Willises asked the Chancellor for guidance how to behave should they demand to see the King. ' "Beg them by all means not to go in, said he, that such a step might be of the utmost mischief to the King" – Should they still persist in going in, "Tell them, that you look upon it as deliberate destruction to the King's health". '[68]

The next dramatic change in the bulletins came on 17 February when Warren, Pepys and Willis announced: 'His Majesty has continued in a state of amendment for some time, and is now in a state of convalescence.' By a curious coincidence, it was on the very day the Irish Parliament presented 'an humble Address . . . to His Royal Highness the Prince of Wales, humbly to request His Royal Highness to take upon himself the Government of this realm, during the continuation of his Majesty's present indisposition, and no longer, and under the style and title of Prince Regent of Ireland' – a message which the Marquis of Buckingham, Lord Lieutenant of Ireland, refused to transmit.

The *London Chronicle* on the same day reported: 'Notwithstanding the happy prospect of his Majesty's intermediate recovery, the Regency will still take place, and continue for some time, a relaxation from business being judged necessary to establish the Sovereign's recovery.' The *Morning Chronicle*'s commentator saw in the mode of the King's recovery an assurance against relapse as well as confirmation of the nature of the illness:

His Majesty's malady has been held to be, not an insanity, but a delirium; and for this reason, that in cases of insanity the disorder is little affected by the pulse, the patient retains his disorder, be the pulse high or low. In cases of delirium the thing is directly the reverse. As the fever decreases, the patient recovers his mental faculties. It has happened exactly so to his Majesty. When his pulse was at 120, his malady was at its height. His pulse now is at 64, and he is perfectly recollected; and it will be a satisfaction to know, that cases of delirium cease with the cause, and scarcely ever return.

While the Regency Bill was waiting for its final reading, the King was entertaining himself at Kew, walking, reading Shakespeare and Pope, practising on the flute, brushing up his Latin, arranging his gardens and hothouses and entertaining the Queen and the princesses. For Willis, who had no French, he translated a letter, as he told Warren with a touch of his old humour, containing 'a remedy for Him as He was mad, & that the prescription was to open a Vein on the top of his head – That it had been sent to Dr. Willis because he was no Physician.'[125]

On 17 February the King saw the Chancellor for the first time against the advice of Warren, but with the sanction of the Willises. As a precautionary measure, the Reverend Thomas Willis was present throughout the twenty-minute interview. On 19 February, when the House of Lords was to begin its third reading of the Regency Bill:

as soon as the prayers were over, the Lord Chancellor left the woolsack, and said 'the intelligence from Kew was that day so favourable every noble lord would agree with him in acknowledging that it would be indecent to proceed farther with the bill when it might become wholly unnecessary . . . he would therefore move the adjournment.' [126]

Pitt proceeded in the same sense in the House of Commons the following day. But first the twenty-nine-year-old Prime Minister, whose loyal policy was beginning to be justified, wrote a hurried note to his mother, telling her that the King continued to advance to recovery: 'if the prospect is . . . confirmed, the plan of the Regency must probably be altered with a view to a very short interval indeed, or perhaps wholly laid aside . . . I could not resist the pleasure of communicating it.'[127]

The bulletin on 20 February told the public that the King 'continues to advance in recovery' and Willis now considered the King so well 'that he recommended, as a preliminary experiment to test the state of his mind, that the chancellor should be authorized to communicate to His Majesty the public events which had occurred during the illness. Of all the men that could have been selected for so delicate an affair,' commented the Duke of Buckingham, 'Thurlow was, perhaps, the worst qualified; but his relation to the Crown as Chancellor left Ministers no alternative.'[128]

Mr Grenville – recently elected Speaker of the House of Commons –

wrote to his brother on 19 February:

Pitt . . . has seen Willis this morning. His account is . . . that . . . the King is *now actually well* . . . and . . . capable of attending to his own affairs as he had been before his illness. He added that the keeping back from the King the present situation of public business and the measures which have been taken by Parliament, did him now more harm than good, because it created a degree of anxiety and uneasiness in his mind. He therefore recommended that the Chancellor, whom the King has already seen, and whom he expressed a wish to see again, might go to him, for the purpose of explaining to him all that has passed. You will easily imagine that this will be an anxious trial for us, because if anything can bring back the agitation of his mind, it must be such a recital as Thurlow must have to make . . . . If the experiment succeeds, you need not be told that we shall not feel ourselves disposed, nor indeed at liberty, to give up the King's authority (he being well) into the hands of . . . the Prince of Wales; and the less so, because we now *know* that he and his friends . . . have take the resolution of making a change at all events, and of taking all the offices of the country into their own hands.[129]

Grenville followed this letter up the next day:

Thurlow was with the King to-day for two hours. He did not enter into particulars of what had been done, but only in general terms. He says that he never saw, at any period, the King more composed, collected, or distinct, and that there was not the least trace or appearance of disorder . . . You must not expect to hear from me on any other subject than the King's recovery; for nobody here writes, talks, thinks, or dreams of anything else.[130]

After the Chancellor's visit and a walk the King was given 'a precautionary dose of 2 grains of Tartar Emetic' to make him vomit. With a clear idea of the difficulties which now confronted him, he said to Greville: 'Believe Me I have no Child's Play before Me, but all will do well by degrees.'[131] There were still occasions in confidential conversation when the King expressed 'wrong ideas', but his equerry found they 'have become too faint from what they have been, that it would not be fair to lay much stress upon Them at this time, but more just to consider them as mists dispersing fast before Sunshine.'

On 21 February the King's old friend Sir Joseph Banks, President of the Royal Society and Director of his Botanic Gardens at Kew, saw him for the first time since the illness and a week later brought him the most recent scientific books and journals to bring him up to date.[132]

How deliberate the King was is shown by items of conversation which Banks reported to Greville. The King spoke of dismissing all the pages who had been about him during his illness and said he would not strain himself by holding a levée for a considerable time. He may well have wished to avoid having to meet 'the rats', as those who deserted him for the Prince of Wales were called, and indeed he did not hold a levée again until September.

The Prince of Wales and the Duke of York, who had so far been refused admission to their father, now made 'a formal demand that they should be allowed to see him; or if not, insisting that the physicians should give in writing the reason for their refusal'. Their mistrust of the motives of Willis, 'the King maker', was obvious. They believed the King was represented as in a better mental state than he was in order to snatch from them the glittering prospect of the impending Regency. But when the King himself was asked, he declined receiving them until he had seen the Chancellor again, and an interview was fixed for 23 February.[133]

On the day, his sons presented themselves two and a half hours after the appointed time. This unheard-of unpunctuality – hardly credible had it not been remarked on by everybody at Kew – may be taken as a measure of the trepidation with which they faced their father, whose state of mind they could not foretell, whose knowledge of what passed politically they could not credit and whose attitude to them they must have dreaded, and an interview which would confirm either their worst hopes or fears. However mixed their feelings, they could not have anticipated that the King had carefully planned the tone of the meeting and how he wished to conduct it. He kept off all painful topics and told them he had brushed up his Latin, learned to play piquet, and such like.

The King purposely confined the conversation to common Subjects [noted Lady Harcourt], & the Queen's dinner being announced they took leave in half an hour and went away. They were evidently surprised at the King's perfect self possession nor did he betray the slightest remains of his Malady.[134]

The manner in which the King stood this acid test of self-restraint was to Lord Bulkeley 'proof that his miraculous recovery is not to be shaken'.[135] In contrast, the princes were 'quite desperate', and 'endeavour to drown their care, disappointments and internal chagrin in wine and dissipation'.

The King himself reported to the Chancellor on the day of the interview:

It must be a satisfaction to the Lord Chancellor to be informed that the Prince of Wales and my second son have been here; care was taken that the conversation should be cordial but without running into particulars. They seemed perfectly satisfied. I chose the meeting should be in the Queen's appartment, that all parties might have that caution which could at the present hour but be advantageous. I desire the Lord Chancellor will if possible call tomorrow . . .[136]

On that same 23 February the King wrote to Pitt that he wished to see him, after an interval of three months:

It is with infinite satisfaction I renew my correspondence with Mr. Pitt . . . I feel the warmest gratitude for the support and anxiety shown by the nation at large during my tedious illness, which I should ill requite if I did not wish to prevent any further delay in those public measures which it may be necessary to bring forward this year, though I must decline entering into a pressure of business.[137]

Pitt attended him the following day. Grenville reported to his brother that Pitt

says there was not the smallest trace or appearance of any disorder; that the King's manner was unusually composed and dignified . . . [he] spoke of his disorder as of a thing past, and which had left no other impression on his mind than that of gratitude for his recovery, and a sense of what he owed to those who had stood by him.[138]

The bulletin of 23 February stated 'His Majesty advances in every respect towards recovery'. In the circle of his friends, an astonished Sir George Baker said 'that he had not, in the whole course of his practice, discovered such a rapid amendment in any patient's health as in that of the King, during so short an interval'.[139]

Mr Storer reported triumphantly to Mr Eden:

The vessel has righted again. Ministry is perfectly afloat . . . The King has seen the Chancellor, the Prince of Wales, and the Duke of York . . . If his Majesty's disorder was singular and surprising, his cure is not less so . . . How Burke and Sheridan must be disappointed! Charles Fox has been at Bath taking care of his health at the moment the King recovered his understanding . . . Ireland . . . is in great confusion . . . I believe most people were tired of talking about the King's illness . . . His Majesty has now been so complaisant as to furnish us with a new topic. His recovery will supply us with new events.[140]

The week following the first announcement of the King's improvement and the adjournment of the Regency debate in the Lords brought party fever to a pitch. It was neck and neck between the return of the King and the installation of the Prince of Wales as Regent. So high did political passions run that as at no time before 'has it been so necessary to separate parties in private company. The acrimony is beyond anything you can conceive,' wrote Lord Sydney to Marquis Cornwallis. 'The ladies are as usual at the head of all animosity, and are distinguished by caps, ribands, and other ensigns of party.'[141]

The crescendo of the bulletins came to a climax on 26 February: 'There appears this morning to be an entire cessation of His Majesty's illness,' signed Baker, Pepys and Willis. The *London Gazette* announced the following day that 'By His Majesty's command, the Physicians' Report is to be discontinued from this day.' It was the King's first official act.

4

Restored to Health

The recovery of the King produced a fresh set of differences among the physicians, but with a curious reversal of roles. While the Willises throughout the illness had been accused of making the patient out better than he was, it was now their turn to counsel caution. The 'London Doctors', as the princesses at Kew disparagingly called them,[1] wanted the King to be freed of all semblance of restraint or restriction and to be taken off all medicines. The Willises, on the other hand, in accord with madhouse practice whereby patients were detained for one month after recovery, wanted to maintain some control over him for that period to guard against relapse and ensure that 'wrong ideas' left over from the acute phase of the illness were fully relinquished. In fact, they packed up exactly one month after the King had been declared well.

It was Warren who first urged that all restraint should be lifted. As early as 23 February, John Willis recorded: 'Dr. Warren now hinted at the necessity of the removal of the Nine men and every restraint.' Two days later Reynolds said the same. He hinted at the possibility of a third examination of the physicians to ascertain whether the King was capable of attending to public business, just as in December and January they had deposed that he was incapable, and 'with any restraint about him the Public could not be satisfied of the King's being well'.[2]

The physicians also pressed the Willises to be allowed now to see the King alone. Reynolds said he could not

speak to his reason . . . not having seen him alone . . . and he should not think himself justified in giving his opinion [about the King's capacity to govern] . . . because seeing the King only under controul, he could not be competent to it, and if he should be obliged . . . to say the King yet needed a Physician, it would be a handle to the Opposition for thinking the King therefore incapable of to govern.

Warren, too, thought another parliamentary examination was likely and asked Willis 'what could they say if all restraint was not taken off?' The Chancellor and Pitt also insisted that 'the Men', as the keepers were referred to in the Willis journal, should be removed and suggested that the visits of the physicians should be reduced to mornings only.

On 28 February six of the nine keepers were at last dismissed, leaving only the three Willis had brought down from Lincolnshire. The King himself arranged to dismiss on pension a number of the pages who had attended him,[3] not for any particular reason, the Chancellor told Greville,[4] but 'that from the manner in which they had been obliged to attend on Him during the illness, they had obtained a sort of familiarity, which now would not be pleasing to Him'. Wraxall, however, who kept his ear close to the ground, heard that they 'received their dismission' because they were suspected of divulging or transmitting information to Carlton House, during the critical periods of the King's malady.[5]

On 28 February also, Baker and Reynolds saw the King alone for the first time without a Willis present and reassured themselves that 'the composure of his mind' was not 'the effect of restraint' or fear of dominion by the Willises, but was indeed a measure of his 'degree of restoration'.[6] Next morning, 1 March, the King was seen alone by Warren and Pepys. To Greville 'both expressed Themselves as having been much pleased with their Visit'. Warren had found the King 'more deliberate in his Conversation than what was his accustomed manner, prior to his Illness that is, He thought He spoke slower, & that He waited longer for answers without interrupting'.[7]

In accordance with their policy of continuing treatment for another month, the Willises unbeknown to the other physicians persisted in plying the King with small doses of tartar emetic, and on 2 March Mr Battiscombe bled him half a pint by their order. He had not been bled since November and not surprisingly was 'very impatient before and after', as Dr John reported. This day also began the new arrangement whereby the physicians attended only on alternate days and there was none at Kew that morning.

The Willises watched the King's mind eagerly. When on 26 February they walked to Richmond with him, John Willis noted 'the walk quite right except a hint or two at Lady Pembroke', presumably as they passed her house, adding 'the King appeared yet very wrong upon that Subject' and thereby expressing some hesitation whether he could really be declared sane. In the hope of arguing him out of it, they so pestered him daily with questions that on 28 February he lost his temper and said 'he should be drove mad if he was plagued any more upon the subject'.[2] Yet the King was still haunted by uncertainty about what had in reality passed between himself and Lady Pembroke and what he had lived through in his delirium. And he continued to test his ideas against reality. He even tackled Mr Dundas, one of the Windsor apothecaries, saying 'that he might be wrong',

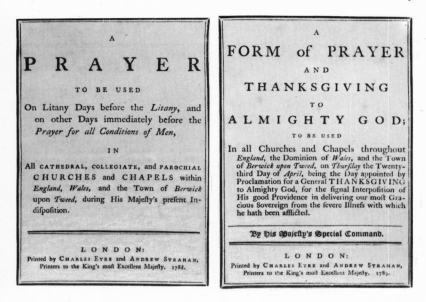

A

P R A Y E R

TO BE USED

On Litany Days before the *Litany*, and
on other Days immediately before the
Prayer for all Conditions of Men,

I N

All CATHEDRAL, COLLEGIATE, and PAROCHIAL
CHURCHES and CHAPELS within
England, *Wales*, and the Town of *Berwick*
upon *Tweed*, during His Majesty's present Indisposition.

L O N D O N:
Printed by CHARLES EYRE and ANDREW STRAHAN,
Printers to the King's most Excellent Majesty. 1788.

A

FORM of PRAYER

A N D

THANKSGIVING

T O

ALMIGHTY GOD;

TO BE USED

In all Churches and Chapels throughout
England, the Dominion of *Wales*, and the Town
of *Berwick upon Tweed*, on *Thursday* the Twenty-
third Day of *April*, being the Day appointed by
Proclamation for a General THANKSGIVING
to Almighty God, for the signal Interposition of
His good Providence in delivering our most Gracious Sovereign from the severe Illness with which
he hath been afflicted.

By His Majesty's Special Command.

L O N D O N:
Printed by CHARLES EYRE and ANDREW STRAHAN,
Printers to the King's most Excellent Majesty. 1789.

5. *George III's illness in 1788 was generally felt as a national disaster and his
courageous triumph over affliction added greatly to his popularity. Early in
November the Privy Council ordered the Archbishop of Canterbury to compose
a form of prayer for his recovery for use throughout the country; and on his
recovery in March 1789 a thanksgiving prayer for 'delivering our most
Gracious Sovereign from the severe Illness with which he hath been afflicted'.*

but he had the impression – 'delusion', as Willis called it – that Dundas
had acted as go-between and now was surprised to hear that all happened
purely in his imagination. Finally, he appealed to Lady Pembroke herself
to clarify his mind. She reassured him that her sentiments had always been
and remained those of a 'most affectionate sister towards an indulgent
brother' as well as a 'most gracious Sovereign'.[8] A similar remnant was the
conviction that he must go to Hanover. All to whom he confided the idea
asked him to give it up, and in fact he never went there.

His normal style of life was rapidly re-established. The Duke of Leeds
saw him on 3 March and found him 'grown very thin and his voice [still]
hoarse . . . His head however, appeared perfectly clear, his memory correct,
and his conversation less hurried and more connected than in general it
used to be.'[9] In the evening he heard music for the first time since the
Windsor concerts were cancelled almost exactly four months before. It
was provided by 'Jones the Welsh Harper', who played chiefly Handel, the
King's favourite composer. He 'slept in his former Apartment [that is
upstairs with the Queen] for the first time' since his arrival at Kew. On

H

6 March he wrote to his son Adolphus, himself recovering at Hanover, thanking him for his 'filial affection . . . during my long and severe illness' and hoping that he would regain his 'former vigour of body' as he had already 'by the mercy of the Allmighty' regained 'that of mind'.[10] The following day the three remaining Willis men departed.

On 9 March a Privy Council was held at Kew and on 10 March the Chancellor put an end to the progress of the Regency Bill and debates which had occupied the exclusive attention of Parliament for four months. He acquainted the assembled Houses that 'a commission had passed the Great Seal with his Majesty's Sign Manual . . . commanding the Commissioners . . . to hold this Parliament, to open and declare certain further causes for holding the same'.[11] The Chancellor then said:

His Majesty being, by the blessing of Providence, happily recovered from the severe indisposition with which He has been afflicted; and being enabled to attend to the public affairs of His Kingdoms, has commanded us to convey to you His warmest acknowledgements for the additional proofs which you have given of your affectionate attachment to His Person, and of your zealous concern for the honour and interests of his Crown, and the security and good government of His dominions. The interruption which has necessarily been occasioned to the public business will, His Majesty doubts not, afford you an additional incitement to apply yourselves, with as little delay as possible, to the different objects of national concern which require your attention.

A 'humble address' in answer to the Speech from the Throne was moved as well as 'a Congratulatory Message to the Queen'.

These legislative deliberations were followed on the same night by the most brilliant, as well as the most universal exhibition of national loyalty and joy, ever witnessed in England. It originated . . . with the people, and was the genuine tribute of their affection . . . London displayed a blaze of light from one extremity to the other; the illuminations extending . . . from Hampstead and Highgate to Clapham, and even as far as Tooting: while the vast distance between Greenwich and Kensington presented the same dazzling appearance.[12]

'Many houses had devices of different sorts in coloured lamps and transparent paintings,' some were 'prodigiously ingenious', wrote Sir Gilbert Elliot.[13] Church bells tolled and cannons fired. The Queen and all the princesses but the youngest accompanied by the two Willises drove unrecognized around London to see the illuminations, an occasion celebrated in an ode by William Cowper. At Kew, the Queen 'had arranged a private illumination of the palace and of the courtyard . . . which she hoped would prove a gratifying surprise to her consort'.[14] 'The King – Providence – Health – and Britannia, were displayed with elegant devises . . . When it was lighted and prepared, the Princess Amelia went to lead her Papa to the front window: but first she dropped on her knees, and presented him with a paper' containing lines scribbled at the Queen's desire by Fanny Burney for the occasion.[15] What a moment for the King, to be allowed to remain by himself for an evening! 'The Queen and princesses did not return from town till one in the morning. They were quite enchanted with the glorious scene they had been beholding.'

The next day, old Dr Francis Willis 'left Kew to go for a week into Lincolnshire his first absence since his arrival' on 5 December, noted Dr John. 'The physicians, all of them,' wrote the Archbishop of Canterbury with emphasis, 'except Dr. Gisborne of the household, have taken their leave.'[16]

On Saturday, 14 March, the King made a triumphant return to Windsor. 'This morning we returned to Windsor,' wrote Fanny Burney in her lively and picturesque way,

with what different sensations from those with which we left it! All illness over, all fears removed, all sorrows lightened. The King was so well as to go on horseback . . . All Windsor came out to meet the King. It was a joy amounting to extacy; I could not keep my eyes dry all day long. A scene so reversed! sadness so sweetly exchanged for thankfulness and delight.[17]

On 21 March, old Dr Francis Willis returned. Next day his youngest son, Dr Robert Darling Willis, came to Windsor, and on 26 March all the medical members of the Willis family left. Their final instructions, which close this volume of the Willis journal, were that the King was to continue 'taking the Bark twice a day and about twice a week to take 3 quarters of a grain at a time of Tartar Emetic and also to use the warm bath, and foot bath occasionally'. In the event of 'too high spirits or too great impatience' one of his pages was instructed 'to add Tartar Emetic to the dose of Bark'.[2]

The King was delighted to be back at Windsor and in harness. After his first night there, he wrote at the end of an official letter to Pitt: 'I have the pleasure of acquainting Mr. Pitt that I have had more sleep last night than any one since my long illness'[18]; and such was his relief at his sleep returning that he also mentioned it to Lord Sydney:

Though it might seem odd to mention one's health in a mere letter of business, I know how much Lord Sydney interests himself in my welfare that I just mention that the being returned to my favourite residence has obtained me a much quieter night than I had experienced since my illness; and the joy that appears in every countenance . . . cannot fail of having a due effect.[19]

The day being Sunday, he received the sacrament from his favourite prelate and friend Richard Hurd, Bishop of Worcester, at nine o'clock and went to prayers at eleven, 'which with the Te Deum lasted more than 2 hours', and again for an hour and a half in the afternoon, recorded John Willis, who, with his brother Thomas, accompanied him. Not until after a full day of worship did he settle down to the gigantic and heart-rending task of studying seriously the political repercussions of his illness. In his early days of recovery from the middle of February the Queen had been anxious to shield him from them to avoid a possible setback. On 18 February, after an evening visit to her apartment upstairs, she 'with difficulty . . . persuaded' him to return to his own because her 'apprehensions were very great of his seeing newspapers and pamphlets that were on her table'.[20]

'To say the truth,' he told the Earl of Lonsdale, 'I have never yet looked into the papers relating to it, as I could not do so till I found myself in a disposition to forgive all those who might have acted in a manner I could not approve . . . I took the Sacrament this day, and shall begin with the papers to-morrow.'[21] Having studied them, he told his brother, the Duke of Gloucester, that the proceedings in Parliament 'had been like taking out a Statute of Lunacy against him' – as indeed only by an 'inquisition in lunacy' could he be legally declared incompetent to manage his and of course the nation's affairs. 'Had it passed,' he declared, 'no power on Earth should have prevailed on him to resume the Government'[22] and he would probably have retired to Hanover.

With the physicians he was 'more than ever displeased . . . after reading the account of the examination by the Committee'.[23] He could not be otherwise with the Prince of Wales, though the Queen held their second son, the Duke of York, 'the most blamable . . . as the King had cautioned him before his illness [against] connecting him with people the Prince of Wales had . . . connected himself with'.[24] He spoke little of how he had been treated, but the memories of it never faded. Many months later he 'talked of the coercion used & asked how could a man sleep with his arms pinioned in a strait waistcoat & his legs tied to the Bed posts'.[25] For a time he held it against all parties concerned, from the Queen through Mr Pitt to General Harcourt, that he had been manoeuvred to Kew by stratagem.

Balls, dances, receptions and parties followed to celebrate, in which the Queen and her family joined but from which the King wisely remained aloof. On 19 March the Queen gave to all those who had been loyal to the King during the crisis 'a new medallion . . . with a Latin inscription in honour of the King's recovery'[26] dated 10 March.

Preparations were advancing for the service of thanksgiving at St Paul's Cathedral, 'an affecting though highly proper act of devotion',[27] as the King himself called it. He had conceived the idea in the last week of his illness in February. But even then the Archbishop and Earl Camden, Lord President of the Council, attempted, though unsuccessfully, to dissuade the King from so trying and strenuous an occasion.[28] 'Many who loved him feared that the excitement of the day might produce a return of his disorder,' wrote George III's loyal biographer Jesse:[29]

[They] therefore endeavoured, though in vain, to divert him from his pious purpose. Among these friendly counsellors was the Archbishop of Canterbury. 'My Lord,' was the King's reply to him, 'I have twice read over the evidence of the physicians on my case, and if I can stand that, I can stand anything.' It was accordingly arranged that the affecting and imposing ceremony should take place on 23rd of April, on which day the King . . . proceeded in solemn procession to St. Paul's.

That the ceremony would be a great strain the King himself realized, as a letter written two days before to Pitt indicates:

I must candidly confess that though now without complaint, I feel more strongly the effects of my late severe and tedious illness than I had expected, though but what had been insinuated; I mean a certain lassitude and want of energy both of mind and body, which must require time, relaxation, and change of scene to restore.[30]

The service lasted three hours and he was away from Buckingham House for five hours.* 'He looks thinner, and is three stone lighter than he was,' wrote Sir Sydney Smith.[31] Sir Gilbert Elliot, who had not seen him since he fell ill, also remarked on how much flesh he had lost. He 'was much struck with the alteration in him . . . the King is quite an object of thinness,' he informed his wife, 'his face as sharp as a knife, and . . . his eyes appeared therefore more prominent than before . . . [He] appears extremely weak by his manner of walking . . . He was dressed in the Windsor uniform, had on a greatcoat which reached to his ankles, and was probably intended to conceal his legs, which are extremely thin.'[32]

The Reverend Dr Francis Willis celebrated the recovery of his patient by paying a subscription of £50 to the charity of the Royal Hospital of Bethlem and so joined the select band of governors.[33] Two letters from him

* How far opposing political views coloured even eye-witness accounts is shown by two descriptions of the King's behaviour during the service. Bishop Tomline, Pitt's tutor and friend who was present in his capacity as Dean of St Paul's, wrote: 'The humility with which his majesty . . . seemed to pour forth his thanksgiving and prayers, made a lasting impression . . . Indeed, throughout the service . . . and in the whole of this interesting and awful scene . . . nothing was so striking, as the earnest and uninterrupted devotion of his majesty' (*Memoirs of . . . William Pitt*, 1821, third edition, vol. 2, pp. 488–9). The Whig Sir Gilbert Elliot, who was also present, told his wife: 'The King's manner was apparently indifferent . . . he looked about with his opera-glass and spoke to the Queen during the greatest part of the service, very much as if he had been at a play' (*Life*, ed. Countess of Minto, 1874, vol. 1, pp. 304–5).

6. *To celebrate the King's recovery in 1789 medals were struck bearing on one side the royal image and on the other a variety of pious tributes. The Reverend Doctor Francis Willis – who claimed the credit for the cure when nature had triumphed over medical art and spontaneous recovery restored the patient – had his own medal struck with his likeness and the message 'Britons Rejoice, Your King's Restored', perhaps the finest piece of advertising ever achieved by a medical man.*

to the King from that period survive and sum up well his social and intellectual background. They confirm Hannah More's opinion that Willis was neither more nor less than 'quite a good, plain, old-fashioned country parson' of seventy-three.[34] The first letter is dated 13 March and was written after he left Kew and before he returned for his final visit to the King at Windsor. It was to thank the King for his present of a gold watch.

Before my weeping eyes left Kew I was introduced to the Embassadors, who unanimously & heartily thank'd me for my best endeavours in restoring your Majesty . . . Then, thou dearest of all Kings . . . forgive me, since of such consequence is your Majesty's health, if I beseech you to give me leave at times to give your Majesty a hint to take especial care of it, particularly to endeavour at all times to have if possible six hours sleep.[35]

The other letter, of 11 May, indicates how protracted the King's convalescence was and how long his debility persisted: 'I have heard, with much concern, that your Majesty complains of want of spirits and weakness of limbs, and that you are much hurt at the reflection of your severe illness.' In a sermonizing vein the old parson in him advised the King, despite his 'severe affliction', to look to its 'good and great effects . . . tho' dearly bought'. His illness, he wrote, had 'drawn out the affections of millions of people, as well as the uncommon esteem of all nations, at the same time that it has expos'd your enemy's and provok'd them to throw out their sting, so as to lose their power of poisoning for the future.' To console the King, he added: 'The lowness of spirits and the weakness of limbs are what were to be expected when the fever, which had so long stimulated the nervous system, was taken off.' And he recommended sea-bathing and 'the bark draughts as before twice or three times a day, for the bark will strengthen and firm the mind as well as the body'.[36]

Encouraged by the 'very kind answers' he received, Willis followed with a third letter, but complained indignantly when he had no reply.[37] He was also 'very indignant at Mr. Pitts offer of £1000 a year to him at his age', having, it was understood, been lured to London with a promise of a pension of £1,500 a year. It was, in fact, not until May the following year that Parliament voted him a pension of £1,000 for twenty-one years.[38] His son Dr John received £650 a year for life, while the London physicians were remunerated at the rate of ten guineas for a visit to Kew and thirty for a visit to Windsor. Sir George Baker's fee in all amounted to £1,380.[39] For the Reverend Thomas Willis, 'who certainly has the most merit in having supported the Old Doctor through his difficulties with the other Physicians', wrote the King to Pitt on 27 August, he suggested 'the natural provision for Him . . . the first vacant Prebendary of Worcester; I have seen so much of him that I can answer for his principles being as will do credit to my Patronizing him.'[40] But Thomas Willis never got this 'natural provision', despite, or because of, his much greater services to the Government during the King's illness in 1801. 'The Warrant for the other Physicians,' the King thought in contrast 'very large considering their conduct but I will not enter on a subject that cannot but give me pain, for I cannot say I find myself either in strength or Spirits so much recruited as I should have hoped.'

Willis senior, however, incurred no hardship by the delay of his reward, because his fame for attending to the King had spread so far that he was soon after called to the Queen of Portugal, whose illness was marked by a 'conviction that she was irrevocably doomed to everlasting perdition'.[41] Although his ministrations were not crowned by success, he was said to have received £20,000.[42]

He saw the King for the last time in his life when he called on him with his son Thomas at St Leonards on 21 September 'on purpose to pay their duty'. Willis assured Lord Harcourt 'of the Kings perfect health, & that there was not the least fear of a relapse'.[43]

Meanwhile, at Windsor throughout May, the King complained of the slow return of his previous energy and health. On 1 May he wrote to Pitt of his displeasure at his third son William, later Duke of Clarence and William IV, who, without his permission, had come home on leave from his naval station in the West Indies. He was sure his return had been engineered by the Prince of Wales to strengthen 'the Opposite faction in my own family'. This back-handed move convinced him all the more of the need to safeguard his loyal Queen and daughters 'from a total dependence on a Successor', as well as to ensure the continuance of 'Executive Government' in case 'it shall please the Allmighty to end my Days' or 'should not I entirely recover the vigour of mind and the inclination of taking the same active part I have done for above twenty-eight Years'. These matters, he wrote, 'hang heavily on my mind' and he only hoped 'a total change of Scene and thorough relaxation . . . should . . . by degrees . . . recover the great shock that so severe an illness has certainly given to my whole nervous system.'[44]

On 5 May he wrote again that 'the lassitude and dejection that has accompanied me since free from fever prevents my being able to decide either quickly or satisfactorily to myself on any subject, and consequently makes me require time on all matters that come before me.'[45] And on 29 May he complained that his proneness to mental fatigue was equalled by his physical exhaustion: 'I am not yet able to copy my own papers, time, air and Sea-bathing', he trusted, would 'restore that tone to my constitution which I am taught to believe I am too unreasonable in having expected would have been effected before this time.'[46]

To recuperate, the King decided to go to Weymouth and he and the royal party left on 25 June. As on his triumphal progress through the West Country – just twelve months before – the route was lined everywhere 'by faces all glee and delight'.[47] At Weymouth he was soon 'in delightful health, and much-improved spirits,' wrote Fanny Burney to her father. But she found

the loyalty of all this place excessive; they have dressed out every street with labels of 'God save the King'; all shops have it over their doors; all the children wear it in their caps . . . The bathing-machines make it their motto over all their windows; and those bathers that belong to the royal dippers wear it in bandeaus on their bonnets . . . and have it again, in large letters, round their waists, to encounter the waves . . . Nor is this all. Think but of the surprise of His Majesty when, the first time of his bathing, he had no sooner popped his royal head under water than a band of music, concealed in a neighbouring machine, struck up 'God save great George our King'.[48]

But it was noticed that if he incautiously 'exposed himself to the excessive hot weather' he soon became 'much indisposed' and 'was soon fatigued'.[49]

Relaxation, air and prolonged excursions had the hoped-for effect, and the King returned to Windsor after twelve weeks much revived. 'I have the pleasure to assure you,' wrote Queen Charlotte to their son Augustus on 24 September, 'that the King is come home much stronger & better for the sea-bathing. He began his Levees yesterday & bore it very well, appeared but little fatigued & seemed very chearfull at night, so I have hopes that we shall soon come to go on in our old way.'[50] As yet, the King wisely did not propose making it a regular function as before 'and not either by business or exercise over-hurry myself but come to both by degrees'.[51]

Illness and convalescence had lasted almost twelve months and he was now to enjoy twelve years of uninterrupted health but for a few minor episodes. In 1790, for instance, while on holiday at Weymouth, he was again sensitive to sunlight and had to give up riding in 'the heat of the sun' as well as driving in his 'sociable'. 'The Queen, therefore, had three double carriages made with cane bodies, and covered in with silk . . . and thus they were enabled to pay noon visits to . . . the country.'[52]

Five years later there was a short return of abdominal symptoms similar to those which had ushered in his illness in 1788. After a period of malaise, he wrote to Pitt on 22 December 1795: 'I shall be prevented from going tomorrow to town by a bileous attack, which is now nearly removed, but the natural consequences of the medicines necessary on such an occasion must in some measure weaken me for a few days . . . it has been attended with no one symptom of feaver.'[53] To the Duke of Portland, he wrote the following day: 'the medicines directed by Dr. Gisborne continue certainly gradually to remove the complaint, and . . . I have every reason to think that the present attack, from being seriously attended to, will in a very few days be entirely removed.'[54] And on 27 December: 'I have had respite enough to pursue the remedies that now have entirely removed the evil . . . yesterday I rode out for the first time, and found myself much the better.'[55] He was well again within a week.[56]

5

What Other Doctors Thought

If the royal malady created a national crisis it also had immediate and far-reaching repercussions on the medical scene. It became the talking point also in medical circles and a number of doctors rushed into print to take issue with the royal physicians about their diagnosis and treatment of the King. Their books also dealt with nervous disorders and mental derangement in general and aired fundamental views on the subject. Because they were topical and controversial they in turn stimulated further publications, so that the great rise of psychiatric literature in the following decades can ultimately be traced to the impact of the King's illness.

DR ROBERT JONES: NERVOUS FEVER

First in the field was Dr Robert Jones, who published at Salisbury on 24 January 1789, one month before the King recovered, *An enquiry into the nature, causes and termination of nervous fevers; together with observations tending to illustrate the method of restoring his Majesty to health and of preventing relapses of his disease* (1789). He was a disciple of Dr John Brown, who in 1780 had formulated and named after himself the well-known Brunonian system of medicine, according to which all diseases could be simply divided into local and general and subdivided further into 'sthenic' and 'asthenic'. For Dr Brown 'Sthenic signified an excess, asthenic a defect, of invigorating or vital power', and since the two conditions were opposites so also were the treatments they required.

Such is the simplicity to which medicine is now reduced, that when the physician comes to the bed-side of a patient, he has only three things to settle in his mind. First, whether the disease be general or local; secondly, if general, whether it be sthenic or asthenic; thirdly, what is its degree? When once he has satisfied himself in these points, all that remains for him to do, is to form his indication or general view of the plan of cure.[1]

Dr Jones set out to show how Brunonian principles could be used to diagnose and treat the King. The fundamental question was whether his illness was 'mania, a sthenic pyrexia', or a fever affecting his nervous system, 'an asthenic pyrexia'. If he was suffering from the former, 'bleeding, blistering, vomiting, and purging . . . cupping, a spare diet . . . and applications of this nature' were required to remove the excess or ebullition of 'invigorating power'. Conversely, such drastic measures would be 'most dangerous' if his illness was 'asthenic'.

From the royal physicians' answers before the parliamentary committee, Dr Jones diagnosed the royal malady as 'neither more nor less than a nervous fever'. This ought to have been treated on the tonic or strengthening plan – the very opposite of that which had been followed. 'Every man, in all descriptions of nervous fevers,' he wrote, 'is rather incoherent' – that is, 'he may labour under a delirium'. It required 'great judgment' not to confuse such cases with 'insanity'. Clearly, the King's 'delirium arises from a weakened condition of the nervous and vascular system in general, but more especially in the brain,' commented Dr Jones, and 'to increase the cause' by lowering treatment, as had been done, 'is not the method to remove the disease'. He was, in fact,

astonished to hear, that his Majesty could sustain, (without being precipitated long before this time into a state of disease;) the weighty, and important business, which, like a millstone, must have hung heavy upon his mind, at the same time that it was reported, that he eat chiefly of vegetable food, and drank nothing but wine and water.

Small wonder that his 'debilitated state of the body' had been made worse by being 'bled, blistered, vomited and purged' while simultaneously being deprived of 'his usual comforts and consolations'. Dr Jones had

not a doubt but that his Majesty has been treated injudiciously, from the beginning of his complaint to the present time; and it will be a duty incumbent upon his physicians . . . to publish a journal of their proceeding. It is full time that the whole of this dismal story should be held out to public notice . . . Their reputations as physicians ought either to stand or fall by their method of treating the King.

The fact that they had confined him in a strait-waistcoat he branded as particularly 'infernal and brutal'. Such a step could be sanctioned only by those 'profoundly ignorant of the principles, and philosophy of the healing art'. For, he asked, what was 'madness' but the consequence of 'the improper treatment of fevers'?

For Drs Warren and Reynolds he had the least regard:

It is said that Dr. Warren, when examined before the Privy Council, made use of the word *insanity*,* as applying to his Majesty's disease, and that he was reprimanded by Lord Camden for such an expression. If the Doctor had made use of such language, it is impossible for any words to be sufficiently severe for the noble earl to make use of, to curb such a wanton and unbounded expression of speech. In the inferior conditions of life, the expression alluded to is equivalent to the destruction of a man's credit and happiness for ever. But in the more exalted situation of a monarch, it not only affects the credit and importance of the nation he governs, but must fall upon his offspring: and the more especially, as this disease is supposed, without any ground for such a supposition, to be *hereditary*. Dr. Reynolds, upon his examination, says, that his Majesty's complaint may last for weeks, months, and years. And I am willing to admit of this prophecy, unless a different plan is pursued than that which has been adopted by the learned Doctor's friends and himself.

Dr Jones's plan to restore 'the King to his accustomed mental and bodily vigour' as speedily as possible was that he should

be indulged in every rational propensity which is agreeable to his mind. His illustrious consort and family ought to have access to him at all times. He should never be contradicted, nor thwarted in any thing that he can request, either in food or drink . . . He should now indulge in animal food, and a proper quantity of wine. Music, provided it is not too loud, will be of great service . . . He should avoid going out into the air . . . otherwise the smallest chilliness . . . will convey it into the head;

and he ought to have read to him 'those books which used to afford him pleasure when he was in a state of health'.

In brief, Dr Jones advised the physicians 'to invigorate, by all possible means, the body, and to afford every consolation to the mind' of their royal patient – no bad precept for psychiatrists of any age.

* The history of 'insanity' as a diagnosis is paralleled by that of 'fever'. Both were anciently considered diseases *sui generis*, until advances in medical and pathological knowledge showed that they resulted from many causes. By curious coincidence the year 1788, in which George III's illness highlighted the fundamental issue in psychiatry – whether 'insanity' was a disease or a symptom – also saw the validity of 'fever' questioned. A pioneer of this new view was Dr Francis Riollay, who in his *Critical introduction to the study of fevers* (1788) wrote that he was induced 'to consider *fever* as a symptom, which many causes occasion; and to account for its several forms and circumstances from *variety* in causes, and *difference* in constitutions' (pp. 67–8). 'This manner of considering fevers,' he concluded (pp. 70–1), 'is attended with several advantages' of which the most important in his opinion was that it 'promises improvement in the methods of cure, by directing the mind towards investigating causes' and treating these rather than their effects. And as he rightly foretold, when causes of fever were identified and it became possible to treat them, the old blunderbuss methods of shocking patients out of their symptoms disappeared. When psychiatry is as far advanced as medicine, the same development may be expected to take place.

MR ANDREW HARPER: INSANITY A DISEASE OF THE MIND

The next to appear in print was Mr Andrew Harper, 'late surgeon to His Majesty's garrison in the Bahama Islands', with a new view of mental derangement, *A treatise on the real cause and cure of insanity* (1789). He set out to rebuff the notion that the King had been insane, and ended up as a pioneer of psychiatric thought. His claim to fame rests on the fact that for the purposes of his argument he redefined insanity as a condition which arises independently of bodily illness from 'some direct and immediate disorder in the operations of the mind'.

Harper wrote in unequivocal terms:

The nature of Insanity has been clearly traced up so far as to render it an unquestionable axiom, that the cause of it must depend upon some specific alteration in the essential operations and movements of the mind, independent and exclusive of every corporal, sympathetic, direct, or indirect excitement, or irritation whatever . . . The mental faculty may suffer a variety of changes and modifications from corporal causes . . . but these . . . have been proved totally dissimilar to Insanity . . . I will therefore take it upon me to define and pronounce the proximate cause and specific existence of Insanity to be a positive, immediate discord, in the intrinsic motions and operations of the mental faculty.

That the King had been physically so ill alone made the royal malady 'totally dissimilar to Insanity'.

What was the background from which this obscure army surgeon propounded such determined views in so difficult a field? He had, as far as can be ascertained, no experience of deranged patients, not even a formal medical education. He had no skills to boast, no learning to flaunt, no private asylum to advertise. In fact, he condemned outright as 'big with ignorance and absurdity' the custom 'of immediately consigning the unfortunate victims of Insanity to the cells of Bedlam, or the dreary mansions of some private confinement'. Unlike Jones, he did not propose rules for preventing relapse of the disorder, but referred to his previously published *Oeconomy of health, containing new and familiar instructions for the attainment of health . . . happiness and longevity.*

His motive for writing was simple. As a good soldier and royalist, he rose to defend his King from the imputation of madness. In particular, he reprimanded Willis for hinting that the King was insane:

No idiosyncratic disposition, no morbid affection, general, or local, nor any physical change or effect . . . can possibly constitute . . . Insanity. How fallacious and destructive then must the opinion of those be, who have ventured to refer the cause of mania to abstemious living, severe exercise and want of sleep [as Willis had before the parliamentary committee]. These causes produce general debility, and . . . predispose to melancholy; but that they should occasion Insanity is utterly impossible.

He also rebuked him for the severity with which he had treated the King, because 'A state of coercion is a state of torture from which the mind, under any circumstances, revolts'.

Harper's sentiments were admirable, and the importance he attached to the physical side of the royal malady correct. But he got carried away and made a general division between disease of mind and of body according to which 'insanity' was an affection of the immaterial organ, a 'mental' illness. With it, he stirred up an issue which still divides psychiatrists into fundamentally opposing schools. Remarkably, it was this part of his *Treatise* which made history. And what in its time was little more than the effusion of an indignant loyal subject was fifty years later elevated to a major contribution to psychiatry. The regimental surgeon whose *métier* were wounds and fractures and who never reached commissioned rank, of whom George III and his physicians probably never heard, had greatness thrust upon him by posterity. The first historian of psychiatry, the learned Dr J. B. Friedreich, named him as the founder in modern times of the psychic as opposed to the somatic school of theories of mental illness.[2] And as such Andrew Harper is remembered to this day.

DR WILLIAM ROWLEY: TRUTH VINDICATED

Dr William Rowley of Savile Row, London, had the misfortune to bring out his *magnum opus* on nervous disorders, *A treatise on female, nervous, hysterical, hypochondriacal, bilious, convulsive diseases; apoplexy and palsy; with thoughts on madness, suicide, &c.*, just before the King fell ill. Its six hundred pages had been two years going through the press. He hoped to present a copy in person and travelled to Windsor for the purpose on 3 November, when it was not yet generally known how ill the King was. Two years later, when he became physician to the St Mary-le-bone Infirmary, he restated his views illustrated on the King's illness in *Truth vindicated: or, the specific differences of mental diseases ascertained ... with facts extracted from the parliamentary reports, and reasons for declaring the case of a great personage to have been only a feverish or symptomatic delirium* (1790). He concluded:

When the circumstances previous to the attack be skilfully considered according to the most approved precepts of medicine, when the actual existence of fever, during the whole time of the complaint, be duly weighed, what are the inferences? The disorder was not a *chronic mental complaint*, because this begins and continues *without fever*. It was not a *phrenitis*, or phrensy, because it did not originate with an *acute continual fever*, nor terminate in a few days. The mental irritation being most *urgent* when the *fever* was most *violent*, clearly proves the irritation to have been a *symptom of fever*, or of some prevailing irritating acrimony. The biliary obstruction, the rash struck in, the cold received by wet feet, the arthritic swellings subsiding, all shew, either singly or collectively, sufficient causes to excite a symptomatic mental irritation, by what physicians call *metastasis*, or the translation of a disease or acrimony from one part to another.

Therefore, to those for whom it remained a question 'what hath been the real complaint of a great Personage', he would answer: 'The disorder was positively a *symptomatic* or *febrile delirium;* and every reason unites to conclude the cure will be permanent.' Three years later, when he published a collected edition of his works, *The rational practice of physic of William Rowley, M.D.* (four volumes, 1793), he commented in the preface:

In volume the second, are treatises on Madness, Suicide, and a short performance on the definitions of mental diseases, proving, that the late affection of His Majesty was not insanity, as supposed by many, but strictly a feverish symptomatic delirium. It may be observed, that the concluding sentence in that book has been verified, where it is declared, '*that the disorder was not madness, and the cure would be permanent*'. It is hoped, that the assertion of this important truth, so interesting to the Royal family and the nation, will not be considered unnecessary by those, who reflect on the many serious circumstances attending that alarming event.

DR JAMES GRAHAM: THE LUNATIC FRINGE OF MEDICINE

Dr James Graham,* self-styled 'Conqueror, under God, of Diseases',[3] heard of the royal malady at Liverpool and at once bent his mind to how best he could assist the King. He composed a prayer which he had 'printed in large Characters, on a very large sheet of paper, signed with my handwriting, and sealed with my seal' and which he hung over his bed to aid his concentration. He then posted to Windsor and on to Hampstead Heath where, by surveying the metropolis, he hoped to diagnose the national as well as the royal malady and propose remedies for both. But the task proved too ambitious and only a two-page prospectus saw the light of day.[4] Fortunately, it suffices to show the kind of contribution he had in mind had he been able to live up to his inspiration. With its florid language, alliterations, repetitiveness, its qualifying phrases, choice of adjectives and

* Dr Graham had achieved notoriety in the 1780's for his extravagantly furbished Temple of Health and Hymen, including a Celestial Bed, in the Adelphi and later in Pall Mall. There he is said to have exhibited Emma Lyon, Nelson's Lady Hamilton, as the goddess of health and fertility. Among the eccentricities he later advocated was 'earth-bathing' as the universal cleanser and healer.

expansiveness of sentiment, it is characteristic of the effusions of a group of psychiatric patients who, once they start to write, cannot stop.

First, An Anatomical, Philosophical, Medical, and Religious Investigation of the . . . causes . . . of the King's late severe, dangerous, and universally lamented corporeal and mental maladies. *Secondly*, A full and clear description, or display, of certain natural, and of certain supernatural, or divine means and medicines which were proposed for his Majesty's . . . recovery . . . Under this head of the work the Author gives humbly his opinion, as a Philosopher and a Physician, of the situation, soil, air, and salubrity, or the contrary of the Royal Palaces at Windsor, Kew, Kensington, St James's Park . . . *Thirdly* . . . A critical and mildly christian review of the form of prayer . . . for the King's recovery, which was read in all the established churches and chapels of England . . . To this part . . . is added . . . a critical and a curious review of the late shrewd and solemn examination of the Royal Patient's Physicians, before the honourable committee, which was for that purpose appointed.

A fourth part of this 'original, eccentric, and most important Work' was to have dealt with the choice of a consort for the Prince of Wales; in fact, none other 'than evangelical wisdom! the virgin daughter of the Great King of Kings!!!' And it subsequently appeared as a separate tract.[5]

But, continued Graham, events had forestalled him:

His Majesty, by the skill and care of his Physicians and Friends – by the suspension of certain mechanical causes of his malady – by hot effervescencies subsiding . . . having, it seems, perfectly recovered his former health of body and mind, just about the time that Dr G.'s *Work* was finished for printing; was the reason for its not appearing . . . He hopes, however, that, when . . . it shall be ushered into the light, it will prove a sterling and standing system of health and happiness to mankind in general . . . For although that the late severe indisposition of our very amiable, and very much-beloved Sovereign, was the motive of this book being written – tho' the Hemorrhage of the national heart be now stopped . . . yet the Author of the Book trusts, that, when published . . . it will be the means of subduing, expelling, and eradicating any species of morbid Virus, or Impurity, which may be insiduously latent or lurking, or more furiously and fatally fermenting, in the blood and other juices of his fellow-creatures at large.

Two years later, in the autumn of 1792, Graham achieved his ambition when at Weymouth he was granted an audience with the King and pressed into his hands his rules of health, confident that they would be of use not only to him but also to his Majesty's forces, 'those brave defenders of our comparatively superiorly favoured and happy island'.[6]

Graham was *en route* to Portugal in response to a 'call' or impulse to restore that country's Queen to health. During the voyage he was observed by Dr William Withering, whose *Account of the Foxglove*, published at

Birmingham in 1785, by introducing digitalis to the medical profession did almost as much to advance the science of therapeutics as Dr Edward Jenner's *Inquiry into the causes and effects of the variolae vaccinae* (1798) did in the field of preventative medicine by introducing vaccination. Withering wrote to a friend from Lisbon:

> I shall give you a sketch of our voyage, a short account of our fellow Travellers . . . the 4th Mess room bed was occupied by . . . Dr. Graham. Graham, the renowned Graham, warned by a vision makes a voyage to Portugal, to cure the Queens insanity. He is either madly or hypocritically religious, some are of one opinion, some of the other, but as I did not choose to be acquainted with him could not form an opinion myself. He lives upon vegetables, Milk, Honey & Water, & reads from the bible from Morning to night. Some of the party at times diverted themselves by drawing him out into conversation, but on these occasions I retired, finding my presence spoiled the sport. He has demanded, though not obtained, an audience of Chevalier Pinto the prime minister here.[7]

The Queen's advisers preferred the advice of Dr Willis.

DR PARGETER AND THE REVEREND JOSEPH TOWNSEND: PSYCHIATRIC DIAGNOSIS

Dr Jones wrote his book to popularize the Brunonian system of medicine, Harper to defend his King from the stigma of insanity, Dr Rowley to put on the medical map 'the specific differences of mental diseases', and Dr Graham to offer his own brand of mystical medicine. All were inspired by the royal malady, and however varied their approach, all agreed that the King suffered from delirium and not insanity. It is well to bear this in mind, because later generations of psychiatrists took the opposite view and called it a mental as opposed to a physical illness.

No sooner had this first wave of publications subsided than the King's illness began to figure discreetly in medical texts. It would be a lengthy and repetitive task to trace the incidental references in the many books on mental and nervous diseases which appeared in the remaining thirty years of his reign. Two, however, merit mention, because each raised an important point.

The first was Dr William Pargeter's *Observations on maniacal disorders*, published at Reading in 1792 and written to illustrate the axiom '*that management did much more than medicine* in the cure of Madness'. Pargeter paid little regard to theory and less to classification, and quoted only so much of classical writers and medical authorities as was necessary to give his modest book the stamp of scholarship without turning it into a parade of learning. It is therefore still readable today and shows what a thinking doctor thought about mental illness just before the end of the century. Pargeter's bow at the royal malady was brief and to the point:

The definition of *madness*, by the consent of all writers, is delirium *without* fever: and here I cannot forbear an attempt to settle a point, concerning which, most people have been too hasty in forming their opinions. Some few years ago, a case in medicine occurred, which agitated this kingdom, and engaged the attention of all *Europe*. This case was universally, I believe, thought to have been maniacal; and lest this idea should be a future reproach to us from other nations, I firmly deny the position in the following syllogism: Quid est insanitas? Insanitas est, delirium sine febre – Erat aegro febris – ergo, Aeger non erat insanus.

Equally delicate in his allusion, though his diagnosis differed, was the Reverend Joseph Townsend, Rector of Pewsey in Wiltshire and erstwhile Edinburgh medical student. Instead of merely joining in the usual argument whether George III's illness was delirium or insanity, he attempted to give it a name. In the second volume of his *Guide to health . . . designed chiefly for the use of students* (1796), Townsend diagnosed the 'case in which the whole nation felt deeply interested' to be '*mania melancholica*' or that 'species of *mania*' which 'is commonly preceded by and alternates with *melancholia*'.

It was a condition brought on by 'anxiety and grief, intemperance, deep study, violent passions and emotions, with disappointed love, and wounded pride', which caused 'a vehement and impetuous circulation of dense and melancholic blood through the weakened and flaccid vessels of the brain'. Following the tenets of the humoral pathologists of earlier centuries, Townsend derived the impure blood from 'affections of the alimentary canal', a theory he considered proved by the fact that the King's 'cure was effected by copious evacuations, after which tonics and astringents were prescribed to restore strength'. Townsend could hardly have dreamt that two centuries later all the causes of his '*mania melancholica*' which he listed, with the exception of 'intemperance', should be resurrected to account for the King's illness, albeit in psychoanalytic garb; and that even his 'diagnosis' should re-emerge in the vernacular as manic-depressive psychosis – both, it must be added, with fateful consequences for the modern image of George III. Psychiatry did not start with Kraepelin and Freud.

PART TWO

The Other Illnesses

6

The Return of the Willises: 1801

In the second week of February 1801, in the midst of a change of ministers, the King was out riding with one of his equerries, General Garth. 'I have not had any sleep this night,' he told him, 'and am very bilious and unwell.'[1] It was the beginning of the second major attack of his illness. Clinically, it turned out to be a replica on a smaller scale of the illness of 1788–9 and it raised the same constitutional issues. If it did not make as much history, it was because a Regency Bill lay ready framed from 1789 and there was no occasion for parliamentary debates and disputes and no examination of the physicians. The acute phase of the illness was also shorter – two weeks as against six – and he recovered physically and mentally much more quickly, so that whether he was delirious or deranged never became an issue.

Now, as then, a week of physical illness with colic, constipation, hoarseness, muscular pain and weakness, sweating, fast pulse and sleeplessness led unexpectedly to acute delirium culminating in coma. Now, as then, the illness was attributed to cold, caught by remaining too long in church on Friday, 13 February, a fast-day when 'the weather was so snowy and cold, that His Majesty became excessively chilled'. He developed 'cramps all over him'[2] and his hoarseness amounted to 'almost a total loss of voice'. At the same time, he was 'constipated and full of bile',[3] troubled by nausea and colic, and his urine was dark. Muscular weakness followed quickly: three days after the onset, on Monday, 16 February, he apologized to Henry Addington, later Lord Sidmouth, his incoming Prime Minister, for 'writing so ill, for I am in bed from a severe cold'.[4] Dr Thomas Gisborne, who had replaced Sir George Baker both as the King's senior physician and as President of the Royal College of Physicians, treated him hopefully with James's powder.[5]

On the same day the Reverend Thomas Willis, with whom the King seems to have kept in contact since 1789 and who periodically visited him, happened to call at the Queen's House, or Buckingham House, now Buckingham Palace, and found him suffering from 'a very bad cold and hoarseness', but despite close scrutiny detected no marks of mental disturbance.⁶ For an hour they discussed the question of Catholic Emancipation, which was uppermost in the King's mind and which because of his uncompromising opposition to it had led to Pitt's resignation as Prime Minister on 5 February. The next day, 17 February, and the fifth of the illness, Addington observed – just as Baker had on 22 October 1788 – that the King's 'manner was more hurried and his countenance more heated than usual'.² But the following day he talked 'most sensibly and judiciously on all subjects' to the Duke of Portland, though his voice was rough and hoarse.⁷

On 19 February, Addington found him 'so much indisposed that he dreaded the effect which the reception of his new ministers in council [the next day] . . . might produce on his health'.⁵ 'At the evening party,' Pitt told Rose, 'the King's conversation and conduct' were 'very extravagant', and 'it was evident . . . that His Majesty's mind was not in a proper state'.⁸ At night, Gisborne gave him 'a strong emetic',⁹ and next morning 'he discharged a great quantity of bile', and was better. He had a Council at the Queen's House as he was too weak to go out, but 'talked to the Ministers in his usual manner'⁸ and 'behaved with great dignity and calmness'.²

After the meeting, Lord Eldon, the incoming Chancellor who, like Addington, had not yet received his seals, had an audience with the King lasting two hours 'during the whole of which time he was as rational and collected as he [Eldon] had ever seen him'.¹⁰ But the King felt iller than he cared to admit and his symptoms revived memories of his sufferings thirteen years before. To Eldon he brought up those painful times: 'He talked to his Lordship of his last malady,' wrote Rose, 'stating many particulars that occurred to him during the continuance of it, and especially dwelt on his feelings during some lucid intervals. The King also quoted to Lord Eldon the questions which his Lordship, as a member of the Privy Council [at that time], had asked the physicians.' To Addington he also admitted he was not at all well. He said, 'My nerves are weak. I am sensible of that. Your father [Dr Anthony Addington] said twelve years ago, that quiet was what I wanted, and that I must have.'¹¹

Neither Addington nor Pitt heard anything untoward the next day, Saturday, 21 February, and 'concluded that all was well'.⁸ But it was not. The King was 'very bilious'⁹ and Gisborne, recollecting how rapidly delirium and other grave nervous symptoms had developed in 1788 and how Baker was blamed for not calling in further aid earlier, 'proposed to His Majesty to call in a second physician, to which the King consented after some difficulty and fixed upon Dr. Reynolds'.⁶ In the afternoon, Thomas Willis called again to inquire about the King's cold. He found him sitting up surrounded by the Queen and the princesses and was greatly surprised to observe 'strong marks of fever and irritation'. When they were alone, the King admitted with great emotion:

I do feel myself very ill, I am much weaker than I was, and I have prayed to God all night that I might die, or that he would spare my reason . . . if it should be otherwise, for God's sake keep from me your father and a regency.

Willis tried to calm him by assuring him that rest and medicines would quickly effect a cure. The King, having regained his composure, attempted to converse with his visitor and related

what had passed the day before, when he had received part of the new administration and taken leave of some of the old. In this relation which lasted two hours his Majesty shewed himself to be in so feverish a state as wholly to render him incapable of getting through one anecdote without digressing first to another. He was in short constantly promising that he would treat me with no more episodes as he called them, yet was he every moment varying to fresh matter, and hardly ever coming to the point immediately proposed. And all this time his Majesty, holding my arm very fast, walked eagerly about the room.[6]

This combination of mental and physical restlessness was what in 1788–9 was called 'an agitation' or 'hurry of spirits'.

In the evening Reynolds came with Gisborne and was struck with the similarity of appearances to those of October–November 1788, and his condition worsened hourly. 'The King's fever appearing rapidly to increase and to become alarming,' wrote Willis, the physicians attempted to check it with another dose of tartar emetic. It was 'given in his tea without his knowledge . . . but the desired effect was not produced.'[6] By midnight he was delirious. Willis, who had remained in the house, was called because 'his Majesty was in his nightgown and half undressed, in which state he had been some time', so confused that he no longer knew what he was doing. Nor did he recognize Willis, and it took them an hour and a half to get him to bed. But no sooner down, he got up and wandered about, ending up in the Queen's chamber, as he had at Windsor in 1788.

Next morning the Duke of York, acting for the royal family, and Mr Addington, acting for the Government, asked Thomas Willis to send for his medical brother Dr John, who arrived at lunchtime. The King, less confused in daytime than at night, recognized him and was horrified to see one he had hoped never to see again. He tried 'to avoid him by going quickly into another room . . . and then suddenly went in a hurry down-stairs . . . into his own room below.'[6] There the Willises cornered him and told him they would not 'suffer him again to leave his own apartment' until he was well. To enforce control, Thomas Willis also sent 'to Mr.

Warburton of Hoxton', owner of a number of large private madhouses which became notorious some fourteen years later as the result of a parliamentary inquiry chaired by George Rose, for 'four of his most respectable men to attend and sit up with His Majesty'.[6] Two arrived that evening and 'were put about Him immediately'.

A hastily composed bulletin at the Queen's House stated: 'The King had a cold, and an indifferent night, and was a little feverish.' Lord Auckland 'thought this was an ill-sounding account, considering the King's constitution,'[12] and events proved him right. The King was very ill in the night, 'in the height of a phrenzy fever – as bad as at the worst period . . . in 1788',[13] said Dr John Willis. Next day, Monday, 23 February, the third brother, Dr Robert Darling Willis, who was too young to have played any part in the previous illness, arrived. Once again, Willises were in control, but this time without their father. The Reverend Dr Francis Willis was not called, explained Addington, because 'he is eighty-three, but he is also rough and violent'.[14] His erstwhile antagonist Dr Richard Warren had died in 1797, attended by Sir George Baker.

After a night during which the King's delirium was at its height, he lapsed into coma. He 'lay for many hours without speaking, and it would seem, unconscious of what passed around him'.[15] 'The King is *really ill*,' wrote Lady Malmesbury to Lady Minto, 'he had been unwell for some days, and it is called cold and bile, but now there is . . . no doubt about the matter . . . The King's pulse was at 144 yesterday. Farquhar [Sir Walter Farquhar, physician to the Prince of Wales] says that so high a pulse must be attended with the greatest danger to life.'[16] So, too, thought the King's doctors, and the Privy Council ordered immediate public prayers for the King's recovery.[15]

Again the spectre of a regency, even succession, arose and the Prince of Wales lost no time sounding out the new ministers. He sent for Addington, but was referred to Pitt 'as his father's actual Minister on the present distressing occasion'.[17] Government indeed

was in a most anomalous, nay, unprecedented state. Here was one Cabinet in progress of formation, and sanctioned by the King. Here was another Cabinet which had resigned, but still holding the seals of office and alone competent to do any official act. Here was Mr. Addington Prime Minister *de jure*. Here was Mr. Pitt Prime Minister *de facto*. It was only by the entire cordiality at this time between the two statesmen that confusion was avoided. They held several familiar conferences on the painful, but, as it seemed, unavoidable and close question of a Regency.[15]

In his conference with the Prince, Pitt, who was most anxious to avoid a repetition of the crisis of 1788–9, insisted that no political capital was made out of the present calamity, and demanded 'that his Royal Highness would forbear to advise with those who had for a long time acted in direct opposition to His Majesty's Government'. To this 'express condition' the Prince agreed. To refresh his mind in preparation for a regency, Pitt obtained from Rose 'a printed copy of the Regency Bill which passed the House of Commons and was rejected [on the King's recovery] in the House of Lords, in February 19th, 1789 . . . with MS. alterations . . . of the amendments made by the Lords'.[18] Two days later he saw the Prince again 'and frankly stated his intention to propose, and press if the necessity should arise, a measure of restricted Regency . . . "Every one concerned," added Pitt, "not even excepting your Royal Highness, cannot do better than accord with what was then most evidently the clear sense of the Legislature, expressed in a manner not to be mistaken".' In this, too, the Prince acquiesced.[19]

Even without the active participation of their figurehead, the Whigs saw in the King's serious illness a 'brilliant prospect' and soon 'all the leading members of Opposition were in continual conclave; speculating, anticipating, and arranging'.[20] From details of his condition which leaked out from the Queen's House, it was even suspected that as in 1788 'some one or more of the servants have already been tampered with again by them'.[17] Their hopes, however, faded as quickly as they rose.

The leading politicians tacitly agreed to avoid public or parliamentary discussion of the illness and its possible consequences, at least until the nature of the King's illness had declared itself and some idea of its outcome could be formed. When 'one very foolish Member' in eager haste made a motion in the House on 27 February for an examination of the physicians on the 1788 model as a preliminary to a possible constitutional change, it was Sheridan for the Whigs who moved the adjournment to get rid of it, for which Pitt paid him handsome tribute. Fox purposely stayed away from the House 'lest he should be thought to give countenance to that mischievous course'.[18,19] How Burke would have behaved cannot be guessed: like Warren, he had been dead four years.

Besides, the King had not yet got over the acute phase of his illness and it was in the balance whether he would survive. The physicians had indeed given it as their declared opinion that he was so ill 'that there was no room to fear a lasting derangement of intellects; that he would either recover, or sink under the illness; and that . . . at his time of life [sixty-three], the probability of one of the events happening much sooner than in 1788, was very great'.[21] His condition continued so critical that for a fortnight the physicians came three times a day, while the three Willis brothers, supported by Warburton's men, were in constant attendance.[22]

The Willis trio now wielded remarkable power, the two doctors by commanding the sickroom and the clergyman because he had the confidence of the ministers and the trust of the King. When on 24 February the King emerged from coma and was very confused, Addington was allowed to see him for a moment and convinced himself of 'strong marks of Delirium'.[6] Yet at midday the outgoing Chancellor, Lord Loughborough, arrived to obtain 'the King's signature to a Commission for giving the Royal Assent to an Act of Parliament', the repeal of the Brown Bread Act, an emergency measure of the previous year which all parties agreed was proving injurious.[23] Not being permitted into the sickroom, Loughborough asked Thomas Willis to procure the King's signature. Willis

seeming to hesitate about carrying it to the King, the Chancellor said he would be responsible . . . and repeated 'I will take all the responsibility upon myself'. I [Thomas Willis] then took it immediately to the King, and informed his Majesty that I had brought the Bread Bill for his Majesty to sign, if his Majesty pleased. I laid it before him and he immediately wrote George very well, but on finding some difficulty in getting Him to proceed with the R., I took it away for some time and then brought it to Him again, and begged of Him to sign for the sake of his People . . . 'If it be necessary, said He . . . I will write as good an R. as ever I did' . . . and the R. was a good one accordingly.[6]

Nothing more unconstitutional can be imagined. Willis, who held no office whatsoever, was the solitary witness to a legislative act. Did the King understand what he was putting his sign manual to? Was it, in fact, his signature? When the story leaked out, Loughborough stated publicly that the King 'was in the perfect possession of his understanding' when he signed the Bill in his presence.[15] Privately to George Rose, he admitted that he had not even seen the King, but 'had sent the commission in to the King by Dr. [Mr] Willis, who brought it back signed, and told him there would be no difficulty in obtaining the royal signature to a dozen papers respecting which no detailed statements were necessary'.[24] Soon, Thomas Willis manoeuvred himself into the position of confidential agent between the King and his ministers and, in effect, became the power behind the throne, through whom all approaches to the King had to go. 'Executive government,' said Rose bitterly to Pitt, was 'therefore, *pro tanto*, in the hands of that gentleman.'[25]

In the evening the King's pulse rose to 130. Malmesbury considered this not unfavourable, as it proved 'his mental derangement . . . to be only the effect of delirium in consequence of fever, but it puts his life in very great danger'.[26] Bulletins were issued from 22 February with variations on the themes of fever, sleeplessness and irritation. On 25 February it was stated: 'His Majesty's fever continues, but the symptoms are not worse.' The pulse in the evening was 110 and Charles Abbot, Chief Secretary for Ireland in the incoming administration, Speaker of the House of Commons 1802–17, and later Lord Colchester, heard that the disorder was 'turning to a black jaundice'[27] – which, since he was not jaundiced, meant that his water was dark.

On 26 February the King's health, as reported by the physicians, was 'the same as before, but the private accounts were more favourable.' Rose learnt that he had 'a good deal of fever, which is thought fortunate, and other symptoms which are stated to have preceded recovery . . . in 1789'.[28] 'All that relate to pulse, tongue, skin, &c. bespeak amendment,' Addington told Lord Colchester from what he could gather on his twice-daily visits to the Palace.[29]

Since not even the Queen and the princesses were allowed to see the patient, the Willises not only had control over him and his contact with the outside world, but also dictated what the world learnt about him. On Friday, 27 February, the bulletin stated 'The King's fever continues but without any increase.' Private intelligence was 'that he was quieter yesterday afternoon, and slept well; but about two o'clock in the morning the irritation returned, and the fever rose with it.'[30] Dr John Willis told the Prince of Wales that the King was now so confused that he 'could not only not understand what he read were he disposed to read, but that he could not . . . know a single letter'.[31]

On Saturday, 28 February, the bulletin read: 'His Majesty's fever continues but is somewhat abated.' Rose heard that 'the symptoms of derangement' were less marked and there was 'a reasonable degree of perspiration',[32] an observation which always made them hope he was throwing off the morbific matter. Lord Colchester was told: 'The Willises think the King may recover very speedily indeed; at a reasonable allowance within ten days, and to a certainty within three weeks.'[33] Pitt, too, was so encouraged by the news to believe it now 'unnecessary to deliberate on modes of Regency'.

On Sunday morning, 1 March, it was announced that the 'fever continued to abate' and the King was better in all respects. Even his obstinate constipation had at last yielded to calomel. But that very evening recovery was interrupted by a relapse which quickly reached another dangerous climax. He had no sleep at all and became 'very irritable', that is delirious, again. Next morning's bulletin was unfavourable: 'The King's fever increased last night, and has not since abated.' Malmesbury rightly feared 'more now for his life than for any thing else'.[34] Dr Reynolds was also gloomy and found 'the King was worse last night than ever'.[35] On Monday, 2 March, he was 'so much worse' again that the physicians doubted whether he could survive[34] and the royal family, including for the first time the Prince of Wales, assembled outside the sickroom in hourly expectation of his death. Pitt, who called in the afternoon of the crisis, told Rose

that the King had been so ill . . . as to occasion the most serious alarms . . . from the violent turn the disorder was taking; that his person had undergone a visible change; and . . . the physicians were in great despondency . . . but that about five o'clock in the afternoon the disorder was at a crisis, when his Majesty fell into a sleep, which was considered as the thing to lead to the best hope . . . At the crisis, his pulse was 136.[36]

Willis's account was:

He was very restless and unquiet . . . and at the recommendation of Dr. Reynolds his Majesty's feet were put into hot water and vinegar for a quarter of an hour. Soon after this his Majesty put on such an appearance of being exhausted, that his life was despaired of. His pulse too had rapidly increased so that Dr. John thought it absolutely necessary to inform the Duke of York immediately of his fears and also Mr. Addington. And Mr. Addington sent immediately for the Prince of Wales. They all met together about three o'clock at the Queen's House and the result of the meeting was, that Drs. Gisborne and Reynolds, Drs. John and Robert W. perceiving the exhausted state of the King, they gave Him a strong dose of Musk [a powerful nervous stimulant], which had the effect of composing him to sleep for an hour and a half which he had not had for, I think, nearly 48 hours . . . He waked with a much slower pulse and . . . appearing better, so that the physicians were enabled to give a favourable account to the Prince of Wales in the evening. If the report had been otherwise it was intended that other physicians should have been called in aid. The medicines of today since two o'clock were chiefly composed of musk and bark. His nourishment jellies and wine.[6]

To ensure more sleep, they laid the King's head that night on a bag of warm hops – a folk-remedy which Addington had remembered from his father's practice and which earned the son the nickname 'The Doctor' – and he slept eight and a quarter hours. In the morning, he awoke tranquil 'with the fever abated'[34] and 'asked such questions as he was incapable of for some days before'.[6] For the first time he took notice of his surroundings, observed that he was not lying in his usual bed and asked where he was. 'He was afraid he had been ill a long time,' he said, and inquiring how long for, was told eight days.[37] 'The alteration for the better appeared to be most extraordinary,' said Pitt with relief,[36] and jubilant crowds gathered round Buckingham House to celebrate the King's recovery.

Much of this and the next day the King lay in a state of 'insensibility and stupor'.[6] His teeth were clenched and he seemed unable to swallow. At night, he heaved as if he were going to be sick. 'Extreme nervous irritability,' his physicians called it, and they feared 'a paralytic stroke' was developing.

On 4 March in the afternoon 'his Majesty began to get out of that state', and was cooperative and tractable. On 5 March he was able to feed himself, and his hands were strong and steady enough to hold a cup. 'With few exceptions of irritation, the whole day passed with increasing good symptoms,' in the words of the Willis journal. His appetite returned, but he was still kept on a low meat-free diet of potatoes and rice to starve his fever.

Sleep still eluded him. On 6 March he had only three hours, but was 'quite collected in the morning and asked whether he might get up'. The bulletin announced: 'His Majesty's fever had not yet subsided, but still continued to abate.' Dr Gisborne told Sir Walter Farquhar that the pulse had fallen to 72 and 'everything quite in a promising way'.[38] The King saw the Queen for a short time, was rational, 'but once or twice a little hurried, of which he was sensible, and checked himself. He asked Dr. [John] Willis the state of business in the House of Commons, and ... desired the Doctor would write to Mr. Addington to inform him how well he was.' Rose was relieved that the King recollected the events before his illness, because it showed that it had not resulted in 'a state of fatuity'.[39]

On Saturday, 7 March, the bulletin stated that the King's condition 'gives the fairest prospect of a speedy recovery'.[40] Malmesbury recorded joyfully: 'His Majesty recovered in mind, as well as body. Duke of York with him for the first time ... found him looking pale and ill, but perfectly collected.' As the interview proceeded, the King pressed his son for political news and asked whether there had been any resignations. The Duke answered, 'Sir, it would take us too much time to tell you all this now.' To which the King replied, 'Frederic, you are more nervous than I am; I really feel quite well, and know full well how ill I have been.'[41] The King also put the Willises on the spot by noticing the strangers surrounding him, and asked 'who put the men about him?' At night he became slightly confused – 'more irritable' – again and was given tartar emetic 'which operated violently' and made him worse.

The bulletin of 9 March mentioned 'fast approaching recovery', although he still slept only two or three hours a night. Private accounts were 'that he is much debilitated by the fever'. If the Willises did not say so openly, they at least confided to their journal that the King was 'lower in constitution' than they had expected, and they started him on asses' milk as a restorative. They also observed from their constant contact with him what are today recognized as the cardinal signs of organic impairment of the brain: emotional lability – 'He cries at almost anything'; perplexity leading to catastrophic reaction – when attempting to go through official papers 'He became so puzzled ... that He grew hurried and angry'; and inability to concentrate which led to fidgetiness and purposeless activity:

If he attempted to play the game of drafts he unconsciously turned the board about incessantly; if a table cloth was laid, he also turned it round and round unable to keep his hands still ... In the same manner his state of nerves seemed to compel him to roll up his handkerchiefs ... of which ... some days he had not less than 40 or 50.[6]

The final bulletin was issued on 11 March: 'His Majesty is perfectly free from fever, but it may require some time, as is always necessary after so severe an illness, to complete recovery.'[42] The Prince of Wales and the Duke of Kent were now permitted to see their father, but with Thomas Willis present. Talking to his sons brought to the King's mind another occasion when his life was in danger:

> He said he was glad to find the inquiries made about his health had been very general; the Prince answered, he believed everybody had been to the Queen's House, who could either go there or be carried; to which the King replied, Mr. Fox had not been, but that Mr. Sheridan had, who he verily thought had a respect and regard for him; particularly dwelling on his conduct at Drury Lane Theatre, when the attempt was made on his Majesty's life by the madman [James Hadfield] . . . His Majesty then proceeded to tell what his own conduct on the occasion was; that he had spoken to the Queen in German to quiet her alarm.[43]

The Prince found his father 'was thinner and had lost the ruddiness of his complexion' and that his 'eyes were a good deal affected' which made him complain of 'the looking glass in his room as faulty in the reflection from it'.[43]

On 14 March the King was well enough to receive from Pitt, his Prime Minister since 1784, the seals of office and 'showed the utmost possible kindness to him both in words and manner'.[44] Both parties were much affected, Pitt in particular because a version of the King's illness, assiduously fostered by the scheming and sinister Reverend Thomas Willis, blamed the outbreak on Pitt for having brought forward a measure for Catholic relief, to which Willis was strongly opposed.[45] During the audience the King recollected the stirring political events provoked by his former illness and remarked on the coincidence of dates and that he was then also 'sufficiently recovered to transact business on the 12th of March'.

Hardly a fortnight had passed since the King lay in coma and was hourly expected to die when, on 17 March, he was suffered to preside at a Privy Council meeting, which for constitutional reasons could not be postponed. He got through the business pretty well, but 'the private audiences' afterwards 'were too much for him. He had a great deal to say to each and the more he talked the more he was fatigued and had the less power of restraining himself.'[6]

Progress towards full restoration of health and strength, as in 1789, was slow and trying to all parties. He naturally lacked energy and the physicians realized the danger of his doing more than was in his power. According to Lord Malmesbury they now 'seem less to dread any mental derangement, than that the intellectual faculties should be impaired so much as never to recover their former tone'.[46] In the last week of March, Rose also heard 'various reports respecting his Majesty's health . . . of a doubtful

and unpleasant nature', including the fact that there were 'at least eight
hundred warrants unsigned; and none are returned that were lately sent'.[47]
Physically, too, he was weak and his illness continued to flicker up and
down. His sleep was often deficient, his pulse at times still above 100 and
he had occasional returns of sweating, colic and constipation. No private
person would have been forced back in this fragile state and so soon after
such a serious illness. Although he was able to reason and comment
judiciously on public affairs, as all who saw him testify, as does his correspondence with his ministers, he was 'not so far recovered as to be able to
execute every part of his office without injury'. When he was overtaxed
he became irritable and hurried.

In this anomalous situation of being simultaneously convalescent and
officially in harness, he 'became impatient of control . . . how should he
understand' – tolerate would seem a better expression – 'that he should sit
at the head of his Council in the plenitude of his kingly power at one
moment, and be under the control of one of his subjects at the very next,'
asked the Willises.[6] Their task of managing him, they complained, 'became
tenfold greater' from that time on. Convalescence became as dramatic a
struggle between the King and his keepers as the acute phase of the illness
had between life and death. Full recovery was as vital to the King as it
was to the credit of the Willises, provided it was seen to have been their
achievement. The King himself saw no need for their further attendance,
which, to say the least, had become an encumbrance to him. But the
Willises maintained that only their active supervision and strict control of
his every activity – they called it avoidance of excitement – could guarantee
full restoration. For the Government, too, the prolonged presence of the
Willises was more than a mere safeguard against relapse. The ministers
depended on Thomas Willis to get the endless stream of documents and
commissions signed, and his brothers provided the medical cover for the
King's capacity to do so in case it was called in question in Parliament.

In the background of these conflicting interests hovered the Prince of
Wales, who despite his promise to Pitt was not to be relied upon to abstain
from plotting a regency. He was certainly suspicious of the Willises for
making the King out better than he was, as they were of him for wanting
to declare him incapable for his purpose. And far from there being a strong
Prime Minister, as there had been in 1788, there was the weak and inex-
perienced Addington. Then there was the sad figure of the Queen, who
herself was not well. She was as anxious to do what was best for the King
and accord with his wishes as she was apprehensive of a return of the
disorder. Above all, she wanted to avoid having to decide issues which
could only lead – and did – to friction between her husband and herself.
She therefore wavered between relying on the presence of the Willises
and wanting them to leave.

K

The result was that in his debilitated state the King was almost totally isolated, being surrounded by frightened relatives, impotent politicians and useless doctors, and he became the more rebellious against the Willises' continued control. When he became angry with them, they coolly threatened him with the alternative, which was a parliamentary inquiry. When he took the law into his own hands and challenged them by what mandate they were about him – being fully aware that in contrast to 1788 his regal authority had not been suspended – they countered by appealing to Addington, to the Archbishop of Canterbury and, finally, to the Queen to support the prudence of their presence. In their relentless perseverance there was certainly an element of professional pride. But, more important, they had tasted power: they had control over the King and they held his ministers in the hollow of their hands.

What enormous influence over affairs they had is illustrated in an entry in Thomas Willis's journal for 18 March:

Mr. Addington consulted me at this time about the propriety of making a proposition for Peace [with France] to the King and asked me whether I thought he would accede to it, and if so, the properest mode of proposing it. It was agreed that a resolution of the Cabinet Council to that purpose should be couched in a few lines and in such a manner that the King should have little to answer but that he approves or disapproves.

Two days later, on 20 March, Addington gave Willis a box containing the Cabinet minutes:

I took the box to his Majesty and introduced the subject by signifying that I understood from Mr. Addington that it contained matter of great importance to which I had adverted before. The King read first the letter from Mr. A. accompanying the Minute. He then observed that it was what he had long wished. But that they had lately been in the habit of sending him round robins against Peace which tho' compelled to agree to he always heartily disapproved of. The King's answer was this 'His Majesty cordially approves of the minute of the Cabinet transmitted by his Chancellor of the Exchequer. The King authorizes him to inform his newly appointed Cabinet of his approbation of their Minute'. It was some time before I could get the King to write the answer which I was anxious for, as I knew the Cabinet Council would sit at a certain hour for the purpose of receiving it. The King's tardiness did not arise from any disinclination to the sort of answer he had written, but from a restlessness in him and an eagerness to talk. I transmitted the answer immediately to Mr. A.[6]

So began the confidential negotiations which led to the Peace of Amiens, preliminary articles for which were signed on 1 October. When on the same day Baron Lenthe sent in a box of Hanoverian state documents for signature, the Willises insisted on scrutinizing them first 'that we migh judge of the propriety of taking in the box'.

How much this situation lent itself to duplicity and intrigue may be seen by events behind the scenes during the week of the Queen's drawing-room. On Sunday, 22 March, Addington warned the Willises that unless the King was not only better but seen to be better by appearing in public it might not be possible to stave off a demand for a parliamentary inquiry. Next day they set to work. Dr John put a blister on the King's back and started him on a course of emetics to keep him low, and the Reverend Thomas enlisted the Queen and the Duke of York in their scheme, which was designed, they said, to ward off a threatened regency. Next, in the best tradition of their father in 1788, they wrote an open letter to Addington, stating that they had 'never seen the King since his illness so well as he had been this morning with those favourable symptoms . . . which are always so much to be depended upon'. They allowed Dr Gisborne to see his patient to add his authority to theirs. On Tuesday they 'proposed to the Queen to have a drawing room on Thursday' and played on her loyalty to the King when she hesitated. She told them to ask the King, and to him they went and 'named it . . . as a wish of the Queen's'. Naturally, to please her, he at once assented. Back they went to the Queen and 'informed her Majesty of his Majesty's consent'. Later that day they allowed Lough-borough to take some commissions in to the King to show he was capable, but told him it would tax the King too much if he resigned his seals of office.

On Wednesday, 25 March, the day before the drawing-room, they advised the King to dismiss Dr Reynolds from further attendance, which the delighted King did 'in a very handsome manner'. As Thomas Willis explained in his journal:

We advised the King to this step, because in the first place he [Dr Reynolds] was not useful in the case itself, and secondly by reason of his practice in the town the King's situation was not likely to be kept so private by his attendance upon him – and so long as Dr. Gisborne remained in attendance state policy was answered.

Having thus covered their flanks, the Willises sent the King with the Queen and two princesses 'out in the coach on an airing round Battersea'. While they were out, Thomas Willis warned the Duke of York

against entrusting too much to the Duke of Kent at present, not that he was likely designedly to betray anything but as he was in the habit of seeing the Prince [of Wales] daily, it was at least judicious to be careful, because it was unnecessary that His Royal Highness should know everything.

On the morning of 26 March, the day of the drawing-room, Dr John made sure that the King would not be able to attend by putting blisters on his legs at breakfast and again at lunchtime. The King was furious and complained bitterly of pain and became 'very angry that there should have been a drawing room' before he was well. No wonder that Malmesbury thought the Queen looked pale and the princesses 'as if they had been weeping'. The King, it was felt, was 'too ill for the Queen to appear in public, and . . . [they] censure her for it'.[48]

Little wonder also that from this time the Queen, like the King, 'imbibed a prejudice against us', as Thomas Willis observed in all innocence. An interview with her afterwards left him 'with as unpleasant an impression as I have ever experienced in my life', and there was now talk of replacing the Willis trio with Sir Francis Milman, who daily attended the Princess Amelia as well as the Queen. By Monday, 30 March, the position of the Willises had become still more precarious. The King

abused me and all of us exceedingly [recorded Thomas] and said he had seen Mr. Addington who told him he was master in his own house. Soon after this Dr. John sent him a medicine [presumably another dose of an emetic to keep him busy]. He [the King] said Mr. Addington had told him that he wanted nothing but asses' milk, and he desired the man who took it in to leave the room for he was determined to take no more medicines.

He also told the Willises to pack up.

But they did not, although they kept out of his way for a few days, so that he believed they had gone, while they busied themselves spreading the tale that the King 'was too well to be confined yet not well enough to be wholly at liberty at his own controul'. As an example of the wrong ideas he still had, they instanced his dislike of them. To the Queen they recommended that he be moved from London. She suggested Windsor. Dr John ominously preferred Kew.

Having failed to soften the King's attitude to them, they decided to beard the lion in his den.

This sort of conduct and distrust continuing so long [wrote Thomas Willis], Dr. John thought it proper to go into his Majesty. The King received him very coldly and asked him why he came. Dr. John answered in order to prevent his Majesty from dealing so liberally in unfounded abuse and misrepresentation. He assured the King that . . . abuse of men who had brought him out of very severe and dangerous fever was a proof of a remnant of the disorder. The King said in reply that it was no proof, for that he had abused him ever since his former illness. Then, said Dr. John, you was not perfectly cured or you could not have abused where you ought to have justly extolled.[6]

But their influence was on the wane. Against their protestations, a Council was held at the Queen's House on 14 April, when Lord Lough-borough at last returned his seals of office and Lord Eldon was sworn in as the new Chancellor. On the same day the 'men' were sent away and thanksgiving prayers for the King's recovery were fixed for the following

Sunday, 19 April. The Prince of Wales broke through the Willis cordon and saw his father for the first time in almost a month. In his memorandum of the meeting he recorded:

> The King began with the happiness he felt at being able the same day to embrace his son and dismiss Dr. Willis's keepers; that being the first day since his illness that any one of his own servants had been permitted to attend him . . . He continually and repeatedly talked of himself as a dying man, determined to go abroad . . . to make over the Government to the Prince . . . He took the Prince to the room, the scene of the late confinement, and complained of the treatment he had experienced in terms the most moving.[49]

The Prince reported the interview to Eldon in the expectation that he would initiate the necessary steps:

> the Prince told his Lordship that it was the intention of his Majesty . . . to devolve the government on him, the Prince; that he wished therefore the Chancellor would consider the proper mode of that being carried into effect; and *that it was the King's intention to retire to Hanover or to America . . .* That the Queen and his brothers wished him to take measures for confining the King; that his Royal Highness very greatly disliked the Willis family being about the King and he was therefore desirous of knowing if they were placed there by any authority, or how they might be got rid of. That his Royal Highness had seen Lord Thurlow [Lord Chancellor at the time of the Regency Crisis] and wished the Chancellor to see him. To all which the Chancellor said very little; refused to see Lord Thurlow . . . that Dr. Willis, &c, were not about the King by any positive authority, but on grounds of propriety and notorious necessity, justifying in the clearest point of view the measure. On many of the points no reply at all was made by his Lordship.[50]

On 16 April the King slept for the first time in the Queen's apartment. Next day he officially said good-bye to the Willises and on Saturday, 18 April, rode out for the first time, to Blackheath to his son's estranged wife, the Princess Caroline of Wales, his niece and daughter-in-law and to his grandchild and only heir to the throne, five-year-old Princess Charlotte.

But the final curtain had not rung down. The very next day, while congregations all over the country heard the Archbishop's prayer on the King's deliverance, word reached Thomas Willis from Princess Elizabeth, who treated him as a confidant and wrote endless interfering letters, that things were not well at the Queen's House and asking him and his brothers to return. It seems that the Queen and her daughters had panicked at the prospect of being left alone with the King. The Willises eagerly responded to the call and now warned of the danger of 'a partial relapse' by 'over-exercise and seeing too many people'. But how were they to stage a comeback? They appealed to Addington, who said 'we should take him again into our power' if the Queen thought it necessary. But she did not wish to be responsible and would not agree without an order from the ministers. Addington protested that he could not give such an authority, which 'could be but negative without coming to Parliament'. In this quandary and under their combined pressure, the Queen at last 'gave up the point, only requesting that she might not be named, or be supposed to know anything that was intended'. Amid this to-ing and fro-ing the Willises, to their chagrin, saw the King in the Mall ride out to start his convalescence at Kew.

They followed in hot pursuit. 'Thwarted in our wish to retain the King in London [wrote Thomas Willis] . . . and constrained to follow him here and there take him anew' aroused sentiments in him and his brothers which could

only be conceived by ourselves who witnessed them on this novel and distressing occasion . . . Besides never having fairly altogether quitted him, and unwilling to forsake the task we had undertaken where great credit was at stake and the completion of which was confidently seen . . . at no great distance . . . these considerations were what induced and determined us, frightful as it was, to execute this cruel scheme.[6]

Their 'cruel scheme' was no other than to waylay the King on his own highway at Kew and detain him by force. Under any other circumstances such a plot would have carried the charge of high treason. That they even contemplated it is a measure of how tenaciously they clung to their patient, not of how ill he was. But they failed to catch him that evening, and the attempt had to be postponed till the next day. The three brothers slept in the Duke of Cumberland's house on Kew Green, Gisborne at the Rose and Crown, and the four Warburton's men, who made up the rear, at the Star and Garter at Kew Bridge. At seven o'clock next morning they assembled outside Kew House, where the King was expected to call for his son Adolphus before his morning ride, hoping by outnumbering him eight to one 'we might succeed in our object without bustle or difficulty'. But the King, instead of coming to Kew House, perhaps sensing that something was afoot, walked to the stables on the Green and returned for breakfast to the Prince of Wales's house, where he was staying.

The Willis contingent were meanwhile left huddled 'in a cold house without even a chair in it, except what was in the room lately fitted out for Prince Adolphus . . . doubting for a long time what to do for the best'. They decided on direct action and went across to the Prince of Wales's house and had Gisborne announced. The King received him with Thomas Willis close behind.

On the King getting sight of me he seemed surprized and would have hastily passed and escaped out of the room [wrote Thomas Willis of this astonishing scene] but I prevented him . . . I spoke to him at once of his situation and the necessity there was that he should be immediately under controul again. His Majesty sat down, turning very pale and . . . looking very sternly at me exclaimed 'Sir, I will never forgive you whilst I live'.

And he never did. Once more the King tried to get past him, but found planted on the other side of the door John Willis with Warburton's men. They conducted him across to Prince Adolphus's apartment at Kew House and there he stayed their prisoner until 19 May, while Thomas Willis and his family moved into a house on Kew Green provided for him by the generosity of the Queen.

Such a cloak-and-dagger kidnapping must be unique in the history of the monarchy and would be beyond credence were it not recorded in Thomas Willis's own words. They kept the King from now on so isolated that he was not even allowed to cross the two hundred yards to where his family lived. Again he was submitted to a regime of tartar emetic, was twice bled and cupped. A postscript the King put to an official letter to Lord Hawkesbury two days later shows how close his confinement was: 'Lord Hawkesbury is desired to send the enclosed to my son, P. Adolphus at Kew by messenger as difficulties are made of letting me send it to him tho' but two rooms off.'[51] And to the Queen he smuggled out a message by hiding it in the drawer of a desk he sent her.[6]

The action of the Willises convinced the Prince of Wales that the King was unlikely to recover and, encouraged by the prospect before him, he again tried to obtain control of the King's person. To achieve it, he had to get rid of the Willises. How to set about it was suggested to him by his friend the Earl of Carlisle:

The first step which appears necessary to be taken . . . is to remonstrate with Ld. Eldon & Mr. Addington, upon their conduct & their supinely suffering the King's health to be tamper'd with by persons who can hardly be called physicians, without applying to the best advice the country can afford. In almost every case of a private individual, before a patient is transfer'd or returned to the care of that part of the Faculty to which Dr. Willis belongs, it is usual to require the fiat of other medical persons to sanction the placing the patient under such care. For if the Mad Doctor was to decide in the first instance upon the necessity of his having the sole management of the case, it is obvious to forsee to what horrible abuses this might tend. Persons perfectly sane might be buried for ever in confinement.[52]

Perhaps the most remarkable feature of this strange situation was how well the King kept his equilibrium and even a sense of humour. He spent his time corresponding directly with his ministers, signing documents and giving directions without a moment's delay or a word out of place. He walked for hours around Kew Gardens, always with a Willis at his elbow, played cards and chess and read and planned his convalescence at Weymouth. On 9 May he was permitted to see the Queen and the princesses and on 12 May received an invitation from George Rose, transmitted through Thomas Willis, to stay at Cuffnells on his way to the coast.

As nobody seemed willing or able to send the Willises off, the King decided to do so himself in unmistakeable manner – he threatened to go on strike. On the Queen's birthday, 19 May, the Chancellor came to see him and found him 'extremely uneasy' at his continued detention. The King declared to him 'he had taken a solemn determination, that unless he was that day allowed to go over to the house where the Queen and his family were, no earthly consideration should induce him to sign his name to any paper or to do one act of government whatever. This resolution he affirmed, with the strongest declaration, that he would abide by, as a gentleman and as a King.'⁵³ With that, he walked unmolested out of the house across the lawn to the Queen.

Addington, to whom they had been so accommodating for so long, allowed the Willises to hang around quietly for another month, to save face.* They still tried to intrigue, but their time was up. When they did see the King, it was from a becoming distance.

On 21 May the King came to London for an open Council at the Queen's House and conducted business in his usual efficient manner, 'looked extremely well and joked as usual with his Ministers after the Council broke up'.⁵⁴ On 31 May he considered himself fully recovered as he wrote to his friend the Bishop of Worcester:

After a most tedious and severe illness, from which, by the interposition of Divine Providence, I have most wonderfully escaped the jaws of death, I find myself enabled to pursue one of my most agreeable occupations, that of writing to you . . . my health is daily improving, though I cannot boast of the same strength and spirits I enjoyed before. Still, with quiet and sea-bathing, I trust they will soon be regained.⁵⁵

Early in June, from too much exposure to the sun, he had a bilious attack reminiscent of that in the summer of 1788, and for a few days appeared 'very quiet, very heavy, and very sleepy',⁵⁶ but soon recovered. On 10 June Thomas Willis made a last attempt to gain for his family the credit for the King's recovery, when he told Rose 'that unfortunately the King had taken a decided aversion to himself and to the other medical people about him but . . . was now almost entirely well, and that there was every appearance that he would remain so'.⁵⁷ Arrangements were going ahead at Weymouth

---

* The prolonged presence of the Willises – for yet another month – is responsible for the current notion that the King 'was forced to live . . . in complete seclusion at Kew, under the care of the Willises; he was not sufficiently recovered to be out of their hands until 28 June' (*Dictionary of National Biography*).

to receive him at Gloucester House, which he had lately purchased from his brother, the Duke of Gloucester. Among the alterations made were the installation of 'hot and cold baths ... under the direction of the physicians'.[57] The faithful and unsophisticated Gisborne advised him to take it easy, to rest an hour in the afternoon, and 'avoid ... exposure to the sun'.[58]

On 21 June, preparatory to his departure, Lord Chancellor Eldon wrote a long, effusive letter to the King, recommending that he take with him 'at least for the present ... Dr. Robert Willis, who, *as being of the College* [of Physicians], attends your Majesty as a regular physician'[59] – that is, not as a mad-doctor. The King replied immediately, thanking the Chancellor for the attachment he bore him,

of which the letter now before him is a fresh proof; but, at the same time, he cannot but in the strongest manner decline the idea of having Dr. Robert Willis about him. The line of practice followed with great credit by that gentleman renders it incompatible with the King's feelings that he should, now by the goodness of Divine Providence restored to reason, consult a person of that description. His Majesty is satisfied with the zeal and attention of Dr. Gisborne, in whose absence he will consult Sir Francis Milman; but cannot bear the idea of consulting any of the Willis family.[60]

On 29 June the Willises stood among the crowd on Kew Green who waved their Majesties, the princesses and Prince Adolphus off to Weymouth. 'Here end our labours,' Thomas Willis piously entered in his journal. Two years later the Willises were compensated for them 'by the hand of Dr. Gisborne', to whom Addington paid a lump sum so as to save the King the pain of seeing their name in the Civil List, to the tune of: Dr John £5,000, Dr Robert £3,000 and Thomas £2,000.[61]

The royal party broke their journey to Weymouth at Cuffnells, George Rose's seat. There a special Council meeting was held on 1 July, at which Glenbervie saw the King. He 'found him very much altered indeed, and instead of that fullness and roundness of limbs and countenance, an emaciated face and person with his clothes hanging upon him. But his complexion is clear, and those about him say he has got flesh and strength much beyond what he had a month ago.'[62]

On 8 July the King informed his Prime Minister from Weymouth that his sleep was 'now perfect' and apologized for not being able to deal immediately with the papers Addington had sent on account of having broken the key in opening the War Office box the previous day. He added: 'The King finds ... that it is necessary to avoid any hurry; even the event of breaking the key gave more uneasiness than it ought'[63] – one of the many instances which reveal what a good judge the King was of himself.

Loughborough, his late Chancellor, now Earl Rosslyn, visited him at

Weymouth in August and gave Lord Auckland his impression:

I can with perfect satisfaction confirm to you all that you may have heard of their Majesty's perfect health. The King, I think, has at no time when I have had the means of seeing him every day, and often all the day, appeared to be in so steady a state of health . . . his manner is much more composed, and he is always ready to enter into conversation when it is going on, though he does not always start it. He is become also more moderate in his exercise, and admits that it is possible to be fatigued.[64]

The King returned from Weymouth less robust than he had hoped. 'Sea-bathing has had its usual success with me,' he wrote to Bishop Hurd on 24 October from Windsor, 'and in truth it was never more necessary, for the severe fever I had the last winter left many unpleasant sensations. These . . . are nearly removed. I am forced to be very careful, and to avoid every thing of fatigue . . . but I feel I am gradually gaining ground.'[65] Fortunately, he had learnt to be philosophical also about his health. He said to Lord Malmesbury, 'You and I have moved on the active theatre of this world these thirty years; if we are not become wise enough to consider every event which happens quietly, and with acquiescence, we must have lived very negligently.'[66]

7

Recurrence: 1804

For three years all went well. Then, in February 1804, the King suffered a short-lived but sharp recurrence preceded by a premonitory attack of pain and weakness. In the third week of January he was said to have caught cold, attributed as in 1788 to remaining in wet clothes. It was followed by what the King himself called a 'rheumatic attack'[1] accompanied by malaise and 'hurry'. Within a few days he became 'too lame to walk without a cane'.[2] His foot swelled[3] and it was thought he either had 'a slight attack of gout',[4] 'a sort of paralysis'[5] or 'dropsy'.[6] The levée on 25 January was cancelled, but he presided as usual over a Privy Council held for his convenience at Buckingham House.[7]

He improved only to relapse in the second week of February, when the illness rapidly reached a climax. He developed strong 'symptoms of bile'[8] and 'high . . . fever' which 'created great apprehensions for his life'[5] and was 'in immense danger for forty-eight hours'.[2] The bulletins stated that he was 'much indisposed'[9] and his family considered 'the case . . . very precarious'.[8] He recovered with 'his mind much affected'[5] by 'great agitation and hurries'.[6] Though 'the mania . . . was by no means so strong as at former times' and he 'was never so completely alienated as in 1788, and in 1801', his 'constitution seemed weaker, and to have suffered more'.[2]

As soon as the physicians – Sir Francis Milman, Sir Lucas Pepys and Drs Reynolds and William Heberden junior* – informed Addington that

* William Heberden, the younger (1767–1845), practised in London, but was so well connected through his father that 'from the first commencement of his career' he was 'above hospital practice' (*A picture of . . . the Royal College of Physicians*, ed. W. Nisbet, 1817, pp. 64–6). He was appointed physician in ordinary to the Queen in 1806, and to the King in 1809. On the death of his wife in 1812 he gave up medical practice, except for his attendance on the King, to devote himself to the education of his nine children. From 1829, when he lost a son and a daughter, he turned his attention entirely to theological subjects. During the years of his faithful attendance on George III he was praised particularly for his prudent conduct 'in his intercourse with the jarring interests' which prevailed, and he was certainly the most humane and enlightened among the royal physicians.

the King appeared to be suffering the third attack of his old complaint, Addington sent for the Willises. They refused to take over unless this time they were given official authority, which Addington provided by means of 'an order from the Cabinet Council'.[10] Armed with it, they presented themselves at the Queen's House on the morning of Monday, 13 February, 'with the intention of their being introduced into the King's apartment to attend him'. But they found their entry barred by two of the King's sons, the Dukes of Kent and Cumberland. A hurried conference between the Duke of Kent and Addington followed. The Duke told the Prime Minister of 'a solemn promise & engagement' which he and his brother had given the King 'subsequent to his last illness, when his mind was perfectly restored, and at different periods since . . . [that] in the event of its being the will of Providence that he should again be afflicted, as he had been before, *we* should use every means in our power to prevent anyone of the Willis family from being placed about him,' and that the King had delivered this sentiment 'relative to *every* member of the Willis family'.[10] They feared that to see them 'would be productive of an irritation of mind for which the worst consequences might be apprehended'.

But these forceful representations did not convince Addington. He seems to have been more concerned with the welfare of his administration than with that of the King. Next day, 14 February, he turned for advice to Milman and Heberden, who were even more strongly opposed to the Willises and told Addington unequivocally that 'in the present state of the King's health, such a measure would in all probability produce *convulsions* which might be *fatal*'[11] – so delicately was the King's nervous system poised. But Addington was not Pitt – 'Pitt is to Addington as London is to Paddington' went the old ditty – and he remained undecided. At an emergency Cabinet meeting the same evening he confronted Milman with Dr John Willis,[11] but still came to no conclusion. Only after a further communication from the royal dukes did Addington drop the Willises. The dukes declared 'that if, notwithstanding this representation, the two physicians, Doctors Willis, are called upon to attend his Majesty, the measure is to be considered to be totally and entirely that of the *Cabinet*, and that *we* in no shape whatever have participated in it.'[12]

Dr Samuel Foart Simmons, physician to St Luke's Hospital for Lunatics (founded in 1750 and opened in 1751 by Dr William Battie as an alternative to Bethlem Hospital), was called instead. Even so, to safeguard himself in case things went wrong and to mollify the Willises, Addington asked Lord Colchester 'to contradict absolutely the assertion in the public papers that he, Mr. Addington, had been averse to the Willises being introduced. On the contrary, he had from the first said that, so soon as it was said to be proper, he would take them in his own carriage' and, in fact, they waited around Downing Street for some days longer.[5]

Meanwhile, fearing they might have offended the Prime Minister and he refuse help were it needed, the Queen and nine of her children – with the notable and deliberate exception of the Prince of Wales[13] – put the onus of the King's care squarely on Addington by sending him a declaration accepting 'with thanks the offer which has been made to us by his Majesty's confidential servants to relieve us from the care and superintendence of his Majesty on this trying occasion'.[14] The royal family knew only too well the difficulties every illness of the King had led to with the Queen. Now, on this third occasion, a deepening breach was feared which all wished to avoid. In the event they were not successful.

On 17 February the bulletin announced that the King was out of danger, 'had several hours sleep in the night, and appeared much refreshed to-day'.[5] By 20 February he was 'recovering fast', having had the previous day 'a long interval of reason and composure'.[15] Despite this favourable turn, the new and anxious mad-doctor, watched over by an equally anxious Prime Minister, proved more a change in name from the Willises than in methods. He tied the King in a strait-waistcoat every day and presumably all day. But Addington made nothing of it, commenting, 'He submits cheerfully to the restraints which he believes to be necessary, and is perfectly contented under the management of Dr. Simmons.'[15] This hardly tallies with what the King thought of Simmons and his treatment. Indeed, the similarities between him and old Willis extended beyond their methods of managing patients. Simmons, too, brought with him a son as well as his keepers, and paraded the same therapeutic optimism. He told Addington that although 'relapses in this disorder are frequent, and many persons return to St. Luke's at intervals . . . the attack is always slighter upon each successive fit'. Since the King was already on the way to recovery it is not surprising that Simmons proved right.

On 21 February the physicians told Lord Castlereagh that, had the Chancellor seen the King, he 'would have found him, to all appearance, as well in understanding as before the illness'. Two days later, Sir Francis Milman declared him to be 'perfect wisdom'.[15] By 26 February he was so well that the Archbishop of Canterbury issued 'a thanksgiving . . . for the happy prospect of his Majesty's speedy recovery',[16] while the bulletin stated more cautiously that ' "though the King was going favourably, any rapid amendment was not to be expected". This report . . . excited some disapprobation, and occasioned several questions and remarks in parliament,' since it threw doubt on whether the King's recovery was genuine or political. In the House of Lords 'some part of the Opposition [Lords Fitzwilliam and Carlisle] called it in question, and held rather unfair language on it.'[17] In the Commons, Addington explained 'that the physicians only meant to intimate by the words objected to, that although the King was now perfectly competent to any act of government, it would be prudent for some time to spare him all unnecessary exertion of mind.'[18] The Archbishop, owing to his 'declining state of mind', had apparently overlooked the usual procedure of submitting his prayer to the Privy Council and he was warned to refrain from 'such proceedings for the future'. The physicians were also taken to task for issuing such a badly worded bulletin as to give the ministers an uncomfortable time. In defence, 'They stated that, so little was that their meaning [that the recovery would be protracted], that they actually prepared two forms, the first of which would have been, that His Majesty was in a progressive state of recovery; but that they had adopted the latter from a desire to repress any over-hasty expectation in the public.'

Eldon, however, had benefited by the mistakes of his predecessors, and was not going to be caught out as Loughborough had been over allowing the King to sign bills. The very day when questions were asked in the House, he arranged an examination of the physicians by the Cabinet. All agreed that the King was 'perfectly competent' to put his sign manual to any act or instrument which had been explained to him; that the illness would not be of long duration; that he would recover sooner if not 'hurried with company and business' and that, accordingly, 'long arguments or fatiguing discussion' should be avoided.[19] The physicians also stated that 'if he went on for the next ten days as he had for the last ten days, he would be perfectly well'.[20] On 5 March, Eldon obtained a further precautionary mandate from the doctors, who confirmed 'that his Majesty is fully competent to transact business with his Parliament by Commission and Message'.[19]

Recovery proceeded without interruption. On 7 March Simmons told Addington 'that he had the happiness to say His Majesty was better to-day than at any time since the illness'[21]; and on 22 March the bulletin read: 'His Majesty is much better, and in our opinion a short time will perfect his recovery.'[22] The 'short time' was, however, long in coming. For much of the year the King's behaviour and conversation, when off his guard in private and on social occasions, showed that the illness had taken out of him more than the short duration of the attack signalled, to which his advancing years contributed. He seems to have reserved his best power for affairs of state, and vented his anger and irritability and 'wrong ideas' more freely at home – as patients in a reduced state will. As in 1801, the royal family saw a worse side of him than his ministers, and what was no more than the aftermath of the illness gave rise to contradictory reports of his capacity and to doubts whether the illness had really ceased. 'He was apparently quite himself when talking business, and to his Ministers,' observed Lord Malmesbury. 'He then collected and *re*collected himself; but, in his family and usual society, his manners and conversation were far from steady – fanciful, suspicious, &c.'[23] He fretted at what he felt was unnecessary supervision by the physicians and in particular at the pro-longed attendance of 'that horrible doctor' Simmons[24] with his 'shabby' men.[25] He became 'very much inflamed' when he heard that the Willises had as much as been in the house when he was ill,[26] while the Willises made it known that they had refused to attend, because 'they were paid so shabbily by Addington [for 1801] that they would not return to the Court'.[27]

Pitt, who after a week's negotiation with the King had come back as Prime Minister on 12 May, soon had to intervene once again between the King and the doctors on behalf of the Queen. On 16 May he and Eldon addressed the King literally 'to implore' him to give 'strict and uniform compliance' to his physicians' advice both for 'the perfect re-establishment and preservation of your Majesty's health' and 'to guard against the danger of any relapse'.[28] They enclosed the declared opinion of his physicians requesting that he should 'be graciously pleased to consent, for a short time longer, to proper management'. Having heard the King was contemplating taking the Cheltenham waters again, the physicians added that 'they would be neither useful or proper'.[29] On 1 June, after a clandestine meeting at the house of Sir Lucas Pepys, Pitt and Eldon wrote again in a similar vein, enclosing another medical certificate because the King was rebelling against the continued attendance of Simmons.[30] History, especially that of 1801, was really repeating itself, almost to the very month.

Said Rose, 'How Mr. Pitt can carry on the government creditably, if the King is to be in the hands of his physicians I cannot discover; nor how he can well resist an inquiry and examination of the physicians, if that shall be pressed in the House.'[31] This was obvious to the Opposition, too, and every unfavourable medical feature strengthened the hand of the Prince of Wales and enhanced his political importance. He procured inside information from Kew through his younger brother the Duke of Kent, who reported on 17 May:

The hurry when with the family and consequently, either wholly, or nearly without control, continue the same, and a variety of shades, and some of these highly unpleasant, manifest themselves . . . A great coolness towards our mother is predominant, and a general asperity towards the whole family collectively upon the subject of his confinement frequently shewn. It appears he has till last evening entertained daily and even hourly expectations of his total release from medical attendance and restraint; but it was thought expedient, thro' the medium of the Chancellor to state to him in writing that he had not yet made sufficient progress in his convalescence for that to take place . . . this . . . excited a good deal of ill humour.[32]

The poor patient, valiantly struggling against physical weakness and to adjust mentally to a resumption of normal life, was hemmed in and

obstructed on all sides. The innate fear and intolerance of mental instability in those around him were so strong that even this sign of returning
health was turned against him and instanced as evidence of unsound mind.
And yet, had he meekly submitted to further confinement and restraint,
it would have been construed the same way, and medically speaking would
have been a much more unfavourable sign.

On 3 June the Duke of Kent reported 'a wonderful change in . . .
manner from anything I have ever seen since the commencement of his
confinement, inasmuch as instead of hurry, violence and ill humour, there
was unusual calmness, quiet, and good nature . . . like his old ways.' But
he remained 'coolly civil' to his family. His physical health was, however,
'unusually bad', 'no ruddiness on his cheek' and he had 'a tremor in his
limbs'.[33] He reported again on 9 June that their father continued calm
but that the 'symptoms of bodily infirmity' were 'very visible, the principal
of which are an extreme lethargic tendency, a great faintness from heat,
legs . . . swelled at night, a very bilious, or rather livid skin . . . a singular
catch in the throat . . . and an uncommon deficiency of sight and hearing'.[34]

Armed with this inside information and 'four reports of his Majesty's
physicians' of 31 May and 5, 9 and 16 June and their formal answers to
the questions he had put to them, the Prince now moved into the attack
with a letter to the Chancellor. He accused the ministers of conspiring to
hide the King's real state from Parliament and the country, pretending he
was well while still under the control not only of physicians but also, and
worse, of 'inferior attendants . . . introduced into his service since his
illness by Doctor Symmonds'. He declared it his 'indispensible duty to
make his solemn protest, as the King's son, as the first subject of the
Empire, and as the Heir Apparent of his Throne' and to demand that the
situation be remedied 'by some authority already known to the law' – the
Regency Bill of 1789 – or brought into the open and 'referr'd to Parliamentary decision'.[35]

Chancellor Eldon was in no hurry to reply, but did so a week later to say
that 'in the judgment of the physicians, his Majesty is [now] well'.[36] The
Prince, however, was not so easily put off. On 1 July he called the physicians for another interrogation to Carlton House and demanded from now
on to 'receive a daily communication of the state of his Majesty's health'.[37]
And again he drew the Chancellor's attention to 'so extraordinary a
circumstance as a King of England whilst exercising his Regal powers
being kept under any personal restraint'[38] – a standpoint the same as his
father's, but expressed with the opposite end in view. At the same time,
the Prince tried to ingratiate himself with the Queen again to obtain her
support in having the King declared incapable.

But the King really was much better. On 20 July he moved from Kew to Windsor and freedom, and although Simmons continued as was customary for another month 'in the house, he is never seen'.[39]

On 31 July the King 'came in person and prorogued Parliament. He looked extremely well, and read his Speech well with great animation.'[40] Others found him mentally well, but in 'appearance much altered, he looks twenty years older'.[41] Full of pride in his achievement, the King told Pitt he 'felt no fatigue from the ceremony ... as he was conscious of acting as he ought; and the sentiments of the Speech were so thoroughly his own that they could not but invigorate him'.[42]

On 20 August Simmons left, and four days later the King set out for Weymouth. Two days after his arrival there, he wrote to Pitt

as to the King's health, it is perfectly good, and the quiet of the place and salubrity of the air must daily increase his strength. By the advice of Sir Francis Milman, who is here, the King will bathe in the tepid bath, in lieu of the going into the open sea, His Majesty feels this a sacrifice, but will religiously stick to this advice, but does not admire the reasoning, as it is grounded on sixty-six being too far advanced in life for that remedy proving efficacious.[43]

The kindly and well-meaning Heberden, who in contrast to the others saw not simply an illness but the patient as a person, and always unreservedly took the King's side, visited him at Weymouth. His 'very decided opinion', as given on 9 September to Lord Camden, was

that the King is advanced very much in his recovery, since he has been here – that those irritations of temper to which he had been subject subside gradually, that the hurry and agitation of spirits are also subsided except when called forth by extraordinary exertion, as was the case yesterday when the King gave a fête on his Wedding Day, and that except want of rest at night he observes nothing either in the King's state of health or manner that he thinks is not as it ought to be ... He observes that on the part of the Queen and some of the Princesses there is an impression that the King is not as well as he really is, that on that account there is a suspicion which is discernable to the King in their manner to him, that he is hurt and irritated by this behaviour and that though he thinks there is some improvement in the domestic management he is far from being comfortable. He has endeavoured and trusts he has made some impression to convince the Queen that his Majesty is really well except that his nerves have not yet recovered their former tone and he is therefore subject to irritation and hurry, and that he takes too little sleep, and that the way to make him quite well now is to shew that they think him so.[44]

At the end of September the King suffered from 'severe headaches ... very dissimilar to his usual nervous affections since then he was very cold, whereas now as he describes the sensation himself, his face & hands are burning during the pain'. Milman feared 'an immediate apoplexy',[45] but the symptoms passed without complications, his recovery continued, and it was said that 'if things were well in the family he would probably be completely well'.[46] By the middle of October he had regained his sleep and lost much of his irritability. Moments of relaxation from business were 'still now and then marked with singularities' and 'his character and habits' appeared 'in some respects materially altered',[46] but he transacted business and corresponded as well as ever. By early November he was fully well,[47] and at dinner a month later Glenbervie found him 'in very pleasant spirits and very narrative'.[48]

However, the breach with the Queen was not healed:

At the Wedding Fête it was presumed that the King would be allowed to sleep with the Queen, which hitherto [since the illness] had not been the case, but the same precautions were taken to prevent his monopolizing the room. These . . . are . . . the occupation of the bedchamber by the two German ladies at an early hour. When the Queen retires there, two or three of the Princesses constantly attend upon her & stay until the King leaves the apartment . . . I have never been able to ascertain the cause of the Queen's disgust for the King since his last illness, for disgust it amounts to, but no doubt she must have very good reason to resist nature, her duty, the advice of the physicians, & the entreaties of the Ministers, for all have much interested themselves in this affair.[49]

Even the King's threat to take a mistress seems to have been in vain. 'He never mentions her with disrespect,' wrote Lord Auckland, 'but he marks unequivocally, and by many facts, that he is dissatisfied with her, and is come to a decided system of checking her knowledge of what is going forward, and her interference between him and the heir, &c., &c.'[50] On his return from Weymouth the King arranged to live separately, although they remained friends and appeared together in public, and he had 'all the books and pictures' removed from the Queen's House to Windsor Castle.[51]

On 12 November the Prince of Wales saw his father for the first time since his illness began, having first sent an assurance to the King through Lord Eldon of his 'most dutiful & affectionate sentiments towards your Majesty'.[52] The 'interview yesterday at Kew was every way *decent*,' reported the King to Eldon, 'as both parties avoided any subjects but those of the most trifling kind' and it remained for the Prince's 'future conduct to show whether the sentiments . . . are genuine'.[53] To the Prince he 'appeared much fallen away',[54] and privately he expressed 'great *lamentations* at having found the King so much *broken in all respects*'.[55] He was never the same again, although he kept free from attacks for six years.

By 1805 the signs and symptoms of cerebral irritation had disappeared, family friction had been smoothed, and the King settled down to his new routine at Windsor. His remaining complaint of 'rheumatic pains' also slowly passed off.[56] But a new misfortune struck him. In June 1804 it was observed that he had 'an uncommon deficiency of sight'. At the end of October, while visiting Rose at Cuffnells on his return from Weymouth, he told him that 'he had nearly lost the sight of his right eye, and that it was with the greatest difficulty he could read a newspaper by candle-light with *any* spectacles he could get'.[57]

Now in the summer of 1805 the vision in his other eye also became impaired. On 3 July it was officially learnt 'that the King had for some time lost the use of one eye by the formation of a cataract, and that another was forming in the other eye'.[58] Sir Joseph Banks told the Speaker of the House of Commons that the King's right eye was completely blind and vision in the left so limited that he had been unable 'to read a word for some time'. It was, however, hoped that the cataracts would soon be ripe for couching.* For the time being, Pitt 'recommended Colonel Herbert Taylor, the Duke of York's military Secretary, to be the confidential person employed in reading despatches to the King, and writing for him during his blindness'.[59]

It is a remarkable testimony to George III's energy and application to duty that until his sixty-eighth year he conducted all his vast official and private correspondence himself without any assistance whatever, even making the copies of his own letters. This further blow he took with stoic calm, at least outwardly. 'I am sure your Lordship will have particular satisfaction in hearing that the King has borne this *last calamity* . . . with all the fortitude and resignation which you so well know belongs to his character,' wrote Lord Hawkesbury on 8 July on behalf of the King to the venerable prelate of Worcester, 'his spirits are cheerful, and . . . his general health has in no respect been impaired'.[60] At Weymouth later in the month he suffered 'a considerable inflammation in his eyes' which threatened total loss of vision. His oculist, J. W. Phipps, later Sir Jonathan Wathen Waller, was called and 'said that the inflammation might produce much good or much evil'. He ordered leeches to be applied and they made the King 'easier'.[61] 'You will I am sure rejoice to hear the dear King's eyes are much better,' wrote the Queen to the Countess of Chatham, Pitt's sister-in-law, on 3 August. 'The inflammation which he had reason to fear [has] not only much abated, but hath proved the means of dissolving the skinn which threatened the cataract. Mr. Phipps gives us hopes' and advised 'avoiding dusty roads, great lights, & above all not overstraining the eye.'[62] As the inflammation subsided the King's vision returned to what it had been and he remained pathetically hopeful for a time that it was improving, as he wrote to Bishop Hurd:

No one ever experienced a more striking instance of the protection of

---

* The operation of couching was in fact never attempted, although its feasibility was considered by the Queen's Council as late as 1811.

7a. *A specimen of the King's clear normal handwriting punctiliously dated, as was his custom, 'Windsor May 9th 1789. 35 m[inutes] p[ast] 6. P M'.*

TRANSCRIPT
Windsor Castle Augt. 1809
Of the above value £4,000
to be placed in the hands of
Messrs Drummond [his bankers]
for King's
Private [?Account]
George R.

7b. The effect of almost total blindness twenty years later, when he did not even see that the ink had run out.

Divine Providence than I have done. The cataract was first formed in the left eye, and much advanced in the right one, but, by an unexpected inflammation in the left eye, this had dispelled the apparent mischief in that eye; and that in the other also diminished, so that Mr. Phipps seems sanguine he will effect a cure.[63]

Phipps's hopefulness of a possible restoration of his sight seems to have encouraged the patient to think that his eyes were really improving for a time. Nothing, in fact, halted the rapid progress to total blindness. By September 1805 a great change in his tidy and clear handwriting took place and it became 'much larger, and the characters . . . very indistinct and ill formed'.[64] From November all his correspondence had to be conducted by his amanuensis. Almost the last letter the King wrote was to Pitt, on 15 September 1805. He ended: 'His Majesty's sight will not allow him to add more, as though he gains some ground, he can neither read what is written to him nor what he writes.'[65]

8

The Regency: 1810-12

On 25 October 1810 the King's family gathered around him to celebrate the fiftieth anniversary of his accession. The party was saddened and subdued because the King's youngest and favourite daughter, Amelia, was on her death-bed. The King himself had caught a cold and complained of headache. What nobody could know was that this was also the last occasion when the King appeared in society. He entered the room leaning on the Queen's arm to guide him.

As he went round the circle as usual, it was easy to perceive the dreadful excitement in his countenance . . . He called to him each of his sons separately, and said things to them equally sublime and instructive, but very unlike what he would have said before so many people had he been conscious of the circumstance.[1]

He may have shown 'symptoms of the disorder' a few days before[2] and the Prime Minister, Spencer Perceval, was apparently uneasy about him.[3] Now, within twenty-four hours, it became clear that he had 'a decided return of his former malady'.[4] 'The worst symptom is the great and increasing agitation of mind,' with almost complete sleeplessness and incessant talking which soon became confused.[5] He was attended by Sir Henry Halford,* physician to the Queen, the Prince of Wales and Princess

---

* Sir Henry Halford (formerly Vaughan) (1766–1844), was the royal physician *par excellence*: to Queen Charlotte, George III, George IV, William IV and Queen Victoria, and held the office of President of the Royal College of Physicians from 1820 to his death. 'He had all the advantages of address and manners', which enabled him 'to look grave at whim and caprice' and to 'give importance, plausibility, and fascination, even to the long-winded detail of nothing'. He 'conducted himself with that delicacy, prudence, and good sense, as to gain equally the esteem of the Queen's cabinet, as of the opposition at Carlton House' and 'shewed himself equally adroit as a courtier as eminent as a physician' (*A picture of . . . the Royal College of Physicians*, ed. W. Nisbet, 1817, pp. 1–6). The *Dictionary of National*

Amelia. On 26 October, Halford called in Dr Matthew Baillie and the next day Dr William Heberden junior, whose father had been called in 1788 and who had himself attended in 1804, and the Windsor apothecary Mr David Dundas.

When Perceval saw the King on 29 October 'his conversation was prodigiously hurried, and . . . extremely diffuse, explicit, and indiscreet'.[6] 'Hurry and irascibility abated' the following day, but his conversation was 'unconnected'. This change was favourable, the doctors told Perceval, and in any case 'at the King's now advanced time of life, the same degree of violence was not to be apprehended'. They therefore insisted 'that no resort should be had to any means of restraint, as in the prior instances, lest that which appeared to be now subsiding should be aggravated'.[6] This enlightened attitude to management, the very opposite of the doctrine of repression, reflected not only the change which had gradually taken place in the practice of the mad-business since the King's first attack. In it one may also detect the humane influence of Heberden. But the physicians failed to allow for the King's iron constitution and indomitable energy, and their good resolutions were soon overtaken by events. That very evening he was 'extremely violent, so as to make even the physicians apprehend that recourse must be had to *coercive measures*'.[7] As so often before, he was quieter next morning, 1 November – in 'a state of debility and vacancy of mind' – when the Lord Chancellor found him 'quite incompetent to sign the Commission' to prorogue Parliament. In the afternoon he again became very disturbed and 'it was determined to send immediately for Dr. Simmons'[8] to take charge, as in 1804.

Crisis in the sickroom was, as in 1788, matched by crisis in government. 'You will observe that Parliament is now exactly in the same situation with respect to its meeting as it was in 1788,' wrote Lord Grenville to Earl Grey. 'That attack began about 22nd of October, this about the 25th. Parliament was then prorogued to the 20th of November, now to the 23rd . . . In the two attacks in 1801 and 1804, as Parliament was actually sitting, the thing was in some degree kept from public observation; but in this instance, as in 1788, it must . . . be brought forward.'[4] The outlook for Mr Perceval's administration was, however, the more precarious in proportion as the King's chances of recovery diminished. The question of a Regency 'is undoubtedly materially changed since 1788', wrote Earl Grey. Then 'the King was in the vigour of his life, had not been subject

---

Biography says he 'was a good practical physician . . . but he deprecated physical examination of patients, knew little of pathology, and disliked innovation'. In his diary he deplored that honours for medical men could 'go no higher' than a baronetcy, because of the objection to 'a Lord . . . with propriety taking a fee', but hoped this obstacle would in time be overcome and 'custom would reconcile that, as every thing else'.

to previous attacks of the same nature, and might be expected to resume his functions with a full capacity to discharge them'.[9] Now, however, 'Encreased age and renewal of malady encreases the difficulties with respect to the patient, and draws the publick attention to those other infirmities so as to make a very discouring sum total of disorder,' wrote Thomas Grenville to his brother, 'nor does it follow that what succeeded at an early period with all the advantage of Pitt's power and reputation, can successfully be renewed in the hands of those who have neither power nor reputation.'[10] Yet public feeling arising from 'the general compassion of this melancholy case' was against a return of party strife on the scale of 1788. 'It is not easy to conceive a more terrible visitation of mental misery,' said Lord Auckland, 'than that of feverish insanity added to total blindness.'[11] Party political advantage took second place to securing the smooth continuation of effective government with the least possible distress to the King.

It was with the greatest reluctance that the royal physicians sent for Simmons. When the attack was coming on and before the delirium had reached its height, the King 'had extracted a promise from them, that he should never be left entirely alone with any medical person specially engaged in the department of insanity'[12] and had expressed his 'antipathy to Simmons, and still more to young Simmons'.[13] The Queen also protested to the ministers about it. But Simmons meanwhile arrived at Windsor 'accompanied by his son and four assistants . . . [and] desired to have the sole management of the King, without which, [he said] he could do nothing. This was refused him by the physicians, in consequence of which, he went back with his troop immediately.'[14]

It was now resolved that 'he should be under no coercion or management not superintended by the ordinary physicians',[15] that they should 'control and govern, but to have some of the mad people under them'.[14] This arrangement, they hoped, would avoid the differences and rivalries which had arisen among the doctors in the previous attacks, spare the King's feelings and respect his wishes and their promises to him. On 2 November, Heberden accordingly sent for Mr John Meadows, recently retired apothecary – that is, medical officer – of St Luke's Hospital, who 'brought with him some of the persons usually employed in such cases', namely Mr P. G. Briand, who kept a private madhouse in Kensington Gore, and two of his 'assistants'.[8] Their duties were explained to them,

especially that they were not to be afraid of employing the necessary means of restraint, but were at the same time never to lose sight of the King's rank, that they were to conduct themselves with respect but firmness, that they were to use no familiarity and no unnecessary violence, that they were not to wait for the discretion of the physicians for the employment of the means placed in their hands, but that they would always be liable to the inspection of His Majesty's physicians, one or more of whom would be constantly in attendance.[8]

That day and the next 'the violence of the disorder was at a horrible height', recorded Mr Speaker Abbot, 'the King had taken but little refreshment for the last five days, and nothing but magnesia for the two last. Closed doors and windows were the only restraint, and, if he had been so left, it is apprehended that forty-eight hours more would have put his life beyond the reach of recovery.'[15] On Saturday, 3 November, came Dr Reynolds, who had attended in all previous attacks, and the following day, Sunday, 4 November, 'coercion' – the strait-waistcoat – was for the first time employed and 'after medicine, leeches [to the temples], and a pillow of hops had been applied, sleep ensued for several hours',[15] but his pulse remained high, above 100.[8]

On 6 November, Perceval brought in Dr Robert Darling Willis, much to the physicians' dismay and the royal princes' annoyance.[16] The bulletin stated: 'His Majesty has passed the night with very little sleep, and is not better this morning.' He had slept only half an hour and it was impossible to get him to eat or drink. But he had survived the first crisis and was improving, and the bulletin of 7 November announced that the King 'was better this morning than he had been for five or six days past'; he began to take notice of his surroundings again,[16] and on 11 November 'asked in the morning how long he had been confined, and when told him, he said he had no recollection of the time; that it was the fourth blank in his life; enumerating the three former ones, and the periods of them'.[17] Only now could he comprehend the death of Princess Amelia on 2 November, although attempts had been made before to convey it to him.

On 12 November 'restraint was taken off' and the next day it was noted with relief that he passed two motions.[8] On 14 November an extra evening bulletin announced 'a progressive state of amendment' which enabled Perceval to persuade the House next day to agree to a further adjournment for a fortnight.[18] As after every attack the physicians worried that if the King did too much too soon he would get into 'hurries and flurries' and retard his recovery. They therefore sent him a formal note advising that he 'should command Himself', not give 'multiplied directions', but rest content for the time to be governed rather than govern. The King replied through his secretary with good humour, 'that he would submit entirely to the directions contained in the paper delivered by his physicians'.[8]

On 16 November, when he attempted to go through Princess Amelia's effects, he showed at first 'surprising accuracy; but towards the end puzzled himself, and left off by his own choice, and had the newspaper read to him before he went to bed'.[8] During the night he again became feverish, his pulse rose above 100, he made water frequently and was put in restraint from three o'clock in the morning till the next midday. The bulletin of 17 November announced he had a sleepless night and was 'a little more feverish'. It was the beginning of a relapse which lasted until the second week of December. He rambled incessantly, and at times his speech was indistinct. He 'resisted being bled' and leeches were instead placed on his head. Again, the bulletins varied only between little or no sleep and more or less fever, while the physicians tried to reassure themselves and Perceval that this was merely the 'second stage of his disorder through which he has always gone, before he recovered, in his former attacks'.[19]

On 26 November he was troubled 'by tightness and uneasiness and sometimes undesirable pain in the abdomen, with frequent, ineffectual attempts at stool',[8] and it was feared that 'the fever' was turning into 'a fever of *illness* and not of the brain'. Heberden wondered how long even his constitution could withstand such onslaughts.[20] 'I am told . . . that this last mischief has been a bowel complaint, which, if not stopped, produces danger by weakness, and, if stopped, affects the head,' wrote Thomas Grenville. 'The private reports that circulate from the physicians still speak of hopes of recovery, and attribute the present relapse to a *bilious attack*, which . . . will soon be removed, and then the King will regain the very advanced state of recovery which he had reached before his bilious disorder.'[21]

On 27 November a Privy Council was summoned for the following day to examine the physicians and provide Parliament with a guide how to proceed.

Lord Camden (Lord President) . . . stated to the Board the cause of the summons, and the course proposed to be pursued in examining the physicians, according to the precedent of 1788, putting the same questions as were then put, with one further question: viz., 'Whether there had been any amendment in His Majesty's health, and was there any reason to expect its continuance ?' . . . and the questions were put successively and separately to Dr. Reynolds, Sir Henry Halford, Dr. Heberden and Dr. Willis; the other physician, Dr. Baillie, being necessarily in attendance at Windsor during the absence of the rest [he was separately examined the next day]. *All* spoke with confidence of the King's ultimate recovery . . . Dr. Heberden alone assigned any probable term to the duration of the disorder; and he thought it would be short. Upon an answer of Sir Henry Halford, stating 'that . . . his bodily indisposition had been materially increased' . . . a considerable discussion arose.[21]

Heberden admitted to 'very little experience' of 'this particular Species of Disorder' while Willis naturally claimed the most: 'From my earliest infancy I had opportunities of observing complaints of this nature, as long as I remained under my father's roof,' he said. 'During the last two and twenty Years I have seen a great variety of cases . . . in private practice.'[22]

A copy of the examination was presented to both Houses on 29 November and 'ordered to be printed' for the use of members as the reports of 1788 and 1789 had been; and the physicians' optimism gained Perceval another fortnight's respite, in the same way as the first examination in 1788 had gained respite for Pitt.

At Windsor 'the King's malady fluctuated considerably . . . On the 6th [December] he had a relapse; and the accounts were indifferent till the 11th, when they were considerably improved.'[23] There were 'long intervals of quiet' but also 'strong symptoms of disorder' which 'his Majesty corrects himself frequently, and almost always allows others to correct him'.[24] Rose maintained that the King was 'fully aware of what is going on, and had observed . . . that Mr. Perceval must have had some difficulty in carrying the second adjournment, considering the length of time his disorder had lasted'. Not so propitious were reports of 'fainting fits', that his excitement had to be 'reduced by medicines', of improved physical health but unchanged mental state.[25] Quarrels had started between Willis and the other physicians 'whom he charges with impeding recovery, by interfering too much, and conversing with him'. The bulletins, however, continued studiously non-committal, or, as Lord Auckland complained, they 'are now industriously involved in obscurity by vague references to preceding days, and by comparatives applied to unknown positives' and 'comprized in an artificial ringing of changes of about twenty words'.[26]

On 13 December the pattern of proceedings of 1788 was further repeated when Perceval proposed in the reassembled House an examination of the physicians by a Select Committee of twenty-one, and the same motion was made in the Lords. They were examined by the Commons on 14 and 15 December and by the Lords on 17, 18 and 19 December.

Type of questions and form of answers show a considerably greater degree of sophistication than on the like occasion twenty-two years earlier. The knowledge that the King had recovered from three similar attacks gave the doctors a degree of assurance which their predecessors lacked. Political steam had also to some extent gone out of the illness, as the form of a regency, if one there had to be, was already laid down. The old political opponents, Pitt and Burke, and the old medical rivals, Baker, Warren and Willis, were dead. The physicians in attendance were therefore free to concentrate on the medical issues without fear of political repercussions and in a position frankly to admit ignorance in face of what was for them a clinical problem of insurmountable complexity. They said they had never seen a case like the King's.

All agreed the King was at present incapable, but would recover, although they could not say when; that the illness had been accompanied by 'notable' bodily derangement and fever, which had paralleled the derangement of mind, and they hoped both would subside together. In reply to specific questions, Dr Reynolds was particularly hopeful because 'I have seen his Majesty recover from three attacks of the same disease, in some parts of which I think he has been worse than he is at present.' He stressed the marked fluctuations which at their worst amounted to 'paroxysms'. He understood that the illness 'came on from the anxiety of his mind upon the illness of his daughter', but confessed 'I do not know that I ever saw exactly a case parallel to the King's'. Asked about the causes of the King's previous attacks, he answered: 'I do not know that the first attack [of 1788] was referred to any known cause; in 1801 I did understand there was a cause; I did not understand that in 1804 there was any assignable cause.'*27 He was optimistic, too, because 'the King's memory is entire, his perceptions are entire; and his acuteness is considerable', though 'his judgment . . . was perverted, and . . . his discretion is asleep at times'. When asked whether the word 'fever' in the bulletins meant 'an accession of mental disease, or of bodily indisposition', he answered 'when we have made use of the word fever, the King had fever, though accompanied with an aggravation of the mental disease . . . At times . . . it has perhaps been the most prominent part of his disorder; there have been periods when the King was very seriously ill.'

Dr Baillie confirmed that

during the whole of this indisposition, [the King] has had more or less of bodily indisposition, though sometimes very little, yet it becomes an additional though a slight proof that he may probably recover, that he has that bodily ailment: If there was precisely the state of mind which the King has without bodily ailment, we should say, there was altogether a less chance of the King's recovering.

Concerning his blindness, he considered it

in the earlier periods of an indisposition like the King's . . . probably . . . an advantage; that it would lessen the excitement [by shutting out one source of sensory stimuli]; but . . . on towards recovery . . . the want of sight would be a disadvantage, because he would be deprived of many amusements that could occupy his mind and assist in the complete recovery.

---

* Contemporaries naturally tried to assign a cause for the King's attacks. None was ever advanced for 1788, the most severe one. In 1801 Pitt was blamed for agitating Catholic Emancipation. In 1804 the attack was attributed to the King's annoyance with the Prince of Wales for having published their correspondence about the Prince's military role in case of Napoleonic invasion. The illness of 1810 was thought to have been precipitated by the King's sorrow at the illness and death of Princess Amelia. When the physicians mentioned these causes as possible, they thought that distress of mind had caused disease of the body, in the same way as severe shock may do. Nothing was further from their way of thinking than that psychological stress had brought on a 'mental', in the sense of psychological, illness.

Dr Heberden considered the King's illness

not merely the delirium of fever; nor is it any common case of insanity; it is a derangement attended with more or less of fever, and liable to accessions and remissions . . . connected with his bodily health . . . the whole frame has been more or less disordered, both body and mind . . . [owing to] a peculiarity of constitution, of which I can give no distinct account.

Sir Henry Halford said he had seen no sign of derangement before 25 October, although for three weeks he had reported to the King three times a day on the condition of Princess Amelia, and declared he was not incapacitated until 28 October and that he was 'at present not as well as he was then'.

Dr R. D. Willis deposed that he had 'never seen a person, at his Majesty's age, labouring under a similar complaint to his Majesty's, taking all the circumstances of the complaint together'. He said it had 'never borne the characteristic of insanity; it never gets beyond derangement'. Being asked to enlarge on this distinction, he explained:

I consider the King's derangement more nearly allied to delirium, than insanity; whenever the irritation . . . arises to a certain point, he uniformly becomes delirious. In delirium, the mind is actively employed upon past impressions, upon objects and former scenes, which rapidly pass in succession before the mind, resembling . . . a person talking in his sleep. There is also a considerable disturbance in the general constitution; great restlessness, want of sleep, and total unconsciousness of surrounding objects. In insanity there may be little or no disturbance, apparently, in the general constitution; the mind is occupied upon some fixed assumed idea, to the truth of which, it will pertinaciously adhere, in opposition to the plainest evidence of its falsity; and the individual is acting, always, upon that false impression. In insanity, also, the mind is awake to objects which are present. Taking insanity, therefore, and delirium, as two points, I would place derangement of mind somewhere between them. His Majesty's illness, uniformly, partakes more of the delirium than of the insanity.*

On 17 December the report was introduced to the House of Commons and a similar report on 20 December to the Lords. On 19 December Perceval wrote to the Prince of Wales to inform him that he proposed the next day to introduce a Regency Bill with restrictions, as in Pitt's Bill. In answer, the Prince referred 'to his answer in 1788, upon receiving a similar

---

* A Mrs Anne Mary Crowe was so impressed by what she read in the papers of R. D. Willis's evidence, in particular his distinction between delirium, derangement and insanity, that she addressed to him a public letter, *A letter to Dr. Robert Darling Willis . . . published in the hope of rousing a humane nation to the consideration of the miseries arising from private madhouses* (1811). Giving her own case as an example, she pleaded for 'persons confined under the imputation of insanity in those habitations of woe commonly called Licensed Houses for the Reception of Lunaticks . . . in whose recovery no part of the community is concerned; respecting whom no bulletins are issued'.

communication from Mr. Pitt' which was then assumed to have been drafted for him by Burke.[28] Perceval also received a letter signed by the Prince's six brothers protesting against any limitations as 'perfectly unconstitutional as they are contrary to and subversive of the principles which seated our family upon the throne of this realm'.

At Windsor the King was about to develop another paroxysm. On 21 December 'without any obvious cause he had a violent fit of passion, which left him under great agitation and irritation'.[29] There followed a return of his old abdominal trouble[30] which was attributed 'to a change of diet; he is grown excessively thin, and they order'd him Meat again, but it brought on fever without strengthening'.[31] On 24 December he was believed to be 'at the last gasp'. 'We state with much concern,' read the *London Chronicle* for 25–26 December,

that his Majesty's disorder took so unfavourable and alarming a turn on Monday [24 December] afternoon, about six o'clock, that the most serious consequences were apprehended by the Royal Physicians . . . An inflammation of the bowels, it was supposed, had taken place suddenly. His Majesty continued through the principal part of the night in extreme pain, accompanied by a violent fever, and with the pulse at 120, which was reduced only to 105 by two hours and a half sleep.

An express was sent to Carlton House 'to say that the King was in so violent a paroxysm, that, if it did not speedily abate, must be fatal. The Prince ordered his carriage and went instantly to Windsor.'[32] The attack 'was produced by constipation of the bowels, which effect ceased with the cause,' Willis told Lord Grenville. When it subsided, the King was left 'in a state of increased debility'.

'This last attack has been a fresh paroxysm as violent as the first, and it is beginning to remit,' wrote Lord Grenville on 31 December, 'and so long as this succession of attacks and remissions continued, the actual state from day to day is quite immaterial, and the real question is which will wear out first, the disease or the constitution.'[33]

On 30 December the King was able to get out of bed, but continued sleepless and complained of nausea, colic and constipation, and his stools varied from dark to pale. Sometimes their colour could not be 'distinctly seen, the water being discoloured'.[8] Halford described his conversation as 'that of a person who is intoxicated'. A symptom now appeared which greatly worried the physicians: at night he 'continually adjusted the bedclothes' and in day-time spent many hours aimlessly 'sorting and moving his papers', for both of which he was 'restrained'. At moments of comparative clarity and calm he played 'upon the pianoforte' – the instrument was no less than 'Handel's own harpsichord', according to Lord Auckland.[33] 'As it is productive of some amusement as well as occupation, it is looked upon as a good symptom.'[34]

As his health started to improve, there were reports of 'the delusions' coming to the fore. 'His uppermost idea is that something is to be done about Hanover. It is the same delusion that he had towards the close of his former illness; and from which he recovered gradually by puzzling out his own misconceptions,' wrote the Speaker.[35] On 8 January the physicians reported to Perceval that 'error and delusion' appeared to 'be getting less prominent, and His Majesty has either more power of laying it aside from his mind, or at least more power of concealing it . . . He begins to talk more of his own family, and upon the whole is going on well, though not without considerable marks of remaining indisposition.'[35] They reported in similar vein to the Lord Chancellor on 15 January, when they declared the King as yet 'incompetent to signify his Royal Will and Pleasure as to the Parliament's proceeding', that is on the Regency Bill.

Private accounts said 'that the former delusions have disappeared . . . although there still remain . . . marks of his indisposition', which left doubt about his recovery being speedy.[35] For example, he easily 'grows very impatient and passionate, and when in a passion always talks Latin, as he did within a very few days of the time when he appeared in public as recovered, after his last illness'. On 18 January he 'walked out . . . upon the terrace, for an hour, for the first time'[36] and again the next day 'and desired to go upon a particular part that it might be seen that he was alive'.[35] Three days later, Heberden described his mind as if it 'had been clouded with some confusion' and was now coming to itself again, but that he never spoke of politics 'seemingly as improper to his physician'.[37] Halford's opinion, however, was that the King 'was not the least aware of what is passing, that he has never expressed any surprise at no business being brought to him, and that, speaking of the examination of the physicians, he had said that having heard no more of it, he concluded it had blown over'. However, Halford gave Earl Grey to understand that he (Halford) still had 'a pretty strong opinion that he would ultimately recover'.[38]

On 25 January the physicians

gave it as their written opinion that it was desirable for the King's Ministers to see and explain to him the present state of affairs. They said that His Majesty's *understanding* and *comprehension* were perfect to every purpose of such a communication, but they could not undertake that his judgment would be so upon what it might be proper to do upon such things as he would nevertheless thoroughly comprehend.[39]

In short, they hoped that if he were informed of the progress of the Regency Bill, it would speed his recovery by stimulating him to apply his mind to matters of the moment. Accordingly, the next day, Perceval and Eldon spent more than an hour with him 'during the whole of which time he talked with them in the most collected manner'. However, they

Jan. 6. 1811.   *Sunday.*

Bulletin. His Majesty had a good night and is in all respects as well as he was yesterday.

Pulse 88 — The King had 2½ hours sleep after midnight (down to which the report was continued last night) — The remainder of the night was composed with little or no conversation — His Majesty was up to the W. Closet twice with little or no effect — Some phlegm and a small quantity of bile were brought up by vomiting — The water is of a deeper colour — and leaves a pale blue ring upon the glass near the upper surface —

℞. Ext: Taraxaci ʒr vj.
Aloes Socotor: ʒr: j.
Pilula una inauranda — et bis die sumenda —

9. P.M. — A quiet day — conversation mild — but under the delusion — a little altercation while getting into bed at 7 o'clock — but this soon ended in sleep — which continues ——

---

8. *A page from the Willis Journals (British Museum Add. MSS 41696, folio 77) of 6 January 1811 in the hand of Sir Henry Halford noting that at the end of an attack the urine was still discoloured. His pulse was 88, he had slept only two and half hours, he was still constipated despite being given aloes (he had been to the 'W[ater] Closet twice with little or no effect'); was troubled by persistent nausea but only brought up 'a small quantity of bile' (perhaps the effect of tartar emetic); and his 'water' remained 'of a deeper colour'.*

failed 'to bring the King to talk of public matters . . . as often as they did so, his Majesty turned the conversation with much dexterity, without appearing to avoid such subjects.'[40] Nevertheless, so pleased was the King to see them that he flattered himself that he could distinguish their faces.

On 29 January Perceval went again to Windsor, this time alone, and put the King fully in the picture. The King asked him what had been done since his illness,

whether Parliament had been sitting, and what they had been about. In answer to which Perceval told him, that the same course nearly had been pursued as that which had been approved by His Majesty after his illness in 1789; so as to provide for his finding everything as nearly as possible upon his recovery in the same state as before. That the measure had been carried forward in the House of Lords, and that a few more days would complete it.[41]

The King dwelt on his age – he was coming up to seventy-three – and 'that it was time for him to think of retirement', an opening which Perceval used to impress upon him the arduous duties to which he would be exposed if he returned. Clearly he hoped to persuade the King voluntarily to relinquish his powers. 'He listened with some unwillingness, and said, "He should always be at hand to come forward if he was wanted", and, upon the whole was rather impatient of any pressure upon the subject of resigning his power.' Perceval said afterwards that 'for the first half hour of this conversation, nobody could have supposed from the King's manner that he had been indisposed at all. But the other half hour was not so good'[42] – in other words, the King's concentration failed him.

Two days later 'the Regency Bill was this day read a third time with the amendments from the Lords, and passed'.[43] It only remained for it to receive the royal assent, that dreaded event which three times in the previous twenty-three years had for months agitated the King's ministers, the Opposition and the country. On 30 January the Prince of Wales took a last sounding of the King's physicians, and although they still remained hopeful of ultimate recovery, and said no unfavourable signs had appeared since their examination in Parliament six weeks before, they could not say that it was imminent.[44] All was now set for a change of ministers, which was regarded inevitable. On 5 February

The Chancellor went to Windsor to see his Majesty, in order to satisfy himself that he was not well enough to make it unfit for his Lordship to put the great seal to the commission for giving the royal assent to the Regency Bill; and found the King so well (though not recovered) as some-what to embarrass the noble Lord. He however returned, and sealed the commission; after which *the bill received the royal assent.*[45]

The next day the Regent took the oath of office and the Privy Councillors kissed hands. The effective reign of King George III was over. But the expected did not happen. The ministers were not changed. Behind the scenes, Sir Henry Halford, as much a diplomat as a doctor, had warned the Prince of Wales 'that a change of Ministers would in all probability, as soon as it was communicated to the King, produce such an exacerbation . . . as might put an end to his life; and . . . very strongly forced upon the Prince the reflection, that he might be considered as, or that he would in effect be, guilty of parricide'.[46] And the Queen had also written to the heir in the same sense.[47] The newly installed Regent, in communicating this remarkable and unexpected decision to the Prime Minister – 'his intention not to remove from their situations those whom he finds there as His Majesty's official servants' – stressed that the reason for his decision was not his regard for the present administration but solely 'the irresistible impulse of filial duty and affection to his beloved and afflicted father' and that he wished no act of his 'might, in the smallest degree, have the effect of interfering with the progress of his Sovereign's recovery'.[48] Ironically, on 7 February, the first day of the Regency, the bulletin announced: 'His Majesty seems to be making gradual progress towards recovery', and two days later the Queen was allowed to see her husband, whom she had not seen since the end of October.[49]

The Regency Act vested the care of the King's person during the continuance of his illness in the Queen, and to advise and assist her established the 'Queen's Council' of seven Privy Councillors headed by the Archbishop of Canterbury, and with power of declaring the King well and competent. To it the physicians had to send daily reports and four times a year answer a questionnaire about the state of the King's health and his chances of recovery, and the Council supervised every detail of the sick chamber and the attendance of the physicians, and themselves visited regularly.

The patient continued slowly to improve and was 'constantly asking if not one of the Council is coming', seeming to think, in the words of the Queen, 'that putting it off procrastinates his recovery'.[50] But he was by no means as well as he thought, and the Queen wished her Council to put 'a check to his expectations'. So fast, indeed, was it believed that he had advanced 'to perfect recovery' that when at the end of February the Regent was ill, because he was 'so overcome with business, and in such low spirits', it was half-seriously proposed 'to make the King sub-regent' to act for him.[51]

On 27 February the physicians suggested to the Queen's Council that the King's pages should be reinstated 'about His person' and the attendants withdrawn. So confident was the atmosphere at Windsor that the King could now be treated like any other kind of patient that the Queen wrote to the Archbishop that she wished Sir Henry Halford – not Willis – to have from now on 'the general direction of His Majesty's cure', Dr Reynolds 'though the senior Phisician' having left Windsor 'by the King's own command'. At the same time, to guard the King against his extravagant orders and plans, she requested her Council to inform all those about him 'of the impossibility of their obeying any of His Majesty's commands and ... humbly to state to the King under these circumstance the painful necessity they are under of receiving no direction, but those issued to them by the Queen's Council'.[52] These arrangements were put into effect early in March and on the tenth the Archbishop of Canterbury, accompanied by the Archbishop of York, also a member of the Council, went to Windsor and explained to the King the need and 'the propriety of his continuing some time longer in retirement'.[53] He had apparently expected his immediate resumption, but was now persuaded to convalesce until May.[54]

The King's disappointment was said to have been so profound that it brought on a relapse. A week of increased irritability followed, during which he 'exhibited more delusion'. It was accompanied 'by a violent pain in his stomach which He said little of to the Doctors but *much to us*' – the family – wrote his daughter Princess Elizabeth. 'He said I should have died with pain in my stomach & back',[55] but kept it from his physicians because he feared it might make them 'keep him back' longer. The physicians were inclined to attribute it to the 'change of attendants' giving 'occasion to a greater disclosure of His Majesty's indisposition' rather than to an actual increase of the illness. They remained confident that time alone would be sufficient 'for the extinction of all errors and delusions ... although this period', thought Heberden, might be shortened if he were to be told that 'they cannot declare him well so long as these continue'.

By the end of March he was better again, 'generally conversible and mild in His manner'. On 21 April the physicians reported:

The whole occurrences of the last week have been of the most flattering kind. His Majesty has appeared to make a gradual and uniform progress; has shewn only very slight marks of indisposition at any time; and, as far as we know, for the last few days scarcely any at all. We therefore submit to Her Majesty's Council the propriety of affording His Majesty some further opportunities of exerting himself both as a means of his acquiring greater strength of mind and power of self-control, and also as a measure necessary to assure His medical attendants, that His present apparent freedom from disorder is such as may be depended upon.

They suggested that Colonel Taylor, his secretary, for instance might see him again and that the 'introduction of Lord Arden or Lord St Helens or other noblemen or gentlemen in habits of familiar intercourse with His Majesty, would be useful. We think moreover that His Majesty may with propriety have the comfort of His prayers read by his Chaplain in His Majesty's own room, but not at present in the chapel.' Halford, however, maintained that for full recovery it was essential to maintain 'absolute authority and control' over the King's mind and that 'every deviation from right the moment it was observed' should be checked. The Council authorized the physicians to carry this regime into effect and ordered that they should

collectively and individually interpose and correct every palpable deviation from right the Moment of its coming to their knowledge, and that they will use their best Endeavours to keep alive in His Majesty's mind the Reasons which have been communicated to him, as those, upon which the Council acting under the advice of the Physicians cannot declare His Majesty well, and to point out to His Majesty that the various Plans and Projects which His Majesty dwells upon are considered as inconsistent with his complete Recovery.

Among these were plans for rebuilding his palaces, particularly Kensington, 'projects for a new regulation of the ribbons and Garter',[56] and the institution of 'a Female Order, which is altogether novel, and . . . inconsistent with the dictates of a sound and deliberate judgement' and furthermore does 'not correspond to His Majesty's manly character'.[52] From the last more especially the physicians 'earnestly recommended to His Majesty to withdraw his thoughts'. At times, too, he brought up the subject of Lady Pembroke again, as in 1788, and was again confused about his relationship to her. Grenville recorded that the King had said to his son, 'Is it not a strange thing, Adolphus, that they still refuse to let me go to Lady Pembroke (the old Countess [now in her 75th year]), although everyone knows I am married to her; but what is worst of all, is, that that infamous scoundrel, Halford (Sir Henry), was by at the marriage, and has now the effrontery to deny it to my face!'[57]

In this state, discussion of his treatment centred on whether he should be more strictly controlled or be allowed to find his own level by being given more liberty. Willis was in favour of restraint and excluding as far as possible all sources of 'excitement' until all 'wrong ideas' had disappeared since these were the only symptoms which stood between him and his return. Heberden took the opposite view and held that only by resuming his normal life and activities could the wrong ideas, confined in any case to only two or three subjects, wear off or be dispelled. So strongly did he feel that he addressed the Queen's Council independently of his colleagues on this principle of managing the King at that stage:

It is now more than six months, that His Majesty has been indisposed; and it is become of great moment that His Majesty's mind should, if possible be roused from its disordered actions, and not suffered to degenerate into a state of habitual error . . . it becomes a duty to present to it fit occasions of exertion, if we would have it resume its natural tone . . . At present there is not one moment of the day passed by His Majesty in his usual manner; scarcely one moment that he is not reminded of his unhappy situation, without being assisted to extricate himself from it . . . The very same restraint, which at one time was calculated to allay irritation, becomes at another a cause of increasing it.

Instead of [his normal routine], his Majesty is either led about under the direction of another; or watched and examined by his family during a formal visit; or left to converse with his Physicians, or his Pages, or to amuse himself with the excursions of his own imagination. He has no business to call forth his judgement, no friendly intercourse to relieve his mind, no amusement to recreate his spirits, no company to vary his thoughts, no music to solace his cares: added to which He has no sight to arrest his attention, or to give importance or employment to his solitude . . . If we would have done with schemes & trifles, we must surely not content ourselves with telling the King of his errors; but must study to place him in a situation, that may call forth the energies of his mind, and divert the wanderings of fancy, not by vain expostulation, but by objects of natural interest.

But unfortunately repression won over tolerance, as it had during his previous illnesses. Although Heberden's advice was at least partially followed – the King was allowed to go out riding 'amid the ringing of bells and the rejoicings of the inhabitants of Windsor'[58] and to see his family – his freedom was shortlived. By the end of May he was in the grip of another recurrence, which was promptly blamed on the King's getting over-excited from 'indulging in giving orders of various kinds, and entering upon the detail of many, & sometimes very objectionable plans . . . [with] improper allusions to Hanover, and . . . to the subject of a certain lady'.

Intercourse with his family was prohibited, the keepers were recalled and Colonel Taylor resigned as his secretary: 'The last day of my attendance upon the King,' he confided sadly to his journal on 31 May, 'His Majesty having been replaced under the charge of Doctor's men on that evening.'[59] The Queen blamed the relapse on Heberden's regime, and, tired of the physicians' talk, put Robert Willis in charge of the sickroom in place of Halford. To confirm Willis's authority, the Queen's Council ordered on 1 June 'that nobody be suffered to communicate with the King but with the consent of Dr. Willis and in his presence'.

Just before this recurrence 'very affecting proof of the King's melancholy state', and his insight into it was given at a concert held at Windsor.

It was the Duke of Cambridge's night, who announced . . . that the King himself had made the selection. This consisted of all the finest passages . . . in Handel, *descriptive of madness and blindness*; particularly of those in the opera 'Samson'; there was one also upon madness from love, and the lamentation of Jephtha upon the loss of his daughter; and it closed with 'God Save the King' to make sure the application of all that went before.[60]

As in all attacks mental deterioration was accompanied by physical symptoms, fast pulse, sweating, sleeplessness, nausea, colic and constipation, pain and weakness in the limbs, oppression in the chest. His countenance was flushed, his eyes became suffused and it was observed that they were 'in constant motion'. By the beginning of July 'he appeared sensible that he had been unwell', but relapsed again and 'displayed symptoms which we have observed only in the most distressing periods of his disease. Bursts of passion, gross and indecent allusions, loud and continual talking.' Again he improved and 'exerted himself to overcome the agitation of spirits of which he was very conscious'. But 'indiscretion and trifling, hurry and irritation' continued, and it was evident that yet another 'distinct Paroxysm of his Disorder' was beginning. He had no sleep for many nights and was kept in continual restraint, that is in a strait-waistcoat. On 15 July the physicians thought he was dying and informed the Queen's Council hurriedly:

It gives us great pain to state that the King's symptoms rapidly grew worse . . . yesterday . . . in the evening he was confused and lost. At midnight there appeared much disturbance & agitation in his frame and about 2 o'clock in the morning the King became so violent and unruly as to render Restraint absolutely necessary. His Majesty has not slept an instant and his pulse is become so rapid as to make us observe the whole condition of things with very great anxiety. We take it for granted that, in the present circumstances, the Queen's Council would desire to receive a further account in the evening and therefore we shall hold it our duty to send a second report at 8 PM.

We have found it absolutely necessary to give some written account of the King at the door of the Castle and should be glad to be instructed how far the Council may think it proper that we should send a Bulletin to Town, in the present anxious state of the King's illness.

The day after the crisis they described him as 'lost in mind, perverted in his ideas, and as irritable and violent . . . as at any time of his illness'; and the next day they noted with relief that 'at several different times he has had about ten minutes continued sleep'. On 17 July he was still 'incoherent', but there was 'some return of reason and recollection'. On 20 July he was 'throughout the day in a delirious state, but generally without violence, and not so entirely engrossed in visionary scenery'. It was not until 31 July that they felt there was 'no reason any longer to apprehend any danger to life'. But he was left further reduced and continued to be 'engaged in imaginary scenes' as 'one in an ordinary delirium from fever'. He had lost, wrote Lord Auckland, 'all the vestiges of partial reasoning and recollections which had hitherto been preserved through the whole of the illness'.[61] For weeks 'his mind' remained 'in as bad a state as ever',[62] but his bodily health improved, and by 17 August showed 'no sign of immediate failure, though His Majesty is considerably thinner, and looks older from the effect of the present paroxysm'.

'Continually addresses people dead or alive as if they were present,' reported the physicians on 20 August, and two days later, 'His Majesty considers it folly to ask him any questions about his health, as *He* is eternal'. On 23 August 'when he began to speak after a long silence he said he had been watching the Evil Spirits and that Nine [we believe of the doctors and of the men in attendance] were to sink to Hell . . . and he became extremely angry'. Much of the time he was confined in a strait-waistcoat and to give him quieting medicine – laudanum – or get him to bed was often accomplished only by force and after 'a formidable struggle'.

On 5 September the physicians reported that the King

has scarcely passed any day with so little apparent bodily illness, and so much real mental disorder . . . We have seen His Majesty sometimes in a state of delirium, sometimes strongly impressed by some false images; neither of which states has characterised this day so much, as a degree of irritability which could only be met by coercion, and which was only varied by occasional exclamations and noises apparently without meaning . . . The best we can report is, that His Majesty has rather spoken less, and rather struggled less, as the evening advanced.

On 17 September

at our interview this morning His Majesty showed clearly his incapability of maintaining any steadiness in his ideas and conversation for more than an instant. Several attempts were made to engage His Majesty's attention by the introduction of fresh topics of conversation but the King never failed to decline into some wild unnatural frame of thought after a sentence or two, and we had the mortification of hearing him speak of new arrangements which the *late King* was *now* making – and detail accounts of strange and horrible events which he himself was convinced had occurred in the course of the last night.

There were moments when he emerged from his confusional state and tried to reconcile what he had lived through and what had really been happening. At such times it became most obvious how far his mind had wandered. 'The Patient has two or three times enquired after some part of his family; generally however He has an impression that his sons are dead, or sent away to a distant part of the globe,' noted Heberden. He spent a large part of the day 'in playing upon the harpsichord or flute', but his mind continued to be

engrossed by the wildest and most extravagant fancies. He imagines that he has not only acquired the power of living for ever, but that he can call from the dead whomsoever he pleases, & make them of any age . . . and He actually describes the dress, the conduct, and the conversation of different persons, who are thus recalled into life . . . In short he appears to be living ... in another world, and has lost almost all interest in the concerns of this.

On 3 October he 'waked under his usual excitement ... entirely occupied with his own wild fancies and lost almost immediately the impression of the physicians being in the room'. 'For want of terms more accurately defined respecting different disorders of the human mind, His Majesty's present state might be call'd Insanity,' said Heberden in answer to the Queen's Council's quarterly questionnaire on 5 October, 'but it appears to me to differ materially from ordinary cases of insanity by that perplexity and confusion of ideas, which belong more properly to delirium; while His Majesty's adherence to certain erroneous notions with some degree of consistency partakes of the true character of Insanity.' On 14 October he was 'engaged in imaginary scenery all day ... appeared to amuse himself ... by arranging offices and appointments for a large company whom His Majesty conceived were standing about him'.[2] On 17 October he complained to Halford 'of noises made by the people of His imagination standing about Him and has endeavoured frequently to close his ears against such seeming disturbance'. On 20 October, after having slept for only twenty-five minutes during the night, 'His Majesty thought a certain Lord sat up in his bedroom all last night for the purpose of protecting him, and as that Lord did his business very insufficiently His Majesty did not hesitate to abuse him'. On another day 'his conversation related principally to an inundation, which was to drown the whole of the country, and from which he was making preparation to escape to Denmark'. During this period, too, the physicians complained that he showed a 'determined disregard to cleanliness' or a 'perverse disposition to uncleanliness' – so little did they understand how severely his nervous system was affected.

For long periods he could not eat and threw his food away, and there were bouts of vomiting and other evidence of pain and suffering. Now, too, he showed another sign of damage to the brain which his physicians attributed to 'an irritable state of nerves', namely that 'tears and laughter' followed in 'quick succession'.

The alarm occasioned by this severe setback which had started in July caused panic in the Queen's Council. They wished to bring in other specialists, and on 6 August Drs John Willis, S. F. Simmons and Thomas Monro of Bethlem Hospital assembled for a consultation at Sir Henry Halford's house. But they felt they could make no suggestion without seeing the patient. The Queen was, however, most unwilling to allow this, as she wrote to the Archbishop, not only because of her promise to the King and 'the Prejudice generally imbibed by the King towards Individuals Similarly Circumstanced in regard to H. My.' but in the case of Simmons also because his 'Conduct & Proceedings ... had rendered him *justly* obnoxious to the King, to myself & to the whole Royal Family & to every Individual Attendant'. But the Council insisted. 'The object of . . . urging it is to have it to report at the next meeting of Parliament, that all advice has been resorted to.'[63] Finally, the Queen gave way and permitted John Willis, Simmons and Monro

conjointly [to] have Access, at *stated* Periods to the King's Apartment, in order that They may be enabled by their personal Observation of His Majesty's Habits Demeanour and Condition, both of Body and Mind to form an accurate Judgment of the Extent and Nature of the Disorder, to make their Reports to the Council, and to advise whether any and what alteration of Treatment is likely to produce any Beneficial Change in His Majesty's State. But Her Majesty must expressly and positively object to their Interference in the Management of the Sick Chamber . . . or to Their making Themselves known to the King. She must insist upon Doctor Robert Willis still retaining that Management exclusively, and must solemnly deprecate the Introduction, otherwise than as passive Observer, of any Person, whose known Presence, and whose occasional Address would, in Her firm Opinion, expose the King to the most imminent Danger of His Life, from the Effects of increased Excitement and Agitation.

The Council were still anxious that John Willis and Simmons should share the management with Robert Willis. The Queen remained adamant in refusing Simmons, but at last had to allow John Willis to join his brother. On 23 November, 'Dr. John Willis was introduced to the King . . . His M. was enraged & Dr. Willis answered H.M. firmly – until at length it appeared likely to answer no further purpose to altercate than to exasperate the irritation,' observed Halford. In December the King once more improved, slept and ate better, received his physicians graciously, and his conversation was in part 'good', as for instance on 17 December when 'He talked . . . for an hour in very good humour and with hardly anything that can be specified as wrong'.

Heberden made several attempts to get the system of coercion, seclusion and restraint altered, and for a time he was backed by Halford. As an experiment he read the newspaper to the King, but was able to hold his attention for only a short time. Dr Robert Willis complained promptly of the 'inutility' of this attempt and asked the Queen's Council to prevent any repetition of it, as it ran counter to his system of management of keeping all stimulation from the King. Heberden defended his action as 'the only attempt that has been made . . . to introduce any real ideas to his Majesty's mind, or to relieve the invaried tediousness of silent and solitary confinement, during which the imagination is left to feed on its own inventions'. What, he asked, had been achieved by the other system:

The King has been kept in unedifying confinement and seclusion till the confinement itself has become a source of irritation . . . the aberrations and extravagancies of His imagination . . . have been suffered to increase without notice and without correction, till at length a fresh accession of disorder had been excited, and a fresh recurrence to seclusion and confinement has become necessary . . . Surely then it is not unreasonable to employ every method . . . to avert such a calamity, and to let slip no opportunity, nay rather be premature in seeking opportunity of recalling the attention from the distractions of a disordered imagination to objects of reality and truth.

But by then it was too late. The Queen was committed to the Willises and their methods and she got it into her head that Heberden was motivated by 'pride' and she expected little from his 'manner of managing the King'. To confirm that the brothers Willis alone were in charge of the King, and that the physicians attended for advice only when asked for it but not to play a part in the management or nursing of the King, the Archbishop went to Windsor to enforce the order of June that no one was to see or address the King without permission from and in the presence of the Willises.

In the previous illnesses the differences among the King's doctors were caused by professional jealousies, alleged political affiliations, or pure social snobbery. In the last illness they arose from opposite attitudes to the treatment of the mentally ill. The old school of isolation and seclusion, of coercion and restraint, represented by the Willises clashed with that of Heberden, who wanted to rehabilitate the King by exercising his faculties, focusing his attention, keeping him in touch with reality and maintaining human contact. Their argument exemplified on the person of the King an issue which soon divided institutions throughout the country between 'moral' treatment, that is active cooperation between patient and doctor, and the old 'terrific' system.

Very soon the physicians found themselves excluded from the sickroom altogether, unless the Willises thought the King's bodily health needed attention. Here, too, one can see the historical beginning of a fundamental division in medicine which became deeper as time went by between mind doctors and body doctors. These eminent physicians could hardly accept the inferior role allotted to them without protest, and they soon rued the day they failed to support Heberden in his fight against allowing the mad-doctors to take control. On 8 February 1812 they wrote to the Council threatening to resign:

We the undersigned Physicians [Halford, Baillie, Heberden] do most respectfully submit to Your Lordships the propriety of permitting us to ascertain the state of the King's health from day to day by our own immediate personal enquiries. We stand responsible to the Public for the proper care of His Majesty's bodily health, and we ask only for those opportunities of enquiring into it, without which it is impossible for a physician to do justice either to his Patient, or to himself. We have sufficiently shewn our willingness to bear the humiliation and indignity of being made mute spectators of His Majesty's condition without the power of contributing our services either to His recovery or to His comfort. And we might prevail upon ourselves still to endure the same degradation, were there any prospect of good to arise from the present restrained intercourse with His Majesty, which could not be obtained without so great an injury to our own feelings . . . The majority of us are the more anxious to obtain from your Lordships an indulgence in these our just requests, by being precluded from that resource to which every physician can resort on ordinary occasions by absenting himself from further attendance . . . We [do not] doubt Your Lordships' readiness to receive in good part a representation dictated equally by an anxious zeal to promote His Majesty's recovery and by a just respect to our own characters.

In July, Heberden was still protesting:

I am of opinion that the present medical treatment and management applied to His Majesty's case, are fundamentally and practically wrong. His Majesty appears to be in that state, from which it is not probable that any plan of management will restore him. But, though it is possible indeed that His Majesty may recover of himself, by the natural resources of his constitution, and without external assistance; yet I do believe it to be utterly impossible that the present distant and secret inspection of His Majesty's conduct can ever be in any manner conducive to the reestablishment of His Majesty's mind.

9

The Last Years: 1812-20

In January 1812, as the twelve months of the temporary and restricted Regency were drawing to their close, the physicians were again called before a Parliamentary Committee. It was the last time they were publicly examined. Baillie considered the King's recovery 'highly improbable' because the illness had continued so long, had 'assumed a more determined form than in any of His former illnesses', and in particular because 'His memory seems to be impaired', that is that senility had set in. Heberden regarded the King's condition as so much changed since the paroxysm of July 1811 'that I look upon it as indeed a new complaint', from which recovery could hardly be expected. Monro said he had never seen a patient as old as the King showing 'the same degree of mental disorder', but thought recovery was not hopeless, since there were 'no symptoms of fatuity'. He had seen the King ten times from October to November in company with Simmons and John Willis. Simmons thought the King's age coupled with blindness were against recovery. At St Luke's Hospital he said only one of every four patients over seventy was discharged cured, whereas half of the younger patients recovered. Halford also doubted whether recovery was now possible and spoke of a new accession of the disorder which had started while the committee was sitting. John Willis said that there was at present 'a very great degree of derangement . . . having very much the symptoms of insanity; at the same time rather unusually . . . with delirious characters'. His brother Robert confirmed that recovery was 'all but impossible'.[1]

As the result of their evidence, the Regency was made permanent and the Regent was given full powers. The frequency of bulletins on the King's health, which had for some months been issued only weekly, was now reduced to one a month. They spoke in terms of his bodily health, his state of tranquillity or otherwise, and ended with 'his disorder continues'. King George III had left the political scene and he ceased to appear in the diaries and correspondences which had been so full of him and his illnesses before. He received no visitors and heard no news. The story of his remaining years is recorded only in the journals of his physicians and keepers and their reports to the Queen's Council and the Regent.

The paroxysm reported to the Parliamentary Committee turned out to be severe. As usual, it started with cold, followed by nausea, colic and painful weakness, sleeplessness, fast pulse, incontinence and confusion. On 16 January he 'talked rapidly and violently for 25 hours without intermission' and was so disturbed that he was 'absolutely unable to be approached or assisted'. His 'countenance was flushed . . . and his voice very hoarse', and his urine was dark. For long stretches he was kept continuously in a strait-waistcoat. By 22 January he was much quieter and received the physicians 'in a very kind manner', but they found him 'nervous and enfeebled'. On 31 January he spoke 'in a rational and correct manner, upon the amusements his Majesty took in His recovery from the illness in 1801'. By the middle of February the physicians reported he 'appears to be very quiet this morning, but not having been addressed, we know nothing more of His Majesty's condition of mind or of body than what is obvious in His external appearance'. He was silent but 'was employed in arranging, tying and untying His handkerchiefs and night-caps, buttoning and unbuttoning his waistcoat'. Next day some expression of the King led the physicians 'to believe His Majesty suffers something at present from Rheumatism . . . but his looks betray no character of fever attending'. In March, Heberden observed that he was 'more than usually subject to laugh, which always carries some appearance of imbecillity'. The King had 'grown fuller in body, but without corresponding increase in strength'.

In March another accession of his disorder left him with 'marks of languor and fatigue'. In June the Queen saw the King, possibly for the last time, but stayed only a quarter of an hour. In July there was another paroxysm as severe as the one twelve months before which at its height again made the doctors fear for his life. At Windsor his state was described as 'melancholy', 'pitiful' and 'alarming', and for an hour he had 'dreadful symptoms', which must have been convulsions. Outside the sickroom it was generally believed that he had suffered 'a paralytic stroke'.[2] After it had subsided he was for a long time 'silent and weak on his legs' and more than once complained of 'pains in his limbs' and 'uneasiness in his stomach'.

To Halford in August he

complained loudly of rheumatism – He had made some other complaints in the morning which induced the physician in waiting to address His Majesty – The conversation, if it can be called a conversation when the King only spoke . . . seemed more like the detail of a dream in its extravagant confusion . . . a question to the purpose in view brought down at length a

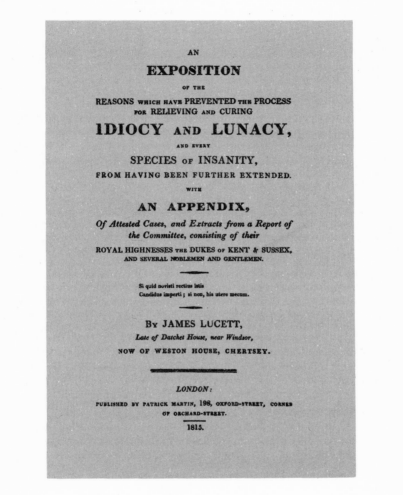

AN

EXPOSITION

OF THE

REASONS WHICH HAVE PREVENTED THE PROCESS
FOR RELIEVING AND CURING

IDIOCY AND LUNACY,

AND EVERY

SPECIES OF INSANITY,

FROM HAVING BEEN FURTHER EXTENDED.

WITH

AN APPENDIX,

*Of Attested Cases, and Extracts from a Report of
the Committee, consisting of their*
ROYAL HIGHNESSES THE DUKES OF KENT & SUSSEX,
AND SEVERAL NOBLEMEN AND GENTLEMEN.

Si quid novisti rectius istis
Candidus imperti ; si non, his utere mecum.

BY JAMES LUCETT,
Late of Datchet House, near Windsor,
NOW OF WESTON HOUSE, CHERTSEY.

LONDON:
PUBLISHED BY PATRICK MARTIN, 198, OXFORD-STREET, CORNER
OF ORCHARD-STREET.

1815.

9. *In 1812 the Dukes of Kent and Sussex, in the hope of helping their father,
interested themselves in a secret process for the 'cure of insanity', practised by
Messrs Delahoyde & Lucett. They set up a committee, raised funds and supervised personally its effect on patients taken from Bethlem Hospital and so
initiated psychiatry's first therapeutic trial. No lasting benefit accrued and in
the spring of 1814 it became clear that they had been taken in. Delahoyde fled
the country and Lucett went to a debtors' prison. On his release he published
this book and restated his claims with an account of his transactions with the
royal dukes.*

heavy denunciation which Dr. Willis's interposition stopped effectually at once.

Yet in September he 'made very sensible observations relative to the Treaty of Amiens which showed there was still no fatuity of mind', and in October 'talked with exact memory of the Seven Years' War [1756–63]'. Such examples show that though his mind continued active, he was going back in time – a feature of ageing which was accentuated in his case since the present ceased to offer variety, events or impressions to fix on. They added urgency to the physicians' sustained pleas that 'it might prevent his mind from decaying so soon as it might otherwise decay' if a much freer communication between the King and those around him were allowed, even encouraged. In April 1813, Halford again urged the Queen's Council on behalf of the physicians that they might be allowed at least 'to converse' with the King: 'I remain of opinion that a more frequent intercourse with His Majesty on the part of His physicians with a view to conversation might be beneficial . . . they would contribute to His Majesty's comfort thereby, being the only channel of communication between Himself and the world.'

In July 1813 the physicians were asked by the Queen's Council whether the secret process for the treatment of insanity canvassed by a Messrs Delahoyde & Lucett which was then undergoing trial under the supervision of the Dukes of Kent and Sussex might be usefully tried on the King. It consisted of pouring cold water on the patient's head from a variable height while his body was confined in a warm bath. They fortunately considered its efficacy unproven and potentially dangerous. Halford alone thought that 'the application of cold . . . might be used with possible advantage in His Majesty's case – as it has been already – but this or any other medical expedient, would require a temporary departure from the system of exclusion'.

Reference to the 'system of exclusion' and seclusion enforced by the Willises, backed by the Queen's Council, brought the physicians back to plead once more that the principle of the King's management based on restriction and confinement should be abandoned: 'The condition of the mind has not only not improved . . . but is in great danger of becoming worse by want of new ideas to be supplied in His Majesty's case by conversation alone . . . I do think that a different system . . . is urgently required.' Halford stressed that the King's case was so out of the ordinary and outside the range of the physicians' experience that 'the wisdom' of the Queen's Council could as well decide the point whether the King's life should not now be enlarged: 'I beg permission to add an earnest entreaty that Her Majesty's Council would not be guided in their decision altogether by the opinions of the Physicians – The King's case appears to have no exact precedent in the records of insanity, and therefore the Physicians do not form their judgement on experience.'

It had ceased to be an issue whether the King would recover sufficiently to resume his authority. All that was left to do was to provide optimal circumstances for him to live out his days at peace and in comfort according to the reduced level of his capacities, and to ease his sufferings during the recurring attacks of painful illness. What had placed George III at such a disadvantage as a patient were the exigencies of being King. Now these had ceased, and yet – however sad to say, he was treated worse than many of his subjects might have been – he was still kept prisoner in close solitary and silent confinement.

Quite apart from the effects of any pathological processes or senile changes in his brain, what could his mind be occupied with but the many and varied scenes of his former life. He relived many of them, arranging ceremonies, concerts, journeys, appointments and promotions, 'reviewing his troops commanded by officers who are long since dead', in 'cheerful

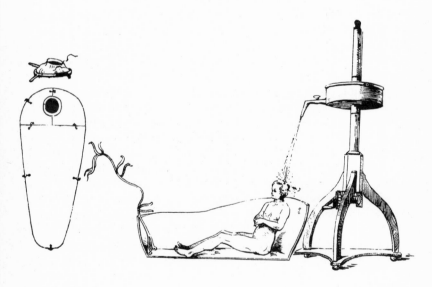

10. *A drawing of 'a portable douche machine' to direct cold water 'upon the head, as well to diminish vascular action, as to repress violence, to overcome obstinacy, and to rouse the patient when indolence or stupor prevails'. The stream of water could be regulated 'to fall on the head of the patient from different heights' according to the needs of the case. (From Sir Alexander Morison's* Cases of mental disease, with practical observations on the medical treatment, *1828, pp. 44–5, 163–4).*

N

conversation with some of his ideal friends', 'disposed to laugh and then to shed tears upon very slight suggestions of persons or things which presented themselves to his imagination'. The long periods of being 'silent and weak on his legs' and when he 'baffled all attempts to fix his attention', periods of apparent contentment and tranquillity when he amused himself playing the flute or the harpsichord and particularly his favourite Handel, were interrupted by the old painful paroxysms.

And so the years rolled by with the King continuing 'to find amusement in the inexhaustible resources of his distempered imagination'. In 1817 it was noticed that he was going deaf and his last source of impressions from the outside world was coming to an end.

At this distance in time it is difficult to understand why the Queen's Council had placed their unswerving trust in the Willises and their system against all the advice of the royal physicians and one must add common humanity. The physicians never gained the right to addresss their patient without the permission and in the presence of a Willis. As late as January 1819 the Council 'Resolved that Sir Henry Halford be requested to converse with the King on Thursday next, if, after communication with Dr. Willis, he shall see no objection to it, in the presence of Lord Arden [a member of the Council] who is resident at Windsor'. And this is what happened: 'Sir Henry address'd the King as soon as His Majesty had dined – and having stated His humble desire to ask His Majesty how he did, and given His name, the King appeared forcibly impress'd – collected Himself – used the manner of a silent, solemn enthusiastic appeal by lifting up His eyes and His hands – but returned no answer – and precluded all further address by striking rapidly the keys of His harpsichord.' The attempt, Halford assured the Council, 'did no harm whatever, for His Majesty went to sleep very soon afterwards'. In contrast, when Heberden, whom the King liked, was with him, 'He spoke more than we have lately heard Him to do, of his own situation, of his confinement, of his taking no exercise, and some other particulars, which might have been consider'd as indications of a natural state of mind, had they not been combined with palpable delusions. The whole was in a perfectly gentle tone and manner.'

Queen Charlotte had died in November 1818 and the Duke of York took over the care of his father and the Queen's Council became the Duke of York's Council. He visited his father at the end of November 1819 and reported to the Prince Regent:

He was amusing himself with playing upon the harpsichord and singing with as strong and firm a voice as ever I heard him . . . but we must not conceal from ourselves that His Majesty is greatly ematiated within the last twelve months . . . the frame is so much weaker that we can no longer look forward . . . to his being preserved to us for any length of time.[3]

The last paroxysm of his illness occurred at Christmas 1819. He had no sleep or rest for fifty-eight hours, during which he talked continually and, the Willis journal adds cryptically, 'gave other remarkable proof of the extraordinary energies of his constitution'. Thereafter he sank.

All reports from the physicians to the Queen's Council were dated and numbered by the Archbishop of Canterbury himself. To number 3075, the last one, he added in his own hand: 'His Majesty expired at 32 Minutes past 8 o'clock P.M., 29 January 1820.' He was in his eighty-second year.

10

Porphyria

This account of George III's illness, gathered from authentic sources, provides the basis on which a modern diagnosis can be made. His medical history shows that he suffered periodically from attacks which followed the same pattern and in which he manifested the same symptoms. These are indicative of a recurrent, widespread and severe disorder of the nervous system. It affected the peripheral nerves, which supply movement and sensation to all parts of the body, causing painful weakness of the arms and legs, so that he could not hold a cup or pen, or walk or stand unaided (even when still able to sit on horseback), hoarseness and difficulty in articulation and swallowing; his muscles wasted and it took months before he regained normal strength and vigour. He suffered from pain in the head and face, became over-sensitive, so that he could not bear the touch of clothes or bedding, wig or necktie, and at times lost the power of feeling, as when he was not aware of blisters being placed upon his legs. Affection of the autonomic nervous system, which controls the heart, blood vessels, gastro-intestinal system and sweat-glands, led to nausea, colic and constipation due to paralysis of the gut; at times the pain was so severe that Baker, for instance, found him doubled up in bed; at times breathing was embarrassed and he had pain and stitches in the chest; racing pulse, flushing and sweating made his doctors think he had 'fever'. When attacks became more severe the brain was involved, leading to giddiness, visual and auditory disturbances, mounting agitation, excitement, over-activity, non-stop rambling, irritability and persistent sleeplessness, confusion typically first by night and then also by day, producing delirium, tremor, rapid movements of his eyes (nystagmus), rigors, stupor and convulsions.

After 1810, when he was in his seventy-third year, there were added to these signs those of progressive senility, aggravated by the repeated onslaughts of his illness which had over the years taken their toll, leaving him reduced, mentally and physically, so that after the old painful paroxysms, which still occurred, recovery was incomplete. To the illness itself were added blindness and in his last years a degree of deafness, both of which excluded him still further from the world.

It is now clear how the royal physicians were defeated in particular by two manifestations of the illness. First, the perplexing physical manifestations by which attacks were ushered in and accompanied, which did not fit any disease with which they were familiar. Second, the mental derangement itself, which started like a delirium but lasted too long after the physical health had improved. This is why in 1788 the doctors argued so fiercely whether he was delirious or insane; and why in 1810, with the hindsight of three previous attacks from which he recovered, they called it a condition midway between delirium and insanity, that is between a toxic-confusional state and a psychosis, as they would now be called, the like of which had 'no precedent' in the annals of medicine.

Their candid confession of ignorance about the underlying condition was wiser than they could have known. Only in the present century did advances in medicine and biochemistry allow Sir Archibald Garrod to put forward the concept of 'inborn errors of metabolism' to account for a group of disorders in which inherited defects of body chemistry lead to an abnormal accumulation of toxic chemical substances which damage the nervous system. Among these is a rare variety, which was clinically defined only in the 1930s, called the porphyrias, because in attacks the urine is of a purple or dark colour, either when it is passed or after it has been left to stand. The biochemical lesion is a disturbance of porphyrin metabolism. These are purple-red pigments which are contained in every cell of the body and give blood its red colour. In the porphyrias their formation and excretion is greatly increased and they or their precursors appear in large amounts in urine and faeces. Their excess in the blood causes widespread intoxication of all parts of the nervous system, peripheral and central. In the group called variegate porphyria there is, in addition, sun-sensitivity and increased fragility of the skin to trauma.[1]

The most important cause is a hereditary factor which is transmitted as a Mendelian dominant; that is, about half the offspring of an affected parent may be expected to inherit the disorder. It may remain symptomless or latent throughout life, or may cause attacks of any degree of severity which are always dangerous and may be fatal. At their height, patients are described as 'ill, paralyzed, delirious, and in agonizing pain',[2] which exactly fits George III. Indeed, his symptoms and their sequence read like a textbook case. The only feature not recorded was hypertension, because blood pressure was not measured at that time, but the repeated crises which made his doctors fear 'a paralytic stroke' or 'imminent dissolution' may well have been hypertensive. Also in keeping with the diagnosis of porphyria is the fact that attacks were ushered in by colds or upper respiratory tract infection, rapid fluctuations in his condition, which are typical, weight loss and protracted convalescence.

Porphyria is a rare condition and is therefore still liable to be missed. If abdominal symptoms are marked, as they were when the royal physicians thought the King had an attack of biliary colic or an acute 'inflammation of the bowels', the patient may be referred to a surgeon with a diagnosis of an abdominal catastrophe. Painful weakness of the limbs due to inflammation of peripheral nerves or neuropathy may lead to a misdiagnosis of rheumatism and perhaps even gout, both of which George III was at various times thought to be suffering from. When mental symptoms occur alone or if they dominate the picture, there is the danger that patients are diagnosed as suffering from any variety of mental illness – just as George III was. Indeed, so commonly does this still happen that in one group of porphyrics reported as recently as 1963 one-third had been admitted in the first place to mental hospitals under such labels as 'depression, schizophrenia, delirium tremens, and acute anxiety state'.[3]

To prove the diagnosis, the physician today would examine urine and stool for the characteristic abnormal constituents. This is, of course, not possible for George III, but fortunately the records of the royal physicians contain six instances in which they describe his urine at the height of attacks as 'dark', 'bilious' or 'bloody', and even noted on occasion that it left a bluish stain on the vessel after it had been poured away. But these were chance observations and did not strike the physicians as noteworthy. They had no reason to pay attention to his urine and even had they noticed discolouration it would have conveyed nothing to them. So little interest did they have in it that at the beginning of 1811, for instance, they remarked that the colour of the stool could not be ascertained because the water was so deeply discoloured.[4]

The exact biochemical fault is not yet fully understood and no specific treatment is known once an attack has started. But it is established that in those who carry the abnormality, certain drugs, such as barbiturates, and 'the pill', act as precipitants, as does excess alcohol consumption, and attacks may be prevented by avoiding them. Other known causes which can bring on attacks are infections and a diet deficient in protein.

George III appears to have had a particularly virulent form of the disease. To an extent this may be attributed to the way he was treated, which at least must have aggravated and prolonged the attacks. He was also kept on 'a low diet' and for long periods was given no meat. He was further reduced by blood-letting, leeches to the temples and cupping, and for months was regularly given vomits and purges. Of all his treatments 'blistering' probably had the worst effect, since it set up a running infection which persisted for weeks. It is also a question how far his ebullitions of passion, his turbulence and obstreperous behaviour were in response to his harsh management and the forcible administration of drugs – often only after a bitter struggle – to bring down his 'fever' and high spirits, slow his pulse, calm his nerves and make him sleep – all of which may have aggravated the underlying condition and certainly exasperated the patient.

II

Retrospect: The Illness of 1765

The illness of 1765 has been left to the last and out of chronological order because of its special significance. It is less important for what happened to the King at the time than for what was made of it afterwards. For this reason it stands by itself and presents its own problems. Whereas in the later illnesses medical facts are plenty and in a sense speak for themselves, the reverse applies to that of 1765, as it does to a less severe one of 1762. Nor was the political scene disturbed by them. In fact, the illness of 1765 did not attract any interest until after the King's death, when with the hindsight of later attacks a whispering campaign was started, hinting that the King may have been deranged even then. Nineteenth-century historians came to accept this speculation as if it were established fact, and George III was stigmatized as a man who had five attacks of insanity between his twenties and old age and was therefore more or less deranged throughout his life. As we shall see, in the twentieth century this 'mental breakdown' as a young man was used to support the theory that he suffered from manic-depressive psychosis. And this diagnosis in turn was taken as revealing that his was a vulnerable and neurotic personality, liable to break down under strain and stress. Such notions could never seriously have been entertained had it been appreciated that the King was mentally deranged for the first time in 1788 and that until the age of fifty he had withstood with impunity the worst vicissitudes of his personal and political life.

In face of the far-reaching and sinister significance with which historical falsification has endowed the illness of 1765, it is intriguing to trace its origin, although this leads away from medicine into the by-ways of historical and literary detection. But first to review the facts.

The illness is best recorded by George Grenville,* who as Prime

* George Grenville (1712–70), Prime Minister in 1763–5, was the father of George, first Marquis of Buckingham (1753–1813); Thomas (1755–1846), statesman and book-collector; and William Wyndham, Baron Grenville (1759–1834), Prime Minister in 1806–7.

Minister saw the King regularly throughout the relevant period. He was ill on and off for a few days at a stretch from the middle of January till the end of March and again in May and July.

The symptoms were violent cold, cough, stitches in the breast, fever, fast pulse, hoarseness, insomnia, fatigue and weight loss. The fact that he was bled, cupped and blistered added to the seriousness of the illness in the eyes of contemporaries. To those in particular who, like Horace Walpole, remembered that in 1762 the King had had a similar attack with 'a violent cough and oppression on his breast . . . was blooded seven times and had three blisters'[1] these features 'showed a tendency to consumption'[2] – a dread disease indeed at the time and often fatal. Lord Holland told Walpole 'he believed the King in a consumption, and not likely to live a year'.[3] This seems to have been also in the royal physicians' minds. Of the brief relapse in July, Sir William Duncan 'said there was very little fever, and nothing to be apprehended at present. The danger to be feared was a violent return in the winter.'[4] 'The idea of the danger in which the King has been lately in terrifies me yet, and I don't wonder that all parties are alarmed,' wrote Mann to Walpole.[5] George III himself must have feared something like it when, in his speech from the throne on 24 April, he recommended provision for a regency in case 'it should please God to put a Period to my Life, whilst my Successor is of tender Years'.[6]

The symptoms closely resembled those of the earlier illness of 1762. This started at the beginning of June, the acute phase was over within ten days and by the end of the month he had recovered. Henry Fox, first Baron Holland, wrote of it:

H.M. was very, very ill. It is amazing & very lucky that H.M.'s illness gave no alarm, considering that the Queen is big with child & the Law of England has made no provision for government when no King or a minor King exists. He go's out now, but he coughs still; &, which no subject of his would be refus'd or refuse himself, he cannot or he will not go to lye in the country air; tho' if there was ever anything malignant in that of London since I was born, it is at this time.[7]

Walpole reported to Mann on 20 June:

The King had one of the last of these strange and universally epidemic colds, which however have seldom been fatal: he had a violent cough and oppression on his breast, which he concealed, just as I had; but my life was of no consequence, and having no physicians in ordinary, I was cured in four nights by James's powders, without bleeding. The King was blooded seven times and had three blisters. Thank God he is safe, and we have escaped a confusion beyond that was ever known, but on the accession of the Queen of Scots – nay, we have not even the successor born.[8]

The Duke of Newcastle, recently retired Prime Minister, received his first report of the doctors having been called to the King on 6 June:

Dr. [William] Duncan ... attended the King today for the first time with Sir Ed[ward] Wilmot ... He is not without uneasyness; He says the King was blooded again this morning and that his blood is very bad. He is very feverish and complains of pains and stitches in his breast with a very bad cough. Duncan has spoken his opinion freely to both the King and Queen, and has told them both that very great care is necessary. He apprehends a blister will be ordered to night, and thinks if things do not mend soon, they will be very alarming.[9]

Lord Chancellor Hardwicke feared 'His Majesty was very ill, for physicians don't deal so roughly with such patients, without necessity. God grant him a speedy recovery.' [10]

The King himself wrote to Lord Bute, his old mentor and now Prime Minister, on 7 June: 'Many thanks for my Dearest Friend's anxiety; I have slept well, the fever is much decreas'd. the Doctors go on pouring manah down my throat; if that has enough effect, they propose asses milk to-morrow, and flatter me with liberty in four or five days, tho' under restrictions, for they say my future health depends on the care taken some time after this disorder.'[11] The same day, the doctors reported: 'The King is much better, tho' he was again blooded this morning. The Pain in his breast has left him, and that was the most alarming Symptom.' [12] Newcastle was informed that 'Yesterday's Bleeding gave speedy Relief. The Blood has proved less inflam'd, than it was found to be before. The Blister likewise had a very good Effect; the Cough being more easy; and the Soreness within almost gone.' Because the pulse remained 'somewhat more quick ... another Bleeding this Evening will become necessary'. But 'matters are in so fair way, that within three or four days, there is no doubt of Recovery'.[13] On 8 June, Newcastle heard 'he was in no kind of danger last night, tho' a Blister was put on; and that he is better today'.[14] On 9 June, Sir Edward Wilmot gave him 'a very satisfactory Account of the King',[15] though he was 'blooded again this morning for the Cough'.[16]

To Bute, the King wrote: 'I have rested extremely well and think the fever is over tho the Doctor has not been here yet to give his opinion; but the cough is still troublesome, and I am not free from complaint on my breast.'[17] Dr Duncan reported he 'mends every day ... His Majesty is up all day and the Queen has never quitted his bed'.[18] Newcastle's correspondent wrote: '[Dr] Duncan assures me that the King is a great deal better and I believe the danger is quite over. I have obey'd your Grace's Commands in sending you these Accounts so long as there was ground for apprehension. It is now needless I should continue to give you Accounts of H.M.'s health.'[19] And Sir Edward Wilmot declared, 'His Majesty wanted nothing to compleat his cure, but a westerly wind.'[20]

A

TREATISE

OF THE

EXTRAORDINARY VIRTUES

AND

EFFECTS

OF

ASSES MILK,

In the CURE of various DISEASES,

Particularly the

GOUT, SCURVY, and NERVOUS DISORDERS;

And of its peculiar nouriſhing and reſtorative Qualities in all Conſumptive Diſorders, and even the Decays of Old Age.

Illuſtrated with ſeveral remarkable CASES.

Tranſlated from the LATIN *of the celebrated*
FREDERICK HOFFMAN, *M. D.*
Principal Phyſician to his preſent Majeſty the King of Pruſſia, *and Member of the Royal Societies of* London *and* Berlin.

LONDON:
Printed for JOHN WHISTON and BENJAMIN WHITE, in *Fleet-ſtreet.* MDCCLIV.

(Price One Shilling.)

11. *In 1762 and again in 1765 George III's doctors prescribed asses' milk. It was the sovereign remedy for consumption and had the authority of the eminent Dr Friedrich Hoffmann, professor of medicine in the University of Halle and physician to Frederic the Great. His* Treatise *on the subject is shown here in its English translation (1754). Dr Hoffmann wrote: 'I could recount many instances of consumptive people who were afflicted with an obstinate cough, a fever and an amazing waste of the whole body; and who, after an ineffectual trial of other remedies . . . took a long continued course of Asses milk . . . and perfectly recovered.'*

By 15 June the King was able to write to Bute: 'I continue well, but much fatigu'd; the Doctors have not been here this evening, but send [Caesar] Hawkins as their ambassador with strong enjunctions not to have any Levée or Drawing Room these eight or ten days that the danger of it was greater than I could imagine, but otherwise they are more indulgent.'[21] The *Gentleman's Magazine* reported that on that day 'Their Majesties went to Richmond to breakfast, being the first time of their going abroad since his Majesty's indisposition. Preparation are making at St. James's that the apartments may be in readiness against the Queen's lying-in' (the Prince of Wales was born on 12 August 1762). Besides rest, he had now been advised 'by the medical people' – or 'Aesculapians', as he also called them – to have himself driven out to take the air. Although still troubled by 'a slight cold' and 'pain in the breast', and 'fatigu'd',[22] he attended the drawing-room on 24 June for the first time in three weeks.[23]

Pain in the chest with cough, fever, fast pulse and fatigue amounted, as his doctors feared, to more than an ordinary cold. What they had in mind was a consumption. This is why they watched him so carefully, hoped for a westerly, treated him so vigorously and prescribed asses' milk; and why Mann answered Walpole from Italy: 'Though the danger which the King was lately in is over, the description of it still alarms me.'[24]

In 1765 he had the same symptoms, which suggests a recurrence of the same disease. His doctors thought so, too, and those who were in the know feared a return of 'consumption'. It started on 13 January, when 'Sir William Duncan came to let Mr. Grenville know that he had been with the King, who had a violent cold, had passed a restless night, and complained of stitches in his breast. His Majesty was blooded 14 ounces; he told Sir William he felt the cold seize him as he came out of the House of Lords.'[25] The next day he was better and the day after Grenville 'found him perfectly cheerful and good-humoured'.[26] On 25 February, there was a relapse. 'The King was blooded, and kept his bed with a feverish cold,' Grenville recorded in his diary; on 26 February, 'The King all this time continues ill, and sees none of his ministers'; and on 3 March, 'The King had a good night, but waked in the morning with a return of fever and pain upon his breast; he was blooded in the foot.'[27] On 5 March, he received a note from the King: 'I am obliged to Mr. Grenville for his expressions on my being so much mended; the physicians, on my naming that I feel as yet some weakness in the breast, have renewed their injunctions of not talking, and particularly on business; if there are any warrants ready for my signature, I wish Mr. Grenville would at any time send them in a box, as also a summary account of the debate of yesterday, which I am curious to hear ... I return the papers signed.'[28]

On 6 March, 'the King was not so well as he had been; his pulse rose in the morning, but sunk again at night, and he was much better and quite cheerful in the evening.' In his letter to Grenville of 9 March there is no mention of illness, and the next day 'Mr. Grenville went to the King according to his orders; he found him very cheerful, and his complexion clear, but a good deal thinner than before his illness. His Majesty talked very easily with him, told him he had seen nobody, and should still keep quiet for some time, and that he would send to him again soon.'[29]

On 22 March, the King was not so well again 'from some little additional cough and pain in the breast';[30] he was cupped and his physicians still 'desired him to keep quiet'. But when Grenville saw him again on 25 March he was 'well to all appearance – he had been out to take the air; he kept Mr. Grenville a long time, talked a great deal with good humour, and coughed but once during the whole conversation.'[31]

There was another bout of 'fever' in the last week of May, when 'the physicians were ordered to attend the King . . . He gave Sir William Duncan his hand to feel his pulse, which was quick, but bid him not to mind it, because he had been hurried for some days past, but he had eaten very little and had no fever.' He told them 'he never had slept above two hours for several days past.'[32] Three days later he was well again. At the end of July he 'had a slight return of his former complaint, and was blooded yesterday, but I know for certain that his physicians are not under any apprehensions,' wrote Mr Whately to Grenville on 24 July;[33] and Mr Jenkinson (later Lord Liverpool) to the same the following day:

We have no news but that the King has been again indisposed. He was blooded on Tuesday morning; his disorder was the same as that he had in the winter. Sir William Duncan said there was very little fever, and nothing to be apprehended at present. The danger to be feared was a violent return in the winter. The King had no levée yesterday, but today he came to the drawing-room, and the Queen was there for the last time before her lying-in [their third child, later William IV, was born in August].[34]

At the beginning of February 1766 he suffered a return of cold and fever, 'was blooded, looked flushed and heated, but had not much fever'. He cancelled the levée, but within four days was perfectly recovered.[35]

These are the facts. How, then, did it come about that historians and biographers have for the last hundred years called the illness of 1765 an attack of insanity? Certainly no one thought so at the time, not even Grenville, who was by no means a friend of the King, nor any of the leading political figures such as Bedford, Chatham, Grafton, Liverpool, Rockingham and Sandwich. Indeed, in some quarters there was a feeling that he was not as ill as was made out: 'The King's confinement makes a great deal of talk,' observed Grenville on 25 March 1765, 'as few people believe him to be as ill as is given out by Lord Bute's friends.'[36] Bute, who named Grenville as his successor in 1763, was thought to have retained the King's confidence, and this was said to have been a source of ill-feeling between Grenville and the King.

Coming to our own time, in the standard Oxford history of the reign it is stated that in 1765 'Melancholia seized him. He had an illness which seems probably to have been the first attack of his madness.'[37] Another modern authority on the period called it a 'fit of madness' or 'the first lunacy'.[38] Sedgwick, in his edition of George III's letters to Lord Bute, added to what he himself called 'the mythology of George III' by suggesting that the reason why so few of the King's personal papers prior to March 1765 survive was that 'they were deliberately destroyed at the time of his first attack of insanity at the beginning of 1765'.[39] Even Sir Lewis Namier, who did so much to revise the image of this 'much maligned monarch', accepted 1765 as 'the first recorded fit . . . of manic depression'.[40] So firmly was the myth entrenched.

In fact, it was not until half a century after the event and with the hindsight of the derangement which accompanied later attacks that a rumour started that the period of obscure intermittent ill-health of 1765 had been of the same nature. At first only hinted at as a possibility, after the King's death it found its way into print as a probability and eventually by repetition became accepted as fact. Once this was so, no historian or biographer could afford not to repeat it, whether he believed it or not. The fact that not a single contemporary observed mental symptoms was interpreted as proving how successfully Court and Government must have hidden it. Even the word 'alarming', which meant neither more nor less than that his life was thought to be in danger, came to be interpreted as a euphemism for 'mental'. Facts have their limits, but theories seemingly none.

Court and Government circles apart, outsiders who left records also knew nothing of mental symptoms. 'The ingenious and learned Monsieur Grosley,' for instance, antiquary and fellow of the Royal Society, who visited England in the spring of 1765, 'prompted by his insatiable thirst after knowledge', gathered no more than that the King had 'a slight indisposition, which had been represented as much more considerable than it really was',[41] namely not just a cold with fever but a consumption. He explained that exaggerated reports 'had even reached France' that 'the ill state of that prince's health' was such that 'his majesty would immediately cross the seas in order to drink the Barège waters'. These celebrated waters 'duly drunk with milk', wrote the English physician resident there, Sir Christopher Meighan, in 1764, 'correct the impurieties, renew the mass of fluids, replenish it with nutritive balsam, regulate the tone of the solids, and restore in both that beneficial correspondence mutually essential to their welfare . . . Certainly no ass's milk, nor any other, can, in consumptive cases, be so restorative and healing as this balsamic emulsion.'[42]

Grosley saw the King repeatedly at 'the parliament-house, and at St. James's-palace' when 'he appeared to be in perfect health'.

But not only was there no whisper of mental derangement: the simplicity of Court life in the early years of George III's reign was such that nothing concerning him could be hidden for long. As Grosley reported:

> George III . . . leads, at his rural seat near Richmond (a seat much inferior in magnificence and lustre to that of many noblemen) a life of the most regular simplicity which he divides entirely between the queen and his books. It is true he comes every week to hold a levée and a drawing room at St. James's; but the court is by no means brilliant; he comes with the Queen in a very plain equipage, escorted by a few light horse . . . At his court he is affability itself. All those he speaks to, he accosts in the most polite manner, and never opens his lips except to say the most obliging things. His palace, which has no guard except at the gate, is open to every Englishman, as well as to every foreigner who is attracted thither by curiosity.[43]

Contemporary chroniclers knew only of bodily indisposition. Mac-Farlane in *The history of the first ten years of the reign of George III* (1783), discussing the Stamp Act, had nothing more to say than:

> About this time the King happened to be indisposed and out of regard therefore to his people, and affection for his own children, he judged it expedient to propose a regency bill, by which he might be enabled to appoint, in case of his decease, the queen, or some other person of the royal family, guardian of the realm, and of the heir apparent, till he should reach the age of eighteen . . .[44]

Belsham in his *Memoirs of the reign of George III* (1802) called it 'an occasional indisposition' which excited 'much alarm in the possible prospect of a long minority, for which no public provision had been made'.[45]

Of the earliest biographers, Holt[46] in 1820 merely wrote that in 1765 the King was 'for some time indisposed'; Baines[47] spoke of 'an illness with which the king was at this period afflicted, and which without being dangerous confined him to his chamber'. Huish in 1821 wrote of 'an alarming disorder, which made him anxious for the safety and welfare of his people and led him to propose a regency bill'.[48] The obituarist in the *Gentleman's Magazine* observed: 'It is believed that, soon after his accession to the Throne, the King had a slight attack of a similar indisposition', as in 1788.[49] Galt, also in 1820, hinted at derangement: 'In March of this year [1765] he was seized with a complaint which continued for several weeks, and which was even then secretly reported to have resembled that malady which since so unhappily secluded him from the view of his subjects, and from the exercise of his royal functions. How far these reports were founded in fact, it is now perhaps impossible to ascertain.'[50]

A good example of how 1820, the year of the King's death, marks a watershed in what was thought of the illness is furnished by Wraxall. In *Historical memoirs of my own time*, published in 1815, he wrote:

A course of systematic abstinence and exercise, had secured George the Third the enjoyment of almost uninterrupted health, down to the time of which I speak [1781]. So little had he been incommoded by sickness, or by indisposition of any kind from the period of his Accession till his memorable seizure in 1788, that scarcely was he ever compelled to absent himself on that account, from a Levée, a Council, or a Drawing-room, during eight and twenty years. One only exception to this remark occurred in the Autumn [*sic*] of 1765, when he was attacked by a disorder that confined him for several weeks: relative to the nature and seat of which Malady, though many conjectures and assertions have been hazarded, in conversation, and even in print, no satisfactory information has ever been given to the world.[51]

In 1836 appeared Wraxall's *Posthumous memoirs of his own time* (he had died in 1831) in which this passage was changed to:

It is with probability conjectured, that the disorder which seized him in the autumn of 1765, the nature of which was mysteriously withheld from the public, affected the brain. In order to subdue that tendency, he thought no prescription so effectual as spare and simple diet.[52]

In this connexion Mrs Papendiek is sometimes quoted as a contemporary who confirmed that the King was mentally ill in 1765. She wrote: 'It was not known beyond the Palace that his Majesty was mentally afflicted.' But she was not a contemporary of the illness – she saw the light of day in July 1765 – and penned her *Memoirs* to amuse her grandchildren as an old lady in the 1830s, not only from memory but 'quite the early part of it from hearsay'. And they were left unfinished when she died in 1839.[53]

The real fount of the legend, and the ultimate source to which every statement that the King was insane in 1765 can be traced, must now be examined. Curiously, it did not originate with a historian, but was a by-product of literary history and seems unbelievably flimsy evidence for so far-reaching a conclusion.

In the year 1820, Robert Anderson published the sixth edition of Tobias Smollett's collected works. In a biographical preface he described Smollett's *Continuation of the complete history of England*, the fifth and last volume, which brought it down to 1765 and had been published in October of that year. Remarking on the fact that in subsequent reprints of this work this section had been omitted, Anderson hazarded a guess as to why: 'It is said, that as soon as the paragraph, p. 444, respecting his Majesty's illness, was observed, the whole edition, unsold, was bought up.'[54] The passage to which Anderson referred as possibly having given offence to the court, seems today harmless enough:

Towards the spring his Majesty was attacked by an illness, which, tho' not dangerous, filled the public with prodigious apprehensions, which were perhaps increased by the very means made use of to save appearances; as nothing of certainty could be gathered from the public papers, but that the state of his health was precarious.[55]

Smollett's 'prodigious apprehensions' clearly were that the life of the young King, whose heir was a three-year-old child, was threatened by consumption – of which, incidentally, Smollett knew himself to be dying at the time he wrote. Contemporaries realized that the death of the King would have caused a constitutional crisis of major proportions. This is what they dreaded, because of the warring state of political factions, the unpopularity of the King's mother, the youthfulness and inexperience of his young Queen, who would have to be considered for a Regency Council, and the knowledge that a regency would last at least fifteen years, until the heir came of age. Despite these reasonable fears, Anderson's wild surmise about the fate of the fifth volume was read as giving substance to the equally unfounded rumour that the King was deranged in 1765. It is all the less likely that the volume was suppressed, since, like so many works of the period, it first appeared in serial parts, the last of which, containing the passage referred to by Anderson, in July 1765.[56] It does not make sense to suggest that the book was bought up while the parts were circulating freely.*

Knapp, the modern authority on Smollett, considered the passage so vague and innocuous as to make it highly improbable that on that account the edition could have been destroyed.[57] He found no evidence anywhere that it had, in fact, been suppressed; and, what is more, discovered that copies were by no means as rare as Anderson had supposed.[58] Indeed, he suggested that circumstances of an altogether different order adequately explained the relative rarity of surviving copies. It may even be that Smollett was not the author of this last part, and for this reason it was not reprinted with his works – a possibility at which eighteenth-century critics hinted. Finally, it must be added that if Smollett was the author he could not have had inside information, or meant more than he said, since he was abroad in search of his own health at the relevant time from June 1763 to July 1765.

It is an astonishing fact that the final step of accepting this version of the 1765 illness and in the escalation from gossip and fancy to fact was taken by no less a historian than Adolphus, who relied on Anderson for his evidence. In the 1840 edition of his much-respected *History of England*, Adolphus wrote:

* It may be that Smollett's interest in, and Anderson's embellishment of, the illness of 1765 are attributable to the fact that both were qualified doctors and so felt tempted to add something to the medical aspect of the case.

o

The malady with which His Majesty was afflicted [in 1765] exhibited symptoms similar to those which in 1788, and during the last years of his life, gave much unhappiness to the nation. I did not mention the fact in former editions of this work, because I knew that the King, and all who loved him, were desirous that it should not be drawn into notice; so anxious were they on this point, that Smollett having intimated it in his Complete History of England, the text was revised in the general impression, a very few copies in the original form were disposed of, and they are now rare.[59]

He went on:

As the King was living at the time of my publication [1802], and the malady utterly unimportant, I omitted all mention of it; nor should I now have deviated from my former course, but that, of late, attempts have been made to impress the opinion that what was only an incidental symptom, was a malady constantly affecting His Majesty's mind. Against the insinuation, may be cited, the testimony of all who, during a reign of fifty years (excluding the last ten), knew, conversed, or transacted business with him.

It must be said that Adolphus, too, wrote without inside information, and merely followed the Anderson–Smollett line. But it throws an interesting light on the Whig view of history which prevailed in the 1840s, that he was aware of a tendency to exaggerate George III's illnesses and to paint him as having been 'insane' all his life. Despite his laudable efforts, the last part of this passage is little quoted and he did not succeed in stemming the tide. On the contrary, everybody who came after him added his own embellishment – as, for instance, the reviewer of the correspondence of William Pitt, Earl of Chatham, in the *Quarterly Review* the same year:

About this time (April 1765), his Majesty had a serious illness – its peculiar character was then unknown, but we have the best authority for believing that it was of the nature of that which thrice [*sic*] after afflicted his Majesty, and finally incapacitated him for the duties of government – and it is highly probable that this illness was produced by the great anxiety which these struggles of faction had produced in the royal mind.[60]

By the time Dr Isaac Ray in 1855 wrote the first medical account of the 'Insanity of King George III', he accepted that

Five times was the King struck down by mental disease. The first time was in the spring of 1765. The particulars of the first attack were studiously concealed by his family, and its true character was not generally known at the time. There seems to be no doubt, however, that its symptoms were similar to those of subsequent attacks.[61]

Paradoxically it was Jesse, that loyal and in general accurate biographer of George III, who in 1867 adopted Adolphus's version of the 1765 illness, presumably on the sheer weight of his authority, and so gave it general currency. Under the heading 'Manifestations of the King's Mental Malady', he wrote:

To the world it was given out that the King's illness at this time [1765] was a cough and fever . . . a humor, which ought to have appeared in his face, had settled upon his chest. His malady, however – notwithstanding the truth was kept so profound a secret by the Court as apparently not to have been suspected even by the Prime Minister [Grenville] – is now known to have been of the same distressing nervous character as those which at intervals deranged his reason in after years.[62]

He even went one step further and with as much or as little justification hinted that the King's 'dangerous illness' in June 1762 was 'probably of longer duration and of a more delicate and distressing character than the Court deemed prudent to disclose'.[63] Nobody, it seems, took the trouble or was in a position to question what had by then been accepted as official history.

To return to the Grenville papers, the main source of what happened. They were published in 1852–3, when the legend of the illness was already firmly entrenched, and their editor's insinuating annotations colour the text and make it appear as if Grenville's own observations gave substance to the King having been deranged. For example, Grenville's diary for 17 March 1765 runs: 'Mr. Grenville went to the Drawing Room, where the Queen told him she was afraid he would not agree with her in wishing that the King would not see his servants so often, nor talk so much upon business.' To this the editor appended a footnote: 'It is probable that the Queen had accurately observed the state of the King's mind during the illness.'[64] It is, however, perfectly clear that the doctors wanted the King to save his voice because he was hoarse and still coughing.

Coming to our own time, this legendary mental breakdown became an essential prop for the theory that the King suffered from manic-depressive psychosis. This recurrent illness, explained psychologically as resulting from unbearable conflict in a predisposed personality, commonly makes its first appearance in the twenties or thirties, when the strains and stresses of life reveal the weakness. So far has the travesty of facts gone that in a recent study of the royal malady a psychoanalytically orientated psychiatrist, Dr Guttmacher, refused to believe that the King was physically ill at all in 1765 unless as 'a complication' of mental illness.[65] 'Every possible subterfuge and prevarication was resorted to' by the Court, he declared, to hide its true nature: 'In all probability, the disorder was purely mental and the clinical reports were falsified.'

Knollenberg, in his *Origin of the American Revolution: 1759–1766*, published in 1960, examined in detail the evidence regarding the King's mental state during this time, because of its bearing on American history.

He is, in fact, the only historian who so far has questioned the accepted version that the King was insane in 1765. His review of the facts led him to denounce Guttmacher's 'suppositions' as 'sheer fancy not supported by a shred of evidence'.[66] He drew particular attention to Guttmacher's tendentious interpretation of Grenville's diary. From the beginning of 1765 the personal relation between the King and Grenville became increasingly strained and after several unsuccessful attempts to form another ministry the King dismissed him in July in favour of the Marquis of Rockingham. Events 'clearly disclosed national cause for the king's indecision and later his coldness to Grenville,' wrote Knollenberg, and, one might add, explain the occasions when the King became 'heated' – not to say lost his temper – with his Prime Minister during their exchanges. To their differences had been added opposition to the King's wish to include his mother, the dowager Princess of Wales, in a regency council. Therefore, when Grenville wrote in his diary that he had 'found the King's countenance and manner a good deal estranged, but he was civil', he was describing the tone of their interview and the King's attitude to him, not the King's mental state. Such phrases taken out of context were, however, used by Guttmacher to show that the King was deranged. From study of the same material, but with knowledge of the political background, Jesse came to the opposite conclusion – namely, that the mental nature of the illness must have been hidden so successfully 'as apparently not to have been suspected even by the Prime Minister'.

There is not only no evidence that the King was ever deranged before 1788, but there is ample evidence that he continued to conduct affairs of state throughout his earlier illnesses, which is proof positive that he was not. Because the issue is so important from many angles – historical, biographical, medical and simply to establish the facts – some of this evidence is assembled here.

A check of the Privy Council minutes[67] for his attendances in 1765 shows that in January he was absent from the only meeting on the 4th; in February he was present at all four meetings on the 1st, 6th, 14th and 22nd; in March he was present at the two meetings held on the 19th and 29th, the latter held not at St James's but at the Queen's House, indicating that the King was mentally well but physically incapacitated; in April he was absent on the 5th, 12th and 25th, but present on the 22nd; in May he attended all five meetings; in June he was present on the 5th, 10th, 12th and 26th, but absent on the 3rd and 19th.

The fact that Grenville did not see the King from 25 February until 10 March has been taken to indicate that this was the time of the King's worst alienation, so that not even his Prime Minister was allowed to see him.[68] But Grenville himself was indisposed at the beginning of this period.[69] And the Sandwich Diplomatic Correspondence shows that the King transacted business on 26 February, 1 and 4 March, and scrawled on a note of 1 March: 'Having been blooded this box is but just delivered to me; I desire Lord Sandwich will order the necessary instruments to be prepared and sent for my signature'.[70] In addition, a letter written by Grenville on 3 March adds further details of the King's health at that time and shows that there is no foundation whatever for supposing that he was deranged:

I have this moment received a very authentic account of His Majesty's health which . . . is in all respects much more satisfactory than what I understood has been reported. The alarm which had been spread was thank God beyond the truth. After a very good night without any fever at all the King was seized this morning at 7 o'clock with a fit of coughing which brought on a quickness of pulse and a soreness in his breast. The physicians thought proper to bleed him ten to twelve ounces to prevent the effects of any inflammation. This was done accordingly and His Majesty has grown much better ever since. He was up in the Queen's dressing room at 8 o'clock this evening and his pulse very little if at all quicker or harder than it was last night. The physicians I believe are at present under no apprehension from anything which they see, but I do not wonder at all at the general concern and anxiety which those who are informed of the exact state of the king's health express upon an occasion in which the happiness of all is so nearly concerned.[71]

And on 5 March the King wrote from the Queen's House to Grenville:

I am obliged to Mr. Grenville for his expressions on my being so much mended; the physicians, on my naming that I feel as yet some weakness in the breast, have renewed their injunctions of not talking, and particularly on business; if there are any warrants ready for my signature, I wish Mr. Grenville would at any time send them . . . as also a summary account of the debate of yesterday, which I am curious to hear . . . I return the papers signed.[72]

Although absent from the Privy Council in the first half of April, the King continued to transact business.[73] 'On the 1st of April the King withdrew to Richmond for a week, but returned unexpectedly on the 3rd and 4th to his levée and drawing-room. This sudden appearance was at that time supposed calculated to prevent any notion of his being ill,' noted Horace Walpole.[74]

The Hanoverian representative at St James's, in his regular dispatches to the Hanoverian Privy Council,[75] first mentioned on 26 February that the King 'had been indisposed a few days with a cold, for which he was blooded', but that he was recovering and that he had found him that day 'quite sprightly' ('*ganz munter*'). On 5 March, he reported home that there had been an unexpected return of fever and that he had therefore refrained from molesting the King with dispatches. On 19 March, he reported full restoration and on 29 March he had an audience and found the King well but for 'a slight residual cough'.

Further proof can be extracted from the examination on oath of the royal physicians by parliamentary committees. None of them had any inkling of a breakdown before 1788. In January 1789, when Willis was asked: 'Does Dr. Willis consider His Majesty's Age as making a material Difference in the Chance of His Majesty's recovering or not recovering, after duly attending to all the Circumstances of His Majesty's Case which have fallen within his Observation, and come to his Knowledge?', he answered: 'I do not judge that the Age is of any Signification, unless the Patient has been afflicted before with the same Malady.'[76] Dr Reynolds, the only physician who attended the King in all attacks from 1788, deposed before the parliamentary committee in December 1810 that the first attack occurred in 1788.[77]

Although none of the physicians who were called in 1788 had attended in 1765, it is inconceivable that these senior fellows of the College of Physicians would not have heard from their colleagues or from the royal family had there been any suspicion of previous derangement. One of their number, Dr Richard Warren, had, in fact, been physician in ordinary since 1763, when he succeeded his father-in-law, Dr Peter Shaw, in the office. He must have been informed, even if he did not attend himself, of what was wrong with the King. Had there been such a history, he would certainly have revealed it in 1788, since his sympathies during the Regency Crisis were on the side of the Prince of Wales.

That derangement came like a bolt from the blue in 1788 also explains Baker's consternation, as appears from his diary, when the King suddenly became delirious while under his sole care. He had not even a suspicion that such a complication might ensue. Nor can there be any doubt that the Opposition would have ferreted out a fact, even a rumour, of such grave import, since a recurrence of derangement would have provided powerful ammunition for an immediate regency. That the Opposition, in fact, knew nothing of the sort is obvious from Sheridan's speech in the House on 16 January 1789. In order to expose Willis as untrustworthy and a charlatan, he ridiculed his claim before the parliamentary committee that one dose of physic he had given the King had cured 'seven-and-twenty years of extreme study, abstinence, and labour'.[78]

Lastly, there is preserved in the Queen's Council Papers[79] the King's medical history drawn up in 1811 by the royal physicians as the basis for a consultation with three leading 'mad-doctors', Thomas Monro, Samuel Foart Simmons and John Willis. It opens: 'A person of strong constitution & regular habits, had been afflicted about the age of 50 and twice since with derangement of intellect accompanied by great nervous irritability . . . In the latter part of October 1810, when he was in his 73rd year, he suffered a fourth attack of the same kind . . .' By that time, surely, there could have been no possible reason for withholding in a confidential memorandum any detail of the King's case which could provide the slenderest clue to the nature and hence treatment of his illness.

The tradition that George III had his first attack of 'insanity' in 1765 may now be relegated to the realm of mythology. With it much of what has been written about him and many historical judgements will have to be fundamentally revised. The same applies to the medical and psychiatric aspects of the case. Yet the startling fact emerges that although there was no mental derangement, the underlying condition seems to have been the same as that which caused the later attacks, since the physical symptoms which preceded or accompanied them were similar. They resemble those of mild attacks of porphyria: cold, pain, hoarseness, fast pulse, insomnia, fatigue and weight loss. But subsequent attacks were more severe and when they involved the brain deranged his mind.

PART THREE

The Family History

12

Historical Diagnosis

A retrospective diagnosis can hardly ever be made with the same confidence as one in a living patient. But it can be strongly supported if the disorder presents a characteristic clinical picture, if it is rare and above all if it is hereditary. Porphyria almost uniquely fulfils all these criteria. To verify our diagnosis of George III's illness it was therefore only necessary to search for sporadic cases among his ancestors from whom it passed down the generations and among descendants who have inherited it.

This is a very different undertaking from attempting to establish the frequency with which porphyria occurred in this huge and widely flung family, which includes the houses of Hanover, Stuart, Tudor and Prussia, besides innumerable minor branches. How far its ramifications spread can be gathered from Debrett's Coronation edition.

In 1938 every ruling sovereign of Europe, with the exception of the King of the Balkan State of Albania, traces descent from Elizabeth of Bohemia [daughter of James I and great-great-grandmother of George III]. Their Majesties of Denmark, Great Britain, Greece, Jugo-Slavia, the Netherlands, Norway, Roumania and Sweden are descendants of her daughter Sophia; the Kings of Belgium, Bulgaria and Italy of her granddaughter 'Liselotte'.

And even this leaves out of account the deposed monarchs of Germany, Russia and Spain. A systematic investigation of such magnitude would in any case take many students many decades and the results fill many volumes. And still it would be doomed to remain incomplete because of lack of medical information. Furthermore, the condition may be latent and transmitted by someone who shows no symptoms, or only inconspicuous ones.

Our first task was to ascertain whether porphyria actually occurred in the family. We therefore searched for living descendants in whom its existence could be established in the laboratory. Although this meant a bold intrusion into privacy for which we still feel apologetic, we were fortunate to obtain the necessary co-operation which made it possible to diagnose it in four

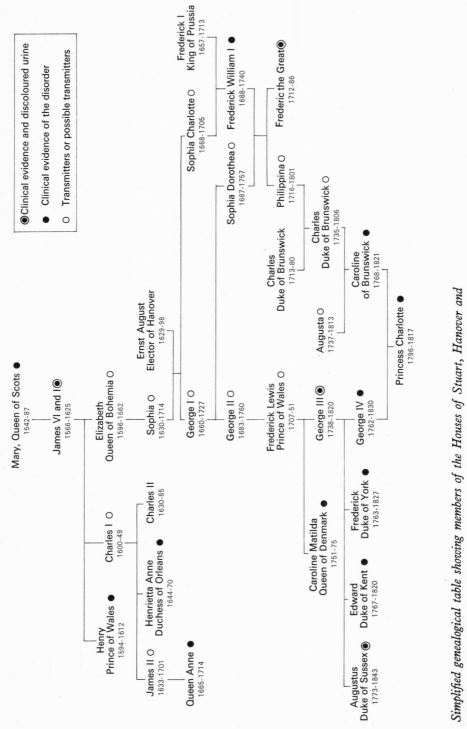

Simplified genealogical table showing members of the Houses of Stuart, Hanover and Prussia mentioned in this study who seem to have suffered from or transmitted porphyria

living family members. This provided the material evidence of necessity lacking in posthumous diagnosis. Furthermore, it was possible to determine from examination of stool and urine specimens by modern methods that the disorder was of the type known as variegate porphyria. Since it is known that the inheritance of the different types of porphyria is specific, these results provided also the key to the particular clinical features to be looked for in ancestors.

Armed with this knowledge we embarked on the historical part of our inquiry. We went first for important figures because it was more likely that their illnesses had made a stir and that records of some kind had been kept. The galaxy of patients assembled in these pages is due to our method of selection and must not create the impression that porphyria is commoner among the great than the not so great. Nor can one deduce from them anything regarding the sex incidence of the disorder. It was obviously impossible to be systematic, since we did not know what we would find. Inevitably many blind trails were followed, but helpful leads also came across the centuries, as when James I told his physician that he had inherited his complaint from his mother. Similar clues in unexpected places emerged until this study reached proportions we had not anticipated and a picture unfolded which revealed the purple thread of porphyria running through the royal houses from the Tudors to the Hanoverians, and from the Hanoverians to the present day.

To convey the sense of suspense and surprise we experienced in the course of this investigation, we do not adhere strictly to a chronological presentation but retain the order in which the discovery of the illness in one patient formed a bridge to the next. The sketches of their medical histories which follow are not intended to be complete but only to bring out the manifestations of the disorder for a convincing picture to emerge. Neither are they potted biographies, although in earlier centuries illness can hardly be separated from political and social background.

It is in the nature of such an investigation that it is open-ended. Doubtless many more cases are to be found. We ourselves could have increased their number, notably among the brothers of George III and his daughters.

Medical facts are not easy to come by and have to be searched out. Matters of health are cavalierly treated in biographical and historical writings, and unfortunately also in selections for publication from correspondences and diaries. It seems to be assumed that illness plays a small part in a man's life and make-up – an opinion which needs no other confutation than the history of George III, though it also applies to George IV and others. A false delicacy which regards medical matters as too personal may prevent biographers from mentioning them. In one instance, that of Lady Arabella Stuart, diagnostically crucial facts were expunged by her laborious Victorian biographer in his transcriptions of original documents. This shows how important it is to go back to original sources, and with luck one may discover new ones. Maybe a medical background is required to appreciate the significance of such data. Even so, a doctor's interpretation is limited by the state of knowledge of his own time. Medical biography or pathography is not necessarily definitive but must be continually revised in the light of medical advances in understanding and delineating disease. Porphyria, which has only been recognized in the last decades, is a good example. On the whole it is less surprising how few medical records exist than how remarkably frank and informative some of them from earlier centuries are.

Facts about health or ill-health are most likely to have been noted when illness impinged on the political scene, as it did when George III's attack in 1788 provoked the Regency Crisis. The astonishing lack of medical information about the first two Georges and George III's father, Frederick Lewis Prince of Wales, may be explained by the fact that their illnesses, if any, remained their private affair. Besides, the end of the seventeenth and the first half of the eighteenth centuries were fallow periods in English medicine, a fact which goes far also to explain why there is almost no authentic medical information to be found about Queen Anne, whose whole life was dogged by ill-health.

The same applies when the political or religious climate fostered suspicion that death was due to foul play. Porphyria, with its 'mysterious' symptoms – sudden onset, agonizing abdominal pain, prostration, followed by rapid improvement or precipitate death – lent itself singularly to this interpretation, as in the cases of Mary Queen of Scots, Henrietta Anne Duchess of Orleans, Queen Caroline Matilda of Denmark and others. In such circumstances a good deal of gossip and speculation about the event has come down and often contains more medical detail.

Informative medical notes are also available in the few exceptional instances when monarchs were served by outstanding physicians, as James I was by Mayerne and George III's sons by the conscientious Hanoverian doctors. Often letters are almost the only source, as in the cases of Frederic the Great and George IV, and a meaningful medical history has to be pieced together from fragments like a mosaic. These days such information would have been exchanged in telephone conversations and so lost. Putting these together is also a safeguard against diagnosing illness during life from the last and fatal illness, as is often done, since a porphyric need not die from the disorder. Conversely, an obscure fatal illness may appear in a very different light if the earlier medical history is taken into account. Queen Victoria's father, for example, is generally believed to have died of pneumonia caught by staying in wet stockings – a hazard to which according to the *Dictionary of National Biography* an astonishing number of the great appear to have succumbed. However, his correspondence reveals that from early manhood he had the tell-tale attacks of 'rheumatism' and 'colic'.

In a medico-historical study covering five centuries one must avoid the pitfall of carrying over contemporary diagnoses literally. Some expertise in medical history is necessary to appreciate the state of medicine at a given period, the theoretical framework in which doctors thought about disease and made their observations, and what observations they were capable of making. Many old medical terms have survived and are in daily use but have changed their meaning in the course of centuries and need to be reinterpreted to understand what doctors had in mind. 'Nephritis', for instance, could not have meant the same to James I's physicians as it does today, and to perpetuate this diagnosis must be misleading. Then not even the circulation of the blood had been discovered and little more was known about the kidneys than that they had to do with urine and when diseased produced stones. James's attacks of 'arthritis' and his mother's 'rheumatism' convey nothing more than that they had pain and could not move their limbs, for which many more causes are known today than diseased joints. In the eighteenth century, after Dr Thomas Sydenham had popularized gout, such symptoms were diagnosed as 'flying' or 'wandering' gout – in contrast to podagra or settled gout – or even 'the ague'. When the physicians called a fever tertian or quartan, they were observing a chronological difference, not implying the presence of malaria, as these terms would today. The term 'fever' itself, before the clinical thermometer came into general use in the nineteenth century, implied no more than malaise and a rapid pulse which, it is known today, occurs also in the absence of fever and in porphyria is indeed a leading symptom in attacks. That peripheral nerves can be directly affected by toxins, causing neuritis or neuropathy – another important feature of porphyria – was not recognized until the late nineteenth century, so that paralysis of limbs was ascribed to diseased nerves within the brain. This is why Frederic the Great's lameness at the age of thirty-five was called an 'apoplexy' or 'hemiplegia' – a diagnosis which stuck. When George IV spoke of a 'stoppage' and the doctors diagnosed 'an obstruction of the bowels' in his consort Caroline, it would be anachronistic to suppose they meant a mechanical obstruction of the gut – such as a tumour – which is what the terms have conveyed since the advent of X-rays and surgery. Rather was it a remnant of the old doctrine that disease originated in imbalance of the four humours, and simply implied blockage of their flow, causing nausea, vomiting and constipation, in much the same way as Mary Queen of Scots' doctors, almost three hundred years earlier, ascribed her troubles to an 'obstruction of the spleen'.

It is fortunate that porphyria can be diagnosed in retrospect with some confidence because attacks present an almost specific combination of seemingly unconnected symptoms: abdominal pain (more rarely pain in the chest), muscular weakness or paralysis, and mental disturbance. In the variegate or mixed type there may also be sun-sensitivity leading to attacks and/or skin lesions with a vesicular rash.

Patients feel gravely ill during attacks and often have a sense of impending doom. The agonizing quality of the pain is only appreciated by the sufferer, so that women tend to be considered 'hysterical', like Mary Queen of Scots, and men oversensitive, like George IV, or 'impatient of pain', like James I. Rapid fluctuations in the condition, which were so marked in George III's case, are characteristic.

In looking for references to urine, one must remember that interest in it changed in the course of medical history. After the time of the 'piss-prophets' who divined everything from it, the intense curiosity in all observable natural phenomena of the early seventeenth century led James I's physician to record minute observations on the colour changes of his urine. In the eighteenth century this early interest receded as no fresh stimulus was forthcoming from new discoveries about kidney function or disease, or new methods of testing it. This explains the paradoxical fact that George III's physicians took much less notice of his urine than James I's and seem rarely to have troubled to inspect it.

13

The Stuarts and the Tudors

JAMES VI OF SCOTLAND AND I OF ENGLAND (1566–1625)

Had King James not taken an active interest in 'unnatural diseases' and defended the reality of demoniacal possession and believed in witches – most of whom suffered from unrecognized neurological or psychiatric disorders – and had he not written a book on it[1] which entitles him to a place in the history of psychiatry, we would hardly have dared so far into the past, or known where to start on George III's ancestry. As it turned out this was a propitious choice, because through him it was possible to establish that porphyria came to the House of Hanover from the Stuarts.

By good fortune he was attended by an outstanding physician, Sir Theodore Turquet de Mayerne (1573–1655). Born near Geneva, he settled in France, where he became Henry IV's physician. James invited him to England and appointed him his first physician. Here he quickly rose to eminence and treated James's Queen, Anne of Denmark, Henry Prince of Wales, Charles I, Charles II and many nobles and notables such as Sir Robert Cecil, Lord Rochester and Inigo Jones. He was a man of wide interests and independent spirit, one of the band of great men who at this period broke out of the confines of traditional Galenic theory and set out simply to observe and to record. They looked upon disease as nature's way of experimenting and started to make experiments of their own to understand what nature did. It was this revolutionary attitude which led Mayerne's contemporary William Harvey to discover the circulation of the blood, and Mayerne himself to note with the greatest care every detail of his patients' condition. This was an innovation without which medicine could not progress and it assured him a place in the history of medicine as the 'first [who] definitely established in England the clinical study of medicine and the method of recording observations'.[2] The British Museum possesses twenty-three volumes of his papers in his own hand, which have luckily survived. Among them are his notes on James, which give a picture almost as informative as a modern account, because not only did he des-

P

cribe his symptoms but also what he thought about them. They are paradoxically much more detailed and therefore all the more revealing than the
journals of George III's physicians. Mayerne combined with his merits as a
clinical observer at the bedside an intense scientific curiosity and is remembered also for his pharmacological and chemical experiments. These two
qualities have resulted in such a clear picture of James's illnesses that a disorder can be diagnosed which was not described until more than three
hundred years later.

The information which Mayerne's manuscripts provide is of two sorts:
daily notes on James's illnesses, at which he was present, and what may be
called a comprehensive medical profile. This is divided into the King's
constitution, habits of body and mind, the disorders to which these made
him liable and those he actually had, arranged under the various symptoms
he displayed. The following extracts give both an insight into Mayerne's
medical thinking and outline the salient features of James's disorder:[3]

James the First, King of Great Britain, was born at Edinburgh in the year
1566, on June 19th, at half-past eleven in the morning, and is now 57 years.
He had a drunken wet-nurse and was suckled for about a year. He has a very
steadfast brain, which was never disturbed by the sea, by drinking wine, or by
driving in a coach.

He is easily affected by cold and suffers in cold and damp weather. His
chest is broad and well formed, and the vital parts contained therein have a
strong and lively warmth and are never afflicted unless from a morbid condition elsewhere in his body . . . The liver is naturally good . . . but liable to obstructions, and inclined to generate much bile. The spleen easily collects
melancholic juices, which is indicated by various symptoms . . . Sometimes he
is melancholy from the spleen . . . he becomes very irascible . . . sometimes
his eyes become yellow but it soon passes off, he glows with heat and his appetite falls off; he sleeps badly. His gullet is narrow causing difficulties in swallowing. He is often constipated and his abdomen swells out with wind . . .
He has by nature a good appetite and properly digests a sufficient quantity . . .
His skin is thin and fragile, so that it itches easily* . . . he sweats easily . . . He
often suffers bruises from knocking against timber, from frequent falls, rub-
bing of greaves and stirrups and other external causes which he carefully
inspects and notes in a book to show to his doctors that they were not due to
an internal disorder and so avoids having to take medicines which he detests.†
All his functions are by nature good, but perverted on occasion and mostly

---

* 'His skin was as soft as Taffeta Sarsnet' and because of it he wore his clothes
loose.[4]

† James refused no medicine so decidedly as senna. And George III abhorred it
so much that he charged Sir George Baker never again to give it to any member of
the royal family and even threatened to prohibit its importation.[5] This may be a remarkable coincidence, but it is also possible that while their gut is paralysed porphyrics cannot tolerate senna.

from disturbance of mind. He is of exquisite sensitiveness and most impatient of pain [or, at least equally probably, Mayerne, as so many, did not appreciate the particular severity of the pain].

Air. – His Majesty bears all changes of air fairly well, in damp weather with a south wind he is attacked by catarrh.

Food. – As regards food there is nothing wrong except that he eats no bread . . . He eats fruit at all hours of the day and night.

Drink. – In drink he errs as to quality, quantity, frequency, time and order. He . . . drinks beer, ale, Spanish wine, sweet French wine . . . and sometimes Alicante wine.

Exercise and rest. – The King used to indulge in most violent exercise in hunting. Now he is quieter and lies and sits more, which is due to the weakness of his knees.

Former illnesses and present inclination to various morbid conditions. – The King did not walk to the sixth year of his age . . . owing to the bad milk of his drunken nurse . . . Between the second and fifth year he had smallpox and measles.

Sleep and waking. – By nature he is a poor sleeper and often at night calls for the servant to read to him aloud.

Affections of the mind. – He is easily and quickly disturbed . . . Sometimes he is melancholy from the spleen exciting disorders.

Excreta. – He blows his nose and sneezes often . . . His stomach is easily made sick if he retains undigested food or bile . . . He then vomits vehemently, so that for two or three days afterwards his face is dotted with red spots. Wind from the stomach precedes illness and he is constipated . . .

Colic. – Very frequently he laboured under painful colic with flatus (an affliction from which his mother also suffered) . . . with vomiting and diarrhoea, preceded by melancholy and nocturnal rigors . . . Fasting, sadness, cold at night produced it . . .

Diarrhoea. – He has been liable to diarrhoea all his life, attacks are usually ushered in by lowness of spirits, heavy breathing, dread of everything and other symptoms . . . pain in the chest, palpitation, sometimes hiccough. In 1610 his life was in acute danger with persistent vomiting. In 1612 after the death of his son another fit of melancholy with the same symptoms, and again in 1619 . . .

In 1619 the attack was accompanied by arthritic and nephritic pains, he lost consciousness, breathing was laboured, great fearfulness and dejection, intermittent pulse and his life was in danger for eight days. It was the most dangerous illness the King ever had.* In 1623 an attack lasted only two or three days but was very severe. It was followed by arthritis and he could not walk for months.

---

* He was so ill that 'false reports' were 'spread abroad of his death' from 'a violent fit of the stone'. He suffered intense pain, was sleepless, could not eat, lost the use of his legs for four months and had to be carried 'in a Neapolitan portative chair'. Later, to strengthen them, 'he bathes them . . . in every stag and buck's belly on the place where he killed them'. ⁵

Fever. – He rarely has fever and if he has it does not last long and is ephemeral.

Nephritis. – For many years past, after hunting, he often had turbid urine and red like Alicante wine (which are His Majesty's own words) but without pain. In July 1613 he passed blood-red urine with frequent severe vomiting, pain in the left kidney and other nephritic symptoms. Later in the year they recurred and again in 1615 when they were even worse.

Arthritis. – Many years ago he had such pain and weakness in the foot that it was left with an odd twist when walking. For several weeks he had to give up all exercise and had to stay in bed or in a chair. In 1616 this weakness continued for more than four months. The following year the pain spread from the foot to both ankles, knees, and shoulders and hands. The pain is acute, and followed by weakness.

Three times in his life he was seized with excruciating pain in his thighs which, as if by spasms of the muscles and tendons, most pertinaciously twitched at night. The leanness, and so to say atrophy, of his legs are apparently due to the intermission of exercise not calling forth the spirits and nourishment to the lower limbs.

As to remedies. – The King laughs at medicine, and holds it so cheap that he declares physicians of very little use and hardly necessary. He asserts the art of medicine to be supported by mere conjectures, and useless because uncertain.

In short James suffered from recurrent attacks of abdominal colic with nausea, vomiting and diarrhoea, fast and at times irregular pulse, painful weakness and spasms of his limbs, and in some of these attacks he was dangerously ill. Mayerne thought the muscular weakness and paralysis were due to the nourishing 'spirits' from the brain not reaching down to the lower parts. These 'animal spirits' were believed to circulate through hollow nerves – in a way analogous to the circulating blood, which Harvey was then investigating. The attacks were followed by wasting, especially – and typically – of those muscles which extend the limbs, and so led to footdrop. At these times he was irritable, suffered from fearful sadness and fits of unconsciousness, and his urine turned the colour of Alicante wine.

Mayerne diagnosed the mental symptoms as melancholy, an excess of black humour from an obstructed liver and spleen, which also caused pain under the ribs and transient yellowness of the eyes.* He called the painful weakness of the limbs 'arthritis' because disease of joints was the only cause then known. He attributed the King's colic and gastro-intestinal symptoms to 'nephritis'. What he thought nephritis was and did to the patient he described in his *Practice of medicine.*[8] The signs were 'nausea, vomiting, with a fixed pain in the loins and a deadness of the thighs'; and the 'intention of cure' was to give medicines to lubricate the urinary passages so that the

---

* Attacks of porphyria are sometimes accompanied by slight transient jaundice.[7]

stone would deliver itself and the patient from pain. Nephritis for Mayerne was therefore synonymous with colic and 'bloody' urine proof of it. One need not smile at Mayerne's seeming medical naivity, because even today it is possible to mistake the colic and discoloured urine of an attack of porphyria for that of stones in the kidney. 'The pain sometimes radiates to the back and even the loins and is then the more likely to be mistaken for renal stones if the urine appears . . . bloody,'[9] states a modern author.

So much for Mayerne's general medical history of King James. His daily notes, a kind of running commentary, in Latin like the rest, are scattered through several volumes of his manuscripts. They have not been used before and contain much more detailed information about the King's symptoms and how they developed. Mayerne described the 'ferocity' of the pain and how at the height of an attack the King suddenly became delirious. He paid particular attention to the colour changes of the urine, which he observed with exemplary assiduity. Obviously he was in his element here, since it is known that his particular hobby was experimenting with pigments. (He is remembered for his chemical contributions in this field and especially for discovering the purple colour necessary for the carnation tints in enamel painting.)[10]

He was – rightly – puzzled by the fact that some features of the discolouration could not be accounted for by assuming the presence of blood. For one thing the sudden transition from 'bloody' urine to clear as water was not in keeping. When a stone leads to bleeding, the urine loses its red colour only gradually and remains smokey for some time. Mayerne discussed at length how this rapid change in colour could be explained and where such an unorthodox stone might have lodged before it was passed. He consulted classical authors, but – of course – could not find any other explanation.[11] How pleased he would have been to hear that today it is recognized that substances other than blood produce red discolouration of the urine, namely the pigments which are passed in porphyria, and that these appear and disappear notoriously rapidly.

In June 1613 the King 'was afflicted with pain in the left side under the ribs . . . which recurred for 24 hours with mounting severity until it was worse than ferocious'.[12] On 12 July on his return from hunting he passed blood-red urine. Shortly afterwards he passed a great quantity which again was clear like water. There followed vomiting, diarrhoea and a fast irregular pulse. Mayerne waited for the obligatory pain which accompanies the passage of a stone, but there was none. Not until night-time did 'nephritic' pain set in, with palpitation and insomnia, and again the urine turned red. Mayerne was relieved when pain appeared, because it confirmed his diagnosis. He reasoned that a stone must have become dislodged by the King's hard riding. But there remained one other fact which did not fit and which he recorded pensively and with remarkable objectivity, namely that

12. *A page from Sir Theodore Turquet de Mayerne's case notes on the illness of James I of England in 1613, in which he described the colour of the King's urine as purple like Alicante wine (British Museum Sloane MS 1679, folio 20v).*

TRANSLATION OF FIGURE 12

12 July 1613

The King rose very early and with great vigour went riding and stag hunting until 2 in the morning. The season and the day were hot, humid and rainy. He had retention of urine. On his return he passed blood-red urine which was turbid with thick red sediment.

Then he breakfasted. After the meal he passed water again and the urine was turbid and reddish, as if lixiviated, with red sand and not at all white.

He passed his water without any pain whatever.

Shortly after he passed water a third time and it was clear.

At night nephritic pain set in from the left kidney; he vomited much and brought up phlegm which gave him relief.

He passed altogether more than six pints of thin urine clear as water with no trace of sediment as if it had been passed through a filter. The abdomen was blown out with flatus up and down.

13 July. In the morning at about 6 o'clock he felt a little better. At nine he got up and the pain in the kidney and ureter returned. The pain radiated to the bladder and the tip of the glans. Micturition was copious, the urine watery with a burning sensation at the end. He vomited phlegm with relief.

The whole of the preceding night he was feverish. In the morning the pulse was hard, febrile, unequal and missing beats as a result of the pain and restlessness.

NB About two months ago after a large meal of cherries he felt heat when making water, and often passed turbid urine as if lixiviated which was soon followed by clear urine.

NOTA This occurred without any preceding exercise; these symptoms were all nephritic.

NB His Majesty told me that since then he had quite often felt heat when passing water so that he himself feared a stone in the bladder.

He also told me that he quite frequently passed water red like Alicante wine without any pain. But not having seen this myself I cannot pass judgement on it; however most probably the water was red from blood.

even in the absence of exercise and without pain the King had also at times passed purplish urine 'like Alicante wine'. The next day when the King was much better Mayerne noted that its colour was 'normal enough'.[13]

On 17 August 1613 the King had another attack while he was staying at 'Beaulieu Niewforest', with 'tormenting pain in the left side or kidney' and 'red urine'. Vomiting became uncontrollable and he retained no medicine. Since to Mayerne's dismay the King 'did not admit the administration of clysters [enemas]' he deliberated whether as a last resort he should be 'immersed in a bath twice perhaps even three times' to alleviate his pain. When the attack was over the colour of the urine returned once more to 'laudible'.[14] How worrying the King's condition had been is shown by a letter Mayerne addressed to Robert Carr, Lord Rochester, the King's secretary, on 22 August in which he 'Wishes four experienced physicians to be joined with himself in the charge of the King's health'.[15]

Similar attacks had occurred in earlier years, in 1611 and 1612, accompanied by 'terrifying sleeplessness, turbulent nights, laboured breathing, palpitation' and the appearance of 'frank delirium with hallucinations'. At that time the King's condition was so ominous that Mayerne was alarmed that he might be developing 'water on the brain',[16] meaning he feared inflammation had spread to the brain – exactly what George III's physicians feared 175 years later, so little had medicine advanced in this field.

Mayerne's account of the illness is a description of porphyria in all but name. So complete is it that it is even possible to identify it as the variegate type, for after having mentioned in his general account King James's fragile and easily injured skin he described in his notes for 1611 his typical sensitivity to sunlight. He recorded that in the hot summer the King became 'so overheated' by exposure to the 'blazing sun' that his face, especially his forehead, broke out in 'a vesicular rash' and he suffered from violent headache vomiting and 'arthritic' pains – in other words it brought on an attack. One can be sure that it was a sun-sensitivity rash because of its typical location and appearance. This also explains Mayerne's disappointment that none of his many lotions and ointments – for all of which he entered the full prescriptions in his journal – did any good and why the rash subsided and the skin healed only at the end of September, when the sun was 'less violent'.[17]

The diagnosis of porphyria throws light also on James's last illness in 1625. He had one of his usual attacks and his physicians (Mayerne was absent) anticipated little danger – for which they were later severely taken to task – when he suddenly took a turn for the worse, went into convulsions, and died. His death was so unexpected that his erstwhile favourite, the Duke of Buckingham, was suspected of having poisoned him by surreptitiously laying 'a plaister on his stomach'[18] – testimony to the fact that as in all attacks he had abdominal pain.

And when it came to the postmortem examination nothing much was found. The left kidney, long suspected by Mayerne to be full of mischievous stones, was healthy. The right was of minute size, less than an inch in length. It was obviously one of the not-so-rare congenital malformations which never function and so could not have brought forth one stone.

His doctors and the *Dictionary of National Biography* ascribed King James's death to a 'tertian fever'. Medical historians and biographers have stuck to Mayerne's diagnosis of nephritis with haematuria (bloody urine) and arthritis, and later, when it became fashionable to diagnose gout, all his symptoms were attributed to it.

HENRY FREDERICK PRINCE OF WALES (1594-1612)

James I's eldest son Henry died on 6 November 1612 at the age of eighteen after a short illness with much the same symptoms which marked his father's attacks: diarrhoea, rapid pulse, insomnia, weakness, laboured breathing, violent headaches, buzzing in the ears, photophobia or sensitivity to light, rigors, muscular twitchings, mounting delirium – 'alienation of braine, ravynge & idle speeches out of purpose' – fits – 'all his former accidents increasing exceedinglie; his boundings being turned into convulsions, his raving & benumminge greater; the feavor more vyolent' [19]– and finally coma. Death came so suddenly to this energetic youth of good constitution that it was rumoured that he also was the victim of poison. Suspicion was even cast on his father, whose motive was supposed to have been jealousy of the boy's popularity. The Venetian ambassador in Savoy reported home on 30 December 1612: 'The French Ambassador said that in France they held that the Prince of Wales died of poison, and added "and what is worse, is that some hold that his father was an accomplice in the murder".'[20]

Mayerne treated him, but his notes on the illness have not survived. The sixteen pages in his manuscripts which they filled are missing and it is presumed that he himself tore them out when 'he endured great obloquy upon the Prince's death'.[21] But summary-apologias in French and Latin by Mayerne are included in a posthumous collection of his works.[22] These show that the illness started on 10 October as a 'tertian fever' (the same diagnosis as the one made in his father's fatal illness), with diarrhoea, restlessness, delirium and insomnia. He rallied for a few days, but on 24 October the symptoms recurred with mounting severity.

Mayerne excluded 'contagious fever' because no one about the Prince was similarly affected. He noted one vitally important detail of his previous health: in the very hot summer of the same year during the 'dog-days' Henry was staying at Woodstock with his parents and 'his drinking companion Lord General Cicill [Edward Cecil]', when he suddenly fell ill. He 'suffered from attacks of fever, hydroa [still today usually called hydroa aestivale to describe a vesicular rash of the face caused by exposure to the sun], and inflammation of his palms and lips so severe that the whole epidermis sloughed off'.[23] Henry had the same sun-sensitivity as his father and seemingly also his fragile skin, because his palms may well have been affected by tennis playing, his favourite occupation.

Even earlier in that year he had not been well. Since the spring a change had been observed in him. He was 'sad and retired, often complaining of a giddy heaviness in the forehead'[24] (frontal headaches are often met with in porphyria), 'his countenance was not as cheerful as it was wont to be, but had heavy darkish looks, with a kind of mixture of melancholy and choler'.[25] He was often so weak and listless that he could not rise from his bed.

Nothing was found at the postmortem examination or in the diplomatic language of the English ambassador, who told the Venetian government: 'To satisfy public opinion . . . the body was opened and a careful examination showed that this blow came solely from the hand of God.'[26] Prince Henry's death is generally ascribed to typhoid fever, the diagnosis put forward as the most likely by Moore in 1885[27] to account for the sudden onset of gastro-intestinal symptoms and delirium. But that was long before porphyria was known.

MARY QUEEN OF SCOTS (1542–87)

Mary Queen of Scots is not only one of history's most tragic figures, she is also one of its great invalids. Contemporaries said she suffered from the spleen, 'rheum' and 'fits of the mother'. Medical historians have somewhat modernized and refined these terms into gastric ulcer, rheumatism and hysteria. From her late teens she had attacks of which the essential features were excruciating pain and vomiting, painful lameness, fits and mental

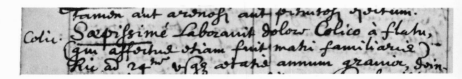

13. *Part of a page of Sir Theodore Turquet de Mayerne's case notes on the illness of James I of England, showing that he had inherited attacks of colic from his mother, Mary Queen of Scots (British Museum Sloane MS 1679, folio 44v). (Translation: 'Very often he laboured under painful colic from flatus (an affliction from which his mother also suffered)')*

disturbance – a combination suggestive of porphyria. So notorious were her attacks of colic that her son James, who never lived with his mother, knew of them and recognized his own affliction in hers, as he told his physician Mayerne.

The most severe attack, in which she nearly died, occurred at Jedburgh in 1566, when she was twenty-four years old. Its rapid onset and alarming symptoms followed by a quick recovery gave rise to the suspicion, still lingering in some quarters, that she was poisoned. She had had attacks of vomiting and colic for some years, when she was suddenly taken ill, became strange in manner, and was nauseated and sleepless. The next day she developed a terrible pain in her side, made worse by every movement, even breathing. She vomited excessively, it is said more than sixty times, until eventually she brought up some 'corrupt' blood. She became delirious and two days later lost her sight and speech, had a series of fits and remained unconscious for some hours. The people around her thought she was dead. Yet within ten days she was up and about again.[28]

In 1570 the same symptoms recurred. She was much

molested with a continewall destillation from her head into her stomack, where of hath growen such debilite and weakness in that part, that she nether hath desire to anie meate, neyther facultie to reteyne that long . . . she is troubled also with incessant provocation to vomitt . . . likewise . . . with a greit inflamation and tension in her left side, under the short ribbes which retchith so farr every waie, that they yet doubt whether it be the inflamation of the stomack, the splene, the wombe, or all of those thre partes together.

She was at the same time

troubled with continual lack of sleep for 10 or 12 days (all which time she has kept her bed) . . . continually afflicted with sighs and pensiveness.

She was also molested with 'vehement fittes of the mother'.[29]

Attacks in later years are described:

she hath complained almost this fortnight of her grief of the spleen which my physician . . . informeth me . . . is *obstructio splenis cum flatu hypochondriaco* wherewith ofttimes, by reason of great pains . . . ascending unto her head and other parts, she is ready to swoon[30] . . . complained much of grief and pain in her side, her heart, and head, and suffered then a painful fit . . . whereat she showed herself somewhat afraid of her life.[31]

In 1572 she was said to have 'unquiet and melancholy fits' and was 'sometimes grieved with passions of her old disease'.[32] On one occasion her colic came upon her so suddenly while on the road that she had to be taken into a wayside house and there called for a midwife, though she was not pregnant, because the pain was so intense that she could only think it was caused by the pangs of childbirth.[33]

She herself described an attack as the 'accustumat dolor of oure syde . . . ane rewme that troublis our head gritalie with a extreme pane, and discendis in the stomack, sa that it makis us lately to laik appetite',[34] and again 'vexed by sickness, with a great vomisement . . . flewme, and colore, the dolour of my syde'.[35] In addition to her 'shivering' and 'convulsive' fits, she had difficulty in swallowing, altered voice, pain and weakness of arms and legs so that at times she could neither write, walk, nor even stand unaided, 'not able to go or stand wherewith she is greatly perplexed'.[36] 'She doubteth a palsy, for she says she wants strength and use of her left arm.'[37] 'Bereft . . . of the use of her right hand.'[38] 'Excuse my writing' she wrote in a letter, 'caused by the weakness of my arm'[39]; 'the weakness . . . and the rheum wherewith we are . . . tormented'[40]; 'not being suffered the command of my legs'.[40]

Attacks often confined her to bed and she was melancholy, excitable or distracted.[41] This mental 'instability' together with her recurrent invalidism and inability to move her limbs, her 'grievous pain in her side' and her equally inexplicable recoveries, impressed those around her as histrionic and put on, and she was believed to feign illness as occasion demanded to gain her ends. Mary Queen of Scots shares with many sufferers from porphyria, living and dead, the fate of being judged 'hysterical'.

The Lady Arabella Stuart (1575–1615) and the Tudors

Whence did porphyria come into the House of Stuart? Had Mary Queen of Scots' mother, Marie de Guise, brought it to these shores from France, or had the Stuarts inherited it from the Tudors and Mary from her father James V of Scotland? It is tempting to look into his medical history because he had bouts of illness with melancholy. Tradition picturesquely has it that he died at the age of thirty of a broken heart after his miserable defeat at Solway Moss, but the theory that it was an illness in which his mind was disturbed has recently been put forward.[42] But of course one is on more and more uncertain medical grounds the further one goes back.

There is however a more promising way open to find out whether porphyria was a Tudor legacy in the person of the Lady Arabella Stuart. She was James VI & I's first cousin, daughter of Charles Stuart, 5th Earl of Lennox, who was the brother of James's father, Henry, Lord Darnley. They shared in addition a great-grandmother in Margaret Tudor, sister of Henry VIII. She was twice married, first to James IV of Scotland and secondly to Archibald Douglas, Earl of Angus. Arabella's grandmother, Margaret Douglas, was therefore the half-sister of James VI & I's grandfather, James V. Arabella descended from the Tudors along a different line from Mary Queen of Scots, and if she also suffered from porphyria it must have come down to her and to James from their common Tudor ancestors.

Arabella stood in line of succession to the English throne next to her cousin James. Some even held her title to be preferable because she – but not James – was born on English soil and so had a right to hold land. On the death of Queen Elizabeth, however, James ascended peacefully and he treated his nearest kinswoman, as he himself stressed, with kindness, although a supposed plot in favour of her claim landed Sir Walter Raleigh in the Tower. Information about her medical history is so mixed in with political events that they cannot be separated. Trouble with James arose only when Arabella intended to marry William Seymour, Viscount Beauchamp, later Earl of Hertford and created Duke of Somerset by Charles II at the Restoration for his loyal services to Charles I. He was in his own right in line of succession as a descendant of Henry VIII's younger sister Mary, who had married the Duke of Suffolk. The simplified genealogical table makes these complicated family connexions clearer. When Arabella actually and clandestinely married Seymour their children might have endangered the succession of James's offspring, since they would have had a claim from both parents. James forestalled such a calamity by consigning Arabella to the Tower in 1611. There she died at the age of forty, not without the cry of poison being raised. Her husband, who was thirteen years her junior, survived her by forty-five years.

Arabella had three attacks of serious illness and during each her mind became deranged. Some simply speak of her as insane during most of her life – a falsification she shared with George III. She suffered from nervous symptoms very similar to those of her relations: she had pain and weakness, headaches and colic. Like her aunt, Mary Queen of Scots, she was thought to feign illness under pressure of adversity, and like her cousin James's her urine was discoloured. It may seem odd that her illnesses occurred when circumstances put her into a corner, but perhaps one should look at it the other way round. Only when there was political commotion was the state of her health noteworthy. Other attacks may well have gone unrecorded.

The first time illness came to notice was in 1603, when she was twenty-eight. Her mother, Elizabeth Cavendish, was dead and Arabella was living with her grandmother, the Countess of Shrewsbury, Bess of Hardwick. There was at that time much friction between these two headstrong women. Arabella yearned for her independence and the free choice of a husband. Her grandmother, ambitious and herself scheming for Arabella's future, was also acutely aware of Arabella's precarious political situation, sandwiched between monarchs and two religions. Rumours were flying through the courts of Europe that she was – or that others were on her behalf – aspiring to the throne of England and that she had embraced the Catholic faith. Nobody could blame the Countess for being on edge – her husband

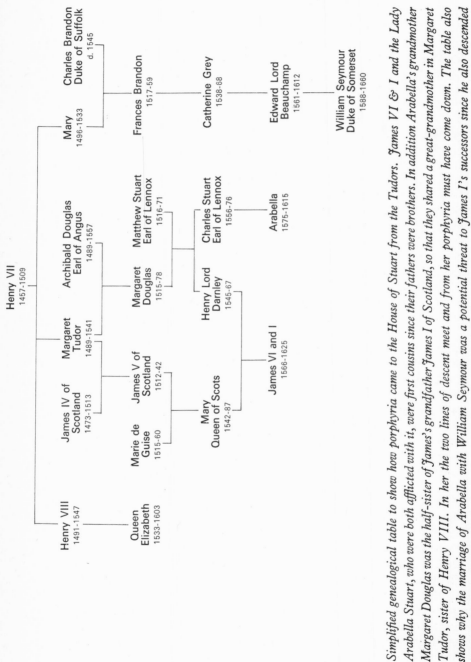

Simplified genealogical table to show how porphyria came to the House of Stuart from the Tudors. James VI & I and the Lady Arabella Stuart, who were both afflicted with it, were first cousins since their fathers were brothers. In addition Arabella's grandmother Margaret Douglas was the half-sister of James's grandfather James I of Scotland, so that they shared a great-grandmother in Margaret Tudor, sister of Henry VIII. In her the two lines of descent meet and from her porphyria must have come down. The table also shows why the marriage of Arabella with William Seymour was a potential threat to James I's successors since he also descended directly from the Tudors.

after all had been Mary Queen of Scots' keeper for many years and both she and Arabella's paternal grandmother, Margaret Douglas, knew the Tower from inside on account of unwelcome marriages. But it looks very much as if their differences at that time were mainly caused by Arabella's disturbed mind.

Queen Elizabeth was greatly perturbed when in January 1603 rumour reached her that Arabella was in secret contact with the Seymour family, intent on contracting a marriage. So vague was the story that some thought Edward Seymour was the chosen one and others that it was his younger brother William, a boy of fifteen. Sir Henry Brounker was immediately dispatched to Hardwick Hall to find out what truth there was in this potentially dangerous match. To him we owe most of the information about Arabella's state of health and more so of mind. He had long conversations with her, but far from getting any information he found her agitated and distracted. When he asked her to put on paper what was in her mind a rambling document resulted. In despair he reminded her that the Queen was anxiously awaiting concrete information and that she should write a letter fit to be submitted to her Majesty. Still she was in no state to comply and produced an effusion 'obscure, in truth ridiculous', showing that 'her wits were distracted throughout'.[43] Her letters in the next few weeks which have survived show how deranged she was. Her biographer, Bradley, wrote:

She can hardly hold the pen, while her words cannot be taken as containing any real meaning. The mysterious lover and suitor of whom one now or later never hears the name is doubtless a blind . . . It is admissible to wonder whether the poor lonely woman had really conceived a fancy to some unknown person, possibly the deceased Earl of Essex.[44]

There was no deep plot, no suitor in reality, it was all a figment of her imagination and wandering mind. How could she otherwise think of the beheaded Essex as her lover ? She was the victim of her delirious mind and, as so often happens, the people around her were hard put to to know where reality ended and delusion began, what to believe and how to handle the situation. One understands better why she and her grandmother were on such bad terms at the time. Brounker had to return to London without anything tangible to pacify Queen Elizabeth's fears.

But Arabella was now not only mentally but also physically seriously ill. Her grandmother wrote to Sir Robert Cecil: 'Arbell hath been very sick with extreme pain of her side . . . I was in great fear for her. She hath had a doctor of physic with her a fortnight together . . . but finds still little ease.'[45] And she added, 'She is so willfully bent, and there is so little reason in most of her doings, that I cannot tell what to make of it.'[46] Her charge became so unmanageable that she again wrote to Cecil 'humbly to beseech her Majesty to have compassion' and send Brounker again to take her away.

The answer she received shows that the court was equally at the end of its tether: 'it is almost impossible to make judgment of whom or what she meaneth (so many contrarities appearing) . . . it will be hard to resolve precisely what should be done.'[47] A few days later she renewed her plea 'for her speedy remove. It may be the change of place will work some alteration in her.'

Arabella herself soon started to harangue Sir Henry Brounker in long epistles which make little sense except when she ends by describing her symptoms: 'I finding myself scarce able to stand on my feet, what for my side and what for my head.'[48] Her next effusion makes her state of mind still clearer. It ends: 'I think the time best spent in tiring you with the idle conceits of my travelling mind, till it make you ashamed to see into what a scribbling melancholy (which is a kind of madness and there are several kinds of it) you have brought me.'[49] 'We are sorry to find,' wrote Cecil to Bess, 'by the strange style of Lady Arabella's letters, that she hath her thoughts no better quieted.'[50]

This was the middle of March and a few weeks later Queen Elizabeth died. James, having ascended without trouble, held nothing against Arabella, released her from confinement under her grandmother, granted her a pension and stipulated only that she should not marry without his consent. She had now recovered both physically and mentally and was readmitted to court life as the first lady of the land after James's Queen. But it took her all summer to convalesce and she repeatedly complained of her bad eyes and that they were 'extreamely swolne'.[51] Sunshine may have affected her face, as it did James's.

The next serious attack of which information survives was in the spring of 1611. The year before it had been rumoured again that she was engaged to marry William Seymour, now aged twenty-two. This time there was substance to it. Both were called before the Privy Council. Despite their denials and promises they were secretly married in July 1610. It was not long before the news reached James's ears. No good was likely to come of it. Wrote a contemporary: 'The great match which was lately stolen betwixt the Lady Arabella and young Beauchamp provides both of safe lodgings; the Lady close prisoner at Sir Thomas Parry's house at Lambeth, and her husband in the Tower.'[52] The pair however managed to keep in communication, probably through bargemen on the Thames, which connected Sir Thomas's house with the Tower. James soon learnt of it and decided this time to take no further risk. He ordered her into the custody of the Bishop of Durham, far enough afield to be out of her husband's reach.

At this precise moment, in March 1611, she fell ill again. The Bishop reported that he had received his prisoner, the Lady Arabella Seymour, at Lambeth Ferry on 14 March and conveyed her to Highgate en route for the North. But they could not proceed, she was 'so weak that it would occasion her death to be removed any further'.[53] After six days she had to be moved to a house in Barnet only a few miles away. The Bishop reported to the Privy Council that 'the Lady Arabella travelled hither, but was very ill on the journey'.[53] Because of her 'ghastly sickness' they were 'compelled the use of the means prescribed, which were employed with all decency and respect'[54] – alluding delicately to the administration of medicines by glysters because of her uncontrollable vomiting. At the end of the journey she had to be lifted from the litter as if she were dead and remained in a state of stupefaction and oblivion, that is coma.

The Privy Council immediately ordered Dr Thomas Moundeford, President of the Royal College of Physicians and physician to both James and Arabella, to investigate. Her illness occurred at too opportune a moment for James not to be understandably suspicious. Dr Moundeford confirmed the Bishop's fear for her life and declared her totally unfit to continue her journey north. The Earl of Shrewsbury wrote to Dr Moundeford on 22 March:

Good Mr. Dr. – I very heartily thank you for your letter, but I am very sorry to hear, as I do, of the increase rather than Diminution of that hon'ble Lady's Weakness and Indisposition of her body, which no doubt is far worse by the disquiet of her mind.[55]

Still James was not satisfied and sent another physician, Dr John Hammond, to make sure she was not feigning. James himself was an expert in such matters and had personally examined in collaboration with Dr Hammond a number of girls suspected of being the victims of witchcraft, and it was an important aspect of their examination to exclude the possibility that these poor creatures were 'counterfeiting'.[56]

Dr Hammond therefore went to work with great care. To his thoroughness we owe the information that Arabella's urine was discoloured. He first entered into 'a discourse' with her about 'her weaknesses and infirmities', that is he took a medical history. He found her 'assuredly very weak, her countenance heavy, pale and wan' and he 'had a sight of her urine and felt her pulse . . . by neither of these,' he informed Dr Moundeford, 'could he warrant either amendment of her grief, or continuance of her life . . . He was inforced to insist in cordials to cherish her to live.'[57] The following day, he found her still dangerously ill, her pulse 'dull and melancholy and her water bad, showing very great obstructions' – that is deeply discoloured. Yet she was 'free from any fever or any specific sickness [that is, one with which he was familiar] and of his conscience he protested she was in no way to travel until God had restored her to some better strength both of body and mind.'[58]

As both physicians agreed that she really was seriously ill James granted her a month's grace, from 25 March, before proceeding to her safer confinement. Meanwhile Sir James Croft was sent to be her custodian and he

reported on 31 March to Lord Salisbury that 'Lady Arabella dressed herself as well as her extreme weakness would permit, and showed readiness to
remove . . . She has had a violent attack in her head.'[59] She was getting over
the attack and was 'somewhat better and lightsomer than heretofore . . .
but she hath as yet not walked the length of her bedchamber . . . neither
do I find her at any time otherwise than in her naked bed, or in her clothes
upon her bed. Concerning her ladyship's mind, it is so much dejected as
she apprehendeth . . . always the worst.'[60]

Not until May had she recovered so far that her departure to Durham
was fixed for early June. She now wrote letters to James imploring him to
recognize her marriage and let her rejoin her husband. But James remained
adamant, and Arabella saw no way out but escape. Disguised as a man, she
secretly left the house, but was still so weak on her legs that as she mounted
a horse which was waiting for her the innkeeper remarked that this 'gentleman' would hardly hold out to London. She made for Greenwich, from
where the couple had planned to flee to France. But the gods were not on
Arabella's side. Before she met her husband she was caught. Her husband
was luckier. He reached France and after her death returned to England and
a successful life. The gates of the Tower closed behind her. Her faithful
physician, Dr Moundeford, suspected of being an accomplice in her escape,
was sent as 'a close prisoner at the Gatehouse' and her custodian Sir James
Croft was 'committed to the Fleet'.[61]

She survived in the Tower for four years, where she continued to have
attacks similar to those of 1603 and 1611. She wrote: 'I have been sick even
unto death, from which it hath pleased God miraculously to deliver me . . .
but find myself so weak,' and again, 'I wish your Lordship would in a few
lines understand my misery, for my weakness is such that writing is very
painful to me.'[62] In March 1613 she was 'ill of convulsions and said to be
distracted'.[63] A Dr Palmer visited her there and found her 'far out of frame
this Midsummer moone'.[64] In September 1614 the Council learnt that
'The Lady Arabella, prisoner in the Tower, is of late fallen into some indisposition of body and mind.'[65] Twelve months later she died.

James ordered an examination of the body, perhaps because shortly
before Sir Thomas Overbury had been poisoned in the Tower. It was performed by Dr Moundeford, assisted by other eminent physicians. Their
report is preserved in the annals of the Royal College of Physicians of
London. It runs:

The cause of her death was a chronic and long sickness; the species of
disease was 'illam jamdiu producem in cachexiam', which increasing as well
by her negligence as by refusal of remedies (for a year she would not allow
doctors to feel her pulse or inspect her urine). By lying in bed she got bed-
sores and confirmed unhealthiness of liver and extreme leanness and so died.[66]

Moundeford must have taken a special interest in Arabella's discoloured urine, otherwise he would not have been piqued at not being allowed to inspect it. It was an extraordinary remark to put into a postmortem report. Did he have King James in mind, whose physician together with Mayerne he also was and of whose Alicante wine-coloured urine he must have known? We do not know. But we do know that with true Victorian delicacy and prudery Arabella's nineteenth-century biographers purged from their quotations all mention of urine both in her lifetime and from the postmortem report, without as much as indicating by the customary three stops that something was omitted. And her many later biographers to our very day left it at that. In medical detection it pays to go back to original sources.

Porphyria, then, must have come down to Arabella and to James from their common great-grandmother Margaret Tudor (1489–1541), daughter of Henry VII. Her daughter Margaret Douglas, Countess of Lennox, Arabella's grandmother, must have transmitted it, and indeed seems herself to have had some of the characteristic symptoms. A neat piece of evidence is contained in a letter to Lord Cecil of January 1567/8. It 'gives information of an important nature in her biography,' says Strickland, 'for she acknowledges as constitutional the same malady which subsequently proved mortal to her; thereby . . . exonerating an enemy generally accused of poisoning her'. She wrote:

Good Mester Sekretary – I am sorry my hap was not to meet you at my last being at Court; and although I was not well in health at the time, I am worse at this present of my old colic, or else I had been [had come] in place of my letters . . . Your assured friend Margaret Lennox.[67]

We have already seen that Margaret Tudor's son, James V, grandfather of James VI & I, showed symptoms pointing to porphyria. These gain significance from the knowledge that he was a carrier of the disorder. From him his daughter Mary Queen of Scots inherited this Tudor legacy.

HENRIETTA ANNE DUCHESS OF ORLEANS (1644–70)

Before leaving George III's ancestors two seventeenth-century Stuarts, four and five generations removed from Mary Queen of Scots, may briefly be mentioned. Their illnesses fall into the pattern, although astonishingly little medical information is available for Queen Anne despite her frequent bouts of invalidism.

Henrietta Anne, youngest daughter of Charles I, sister-in-law of Louis XIV, was married to his only brother Philippe Duke of Orleans and Anjou. She lived at the French court in a whirl of dissipation not on the best terms with a jealous husband. She patronized Racine and Molière and was active in political intrigues. She had just returned from England in the summer of 1670 where she had negotiated the secret Treaty of Dover, also known as the 'Traité de Madame' between her brother Charles II and Louis XIV, when at the age of twenty-six after a short illness she unexpectedly died. Suspicion of having connived at poisoning her fell on her husband and according to the *Gentleman's Magazine* all Europe believed this.[68]

Her illness started in June.[69] She had been depressed in spirits for some days and had complained of lassitude and pain in her side and stomach. It was a very hot day when she suddenly became much worse and to relieve the pain went bathing in the Seine against her physicians' advice. On getting out of the water she collapsed. She was given chicory water to drink and this was later taken to have been the vehicle of poison, although it was her habitual drink. She started to vomit, pressed her hands to her side and in great distress cried: 'Oh, what a stitch in my side! oh, what a pain, I cannot bear it.' She lost the use of her legs and had to be carried to her bed. With tears in her eyes she said she suffered inconceivably from terrible pain in the pit of the stomach and screamed more than ever, rolling from one side to the other. Vomiting persisted and she soiled her bed. They called a doctor who pronounced it an 'ordinary, simple colic'. But Henrietta Anne said she knew her disease better than the physician and that she would die. She made 'horrible efforts to vomit' which made 'Monsieur', her husband, say: 'Madame, do your best to vomit that this bile may not choke you.' But the agony of her pain persisted 'as severe as ever, but she had no longer the strength to cry'. Hiccough seized her and 'after 8 howers infinite torment in her stomach and bowels shee died, the most lamented'.[70] Nothing 'unnatural' was found at the postmortem examination.

Her fatal illness did not come out of the blue. After her death her brother-in-law, Louis XIV, said that 'above three years since, she very often complained of a pricking pain in her side, which forced her to lie down three or four hours together on the ground, finding no ease in any posture she placed herself in'. Only a few weeks before her death on her journey to England she was ill, her digestion considerably impaired so that she could only take milk, felt prostrate and could not sleep.

She had been ill earlier. At the age of eighteen she could not walk for some weeks and had to be carried in a litter, lost weight and could not sleep. In 1688 her health again gave rise to anxiety. Her husband wrote to Charles II, with whom she had a regular correspondence:

Madame begs me to excuse her to you that she does not write; but for six days she has had head-aches so violent that she has her shutters always closed; she has been bled in the foot, and has tried many other remedies, but they have not relieved her at all.

Her mother Henrietta Maria, who lived in Paris, apparently thought that only praying could restore her daughter to health, as appears from a letter Charles II addressed to Henrietta Anne on 7 May 1668:

> I will not go about to decide the dispute between Mam's Mass and Mr. de Mayerne's pills, but I am sure the suddenness of your recovery is as near a miracle as anything can be. And though you find yourself very well . . . have a care of your diet . . . Above all . . . of strong broths and gravy in the morning.[71]

Mayerne's pills seem to have been a family nostrum because he himself was dead by then, but he had attended, besides Henrietta Anne's grandfather James I, her grandmother Anne of Denmark, her uncle Henry Prince of Wales, her aunt Queen Elizabeth of Bohemia and some of her children, and her father Charles I while he was still Duke of York. Mayerne's journals may justly be called the medical annals of the court of England of that period.

The many panegyrics in verse and prose expressing grief at Henrietta Anne's untimely death made John Wilmot, Earl of Rochester, exclaim: 'never was anyone so regretted since dying was the fashion'. She had two daughters: Anne, who married into the House of Savoy, and the elder, Marie Louise, who became the Queen of Charles II of Spain. She died at the age of eighteen of a mysterious illness, which, it was said, tragically resembled her mother's, and like her she was rumoured to have been poisoned, although some attributed her death to the stifling air of the Spanish court. She had been ill for only three days 'with stomach-ache, nausea, diarrhoea and a feeling of suffocation'.[72] Her husband remarried but again had no children. It was the choice of a successor which led to the political struggle which caused the War of the Spanish Succession.

QUEEN ANNE (1665–1714)

Queen Anne, James I's great-granddaughter, was from the age of twenty a victim to 'flying gout'. It could hardly have been ordinary gout which afflicted her so cruelly all her life. In her limbs it gave rise to pain and weakness, so that she could not stand or walk and often had to be carried, as she was to her coronation at the age of thirty-nine. At thirty-three she told the Duchess of Marlborough that 'the gout is now in my knee as well as my foot, and this time I am a perfect cripple . . . my spirits . . . are indeed mightily sunk with this bad pain, and . . . it is impossible to help having the spleen when one is in such misery.'[73] A year later, in 1699, she explained: 'My not coming yesterday to London was not occasioned by any return of the gout, but it has left so great a weakness in my foot and knees, that I thought if I deferred my journey . . . till next week I should be better able to bear it.'

In 1702 she would have come to town 'if I were able to stir, but when that will be God knows, for my fever is not quite gone and I am still so lame I cannot go without limping'. In 1703 she was still so lame that she 'can hardly walk the length of a room, and that with two sticks'. In October 1706 she mentioned to the Duchess 'a return of my Grips' and being 'really so dispirited for some days' that she could not write. In 1711 she informed the Earl of Oxford that she was unable to open Parliament 'for though I thank God that I am much better than I was, I am not out of pain and the weakness always continues a good while'. The same year she told the Earl: 'I have been in so much pain all the last night and this day . . . If it please God to send me a tolerable good night I intend to write you . . . tomorrow.' Jonathan Swift noted: 'The Queen . . . I fear will be no long liver; for I am told she has sometimes the gout in her bowels.'[74] In July 1711 he wrote: 'The Queen has been extremely ill, so as for four and twenty Hours People were in great Pain; but she hath been since much better, and voided Abundance of Gravel.'[74] In February 1713 he noted that she had gout in the stomach and was lame. At that time she was also tormented with gout in her elbow.

'Gout in the stomach' gave her indigestion and 'hysterical affections'. They called it the vapours when it went to her head. Swift recorded 'she had an Aguish & feaverish Fitt'.[75] She had rigors and convulsions. But between attacks, 'whenever not incapacitated by muscular infirmity occasioned by access of gout or dropsy', she was 'indefatiguable' hunting the stag.[76] She also endured, it is said, seventeen unsuccessful pregnancies and the death at the age of eleven of her third and only surviving child, William Henry, Duke of Gloucester. In 1713 she was 'so much tired with the little fatigue of yesterday' that she told the Earl of Oxford she could not undertake going to St Paul's.[73]

She died in coma at the age of forty-nine. 'Her constitutional gout flew to the brain, and she sank into a state of stupefaction, broken by occasional fits of delirium.'[77] The great Dr John Radcliffe was called to her last illness but refused to attend. He commented: 'Here we are all in the dark, as well as her doctors. At first they said it was an ague, and then gave her Jesuits bark [quinine]. She took but three doses, and that was left off; so that I suppose they found it no ague, or else she would have taken more or none at all. Then it was conjectured to be the gout in her stomach; and now it is thought to be the gout all over,' and he added sarcastically, 'excepting the joints'.[78]

'Her life will never be justly judged,' wrote a commentator, 'if its sufferings are left out of account'[79] – which is as true of her as of some of her relations. It is even possible that the phrase 'Queen Anne is dead' gained currency from her frequent severe illnesses, when 'the gout vibrated fearfully through the Queen's frame from her feet to her stomach' and led to rumours that she had died.

14

The House of Hanover

Coming to George III's own generation, his youngest sister, born four months after their father's death, was nine years old when he ascended the throne in 1760. She was thirteen and a half when at the conclusion of long negotiations he announced in January 1765 in the Speech from the Throne at the opening of Parliament:

> I have now the satisfaction to inform you that I have agreed with my good brother the King of Denmark to cement the union which has long subsisted between the two crowns by the marriage of the Prince Royal of Denmark with my sister the Princess Caroline Matilda, which is to be solemnized as soon as their respective ages will permit.[1]

A ball was given to celebrate the betrothal – it was her first appearance in public. Their ages having advanced by twelve months, George III petitioned Parliament for a marriage portion for her. Denmark and Norway were still united and powerful, since the duchies of Schleswig and Holstein had not yet been annexed by Prussia. Relations with Britain needed strengthening to check the growing influence of Catholic France and of Catherine the Great's Russia, to increase British prestige in the Baltic and add to the security of the Protestant religion. Royal marriages were nothing if not timely instruments of diplomacy.

In October 1766 Caroline Matilda, unenthusiastic from the start about the prospects before her, was married at the Chapel Royal, St James's Palace, her brother the Duke of York standing proxy for the bridegroom. Tears streamed down the hardly adolescent bride's face as she took leave of her friends, family and country the following day and, accompanied part of the way by a small entourage, set out for Copenhagen. They were the first of many the 'Queen of Tears' was to shed. 'The poor Queen of Denmark,' wrote Mrs Carter on 4 October 1766 to Miss Talbot, 'is gone out alone into the wide world: not a creature she knows to attend her any

further than Altona. It is worse than dying . . . they have been telling me
how bitterly she cried in the coach.'

Arrived in the capital of her kingdom she set eyes for the first time on her
husband. She saw a small – some said diminutive – youth of unprepossess-
ing appearance only two months older than herself. On the death of his
father Frederick V six months earlier he had ascended the Danish throne
as Christian VII. The young couple were first cousins, his mother being
Louisa, sister of Frederick Lewis, Prince of Wales, father of George III
and Caroline. She died in 1751 and King Frederick had remarried, so that
awaiting Caroline Matilda was a stepmother-in-law, the Dowager Queen
Juliana Maria of the house of Brunswick-Wolfenbuttel. The coronation
took place with great pomp in May 1767. The following January a son was
born who succeeded in 1808 as Frederick VI, and in July 1771 a daughter,
Louisa Augusta, named after her two grandmothers.

Poor bewildered Caroline Matilda found she had exchanged the unevent-
ful nursery at Kew for the turmoil of a gay, pleasure-seeking court, and
the warm shelter of her family for a cold, dissipated husband who neglected
her for his amusements. While her husband's mental state steadily deteriorated, until eventually he fell into 'idiocy and imbecility', she became em-
broiled in court intrigues and enmeshed in a struggle for power between
rival factions. The story has often been told, and the composer Meyerbeer
even wrote incidental music for it. Struensee, the revolutionary, the unscrupulous, power-seeking upstart, had ensnared her, and she, he and an
accomplice were tried. The two men paid the ultimate penalty. The Queen
– six months before her twenty-first birthday – was imprisoned in the fort-
ress of Kronborg, Hamlet's castle near Elsinore. There she was kept like an
ordinary convict until George III, through his envoy Sir Robert Murray
Keith, threatened Denmark with naval war. It was no empty threat. An
official document gives the list of the ships about to sail for Copenhagen
and the whole fleet was ready under the command of Sir Charles Hardy.[2]
George III demanded not only that his sister be set at liberty forthwith and
retain her title, her divorce not made public, and a pension granted her, but
that all in all she be treated with the respect due to an English princess.
The Danish court was not deaf to the British lion's roar and immediately
fell into line. An English ship landed to take her away, not to England as
she hoped, but to Celle, an old town in the King's Hanoverian dominions,
not far from Hanover. She never saw her children again, nor her native
land, and lived a quiet, simple, charitable life in the castle for the rest of her
days. But her days were numbered.

Little reached the outside world of life in exile at Celle. The curtain
seemed finally to have come down on the tragedy when news of her sudden
death in May 1775 shocked the world. It appeared so 'unnatural' – she was
twenty-three and a half – that wild rumours spread she was the victim of

poison which a kitchen boy had poured into a cup of chocolate. To scotch these rumours, her attendants were interrogated and her chaplain wrote an account of her last days. These depositions of eye-witnesses together with the reports of her physicians to the Hanoverian authorities and to George III direct, preserved in the family archives at Hanover, provide sufficient detail to reconstruct the illness.

Suspicion of having instigated the crime fell on Denmark because a restoration plot was afoot, as was subsequently revealed. In the autumn of 1774 Sir Nathaniel Wraxall, self-appointed negotiator, had been approached by liberal-minded Danes in exile with a plan to restore the banned Queen to reign in place of her now totally incapacitated husband. This position had been usurped by her stepmother-in-law, the Dowager Queen Juliana. She and her circle had reversed the progressive measures introduced by Struensee and opposition to her repressive regime was growing. Anglophile Danes also wanted to see Danish foreign policy, as had been intended in Caroline Matilda's time, which had since veered towards France, re-aligned with Britain. For the plan to succeed it was essential to secure Caroline's willingness and George III's blessing and promise to intervene actively if necessary; in Denmark the ground had also to be prepared. Wraxall therefore travelled busily between the three centres. He had arrived in London from Celle in April 1775 and was awaiting George III's final approval of the proposals he had brought, when news of Caroline Matilda's death put an end to the ambitious project.[3]

Though it sounds more like an adventure story, the episode was in fact real. It is even known what George III felt about it. Six years later in 1781 in a letter to Lord North he wrote:

Lord North's supposition that the letter he transmitted this morning came from Mr. Wraxall, the member for Hindon, proves very just by former letters I have received from him ... Lord North ... may see the gentleman, and settle with him any just demands he can have. Undoubtedly he was sent over by the discontented nobility of Denmark, previous to the death of the late Queen my sister, with a plan of getting her back to Copenhagen, which was introduced to me with a letter from her. Her death, and my delicate situation, having consented to her retiring into my German dominions, prevented me from entering eagerly into this project.[4]

Wraxall had written to ask for £500 to cover his expenses incurred in the venture.

Naturally against this background of conspiracy rumour had it that the Dowager Queen Juliana, finding her position threatened, plotted to do away with her rival. But Caroline Matilda's physicians and attendants were perfectly satisfied that her disease was natural, and so was George III that she died 'of a putrid fever and sore throat'.[4] From Wraxall's visits to Celle in the last months of her life we know she was in flourishing health at least until a few weeks before she fell ill. Her spirits were high as she saw the end of captivity approaching and the prospect within reach of rehabilitating her reputation and being reunited with her children. Clearly she did not suffer from a lingering disease.

May 1775 was exceptionally hot. On the 5th she was not well but took a walk in her beautiful French gardens (still to be enjoyed today), which some called the 'jardin anglais'. She had to return to the castle but found her legs would not carry her, so that she needed help to mount the steps. 'I am so weary,' she said to her maid, 'I must pull myself together, but I can't.' A rash appeared on her arms but vanished on the fourth day. She started to vomit and her throat felt queer. She was sleepless, complained of headache, became restless, and when she attempted to get out of bed could not raise herself. Her pulse rose to twice its normal rate and ultimately became uncountable. Her speech was at first rapid, but soon she began to ramble, and her voice became weak and finally incomprehensible as she seemed unable to move tongue or throat. Towards the end she lay motionless and sank into coma, and she died in the evening of 10 May.

Her chaplain, Pastor Lehzen – father of Queen Victoria's governess – stayed with her throughout the illness. The physicians had warned him to expect a fearful death struggle owing to the overwhelming nature of the infection. But what he saw was 'a spectacle the like of which I have never witnessed'. During her last hours

her speech became softer, indistinct, more difficult to understand . . . one could hardly make out what she meant. Then it became less and less . . . until eventually her tongue lay motionless in her mouth. Her restlessness gave way to a kind of dozing. She appeared like a sleeping person with only slight and occasional jerks as if she had vivid dreams. She remained free from convulsions which we all had dreaded. Her breathing became slower and slower and deeper and deeper, but there was nothing resembling a death rattle. If one moved a little away from her bed it sounded like the breathing of a person in a deep sleep. There was no flicker of movement in her face . . . All of a sudden she had drawn her last breath. One could not help but expect that another breath would follow. But in vain. I have in all my experience never seen a dissolution so devoid of all terror . . . Her arms were resting by her side all the time, she lay in her bed without a flicker, as she had been for I don't know how long.[5]

Her pastor may well never before have witnessed death due to paralysis of vital centres, which he so accurately pictured, because it is very rare. Her physician, Dr Polycarpus Friedrich von Leysser, seems to have realized at the very beginning that her illness was most unusual and alarming, since on the second day he called in George III's physician in ordinary at the court of Hanover, the *Leibmedicus* Dr Johann Georg von Zimmermann.[6] It is an extraordinary coincidence that this scholarly and internationally known doctor later treated several of George III's sons in their attacks of the same disorder, as well as Frederic the Great.

They diagnosed 'a putrid spotted fever' – typhus. This is sometimes also called 'miliary fever' and, bedevilled by a printer's error, has gone into accounts of Caroline Matilda's death as 'military fever'. Epidemics were well recognized and had ravished Europe for centuries. But there was no outbreak at the time she was supposed to have succumbed to it, and how she acquired it remained a mystery. A garbled version was put out that she caught it from looking at a page in his coffin who had died of a fever and sore throat the day before she fell ill. Her maid did not accept this story. She told Wraxall, 'I neither believe a body could communicate any infection, nor that she stayed long enough, had there been any, to receive it.' But Caroline Matilda told her maid the next morning that the image of the dead page had filled her with terror all night.[7] Her disturbed night may well have been a sign of beginning delirium, but to her physicians it suggested the cause of her illness. It has long since been discovered that typhus is not contagious in this way and only follows the bite of a louse. And what is known of the page's illness makes it certain that it was not typhus. Lastly, an infection of this kind could not take effect within hours.

The shrewd Wraxall also did not believe her doctor's diagnosis, albeit history books accepted it. He wrote:

She was of a very full habit . . . [and] had been twice attacked with fever, similar to that which carried her off, in the course of the year preceding her decease. The month of May 1775 began with very warm weather; and the Queen who was accustomed to use violent exercise, had probably overheated her blood by walking. When these particulars are impartially considered, they sufficiently explain the cause of her death, without having recourse to poison or infection.[8]

Wraxall was quite right in taking her earlier medical history into account. It worried her physicians also that this was the third attack of the same kind within a few months. They reported to George III the day before she died that 'Their anxieties were greatly increased by the fact that she had had two similar attacks with fever and a skin rash from 18 to 24 November last year and again from 24 December to 7 January this year and by recurring these attacks become increasingly dangerous.'[9] Caroline Matilda knew this too when she said to Dr von Leysser on the second day, 'This time you cannot save me, I know I shall die.' This of course makes an infection very unlikely and altogether rules out typhus fever. The clinical picture however would fit that of an acute attack of porphyria, starting with a rash on her exposed arms, followed by an ascending type of muscular paralysis which quickly spread to vital nerve centres and brought her breathing and heartbeat to a standstill.

It is significant that even earlier in her life she had had milder attacks of an obscure nature. When her mother came to visit her in Denmark in June 1770 she was prevented from going to meet her in Schleswig because of a sudden indisposition. Since it had passed as suddenly as it had appeared some thought she was feigning. What she actually had was an attack of colic, with which her brother's attacks so conspicuously also started. We know this from a report the English envoy, Gunning, sent to London in September 1770 when she had another attack: 'I had the mortification to find her Majesty was so much indisposed by a fresh attack of cholick as to render my admission to her impracticable.' Earlier still, in October 1769, she had been ill and so depressed that she would not listen to her physicians, refused medicines, 'turned her face to the wall and prayed for death'.[10] Gunning sent the following dispatch to London:

> I am extremely sorry to acquaint your Lordship that the state of the Queen of Denmark's health has lately presented some very unfavourable symptoms; which have given such apprehensions to her physicians, as to make them think that a perfect reestablishment may be attended with some difficulty . . . I cannot help desiring your Lordship to represent to his Majesty that, though there appears no immediate danger, yet the situation the Queen of Denmark is at present in is too critical not to make it highly necessary to obviate worse symptoms . . . I believe that she would be wrought upon by nothing more successfully than by some affectionate expostulations from the King, upon the very great importance of her life.[10]

It is not known whether and what George III wrote to cheer her up. Fate had something different in store for the hapless Queen. Her husband insisted that she be seen by his own physician. He may have delivered her from that attack, but it was he who precipitated her into disaster. He was Johann Friedrich Struensee, who, before he flung himself into politics which cost him his head, had practised as a physician. It was their first meeting.

Among the obituaries of Queen Caroline Matilda preserved in the Hanoverian family archives is an anonymous article describing the deep sorrow and grief of the people of Celle. 'The death of this amiable princess,' lamented the author, 'most strikingly reminds one of that of Henrietta, Duchess of Orleans in the last century.'[11] They were, it is true, of the same age, both had two children, both died rapidly of an unexplained illness and both were rumoured to have been poisoned. What the writer could not have known is that they both died of the same hereditary disorder.

Caroline Matilda and George III were known for their 'infinite likeness of countenance'. Contemporaries also remarked on a peculiar quickness of speech which they both showed when excited.

GEORGE IV (1762–1830)

Greater contrast of character, habits and conduct of life than between George III and his eldest son can hardly be imagined. Yet their medical histories show much similarity, save only that George IV did not suffer from episodes of obvious derangement. In essence the attacks which incapacitated him periodically from his teens throughout his life consisted of abdominal colic, painful weakness of the limbs so that at times he was almost paralysed, and excitability and impulsiveness or lowness of spirits. Both father and son were dangerously ill for short periods, but each attack was followed by prolonged debility. They started with 'hurry and flurry' and on several occasions they were both affected at the same time. Both went blind at the same age from cataract, but whereas George III became known as 'the blind King', George IV's affliction was hardly known, because it occurred in the last year of his life. Their end however was different. George III died of old age. George IV developed heart disease, to which his intemperance may have contributed.

For the medical biographer there is this great difference: extensive medical records exist for George III but there are none for his son. For this remarkable lack there are a number of reasons. Even of George III's illnesses little would have been known had they not been accompanied by mental derangement. Without it they would not have aroused the interest they did and would have remained his own affair. Even had his son been frankly deranged, public and political life would not have been disrupted as it was in George III's time, because of the decline in the effective power of the Crown. Besides, George IV ascended the throne at the fairly late age of fifty-seven, reigned one sixth of the time his father did and died fourteen years younger.

None of George IV's physicians seems to have left a journal and there is no continuous record of his illnesses, with the exception of what Sir Henry Halford wrote to his wife about his last illness. Any medical records which might have existed would probably have been destroyed, as so many of George IV's own papers were. The papers of Sir William Knighton, who was nearest to him as his secretary, physician and keeper of the Privy Purse, were all burnt by his widow. All one has to go on therefore is what George IV confided in letters to friends or family, and they to him, or what contemporaries noted in their diaries.

With so little readily available information it is not surprising that his biographers have made light and little of his ill-health and have pictured him as a man oversensitive to pain and inclined to evade difficult situations by flight into illness, real or pretended. He is accused of 'indulging' in bloodletting, as in a sport, and taking refuge in large doses of laudanum. But this view of his character cannot be maintained if his medical history is fully appreciated. It would in any case be a very singular bent in a young man for whom the doors to any vice were wide open to seek pleasure in an exercise which is painful, lowering and needs a surgeon to perform.

Far from overdoing his sufferings and 'putting it on', George IV took great care, even precautions, to conceal them – perhaps because he realized, as he must have done, how similar they were to his father's. In fact he admitted his illnesses only to his close friends. To the Countess of Elgin he wrote at the age of thirty-six in 1799, 'I have been between ourselves *very ill indeed*, & it is little known *how ill*.'[12] 'How profoundly kept was the Regent's illness, at least till all shadow of alarm was over,'[13] wrote his daughter Princess Charlotte in 1816. To Lord Liverpool he wrote in 1822 'for two or three days I felt so very unwell, that I began to apprehend that that, which is slowly giving way was coming upon me suddenly ... I write this however *confidentially only to yourself*.'[14] On several occasions he even dissimulated in order to hide that he had an attack. Had not the Duke of Cumberland spread 'a most *villanous* lye' that his illness was *'no other* than that he *was mad'*.[15]

This was in November 1811, when he excused himself from a ball under the pretext of a sprained ankle. 'This took place ten days ago,' wrote W. H. Fremantle to the Marquis of Buckingham,

since which he has *never been out of his bed*. He complained of violent pain, and spasmodic affection; for which he ... took a hundred drops of laudanum every three hours ... which, he says, relieves him from pain: and lays *constantly on his stomach* in bed ... The Duke of Cumberland is going about saying it is all sham ... I think he is so worried and perplexed by all the prospect before him [the approach of the unrestricted Regency] ... it has harassed his mind, and rendered him totally incapable, for want of nerves, of doing anything.

But three weeks later he continued 'very bad' with 'pains in his arms and fingers ... and the loss of all power in them, gave great apprehension of palsy'. On 6 January 1812 he was 'still very unwell, and it is much believed that the attack in his arm is paralytic'. Not until 17 January was 'his first going out after his illness' reported to Buckingham.[16] A few days earlier his daughter had found him 'a great deal thinner, pale ... & a very little hitch in his foot'.[17]

The symptoms of this attack – weakness and pain in his limbs, abdominal colic, sudden onset, loss of weight – impress even the modern layman as something more than gout. Yet this is what his contemporaries thought he was suffering from and biographers have accepted. He is said to have had his first attack in 1806 when he was forty-four.

A very different medical picture emerges from his correspondence. From the age of twenty he had attacks of spasms in the chest, abdominal colic, pain and weakness in his limbs, insomnia, fast pulse, lowness of spirits, states of excitement and 'shattered nerves', and was left languid, wasted and weak. Wraxall, who kept himself almost professionally well informed about Court affairs, noted: 'Long before . . . his thirtieth year he had been bled over a hundred times . . . the first time Dr. Warren was called in . . . [he] declared his pulse could not be counted and resembled a machine completely disorganised.'[18] In March 1781, before he was nineteen, he wrote to his brother Frederick:

the only reason of my not writing to you was that I have been upwards of a month under Sir Richard Jebb's hands, so ill that for two days he was very much alarmed for me . . . I remained cooped up in my bedchamber an entire fortnight without ever tasting anything but barley water or some damned wishy washy stuff of that sort. I was sensible of my danger for those two days when the disorder was at its crisis, and I cannot say I was much affected with any idea except when I thought I never should see either you, my dearest Frederick, or my dear friend Lake again.[19]

In 1787, aged twenty-four, he was 'exceedingly ill'. The *Gentleman's Magazine* reported that on 27 May

About noon His Royal Highness the Prince of Wales was suddenly taken ill with an inward complaint . . . which alarmed his physicians . . . the fever abated but . . . returned so violently . . . as to keep his physicians in anxious suspense.[20]

The Marquis of Ailesbury noted on the King's birthday on 4 June that 'The guns in Park did not fire, that Prince of Wales might not be disturbed'.[21] He had been informed a few days earlier that the Prince of Wales 'was exceedingly ill and worse than Mr. Keate [the surgeon] had ever known him, and besides Sir Richard Jebb and Halifax, Dr. Warren had been called.'[21]

The year 1791 was a year of much ill-health for the Prince of Wales. In May his brother Frederick wrote to him from Berlin:

I cannot let the courier set off without writing a few lines to you to tell you how much I was allarmed at the news of your illness. Warwick Lake, however, has informed me that it is now over, and that you at present require nothing but care and rest. I do not like this kind of attack and beg you for God's sake to take more care of yourself.[22]

Three weeks later the Prince of Wales replied:

As to myself I have been very seriously ill indeed, what with the numberless causes of vexation I have had, & last of all yr. departure, wh. I acknowledge made me suffer more than anything else, & tho' I did everything I possibly cd. to master myself at the time you set out, yet when you was gone I cd. not hold up any longer, but sank under feelings wh. are not easy to be describ'd, & that hurried me on into the violent complaint wh. has more or less hung upon me for some time. I have been blooded five times & not tasted meat ever since you went till within two or three days, & tho' I am near well at present my nerves feel but in a shatter'd state.[23]

In September of the same year he gave his mother a little more detail of his symptoms: 'I have had for some days past a bilious attack, attended with a slight degree of the complaint I suffer'd so much from in the Spring.'[24]

There are further mentions of illness in 1792 and 1793, and in 1796, which left him complaining of 'extreme weakness and lassitude'.[25] This was 'The day after the birth of the Princess Charlotte [when] the Prince was suddenly seized with one of his sudden and mysterious attacks of illness, brought on, no doubt, by the agitation and excitement consequent on the event. The attack, which was very violent, was treated as usual with profuse bleeding . . . The Prince was, or thought he was, in danger of his life.'[26]

In April 1799 his medical attendants sent him to Bath. From there he wrote to his mother:

Perhaps my having been a good deal indispos'd since I have been here, & which always to a certain degree leaves a species of gloomy impression on the mind, makes me consider this place as stupider than it really is . . . I certainly am better & gradually getting better every day, my spasms, from the good effect of the waters, certainly decreasing much as to their violence as well as the frequency of the visits they have been so kind as to make me.[27]

A fortnight later he apologized to the Queen 'for the great stupidity of my letter' and accounted for it by 'my being a little low *still*, owing to the medicines I have been obliged to take to expel my old enemy, *the bile*, & which, thank God, is now accomplish'd, & I feel myself better considerably'.[28] What can have prompted the Prince to speak of expelling the bile and knowing that it was 'now accomplish'd'? He was not jaundiced and therefore cannot have meant that the colour of his skin was paling. This leaves only the surmise that he was alluding in terms fit for the royal ear of his mother to the colour of his urine, a route by which 'bile' was known to be expelled. It is tempting to take this as evidence that during attacks his urine was discoloured.

The Queen was worried that he might take the Bath waters 'improperly' and therefore asked Dr John Turton to write to him. The Prince thanked him for his kind letter and went on:

I have certainly been very unwell since I have been here . . . you know perfectly well though a strong and healthy man by nature . . . still *mine is a very nervous* and so far a *delicate* fibre and that consequently the disorders of the body in general *with me* owe their source to the mind. (This God knows has for some time & a long time too, been too much the case with me, & then any little addition, such as a casual cold, or even any indisposition, no matter how trifling, contributes much to the unhinging the whole system). The waters . . . have been the means of lessening the frequency as well as the violence of my spasmodic attacks . . . and the perseverance will do as much for the spasms which tormented me so much of late.[29]

In 1800, still in this thirties, he was frequently and seriously ill. There was talk in some quarters of his not surviving. In March Fremantle thought, 'it [is] quite impossible he can recover . . . He is reduced beyond idea.'[30] The Prince himself had great apprehensions of approaching sudden death and was copiously and repeatedly bled. In April he wrote of 'a severe return of the spasms on the neck of his bladder'. The explanation for this particular pain is to be found in the discovery, at the postmortem examination, of a congenital diverticulum or pouch in his bladder which contained some hardened matter, evidence that from time to time it became inflamed. In October he had again 'a violent stoppage in my bowels which has given me great pain'.[31]

In 1804, when the King had been seriously ill a short time, the Prince was also suddenly taken ill at Brighton. The Earl of Moira, his friend and staunch supporter, wrote on 5 February to Colonel McMahon: 'Infinite thanks . . . for your having somewhat eased my mind respecting our beloved Prince. With what calamity this country was menaced by his illness,' and to the Prince himself he wrote, perhaps expressing more his personal than the general feeling:

I could not but feel a severely painful shock at the thought that the attack was of a nature which might become formidable. For mercy's sake, Sir, take care of a life so precious not merely to those who are devoted to you but to your country. Believe me, the alarm excited here by the supposed extent of your indisposition proved in the most gratifying manner with what anxiety the public mind fixes itself upon your energy & talents as a resource in the growing difficulties that surround us. Had it not been for the occasion, which was too high a price for the gratification, I should have delighted in the unfeigned exhibition of people's feelings . . . Thank God, the crisis is over.[32]

On 8 February *The Times* reported that the Prince was out of danger. 'There was never known before,' wrote Sheridan to his wife on 27 February, 'anything equal to the agitation of Peoples Minds at this moment [referring to the King's attack], and the Prince just recovered from an illness in which his life was despair'd of for two Days is so nervous and anxious that it is not easy to thwart him tho' he runs a great risk of making himself ill again.'[33]

Glenbervie recorded on 11 February that 'the Prince came to town . . . but as yet not recovered from the illness of which he had a very severe attack at Brightelmstone.'[34] 'He was seized with one of those sudden and mysterious attacks to which he was subject all his life . . . Mrs. Fitzherbert, contrary to her rule, took up her lodgings at the Pavillion in order that she might be nearer the Prince, and she nursed him night and day with unremitting devotion.'[35]

In September 1804 the Dowager Countess of Elgin, governess of Princess Charlotte, reported to the Queen that she had found the Prince 'alass! in the most violent agitation & distress of mind and body. H.R.H. had had a violent cramp and a bowel complaint.'[36]

There was always sufficient reason for contemporaries to attribute the Prince's attacks of sickness to stressful events either in his private or public life. In 1804, not being given permission by the King to go on active service, he had foolishly published the 'Royal correspondence', to the extreme chagrin of his father, who refused to talk to him. Foreign invasion seemed imminent and lastly the King's illness revived once more the excitement and agitation of a possible regency, with all it implied for the Prince.

When he became Regent in February 1811 the Prince, like his father, was very ill. Glenbervie noted that he 'has, during the agitation of these things, had three epileptic fits. He has besides been very ill with sickness, swelled legs, etc. . . . Sir Walter Farquhar has said that the Prince has been very nervous.'[37] He was then within one year the same age as his father when he had his first severe attack in 1788.

At the end of 1811 he had another attack, and what Buckingham knew about it has already been mentioned. 'Lady B[essborough]' wrote to Lord Granville Leveson Gower that

The Prince is, I believe, extremely ill. Farquhar says he suffered such agony of pain all over him that it produces a degree of irritation on his nerves nearly approaching delirium. What will become of us, if as well as our King, our Regent goes mad? It will be a new case in the Annals of history . . . I live in a state of uncertainty and anxiety that stupefies me.[38]

A little later she wrote that the Duke of Cumberland went about 'saying everywhere that his Brother's illness was higher than the foot, and that a blister on the head might be more efficacious than a poultice on the ankle'.[38] And she reported Sir Henry Halford as saying that the Prince Regent 'can hardly write from three of his fingers being compleatly numb'd and useless', which much alarmed the doctor, 'thinking it palsy'.[38]

Twelve months later the Queen wrote to the Prince that she was 'very sorry to learn that gout still continues upon you'.[39] In the autumn of 1813 he wrote to his mother: 'Now that I have recover'd a little the use, both of my senses & my poor hand.'[40] In November Princess Charlotte wrote:

He [her father] was very unwell indeed, wh. is the only excuse to be made for such strange conduct; & was so unwell as to send for Sir Henry [Halford] in the night, who has been 3 times with him today. He is now much better & freer from pain. Sir Henry tells me it was a violent obstruction from irregularity of diet & exercise.[41]

But the attack lasted well into the new year. In January 1814 he wrote: 'After a long and painful confinement, which has scarcely left me strength to hold my pen . . . '[42] In February his daughter wrote to Miss Mercer Elphinstone:

The P.R., I must tell you has been *alarmingly* ill & is *far from* recovered yet. Sir Henry [Halford] says he never saw him so ill in all his life before, & has not scrupled to tell either him or me that another such attack would be *fatal*. It began by a spasm wh. ended in inflammation in his bowels. He was twice blooded & is to be bled all over with leeches, as the pain continues still very great & the pulse high. Sir Henry was 4 times at C[arlton] H[ouse] yesterday . . . He attributes this violent attack to drinking wh. he has been doing a vast deal lately. Laudanum, his old enemy, was administered first, but did not remain in his stomach; however he is dosed with it now to assuage the pain.[43]

Alcohol excess may have brought on an attack of porphyria. As late as March the Duke of Cumberland was grieved 'to the soul' to hear that he was still confined with the gout.[44]

On 24 January *The Times* reported that the Prince Regent was 'recovering from the fit of the gout, which for the time it lasted, was a very sharp one'. Princess Charlotte wrote: 'The P.R. is ill again . . . his legs have dwindled into nothing . . . he talks of having much on his mind & being in a very nervous state.' And a few days later she found him 'vastly better . . . He wheels himself perfectly in a merlin chair . . . He is grown thinner & his legs considerably reduced.'[45] All through the year he suffered from rheumatism, obstruction of the bowels and lowness of spirits.

In 1817, a month after the tragic death of his daughter in childbed, he broke his silence to his mother:

I have been, though without any very serious or actual occasion or call for alarm, still very much & truly indispos'd for the last ten days, & indeed if I were to add for some weeks past, I should be saying no more than the truth. I do not know under what denomination to class the attack, or by what name regularly to define it & call it, for it seems to me to have been a sort of mish-mash, Solomongrundy, Olla podrida kind of a business . . . a good deal of rheumatism, as much of cold, with a little touch of bile to boot . . . In short all this potpourri, has render'd me both bodily as well as mentally quite unfit & indeed quite unable to take up a pen until this day, when I begin to feel myself entering I hope a convalescent state.[46]

A week later he reassured his mother that

I really felt infinitely, infinitely better . . . & I am experiencing hourly amendment . . . that is to say at least my poor stomach does, which I attribute to the having resum'd the use of Brandish's medicine . . . which at present seems . . . to alleviate all those dreadful sufferings I have experienced for some time past.[47]

The year 1820 started fatefully for the royal family. George III died on

29 January, being oblivious that his son Edward had preceded him by one week. The third victim of porphyria was the Prince Regent, now George IV. The day before his father's death he had been taken ill and his condition became rapidly grave so that his life was despaired of. The Princess of Lieven lost no time telling Metternich on 2 February that 'The King is very ill. Heavens, if he should die! Shakespeare's tragedies pale before such a catastrophe. Father and son, in the past, have been buried together. But two Kings!'[48] Creevey wrote to Lord Brougham: 'He is, I apprehend, rapidly approaching death.'[49] And Lord Brougham in turn thought that the King 'has been as near death as any man'.[50]

The first bulletin on 1 February announced: 'The King has been attacked with an inflammation on the lungs. We hope a favourable impression has been made on the complaint [by bleeding]; but His Majesty continues severely indisposed.' Such official language was indeed alarming, and conveyed imminent danger. His symptoms were insomnia, fast pulse, pain in the chest and embarrassed breathing. It was this last symptom which made the physicians think of pneumonia. Had the stethoscope come into general use by then they may well have judged differently. Pain in the chest may occur in porphyria and embarrass respiration. In his early attacks of 1762 and 1765 George III complained mainly of it, in the Duke of Sussex it remained a prominent feature in all attacks and Princess Charlotte had the same symptom. In all it was, at least for a time, mistaken for lung trouble. However, the dangerous state quickly subsided and on 5 February George IV was better. The bulletin of 7 February stated he was 'recovering' so satisfactorily that no more evening bulletins would be issued. On 9 February he was 'almost' and two days later altogether 'free from complaint, but His Majesty will require time to recover his strength'. No more bulletins were issued and his physicians were proud to be able to announce that the inflammation on the lungs had not materialized. They and others were convinced that copious bleeding – 150 ounces was mentioned – had prevented it and saved the patient.

But he was not in a fit state to attend his father's funeral on 15 February. The royal physicians – Sir Henry Halford, Sir William Knighton and Sir Matthew Tierney – wrote to him on 7 February:

We, your Majesty's physicians, venture humbly to approach your Majesty, to implore your Majesty to forego that satisfaction to your feelings which your Majesty attaches to a performance of the last act of filial piety to the late King, your Majesty's father. We are scarcely yet relieved from that state of anxiety and alarm which your Majesty's dangerous illness gave rise to, and from which your Majesty is only just extricated, under the mercy of Heaven.

We cannot therefore contemplate an indulgence of your Majesty's wishes without absolute dismay – seeing the probability of a relapse in consequence of an exposure of your Majesty's person to the night air, in a cathedral, under that anguish of mind which your Majesty was observed by everybody so pain-fully to suffer at the performance of the same sad ceremonies last year [the death of his mother]. And we humbly intreat your Majesty to yield, not to our wishes only, but to those of the whole nation, which would be expressed, we are persuaded, if it were generally known that your Majesty meditated this dangerous effort of respect and piety.[51]

It took him months to recover his strength, as his physicians predicted. At the end of March the Duke of Cumberland wrote to him from Berlin:

The account you give of your returning health is . . . the most gratifying news . . . Nothing proves to me more clearly your returning strength than your handwriting, which appears to me as distinct as ever. That you complain still of being a little nervous does not surprise me.[52]

Contemporaries attributed the severity of his illness to 'agitation of his mind' over his consort Caroline. On his accession she had automatically become Queen of England. This was the very thing he had striven so hard to forestall. It had been the purpose of the 'delicate investigation' in 1807 to obtain a divorce and was soon to be pursued by the 'Bill of Pains and Penalties'. So unbridled was his hatred of her that almost his first action as King was to demand that her name be omitted from the public prayers for the royal family. And, singular as it is, the name of the Queen was banished from the liturgy. How far the vehemence of his behaviour in the first weeks of his reign can be explained – and so at least to a small extent excused – by the excited state of his nerves due to an attack of porphyria is a moot ques-tion. Certain it is that Caroline was not the cause of his illness.

At the end of 1820 he wrote to his brother that he had 'had bile, & my old enemy the gout flying about me . . . which incommoded' him 'a great deal'.[53] In 1822 Princess Lieven reported: 'We left the King very ill; he is tortured by gout and employs the most violent remedies to get rid of it. He looks ghastly . . . is plunged in gloom; he talks about nothing but dying. I have never seen him so wretched; he did everything to pull himself together, but in vain.'[54]

In April 1823 she wrote: 'The King is still in bed and sees nobody but his doctors. He has gout in both knees, the right foot and the left wrist and elbow.'[55] At the same time Sir William Knighton wrote to the Earl of Liverpool: 'The King has written your Lordship one letter today, which is as much as His Majesty could well undertake, for the severity of the pain has left a great languor, besides an embarrassment and weakness of the ner-vous system which precludes the power of much exertion.'[56] In May Princess Lieven wrote:

The Duke of York is the only one who still maintains that the King's health gives no cause for anxiety. Wellington told me that he did not give him eight months to live. I am inclined to think the same . . . It is a fact, since January

6, the King has not enjoyed an hour's health, and often, for three or four weeks at a time, has been very ill indeed. At sixty-two, one does not get over such attacks . . . All eyes are on the Duke of York. The Opposition are furious, for they have nothing to hope from his reign.[57]

In June Mrs Arbuthnot noted in her diary: 'Our King is gone to the Cottage in Windsor Forest to try the effect of country air; he has nearly lost the use of his limbs and cannot walk at all.'[58]

Attacks of pain, spasms, sleeplessness, bowel complaint and nervousness continued and increased in frequency. Indeed, after his accession his health went downhill and fits of rage and temper became more and more a feature of his conduct. His relationships became strained and volatile and even with his trusted secretary Sir William Knighton he fell out from time to time. Mrs Arbuthnot noted in October 1823:

The King began talking about Knighton, abused him & shewed evidently that he feared & hated him as a madman hates his keeper . . . [he] certainly hates him & yet finds him so useful he cannot do without him.[59]

Mrs Arbuthnot's accounts of his relation to Lady Conyngham, and hers to him, leave little doubt that his time was over when passion and lust attracted him to women. What he needed was compassion and a companion in his declining and lonely years. In 1827 he had an attack which particularly affected his left arm and both legs, but Sir Robert Peel stressed in a letter to Sir Henry Halford that he found his mind remained 'composed and tranquil'.[60]

In March 1828 Croker noted that he was

obliged to be carried to and from his carriage; and instead of the open railed gate to the Garden of St. James's, through which His Majesty has driven of late years from the Park, they have in the last two days substituted a close gate to prevent people's seeing the operation of moving His Majesty in and out of his carriage.[61]

In February 1829 'There was a Council at Windsor . . . the King . . . complained a good deal of his health, said he suffered dreadfully from gout & cramp, & Mr. A[rbuthnot] said he thought him dreadfully altered since last year and grown excessively old & infirm.'[62] In May 1829 there was 'no appearance of stone or gravel, but violent irritation . . . only subdued by laudanum' and he 'constantly talked of his brother, the Duke of York, and the similarity of their symptoms and was always comparing them'.[63] The Duke of York had died in 1827 of symptoms indeed very similar.

Many of the symptoms in George IV's last years, such as swollen legs, oppression in the chest on exertion, and increasing languor, pointed to his heart being affected. This was confirmed by the postmortem examination, which showed that his heart muscle was diseased and his blood vessels showed an advanced state of 'ossification' – what today is called arterio-sclerosis. Since attacks of porphyria are accompanied by a rise in blood pressure this development would be in keeping with the diagnosis, although it may have developed independently.

The last illness started in January 1830. The public however was not officially informed until three months later, although the Duke of Wellington advised Sir Henry Halford, who was mainly responsible for the sick-room, not to hold information back. He wrote to him on 18 January: 'I sincerely hope, that the King may feel no farther inconvenience from this Derangement of His Stomach. It is very desirable that the Publick should not be misled on the Subject.'[64] But the diplomatic Sir Henry did not publish the first bulletin until 15 April: 'We regret to state that the King has had a bilious attack, accompanied by an embarrassment in breathing. His Majesty, although free from fever is languid and weak.'

'Bilious attack,' snarled *The Lancet*, established only seven years before, 'is an expression so vague and old-womanish that nothing can be inferred from it.' This was only the overture to a long-drawn-out and acrimonious controversy in its columns after the King's death, with reproaches against the royal physicians – mainly Halford – for withholding information to which the public were entitled. Why, asked the editor, had he not given the King's illness a name? Did he or did he perhaps not realize that he suffered from 'an organic heart disease'?

Little therefore would be known of what went on in the sickroom at Windsor in the King's last months of life were it not that Halford wrote daily to his wife and his letters are preserved in the Halford papers. He lived in the Castle and served the King with great devotion day and night. The letters make distressing reading, and if there is such a thing as expiating one's sins by suffering, George IV went a long way towards it. Confined to his room without sleep for long periods, in great pain and anxiety typical of states of failing circulation, unable to lie down for shortness of breath, with no stomach to eat, his legs swollen and tapped, he lingered on with the aid of opium.

One can understand Halford's reluctance to give details, although Wellington's counsel was to be frank and informative in the bulletins. Wellington wrote to him on 27 April, 'I have just received your letter, and I have thought it best to have the bulletin published. There has been a very general apprehension in respect of the King's health . . . and I am certain that the knowledge of the truth is always the best remedy for such alarms.'[65] All the bulletin contained was: 'The King continued as well as His Majesty has been for several days part, until this morning, when His Majesty is now again better.' But the bulletins continued to give little indication how desperate the King's condition was. All they revealed was that 'the King slept at intervals at night', 'has not slept well' and that his respiration was better, worse or the same. To his wife Halford confided on 21 June: 'H.M. becomes weaker daily – He frightened me yesterday by spitting up blood – as this is probably one of the most likely modes by which His painful existence may be terminated', and he added: 'Our bulletins now admit cough and expectoration.'[66] It actually stated: 'The King's rest has again been broken by the cough & expectoration, and His Majesty feels languid this morning.'

George IV had one more affliction to suffer. In July 1829 he wrote to Sir William Knighton 'my unfortunate eyesight is grown so much more dim . . . that I can scarcely (writing as I am now doing by candlelight) see a single letter that my pen is tracing upon the paper',[56] and in December he wrote again 'though blind as a beetle I endeavour to scribble a few lines'.[67] Greville noted: 'The King has nearly lost his eyesight, and is to be couched as soon as his eyes are in a proper state for the operation. He is in a great fright with his father's fate before him, and indeed nothing is more probable than that he will become blind and mad too; he is already a little of both.'[68] And in February 1830: 'The King very blind – did not know the Lord Chancellor, who was standing close to him, and took him for Peel.'[68] It is known that metabolic disorders such as porphyria predispose to cataract, and besides George III several of George IV's brothers and sisters were likewise afflicted.

In May 1830 he could no longer see to put his sign manual to bills and by an Act of Parliament a stamp was used instead in the presence of three appointed witnesses to whom the King had to signify his assent. Sir Henry Halford, always ready to accept honours and distinctions, hoped to be one of these 'commissioners' but was not chosen.[66]

The sixty-sixth bulletin, on 26 June 1830, stated: 'It has pleased Almighty to take from this world the King's most Excellent Majesty. His Majesty expired at a quarter past three o'clock in the morning, without pain.' Sir Henry, physician to their Majesties King George III and Queen Charlotte, to George IV and Princess Charlotte and later to Queen Victoria, took horse to Bushy Park where he arrived at six in the morning to be the first to inform, and kiss the hand of, his new sovereign, patron and patient, William IV.

PRINCESS CHARLOTTE AUGUSTA (1796–1817)

Unloved and rejected by her father, separated from her mother, tossed about by her parents' discord, Princess Charlotte, only legitimate grandchild of George III, daughter of George IV and heir apparent to the throne, was not much luckier in her inherited constitution.

In May 1816 she married Leopold of Saxe-Coburg, Queen Victoria's maternal uncle. After two miscarriages she was pregnant again and in July 1817 it was announced that a child was expected in October. On 9 October the country was told to expect the happy event in nine or ten days' time. But the date passed without anything happening and a bulletin stated on 21 October that her Royal Highness 'still remains well'. To assuage public anxiety further information appeared in the press:

Claremont, 22 October. Her Royal Highness has occasionally suffered a little from headache, for which it has been necessary, at different times, to extract blood. On one occasion Her Royal Highness submitted to four incisions in the arm without effect in consequence of the veins being deeply buried. On a consultation of the Physicians and Surgeons, it was deemed improper to make any further attempts, and the blood was ordered to be drawn from a vein at the back of the hand, where the operation has several times been successfully performed . . . with great relief to Her Royal Highness.

Her doctors remained confident, and the royal family did not seem to have anticipated anything untoward: her father was shooting in Suffolk, her mother abroad, her old grandmother Queen Charlotte at Bath.

Labour did not start until 3 November. On the morning of the 4th her 'progress was in every respect favourable'; in the evening labour was 'going on very slowly, but we trust favourably'. The following day at 5.30 in the afternoon labour 'has within the last three hours, considerably advanced, and will, it is hoped, within a few hours, be happily completed'. At ten o'clock that night the birth, at nine o'clock, of a stillborn, well-made male child was announced, but the Princess was 'doing extremely well'. Within six hours of delivery she was dead. At six the next morning Lord Sidmouth, who was present as Secretary of the Home Department, informed the Lord Mayor of London 'with the deepest sorrow that . . . Her Royal Highness expired this morning at half-past two o'clock'.

The country was stunned 'as if by an earthquake at the dead of night . . . This melancholy event,' recorded Lord Brougham, 'produced throughout the kingdom feelings of the deepest sorrow and most bitter disappointment . . . it is difficult for persons not living at the time to believe, how universal and how genuine those feelings were. It really was as if every household . . . had lost a favourite child.'[69] Everyone felt the loss of the only direct successor to the throne, everyone was touched by the human tragedy that had befallen the royal family, and every mother-to-be was apt to identify with her fate. The profession was shocked and roused. Charlotte was the first member of the royal family who was delivered by an accoucheur, or 'man-midwife'. Emotions became more confused and unrestrained because of the mystery surrounding the event. There was no satisfactory medical explanation. Controversy, accusations, apologias, discussions, speculation and demands for a full investigation filled the newspapers. A scapegoat had to be found. Jesse Foot, the surgeon, known as a bitter pamphleteer whose jealousy had once turned against the great John Hunter, surgeon-extra-ordinary to George III, took up the campaign and published *Two letters on the necessity of a public inquiry into cause of death of the Princess Charlotte and her infant.*

Naturally the physicians in attendance, Sir Richard Croft and Dr Matthew Baillie, were blamed and in particular Croft, the accoucheur in chief. He was accused of negligence and of mismanaging the confinement and of having delayed too long before calling Dr John Sims, the third of Princess Charlotte's physicians. Malicious aspersions were thrown out that he had prematurely retired from the scene after the child was born and gone to sleep. The Prince Regent, sensible of Croft's unhappy situation, had with admirable magnanimity conveyed to him

His Royal Highness's acknowledgement of the zealous care, and indefatigable attention manifested by Sir Richard Croft towards his beloved daughter during her late eventful confinement; and to express His Royal Highness's entire confidence in the medical skill and ability which he displayed, during the arduous and protracted labour, whereof the issue, under the will of Divine Providence has overwhelmed His Royal Highness with such deep affliction.[70]

But Croft, ostracized by many of his old clientele, never regained his confidence, and when by a fateful chance he found himself a few months later conducting a similar case, took a gun from the wall and shot himself in the patient's home.

What had happened? What had Princess Charlotte died of? The known facts are: after fifty hours in labour she was delivered of a dead boy. The placenta was then removed manually. All seemed well and the physicians retired to the adjoining room. The state dignitaries and the Archbishop of Canterbury, present to witness the birth of a successor to the throne, left. About three hours later Princess Charlotte started to vomit, and when the nurse brought her gruel she was unable to swallow. She continued nauseated and indicated that she had acute pain in the adbomen: 'About one o'clock, the spasms came on, and Her Royal Highness, placing both her hands on her stomach, said "Oh, what pain, it is all here." '[71] Her pulse became rapid and irregular. Extreme restlessness developed and she went into convulsions. Afterwards 'she could not articulate, but sunk into a calm composure, until . . . with a gentle sigh, she expired,'[71] less than three hours later. She was twenty-one.

The *London Medical and Physical Journal* (1817) found her death unexplained and inexplicable. It was not, they argued, due to exhaustion, since 'a labour much longer protracted has often ended happily for mother and child'. Nor was there undue loss of blood. But they wisely singled out one feature: 'During the whole period, and for some time after, no unfavourable symptoms occurred, excepting that her Royal Highness was less exhausted than might have been expected by so tedious a labour and the subsequent events ... [there seemed] no apparent danger, excepting what arose from the almost unnatural composure, not to say cheerfulness, of Her Royal Highness.' Indeed it is an arresting fact that no emotional response to her lifeless infant was observed by anyone. The only possible explanation is that already during labour she had suffered a degree of lightheadedness which impaired her insight and clouded her consciousness. This is also why during her long trial she was never heard to complain or even utter a sigh. Contemporaries, in the awestricken atmosphere of her sudden death, praised this as 'fortitude' and a 'truly humble submission to the will of God'.

However, even before she went into labour, during the early months of pregnancy she had at times, besides headache, 'a morbid excess of animal spirits' – that is states of excitement. These were considered sufficiently serious by her physicians 'to take great care to subdue' by repeated bleedings and other 'lowering' measures such as keeping her on a restricted diet without 'animal food', even without solids.

What was the link connecting her impaired mental state during labour with the periods of excitability and 'agitation' she had shown before ? Was it the same disease process which when mild irritated her nervous system and produced excitement or a manic state, and when more severe impaired her faculties and lowered her awareness, and when at its height caused convulsions and led to paralysis of vital functions and so to death ? Only a look at her previous medical history and a search for other symptoms attributable to an affection of her nervous system can provide the answer.

But first, what other medical contemporaries thought and how her illness and death were interpreted by later physicians.

The *London Medical Repository* (1817) confessed that they too could throw 'very little light upon the immediate cause of death'. They added as the only possible explanation this significant sentence:

We have been informed, that the whole Royal Family are liable to spasms of a violent description, and to this hereditary predisposition and the increased excitability of the amiable Sufferer are we left to ascribe an event which has destroyed the flattering hopes of a nation, and lopped off the fairest stem of its monarchical succession.

There this unaccountable event rested as far as the public were concerned. For the science of midwifery, however, its lesson lived on. The tragedy of 1817 became the classic example of the danger to mother and child if instrumental interference was delayed, and practice changed from the conservative expectant attitude to the dogma of 'early forceps', as it came to be called. Dr W. S. Playfair, in his well-known *Treatise on the science and practice of midwifery* (1878), wrote of the dread of instrumental interference then prevalent . . . It is impossible to read the details of the delivery [of Princess Charlotte] . . . without being forcibly struck with the disastrous results which followed the practice adopted, which, however, was strictly in accordance with that which, up to a quite recent date, has been considered correct by the highest obstetric authorities.

In 1917, on the centenary of her death, *The Lancet* reopened the mystery of this 'tragedy in the annals of English obstetrics' in an editorial headed 'The Vindication of a Medical Reputation'. In the correspondence which followed, the possibility of death from pulmonary embolism or blood clot in the lungs was put forward, only to be rejected. One correspondent rightly drew attention to the fact that the significant finding at the postmortem examination, which the Prince Regent himself had ordered, was not only 'loss of uterine tone', but a general 'atony of the viscera': the stomach was dilated to the extent of holding three pints of fluid, and the large bowel was blown out by air. These findings – we may add today – indicate a general paralysis of vital nerves, that is of the autonomic nervous system, and are consistent with the diagnosis of porphyria.

The case continued to simmer in medical minds and in 1951 Sir Eardly Holland once more reviewed all the available evidence of this 'triple tragedy'. He concluded that obstetricians still could not offer an explanation to clarify what had happened, and he thought it 'unlikely, that there will ever be more exact data for finality'.[72] In this modern authoritarian judgement nothing in her delivery accounted for her death.

To return to the patient. Princess Charlotte's earlier medical history can be gleaned from her own letters and those written about her. From her midteens she had the characteristic attacks of nervous symptoms with abdominal pain and excitability or depression and insomnia followed by exhaustion which her father and grandfather exhibited. Aged sixteen she wrote: 'I am *far from* . . . *well* . . . I sleep but little, or suffer from severe headaches . . . My spirits *rally* but for a *very short time.*' 'I was taken very unwell . . . have been bleeded with leaches, a nasty opperation. . . . I am a good deal pulled down . . . I have been sadly bilious . . . a little would upset me.' At the age of seventeen she was 'suffering from a heavy cold and cough, before wh. I have lost my sleep and appetite.' A little later, 'As to my health and spirits, I cannot say much for either . . . my head aches still very much . . . I am horribly and detestably out of spirits.'[73] Sir Henry Halford reported to the Prince Regent:

The Princess is really not well. She looks ill – and has complain'd for some time past, but more lately of pain in her left side. This is not accompanied, however, with cough. Nor has the Princess difficulty in lying down on either side – nor is the skin hot, tho' . . . the pulse is quick. I am inclined to think it muscular only – but it seem'd prudent to apply a blister.[74]

A week later he found her a little better and thought 'there is more lowness and nervousness . . . than disease itself'.[74]

When Charlotte was eighteen Dr Matthew Baillie reported to her father after visiting her at Weymouth, where she had been sent because of her ill-health, that

she looks better in the countenance than she did a fortnight ago, and has gained a little flesh. Her pulse is still too frequent, for it was yesterday 84 . . . Her Royal Highness complains of distentions of the stomach from indigestion, but has much less of the feeling of constriction in her chest.[74]

She herself wrote:

Last night I had a slight nervous attack again, wh. always affects my spirits as well as my side . . . what I feel on these occasions is oppressed like as if my heart would burst or sigh itself out . . . I must say that I get every day more ignimatical to myself . . . At times I laugh and talk away as *fast* that you would think I had no cares at all.[75]

Being hurried in his speech when an attack was coming on was a feature of George III's early symptoms, as it was with his sister Caroline Matilda. A little later Charlotte was 'rather better . . . but very weak, so much so as to be quite blown and fagged'.[75] Miss Knight, her 'Lady Companion', observed that 'She was much thinner, as she had been reduced by the medicines she had been obliged to take for a pain in her side, occasioned by a bilious disorder, which was erroneously treated as nervous.' She also found her in 'Much agitation, nervous uneasiness and . . . nervous impatience . . . to such a degree as to injure her health.'[76] Charlotte herself mentioned such states repeatedly. 'I am getting over the attack quite well,' she wrote, 'as it is now some days since I got it, and I would not venture upon writing of it all till I was calm and better.'[77] Abdominal colic plagued her, as she told her father in 1816: 'I have been confined to the house with . . . a return of my bilious complaints (which I am sorry to say I am but too liable to).'[78]

A sad, pathetic letter has survived which she wrote on 10 October to her mother in Italy while she was waiting to be confined. It shows that besides spells of excitement she had bouts of severe depression. They cannot be attributed to outside factors. Her family troubles had come to an end with her happy marriage to the man of her choice. They had made their home at Claremont in the country, where they lived away from the bustle of London and to their taste, quietly and almost exclusively for themselves. Yet her letter is full of preoccupation with, even forebodings of, death. She wrote:

Should it be the pleasure of Providence that I servive the hour of approaching danger . . . I fear less to die than to live, the prospect of protracted existence is so blended with dangers and difficulties; so shadowed with clouds and uncertainties, so replete with anxieties and apprehensions that I must shrink from the contemplation of it, and fly for refuge even to the probability of my removal from so joyless an inheritance . . . What cause have I to covet that existence others prize so highly?

And she deplores not being with her mother 'to pour cheerfulness into the sinking heart of her . . . trembling child'.[79]

The medical controversy over this distressing and enigmatic event may now be closed. Although a very rare occurrence, cases have been observed where a fulminating attack of porphyria set in a few hours after confinement with signs of cerebral irritation, spreading paralysis, convulsions and finally respiratory failure. Porphyria had caused a human tragedy and national catastrophe. It was not until the birth of Victoria in 1819 that George III's fifteen children brought forth an heir to the throne.

Is there an explanation why Princess Charlotte's illness started at such early age and was so grave? It could not have been caused by synthetic drugs, which are nowadays known to precipitate fatal attacks of porphyria, because of course they had not been discovered then. Could it have been her inheritance? By its mode of transmission as a dominant Mendelian character she had an even chance of inheriting the disorder from her father. Over and above this her parents were first cousins, so that if her mother also carried the gene Charlotte's risk was doubled. Theoretically, if both her parents were affected, she might even have been endowed with a double inheritance, but such a case has never been observed. It is therefore not known whether it would make the illness show itself earlier or attacks more severe. However, this trend of thought led us to her mother's medical history.

15

The House of Brandenburg-Prussia

Princess Charlotte's mother, Caroline of Brunswick, was the daughter of George III's sister Augusta and Charles William Ferdinand, Duke of Brunswick. George III always sided with her through all the marital troubles of his son and never tired of referring to her pointedly as 'my niece and daughter-in-law'. Lord Malmesbury had been sent to Germany to arrange the marriage and he brought Caroline to England for the wedding. The Prince of Wales saw her for the first time on 5 April 1795 at St James's Palace. She knelt to him as she was instructed to do. 'He raised her (gracefully enough) and embraced her, said barely one word, turned round, retired to a distant part of the apartment and calling me to him, said "Harris, I am not well; pray get me a glass of brandy".' When Malmesbury rejoined the Princess she asked him in astonishment 'Mon Dieu! est ce que le Prince est toujours comme cela ?'[1] If this was not a propitious beginning, it was symbolic of their marriage. But it has never been satisfactorily explained as a psychological phenomenon – despite many attempts – which of the Prince's senses was so offended and produced such instant disgust that it turned into the indomitable and unrelenting hatred which knew no limits, not even of decorum, and with which he persecuted her systematically to her last day. The fact is that after the wedding night to which Princess Charlotte owed her existence they never gave nature another chance. They soon parted altogether and thereafter the Prince of Wales refused to be under the same roof with her even for a party or a ball.

Caroline's fate was so news-worthy, and gave so much food to scandal-mongers and caricaturists at the time and to biographers after her, that little note was taken whether she was ill or well and medical information about her is scanty. Her fatal illness at fifty-three, however, can be somehow reconstructed. After his accession in 1820 George IV was hell-bound on obtaining a divorce. Without it, object as he might, she was his lawful Queen. Her trial for adultery before the House of Lords – a deplorable and

despicable spectacle – known as the Bill of Pains and Penalties, was abandoned in November 1820 because its third reading had produced only a
marginal majority. The coronation took place on 19 July 1821 and while
George IV had succeeded in excluding her from the ceremony, she with
equal determination presented herself at Westminster Abbey on the day
demanding admission. Guards barred her entry. This, her last and bitterest
humiliation, was widely believed to have caused her death shortly after.
The Times, speaking for many, had 'no doubt that the Queen died of a broken
heart . . . [and] suppressed grief'.

She was only seen in public twice more. On 30 July she was taken ill at
Drury Lane Theatre. She had suffered for some days before from sleeplessness, constipation and colic. The *Annual Register* ascribed her illness to
her having taken too large a dose of aperients. She started to vomit and her
pulse was quick.[2] A bulletin on 2 August stated that her Majesty 'has an
obstruction of the bowels, attended with inflammation; the symptoms
though mitigated, are not removed.' It was signed by Dr Pelham Warren,
son of George III's Dr Richard Warren, Dr W. G. Maton, who had treated
the Duke of Kent in his fatal illness the year before, and Dr Henry Holland,
the Queen's friend who had accompanied her when she set out on her
travels abroad in 1814. Her pain was excruciating, she became weak and
was convinced she would not survive. Colic continued with 'excessive sickness at the stomach'. Besides bleeding and opium her Majesty was now
immersed, for about a quarter of an hour, in a warm bath – a procedure
highly regarded for its therapeutic value. The bulletin of 5 August was
signed by two more physicians, Dr Matthew Baillie and Dr H. Ainslie. It
stated that she had passed a tranquil night and was no worse. Some hope of
recovery had brightened the sickroom, although she had no sleep for four
nights. On the 6th her state was still 'more favourable'. Public sympathy
was vociferous, not only for one suddenly stricken with a painful illness, but
because the people on the whole sided with her as the injured party in the
royal quarrel. In fact her illness and death brought George IV's unpopularity to such a peak that for many months he dared not appear in public.
Offers of help and advice poured into Brandenburgh House, where the
Queen lay. A chemist recommended a trial of 'the but lately known remedy
for stoppage of the bowels', to wit croton oil, of which 'one drop is a dose'.
On 8 August she had another sleepless night, but she was described as no
worse. That afternoon the pain returned more violently, she became restless,
then delirious and finally comatose. She went into convulsions, her eyes
became fixed, her muscles paralysed, her breathing increasingly difficult
and in the evening it was announced that 'after an entire absence of sense
and faculty of more than two hours nature gave up the contest'.

This is about all one can gather from official sources – few facts and
fewer clinical observations. Private accounts only add confusion. Lord

Brougham, who as the Queen's counsellor had seen her in her last days to draw up her will, gave Creevey details which the latter had every right to find 'most curious' if he meant that they did not make medical sense. Brougham wrote to Creevey:

On Friday last she lost sixty-four ounces of blood; took first of all 15 grains of calomel, which they think she threw up again in the whole or in part; and then she took 40 grains more of calomel which she kept entirely in her stomach; add to this a quantity of castor oil that would turn the stomach of a horse. Nevertheless, on Friday night the inflammation had subsided, tho' not the obstruction of the liver.[3]

What was meant by the inflammation having subsided but not the obstruction of the liver, or from what symptoms this was divined, it is impossible even to guess.

All the evidence taken together makes her terminal illness suggestive of porphyria but no more. Her earlier history lends some support to this diagnosis, although again facts are few. At the age of fifteen she had an illness which isolated her for some time and there was a suspicion that not only her 'corporeal frame' was affected.[4] While on the Continent from 1814 to 1820 she was occasionally 'afflicted with violent rheumatic pains' and troubled 'by severe spasmodic attacks'. At Milan she was confined with an indisposition when 'both her health and spirits' were affected. There is record of similar incidents but no further details. This is as far as one can go on the physical side, but there is no doubt she was mentally disturbed at times, and many contemporaries considered her 'not a little mad'. She had attacks of excitement and many instances are known where her behaviour was – to say the least – bizarre. For instance at Jerusalem she founded the Order of St Caroline of Jerusalem 'to recompense the faithful Knights who had the honour of accompanying Her Majesty on her pilgrimage to the Holy land' and made her friend Pergami grandmaster and her boy protégé William Austin knight thereof.[5] The story is told that her mother, the old Duchess of Brunswick, George III's sister, was powerless to control her daughter; she grieved over Caroline's errors bitterly. ' "She has this excuse," she once said to Lord Redesdale, "she is not quite right *here* (touching her forehead)" and burst into tears.'[6] Malicious gossip had it that evidence of her mental derangement was kept dark because it would have hindered divorce proceedings.

An objective matter-of-fact description of her mental state in 1819 came from the pen of James Brougham, who had been sent out to Italy by his brother, Lord Brougham, to find out on what conditions she would agree to a divorce. He found her unstable and morbidly suspicious. He reported:

I have had several very serious discussions with her on the subject of her giving up England, and all claims to be Queen and even of having a divorce

s

immediately . . . All she wants is to pass the remainder of her life quietly. She has not the spirits she used to have . . . To be sure she is in a state of constant hot water. Great part is imaginary, but still if she *has the fear*, it matters little whether there are grounds or not. For instance, she thinks there are people hired to kill or poison her, and the kitchen is watched accordingly – two servants parade the hall all night, besides the guards on the outside. Pistols, blunderbusses etc. in my room, besides the dogs etc.[7]

If Caroline of Brunswick had porphyria, this metabolic disorder may well have been the very only thing which, unbeknown to themselves, George IV and his Queen had in common. In fact her chances of inheriting it were greater than her escaping it. It might have come to her through her mother, George III's sister Augusta, along the line of the Georges down from James I's granddaughter Sophia, Electress of Hanover. Her father came of the same stock and stood to the Electress in the same relation since he and her mother were second cousins.

On the death of King William III and because his successor Queen Anne had no heir, in 1701 Parliament passed the Act of Settlement to safeguard the crown from passing after her to the Catholic descendants of James II, the Old and the Young Pretenders. It transferred succession to the protestant granddaughter of James I, Sophia Electress of Hanover, and her issue. However she was survived by Queen Anne by a few weeks and Sophia's son ascended the throne as King George I in 1714. Her daughter Sophia Charlotte married King Frederick I of Prussia, from whom Queen Caroline of Brunswick, George IV's consort, descended. In her the two lines, the Hanoverian on her mother's side and the Brandenburg-Prussian on her father's, combined, and so increased her chances of inheriting the disorder from either or both parents, as in the case of her daughter Princess Charlotte. In this middle branch of the house of Brunswick from which Caroline descended there was much nervous illness. It died out in the 1880s.

In theory then porphyria may have occurred with equal or even greater likelihood in the Prussian line than in the Hanoverian because of more frequent cousin marriages. However, in tracing it through the generations it must be remembered that the metabolic disorder may be present and therefore transmitted without causing symptoms, or only minor ones which would not be recorded or are inconclusive. The Electress Sophia's daughter, Sophia Charlotte, who would have introduced the gene into the Prussian family, died in her thirties after a short illness with features consistent with porphyria, but not enough is known. It is otherwise with Sophia's great-grandson Frederic the Great. And if he had it as well as his cousin-german George III, it must have come down from their common ancestor, the Electress Sophia, through intervening generations.

FREDERIC II OF PRUSSIA, 'THE GREAT' (1712–86)

Proverbially the monarch on crutches, victim of gout and indigestion, Frederic the Great is also the one about whom most was written and who wrote the most. When Carlyle was engaged on his six-volume biography in the 1850s he complained that the literature already amounted to 'waggon-loads', and it has grown ever since. Paradoxically, his medical history is poorly documented – he changed doctors too often for any one to have an overall picture. He also objected to having his sufferings made public and although well-informed on medical matters himself and in close touch with many leading physicians – or perhaps because of it – remained distrustful of the medical art for his own person.

In his last illness in 1786 he was attended by two physicians successively and both published accounts of it. One was Dr von Zimmermann, who had attended Queen Caroline Matilda of Denmark. His book, all three volumes of it, was an ambitious political history of the reign of Frederic the Great but contains almost nothing of medical interest except that it relates how 'When the gout racked his whole body he named the sites of the most excruciating pain after the English Opposition; he used to say "Mr. Burke is busy in my knees and Mr. Fox belabours my feet." ' [8] The account of the other physician, Dr Selle, is rather more medical but still not sufficient for a modern diagnosis. However, his description of the King's early medical history gives a picture which would tally with attacks of porphyria. He wrote:

In his early years the King suffered from a peculiar debility and sensitivity of his stomach with much vomiting, attacks of colic and obstruction of the bowels . . . From his 28th year he had attacks of gout . . . At 35 he was attacked by a hemiplegia which however quickly yielded to antiphlogistic treatment. [9]

Here then was colic, constipation, pain and weakness of the limbs and 'a hemiplegia' which was shortlived if one discounts the therapeutic confidence of the time. At that time every paralysis was attributed to something having happened in the brain, such as a stroke. It was not known that muscles can lose their power when peripheral nerves are affected by some pathological process or toxin, a condition known today as peripheral neuritis or neuropathy. This was in fact only recognized at the end of the nineteenth century. Frederic's physicians therefore had no choice but to refer all lameness to the central nervous system and call it a hemiplegia. Yet medical historians, perhaps because they know more history than medicine, have surprisingly rarely re-thought famous illnesses in the light of advancing knowledge. They have simply accepted Frederic's doctors' diagnosis and perpetuated the story that he had a stroke at that young age. Frederic himself described his illness somewhat less misleadingly to Voltaire in a letter written nine days after its onset, when it had already subsided, as 'une attaque d'apoplexie imparfaite' from which only his age and constitution had 'recalled him to life'.[10]

Thanks to Frederic being an indefatigable correspondent it is possible to cull many details of his illnesses from his letters. They leave no room for doubt about the diagnosis. In 1732, still in his teens, he had 'horrible headaches, migraine, an upset stomach'.[11] He had hoped, he confessed with disappointment, to recover more speedily, but continued 'at war' with his stomach and had 'lost a terrible amount of weight during the attack'. At twenty-four 'migraine is epidemic' with him, he suffered from severe headaches and was so weak that 'it needs a mere bagatelle to throw us over, and a nothing to destroy us'. He was so melancholic that he wrote, 'We can glory in nothing but our miseries.' At twenty-five he had to take medicines 'to cure my abysmal stomach . . . what does it matter, we must die some time whether of gout, gravel, the King's evil or colic.' At thirty-four 'An obstruct-tion . . . has turned into gout . . . my tormenting headache threatens to paralyse my right arm and gravel my left.' Aged thirty-five he had his most severe attack, when he was said to have had 'a hemiplegia'. How ill he felt he told a friend: 'Once again I have escaped from Pluto's realm, but I was only one station away from the Styx and heard Cerberus howl.'[12] 'I have most wonderfully escaped the jaws of death,' wrote George III to his friend Bishop Hurd after his attack of 1801. The feeling of impending death is a common experience at the height of a severe attack of porphyria.

Of all Frederic's correspondence, most informative medically are his uninhibited letters to his valet, his 'old factotum' as Voltaire called him. They were discovered scattered in private hands in the 1920s and to our knowledge have not been studied from this angle. How intimate they are is evident from the fact that Frederic did not write in French, as was his custom, but in German, for the benefit of his servant. He knew German and its spelling so imperfectly that the editor had to annotate some passages to make his meaning clear.[13] (The translation is ours.) To him Frederic confided in 1745, aged thirty-three, 'My health has suffered considerably [from the hardships of the campaign]. I cannot sleep at night because of palpitation, cramp and colic.' A little later his 'chief complaint' was of being 'still constipated like a Turk'. Three weeks after his 'hemiplegia' he wrote 'my doctor is an optimist if he really believes that strokes and renal colics are nature's way of restoring health; I speak from bitter experience, being so weak that the smallest exertion bowls me over.' He also had pain 'in the spleen and kidney', but whether this was due to 'an obstruction or a tumor' he did not know. The colic was 'under the ribs radiating to the back', he suffered severely from cramp, vomited much, had pain in the arms 'as if paralysed'.

After suffering for a month he foamed in desperation: 'The whole illness, the physicians have now at last discovered, is the result of a kidney disease, after they have tortured my colon for four weeks like a pack of hounds.' What else could have made his doctors suddenly so certain that his kidneys were diseased but that they had observed 'bloody' urine? They had no other means of diagnosing it than by inspecting the appearance of the urine. Colic, constipation, pain and weakness in the limbs, and insomnia persisted for more than two months and his convalescence from this attack was slow.

In 1775 he consoled his valet, who was also ill: 'You can't piss, and I can't walk.'[13] To Voltaire he wrote at the end of the year: 'Gout held me tied and garrotted for four weeks; gout in both feet, both knees, both hands; and such was its extreme liberality, in both arms as well. At present the fever and the pain have subsided and I only suffer from very great exhaustion.'[14]

Three weeks later he apologized to him for not writing for so long but 'I am emerging from my fourteenth attack of gout. Never has it tormented me quite so much and robbed me nearly of the use of all my limbs.'[14] But a few weeks later, early in 1776, he had suffered another 'violent attack of gout which left me very low'.[14] He had been so ill that there were fears he might not survive.

Attacks recurred throughout his life. As a precaution he visited spas regularly and was bled four times a year. In between he was capable of great exertion and of enduring much hardship.

FREDERICK WILLIAM I KING OF PRUSSIA (1688–1740)

Frederic the Great could have inherited porphyria from either or both his parents, who were first cousins. His father certainly had characteristic attacks of colic and painful lameness from early life. At the age of thirty-one an attack was so severe that he nearly died. His doctors diagnosed 'nephritic colic', as they did in his son and in his distant ancestor James I. At thirty-nine he had 'violent fits of the gout'. He lost his sleep, he was mentally acutely disturbed and his temper became uncontrollable. His daughter Wilhelmina of Baireuth – Frederic the Great's favourite sister – wrote in her diary that 'he worried himself into melancholy and hypochondria'. He developed 'a fit of religious mania' and he spoke of abdicating.[15] In 1729, when he was forty-one, he had his most serious attack, with the same symptoms, and for some time afterwards was unable to walk and had to be wheeled about the house. It is said that to distract himself from his sufferings he painted – a talent with which many members of the Prussian and Hanoverian houses are gifted – and signed his pictures *Friedericus Wilhelminus in tormentis pinxit*.[16]

The disorder must have been transmitted to Frederick William I by his mother Sophia Charlotte, sister of George I, who died at the age of thirty-seven. Among Frederic the Great's thirteen brothers and sisters there are a number whose medical histories suggest that they also suffered from the family disorder.

16

George III's Other Sons

There is an extraordinary link between the royal porphyrics of Prussia and England, in the person of Dr von Zimmermann (1728–95), physician and author of international repute. To him as royal physician the Hanoverian Privy Council turned for advice and guidance when news reached them in November 1788 that George III was seriously ill. He replied on 21 November:

How can I possibly advise on the distressing and highly dangerous illness of our most gracious sovereign, when I have not even received enough information to form an opinion of the nature of the illness! It is impossible – and would not be justified – to rely on what the English newspapers say, which are so often, and especially in a case like this, full of lies. I read the few lines of 7 and 11 [November] from London, but am no wiser for it. And the same goes for those of 14. No doctor on earth could divine what the King was suffering from without knowing the facts – still less suggest treatment.

From the first dispatches it sounded as if the King had an apoplectic fit. But the news today is of a violent fever with a pulse rate of 130 which has severely affected the head . . . as might happen in an apoplexy. All I know therefore is of high fever and a delirium. But not a single symptom is described which enables one to decide whether it is an inflammatory, a bilious, or a putrid fever.

For all I am told, it might be something very different altogether: perhaps some gouty matter, or even water may have settled on the brain and produced these terrible and threatening symptoms.

By the time this letter reaches England everything may well have been decided. Should it please Providence – as I profoundly wish and pray – that his Majesty will be spared, I confidently expect that the delirium will vanish as soon as the fever has abated of which the disturbance of the brain is only a symptom.[1]

He ended his letter by agreeing to go to The Hague, as the Privy Council had instructed him to do, to be at least nearer to the source of news, and in case the royal physicians in London should call him to the King's bedside. But he warned them that professionally his situation would continue to be unenviable and embarrassing, to say the least, unless he received reliable and detailed descriptions of the symptoms.

He arrived at The Hague on 1 December and reported to Hanover that two English mails had brought nothing from London, and that he therefore still knew nothing about the King, not even how his terrible illness began. 'I therefore implore you fervently to persuade at least one of the King's physicians to send me a frank, detailed, professional account of how the illness developed.'

He next wrote from The Hague on 5 December – the very day the Reverend Dr Francis Willis took charge of the royal sickroom at Kew Palace. Still he was without information. He complained bitterly of having been exposed to this fruitless and hazardous journey through Holland with roads covered in deep snow so that they could not be recognized, where rivers and canals were icebound, and the mail long delayed by these inclement conditions and two postillions had already perished by the wayside. How still more dangerous his return journey would be! And he growled:

> That the purpose of the privy councillors, with which they sent me to The Hague, would never be fulfilled, I myself knew from the outset and General Freytag knew it as well as I did. It was a foregone conclusion that the English physicians would in no circumstances whatsoever permit me only the smallest participation in the treatment of the King. Since the councillors did not seem to realize this, I had no choice but to obey their orders.

Exhausted, outraged and no wiser he returned home to Hanover.

Even if Dr von Zimmermann never came to play an active part in George III's treatment it is valuable to learn what an experienced physician of his day made of the King's illness. And after all he had treated his sister Queen Caroline Matilda, three of his sons and his cousin-german Frederic the Great.

FREDERICK AUGUSTUS DUKE OF YORK (1763–1827)

It was through the good offices of George III's second son Frederick that Dr Zimmermann came to attend Frederic the Great. 'I think it my duty to acquaint you, Sir,' wrote Frederick to his father in June 1786, 'that this morning I had a letter from the King of Prussia in which he begs me to send Doctor Zimmermann to Potsdam: he set out about two hours after the King's letter arrived.'[2] Frederick himself had been Zimmermann's patient at the age of twenty in 1783, when he was seriously ill. Even that was not his first attack: 'I am most excessively alarmed & terribly uneasy . . . that you have again been seriously ill,' wrote the Prince of Wales.[3] What actually ailed him we know only indirectly from what Zimmermann five years later reported to George III about Augustus Duke of Sussex, namely that his symptoms were identical with his brother's. Zimmermann's records of Augustus's illness are so detailed that they leave no room for doubt also about Frederick's.

In the summer of 1784 'the excessive heat of the weather' had caused 'a feverish cold . . . of the aguish kind'.[4] The following year he wrote to his father: 'Dr. Zimmermann has insisted upon my going to Pyrmont to drink the waters and bathe there, as the only thing which would thoroughly cure me of the terrible cramps and spasms in my stomach, to which I have been very subject for the last two years.'[5] In July 1789 the Prince of Wales wrote to their father, who himself was convalescing at Weymouth, to warn him 'that some vague & untrue reports might reach your Majesty' and to inform him 'respecting the state of my brother the Duke of York's health'.

After suffering excessively for four or five days, & having been extremely disciplin'd during yt. time by means of James's Powders & bleeding, the disorder seem'd to be advancing to an alarming height this morning, & Dr. Moseley, the physician who has hitherto attended my brother, appearing very uneasy, I judg'd it necessary to call in Dr. Warren, who within the last three hours pronounc'd the disorder to have taken a favourable turn & to be decidedly the measles, wh. have spread in a very large eruption all over his countenance. The Dr. has judg'd it right to bleed him again . . . [But five days later] he was siez'd with a complaint in his bowels . . . [and] complained of an increase of tightness on his breast, which made the physicians think it necessary for him to lose about eight ounces of blood.[6]

His pain was so severe that he had to take laudanum and 'composing pills' to sleep. If it really was measles it was a strange attack, occurring rather later than usual with the rash confined to the face and accompanied by severe systemic and gastro-intestinal symptoms. It may have been an attack of porphyria with a sun-rash in the face. Alternatively, if it was the measles as Dr Warren thought, it may have brought on an attack of porphyria, as infections are known to do.

In September of the same year he was attacked by a 'very unlucky and very violent intermitting feaver which . . . has reduced me so exceedingly low that it will require considerable time for me to recover'.[7] In June 1796 he 'was so exceedingly unwell all day yesterday, and though perfectly free from spasm today, yet so exceedingly weak'.[8] His brother found him 'extremely ill indeed, and hardly able to speak'.[9] In July The Times reported that the Duke of York had a return of his 'stomach complaint'. In 1797 he informed the Prince of Wales that 'in the present moment I cannot think of absenting myself from London, nor am I indeed as yet sufficiently recovered from the ague to play any tricks.'[10] In 1820 George IV wrote to him: 'It grieves me much to learn that you have been indispos'd . . . You talk of an attack of bile; I also have had my share of it . . . and my old enemy the gout flying about me.'[11] Princess Lieven 'saw the Duke of York for the first time since his illness [in 1823]. He thought he was going to die. He is half the man he was and as weak as a cat, but not as regards his mind!'[12]

In March 1826 the Duke of Cumberland wrote to Sir Henry Halford:

Excuse my troubling you . . . but the last Accounts of my brother's health have so alarmed me that I do beseech you to write me only *two* lines, that I may really know how he is. I understand . . . he had a violent attack of Gout, which fell upon his bowels, for which he has been twice blooded in 24 hours.[13]

In May Mrs Arbuthnot found that 'The poor Duke looked very ill, scarcely spoke & ate nothing. I am sadly afraid he is in a bad way, for he is grown very thin, never sleeps and has constant spasms in his stomach. Sir Henry Halford is very uneasy about him, and attributes his illness a good deal to mental uneasiness. He is overwhelmed with debt . . . '[14]

His fatal illness was long drawn out. It was said to have been 'dropsy'. And if this is not a diagnosis, it was certainly a symptom of increasing heart failure, for which his water-logged legs were repeatedly tapped. He said to the bishop who administered the sacrament: 'I have in the course of my life faced death in various shapes and I am now doomed to view its approach in a slow and lingering form . . . I admit that my life has not been pure and there has been much in the course of it that I wish had been otherwise.'[15] Since George III's death he was heir presumptive to the throne, but his elder brother George IV survived him by three years. He married in 1791 Frederica Princess Royal of Prussia, Frederic the Great's niece, but they had no children.

AUGUSTUS FREDERICK DUKE OF SUSSEX (1773–1843)

Augustus, George III's sixth son was, like his brother Frederick, Dr von Zimmermann's patient while he was living at Hanover with his brothers. We owe to Dr Zimmermann and his three colleagues, Drs Stromeyer, Richter and Fischer, who attended the Prince during his illness, a most informative account of a series of dangerous attacks which befell Augustus while he was still in his teens. It is contained in regular medical reports to the Hanoverian authorities and to George III direct, preserved in the family archives at Hanover.[16]

The illness started in early August 1788 when he was fifteen. He fell ill with what his physicians called a 'most fearful paroxysm', during which his life hung in the balance several times. His attacks waxed and waned for about eight weeks. They described his symptoms and condition in great detail: insomnia, fast pulse, a 'spastic condition of his bowels' (that is obstinate constipation), headache, giddiness, great exhaustion and muscular weakness. But the most alarming symptom was 'a spasmodic constriction of the chest' which was accompanied by 'excruciating pain' and made respiration so difficult that on several occasions his face was discoloured and he was in acute danger of suffocation. Although it resembled 'convulsive asthma' they considered the condition as something much more complicated because of the severity of the pain and other symptoms. They observed his urine carefully and noted that during his four major attacks it was 'deeply discoloured', 'reddish-brown', or 'deep amber' and each time when the attack had subsided 'the colour returned to normal'. Presumably when they noted that 'his body was still full of impurities' they were also referring to the fact that his urine was still dark-coloured.

By October he was on the road to recovery, but had lost much weight, was weak and himself felt 'as if coming out of a long faint'.[16] The Duke of Cumberland wrote to George III on 2 October 1788: 'I am very happy to tell you that Augustus passed a very good night & finds himself so much better today as to have been able to set up half an hour . . . I hope with all my heart that he may continue to recover daily & be soon again a stout man.'[17] The physicians advised George III to send Augustus to a warm climate to prevent recurrences. He spent two years in the South of France and Italy, but attacks recurred.

Zimmermann reported to George III that this was a very complicated illness, which the physicians found difficult to give a name to. It resembled closely that of his brother Frederick in 1783. Zimmermann referred the King for details of his symptoms to the reports he had then sent to their Majesties, together with a full consultation of the case. About the nature and prognosis of the illness he concluded:

As regards the likelihood of recurrences we believe His Royal Highness has a peculiar disposition to paroxysms of a violent kind, but in what this disposition consists we cannot determine . . . it may be some bodily irritation which settles mainly on the chest. We are however all agreed that there is no ulceration of the lungs . . . It has come to our knowledge that several members of the Royal Family and in particular his Royal Highness the Duke of York and Prince Edward [Duke of Kent] are subject to the same paroxysms and this arouses our suspicion of a hereditary predisposition.

It is interesting that Zimmermann hinted at a hereditary condition in the same sense as Dr William Heberden had done to the parliamentary inquiry into George III's illness in 1810 when he spoke of 'a peculiarity of constitution of which I can give no distinct account'. Augustus's pains and spasms, although they also affected his stomach, were most pronounced in the chest and this made his physicians consider, but reject, the possibility of an inflammation of the lungs. The same happened when George III was ill in 1762 and in 1765. His pain in the chest with embarrassed respiration led to fears that he was developing 'a consumption'. When George IV had the same symptoms his doctors diagnosed 'an inflammation on the lungs', but soon corrected themselves.

Augustus had many more such bad spells. In 1790 he described a near fatal one to his father:

> Such a painful and long illness I have not yet had. Seven times blooded, two blisters ... Such a day as ... Friday was dreadful, so just between life and death, all my faculties for a good four hours so entirely gone, that what passed that time I am quite ignorant of ... I am weak, Sir, and cannot write more.[17]

He also developed the tell-tale muscular pain and weakness. In March 1792 the King acknowledged a letter from Sir William Hamilton 'concerning the rheumatick fever that has seized my son Augustus'.[17] In January 1795 Augustus wrote to the Prince of Wales from Naples: 'Excuse my scrawl, but the agitation of my mind as well as the weakness of my body, which is worn out by the want of six nights' sleep, must plead my apology.'[18] In 1802 he was again 'attacked with one of his violent spasms'.[19] In October 1806 he wrote to the Prince of Wales:

> It is from a sick chair and not from a sick bed that I address you these few lines, to which I have been confined for these last eleven days without moving ... what I go through no one can conceive who has not been an eye-witness of my sufferings, besides which all the physicians ... have informed me of the state of my health which they declare dangerous ... the body getting weaker also affects the mind and makes me view my situation in the most melancholy and desperate colours possible ... scarcely able one moment to close my eyes.[20]

And the Duke of Kent reported to the Prince of Wales on the same day

> the full sentiments entertained by the Duke of Sussex's physicians of his present deplorable state of health ... His situation is considered both by Sir Walter Farquhar and by Dr. Fryer to be *extremely precarious* ... it being next to impossible but that he must at length sink under the repeated attacks ... the latter of these two gentlemen who is in the habit of daily attendance ... has presented to me the unusual despondency of mind which he had of late remarked in him, and particularly during his recent attacks, which lasted fourteen days without intermission ... there is an alarming degree of hypochondria which seems to menace the most fatal consequences.[20]

In August 1811 a bulletin from Windsor read: 'The Duke of Sussex is rather better; but not out of danger. The complaint is understood to be an affection of the bladder.' Did he again pass discoloured urine, as he had at Hanover, for this diagnosis to be suggested?

In 1812 Princess Charlotte reported on 'a splendid dinner, where all dined except the Duke of Sussex, who is again ill with one of his attacks'.[21]

In the subsequent thirty-one years of his life, attacks seem to have diminished, as they sometimes do. But he had the misfortune of going blind from cataract, as did George III, and George IV, William IV, the Duke of Cumberland and their sister Sophia. Among the many public and charitable activities of this, the most liberal and progressive of George III's sons, was the presidency of the Royal Society. In 1834

A letter was read from his Royal Highness, the president, in which after expressing his extreme regret that the state of his eyesight prevented his attendance he says: 'Should the gentlemen kindly vote me again in the chair, aware as they are of my present infirmities, I can only accept the proffered offer upon an understanding, that should I not be better at this period next year, I may now be considered as giving them notice that I shall consider myself bound in duty to resign an office, the duty of which I am no longer able to perform'.[22]

His cataract was 'couched' successfully and he served two more years until he resigned in 1838.

The Duke of Sussex had two children by his unofficial marriage to Lady Augusta Murray, a daughter, Augusta, and a son, Augustus D'Este. Neither left issue. The son was a lifelong hypochondriac who suffered from intermittent lameness which he described in minute detail in a diary which is published.[23] It has been assumed that he suffered from an atypical multiple sclerosis, but in the light of his father's and grandfather's illnesses he too may have been a porphyric.

EDWARD DUKE OF KENT (1767–1820)

In some quarters it was known that a royal malady was affecting several members of the family. Dr Zimmermann had said as much to the King in his report on Augustus. The medical journals took it into consideration when discussing Princess Charlotte's death. Dr William Heberden also had a familial disorder in mind to explain George III's illness. Sir Robert Thomas Wilson, who visited the King at Weymouth in 1804, learnt from Sir Francis Milman 'that the King is not the only one of his family likely to be affected with this grievous malady'. A younger princess, probably Sophia, was subject to the same 'spasms'. An 'eminent surgeon' told him that he feared 'in one of those attacks, she will lose her life – say rather, her senses for ever, for to that misfortune is more than one of these Royal personages doomed.'[24]

Those of George III's sons who were also affected certainly recognized that their complaints were alike. George IV in particular was often deeply distressed to witness his brother Frederick's suffering in his last illness and was obsessed by it as a foreboding of his own end – as indeed it turned out to be. The brothers must also have realized that their attacks were accompanied by the same aches and pains as their father's, but they do not seem to have said so openly, at least not in their accessible correspondence. After all, to have admitted this frightening fact would have meant facing the dread of developing mental disturbance, a possibility which must have hung over them like the sword of Damocles. The Duke of Kent was the only one who dared to give expression to it and then only under considerable pressure. He had brought his father's wrath upon himself for debts incurred at Hanover and for returning to England from Geneva without permission. Now, in December 1790, at the age of twenty-three, he was serving in the Army at Gibraltar and anxious to re-establish himself in his father's eyes, one reason why he was such a martinet in his regiment. But he had fallen ill with severe bilious attacks and was advised to ask for a transfer to a cooler climate. In this difficult situation he wrote to his father:

My health has so very materially suffered during the immoderate heat of last summer that the Surgeon General of our Garrison, who has constantly attended me during the frequent bilious attacks from which I have felt the most violent and serious effects, has given it as his positive opinion that by my remaining here another summer my health would be exposed not only to the most prejudicial but perhaps the most fatal attacks of a complaint, the severity of which, is, I believe, not unknown to your Majesty.[25]

What George III thought when he read of Edward's bilious attacks is not known, but it must have passed through his mind that his illness two years earlier had also started with what the doctors had called biliary colic.

It was not the Duke of Kent's first symptom of porphyria. In 1787 he had been sent to live in Switzerland for two years for his health. From Geneva, aged twenty-one, he had written to his father: 'The first lines which my hand is able to trace since my recovery from a violent rheumatism . . . which nearly deprived me of the total use of both my hands, my duty as well as my inclination lead me to address to your Majesty.'[26] This letter reached George III on his return from Cheltenham, where he had gone to get rid of his own bilious attack, and in the short interval of freedom before his severest attack flared up in October 1788 with the same complaint.

The Duke of Kent in fact suffered periodically all through his life from attacks of abdominal colic, pain and weakness of his limbs, and he also developed skin lesions. His severest attacks occurred in summer because he was sensitive to the sun, as he well knew. Between attacks he enjoyed robust health and was of such hardy constitution and fine physique – he was more than six foot tall – that those who knew nothing of these spells of illness were at a loss to understand his rapid end and looked on it as a mysterious dispensation of Providence which fitted well with his own superstitious vein.

In January 1791, still at Gibraltar, he complained to his brother:

I have suffered so much from violent bilious attacks ever since I have been

here, that I found it necessary to take the opinions of the medical people . . .
they all agreed that this climate was extremely prejudicial to my health, and
that particularly by my remaining here the six hot months very serious consequences might attend it.[27]

His plea to be moved was granted, but he was not allowed home because
his father wanted to keep him out of range of the clutches and political
mischief of the Prince of Wales. He sailed direct to America, where he was
posted to Halifax, Nova Scotia, as Major-General. There his attacks continued. In 1798 he pleaded not to be 'compelled to pass an eighth winter in
this trying climate, from the changeableness, and severity of which I have
for the three last suffered incredibly' and 'so severely from rheumatic
attacks'.[28]

He was invalided home. But the following year, 1799, he was sent out
again, this time promoted to Commander-in-Chief of the forces in British
North America. The Duke of York was sorry to hear that while in England
he had had 'so bad an attack of rheumatism'.[29] The crossing to Halifax took
forty-three days and on arrival he wrote to his friend the banker Thomas
Coutts that his health was still not of the best 'which I account for by having embarked too soon after a prodigious severe rheumatick attack'.[30]

In the summer of 1800, now aged thirty-two, he wrote to his father from
Halifax: 'I have had one of the severest bilious attacks I ever yet experienced, and . . . a very violent rheumatism settled in my head for several
days.'[31] His skin was also affected. He complained of

being unable for six weeks to wear anything but a pair of loose trowsers, from
a very troublesome humour which, after shewing itself in several parts of my
body, at length settled in my leg; indeed at this moment I am writing, one of
my eyes is nearly closed from the same cause.[32]

He was permitted to return to England in September the same year. In
1802 he was sent out again to Gibraltar, this time as Governor. From there
in June he wrote to the Prince of Wales:

My health is as good as I had a right to expect in the midst of this trying
heat, and that on the whole I think myself less bilious in some degree than I
had apprehended.[33]

As winter set in he improved, as he told Thomas Coutts:

My general health since the weather began to cool about the middle of
October, has been good, but within these few days, I have had a pretty smart
return of the rheumatick attacks, which are the consequence of the repeated
changes of climate, I have experienced for these last thirteen years.[34]

He was ordered home again in 1803, this time not for reasons of health
but because his too severe military discipline was sharply criticized. So
ended his soldiering career. In England he continued to be plagued from

time to time by 'biliousness', as he told Thomas Coutts in 1809; and a year later he wrote to him that his 'head [was] very painfull from a severe bilious attack which it has led to'.[35]

From 1815 he resided on the Continent. It was a way of living cheaply and so of reducing his substantial debts. To secure an increased grant from Parliament by getting married was another means of escaping from chronic financial embarrassment. An additional incentive to this step was the public outcry for an heir to the throne after the death of Princess Charlotte in 1817. Valiantly combining private and public motives the fifty-year-old Duke decided to marry. He chose for his bride Victoria of Saxe-Coburg, Princess of Leiningen, a widow with two children. They were married in England in 1818 and returned to live in Germany. In April 1819, a few weeks before the Duchess's confinement, they hazarded the journey back, and on 24 May the future Queen Victoria saw the light of day on English soil. Soon after, the family of three settled quietly at Sidmouth to a simple country life.

There, on 13 January 1820, the Duke was suddenly taken ill. Hardly had the news become known when it was overtaken by the announcement of his death. People, if not stunned, were puzzled by this unexpected event. When the Duke of Cumberland heard of it at Berlin a fortnight later he wrote to their eldest brother the Prince of Wales:

> I can safely declare that I never was so struck in my life as with the late melancholy account of poor Edward's death ... I should have thought he would have outlived us all from his regular habits of life which he has pursued ever since I can recollect any thing.[36]

The Duke of Kent's death was not a national loss. What difference it might have made to Queen Victoria – to whom he does not seem to have passed the disorder – had she not lost her father before she was a year old nobody can tell. It was a blow to the Duchess. Her cruel bereavement, it was pointed out at the time, uncannily resembled that of her brother Leopold, who, equally suddenly and by a mysterious death, had lost his young wife, Princess Charlotte.

Had his death occurred in the seventeenth century or earlier and had he been a politically significant figure, no doubt someone would have raised the alarm that he had been poisoned. No such suspicion arose in the more enlightened yet medically still unsophisticated early nineteenth century. It was accepted that he simply caught cold, which spread to his lungs and killed him. And this was attributed to his imprudence in not changing out of wet stockings after a long walk on a rainy day! 'You will be surprised,' wrote Croker to a friend, 'at the Duke of Kent's death. He was the strongest of the strong; never before ill in all his life, and now to die of a cold, when half the kingdom had colds with impunity.'[37]

The first bulletin was issued on 15 January: 'His Royal Highness is . . . indisposed with a severe cold, which has confined him to his room.' Two days later he developed 'most alarming symptoms' which were attributed to 'an inflammation on the chest'. The following day it was stated that the illness had 'terminated in pleuritic inflammation and cough', a diagnosis doubtless made because of pain. From the beginning his physicians took a serious view of the illness and at once started energetic treatment. They bled him 'copiously', applied blisters and leeches and cupped him. They plied him with castor oil and febrifugia. The symptoms 'considerably abated' but respiration was still embarrassed and he continued to complain of pain. On the 20th he relapsed and 'his danger considerably increased'. He rallied once more, but on 23 January he died. 'His complaint,' wrote The Times, 'was inflammation of the lungs so violent as to baffle the utmost efforts of medical skill.'

Some further details of his illness became known. His first symptom on returning home was hoarseness, then a cold developed, with pain in the chest and difficulty in breathing. Persistent hiccough set in and at the end he was delirious. It is hardly possible today to decide with certainty whether he died of pneumonia or an acute attack of porphyria or a combination of both. A respiratory tract infection may well have brought on, as it often does, a flare-up. Conversely, an attack of porphyria may have caused respiratory embarrassment which in turn favoured the development of pneumonia. His physician, Dr W. G. Maton, also thought there was more to it than pneumonia and pleurisy. Three days before the Duke died, Dr Maton reported to Lord Sidmouth:

I found His Royal Highness labouring under a most severe inflammation in the region of the diaphragm, which has been succeeded by an obstinate singultus [hiccough] and a train of other obstinate symptoms, which I do not believe it possible for medicine to conquer.[38]

How tantalizing not to be told what these 'other obstinate symptoms' were. The Duke was embalmed and had anything of note been found in the lungs it would have been made public, if only to confirm his doctors' diagnosis and justify their treatment. But nothing transpired.

That he was not free from bilious attacks even towards the end of his life is shown by the following curious anecdote. He is said to have had great feeling for other people's sufferings and when his wife was carrying Victoria he had stomach pains in sympathy with her, according to modern psychologically-minded biographers.[39] This was taken as an example of the primitive custom called couvade by which husbands pretend to undergo the sufferings of their parturient wives. Thus, because the medical significance of his abdominal colic was not appreciated, it was endowed with psychological significance, as so often happens when physical symptoms do not

T

find ready explanation in contemporary medicine or the doctor's knowledge,

Six days after the Duke of Kent died, his father's sufferings came to a close on 29 January 1820. His brother the Prince of Wales, now George IV, lay dangerously ill at the same time – and from the same disease.

Pulling these historical threads together suggests that this hereditary metabolic disorder came to the House of Hanover from the Stuarts through James VI & I's granddaughter Sophia, Electress of Hanover, mother of George I, and through her daughter Sophia Charlotte was introduced into the Brandenburg-Prussian House and so affected Frederic the Great. Evidence of it was found as far back as the Tudors and it still occurs in living family members, thus spanning fifteen generations and almost five hundred years.

The mysterious and sometimes dramatic features of attacks gave rise on five occasions to the suspicion of foul play and created a *cause célèbre*: the near fatal illness of Mary Queen of Scots in 1566 at Jedburgh; and the deaths of Henry Prince of Wales in 1612, of James VI & I in 1625, of Henrietta Anne, Duchess of Orleans, daughter of Charles I and sister-in-law of Louis XIV, in 1670, and of George III's sister Caroline Matilda, hapless Queen of Denmark and Norway, in 1775. In all these cases relatives or friends were implicated in a supposed crime, which, even if not sustained, cast a shadow over their characters which it may be interesting to follow up and rectify.

The victims of the disorder themselves, particularly Mary Queen of Scots and George IV, will now demand more sympathy from biographers, as their sufferings are seen to have been real and severe. Even James I's much speculated-upon relation with men like Buckingham, may find an explanation in his need for close friends – favourites to whom he could delegate state business during his frequent bouts of incapacitating illness.

Porphyria may justly be called a royal malady and command the historian's respect. It caused directly two national disasters: the Regency Crisis in 1788 and the catastrophe of 1817, when Princess Charlotte died in childbed with her infant. This tragedy threatened the Hanoverian succession with extinction and left the nation without an heir apparent until the birth in 1819 of Victoria. It is not impossible that porphyria also contributed to Queen Anne leaving no heir, a calamity which necessitated safeguarding the Protestant succession by the Act of Settlement of 1701, by which the crown was transferred from the Catholic House of Stuart to that of Hanover and so brought George I and his descendants to the English throne.

PART FOUR

Georgian Psychiatry

Dr Francis Willis: Insanity Proved Curable

Had it not been for the glare of publicity which fell upon the man and his methods, the Reverend Dr Francis Willis would have remained no more than he aspired to be – the successful medically qualified keeper of a provincial private madhouse. But by being called to manage the King and justify himself before parliamentary committees he made his mark in medical history for propagating the notion that insanity was curable.

Academic or scientific pretensions he had none, though he was Master of Arts (1741) and Doctor of Medicine (1759) of the University of Oxford. He was a clerk in holy orders when he proceeded to a medical degree to regularize his practice among his parishioners and so added to the cure of souls the physic of the body. From his pre-medical days, when he is said to have been in danger of prosecution by the local doctors for practising irregularly without a qualification or even a licence from his bishop, dates the first of his only two contributions to the literature: 'The Case of a Shepherd near Lincoln', 'published at the request of the Rev. Mr. Willis' by Dr Robert James in his *Dissertation on fevers*.[1] It was written about 1750 and tells of 'one Isaac' to whom Willis was called 'to read the departing prayer', he having 'lost his senses for five days last past'. Instead of sharing in his wife's despair, Willis 'ordered her to give him a clyster immediately, and apply a blister to his back and head'. After that they gave him 'a paper of Dr. James's Powder' which caused 'convulsive twitchings' and vomiting. Soon after the patient brought up 'three worms, one of which was upwards of a foot long'. Two more doses of the powder the next day 'brought up two more . . . and in four days after, Mr. Willis saw him in a market, seven miles from home, very well, selling sheep'. Dr James commented a 'very remarkable . . . case' and Willis 'esteeming it a part of his duty to communicate this to the world, has desired it to be made public'.

Willis's only other contribution to medical literature was a case report written while he was in regular practice at Dunston, from where he helped to found and became physician to the General Hospital at nearby Lincoln.[2] His neighbour Sir Francis Dashwood communicated on his behalf to that august body the Royal Society of London 'An Account of an extraordinary Case of a Lady, who swallowed Euphorbium' which was printed in their *Philosophical Transactions* in 1760 and reprinted in *The Medical Museum*, 1763.[3]

In fact the patient was his wife, and what she had swallowed was a powerful caustic and counter-irritant strictly for 'external use'. It was recommended in the *Dispensatory* of the Royal College of Physicians for cleaning ulcers and raising blisters and was the active ingredient in the 'Emplastrum Cephalicum' which 'is laid upon the Head to draw out serous humours, and make a Revulsion'. It was also recommended to be 'apply'd to the Feet in Fevers' to draw that disease out through the lower parts.[4] One can imagine the havoc wrought in Mrs Willis's inside, but fortunately she recovered to 'a perfect state of health'.

'Having very early succeeded in the cure of a decided case of derangement, and been equally fortunate in other similar cases', Willis began to specialize in the mad-business and opened his own establishment at Greatford near Stamford in Lincolnshire in 1776. He cannot be classed among the charlatans of history if that term is taken to mean those practitioners who 'adopt extraordinary modes of obtruding themselves and their *wonderful* abilities on the notice of the publick', as they were described by a contemporary.[5] He did well enough without advertising, although his practice was by no means as extensive as he and others claimed, judging from the admissions to his house entered in the register at the Royal College of Physicians.[6]

His double qualification in divinity and medicine which earned him the sobriquet 'the Duplicate Doctor' was not uncommon. He was in the line of 'clerical mad-doctors' which can be traced back to Timothe Bright, physician to St Bartholomew's Hospital, whose *Treatise of melancholie* (1586) was the first psychiatric treatise published in this country and who left medicine for the church.[7] In the seventeenth century the Reverend John Ashbourne of Suffolk gained fame for 'great skill in curing mad people' in his house. He ended as the first psychiatric martyr on record when in 1661 a patient ran him through with a pitchfork.[8] Nearer Willis's time the Reverend Lewis Southcomb of Rose Ash in Devon also practised in this field and distilled his experience in a book called *Peace of mind and health of body united* (1750).

Very little is known about Willis apart from his public appearance in 1788–9 and only glimpses of the man and his methods can be gathered. He is said to have been adept at controlling patients by his gaze. It was reported that

On his first meeting a new patient, his usually friendly and smiling countenance changed its expression. He suddenly became a different figure com-

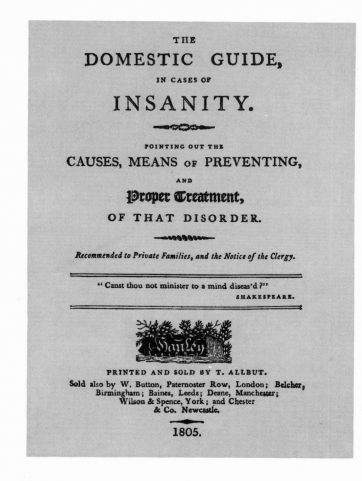

THE
DOMESTIC GUIDE,
IN CASES OF
INSANITY.

POINTING OUT THE
CAUSES, MEANS OF PREVENTING,
AND
𝔓roper 𝔗reatment,
OF THAT DISORDER.

Recommended to Private Families, and the Notice of the Clergy.

" Canst thou not minister to a mind diseas'd ?"
SHAKESPEARE.

PRINTED AND SOLD BY T. ALLBUT.
Sold also by W. Button, Paternoster Row, London; Belcher,
Birmingham; Baines, Leeds; Deane, Manchester;
Wilson & Spence, York; and Chester
& Co. Newcastle.

1805.

14. '*If it be proper to diffuse the general knowledge of any Disease, it must be of Insanity,*' *wrote Mr Thomas Bakewell, owner of a private madhouse, Spring Vale near Stone in Staffordshire, introducing the first popular* '*Insanity Today*' *type of book. He did not* '*venture to recommend*' *it* '*to the notice of medical men*', *since* '*there is scarce a gentleman of the faculty . . . but would gladly give up this part of his practice*'. *Instead he begged* '*leave to solicit the attention of the clergy*' *and in passing paid the Reverend Dr Francis Willis a compliment:* '*They generally have it in their power to command that leisure, and attention to their instructions, which are so necessary in the proper treatment of this disorder. The gentleman, to whom a nation feels grateful for what he has accomplished, is, I understand, a clergyman. No one will presume to say, that he has disgraced his profession, by paying attention to this disease.*'

manding the respect even of maniacs. His piercing eye seemed to read their hearts and divine their thoughts as they formed and before they were even uttered. In this way he gained control over them which he used as a means of cure.[9]

Even the fiery Edmund Burke is reported to have flinched and turned away when Willis 'fixed' on him. The occasion was the examination 'of the Physicians who have attended His Majesty . . . Touching the present State of His Majesty's Health' in January 1789. It transpired that, against their agreed plan of management, Willis had allowed the King a razor to shave himself, and his colleagues charged him with rashness, not to say malpractice.

Burke also was very severe on this point, and authoritatively and loudly demanded to know, 'If the Royal patient had become outrageous at the moment, what power the Doctor possessed of instantaneously terrifying him into obedience ?'

'Place the candles between us, Mr. Burke,' replied the Doctor, in an equally authoritative tone – 'and I'll give you an answer. There, Sir! by the EYE! I should have looked at him *thus*, Sir – *thus*!'

Burke instantaneously averted his head, and, making no reply, evidently acknowledged this *basiliskan* authority.[10]

R. B. Sheridan, who was on the same parliamentary committee, tried to perplex Dr Willis 'with a long string of questions . . . Willis said, "Pray, sir, before you begin, be so good as to snuff those candles that we may see clear, for I always like to see the face of the man I am speaking to." ' This so confounded Sheridan 'that he could not get on in his examination, and for once in his life he was nonplussed,'[11] and like Burke retired from the unequal combat.

Dr Uwins heard that he believed 'he owed a great proportion of his patients to the importation of China tea into Britain'. Tea-drinking was widely held to be a dangerous vice causing nervous disorders.[12] But to single out the China variety was Willis's own idea. Uwins, who related this, himself did not believe it was particularly harmful. 'In this assertion,' he wrote, Willis

might be correct in one sense, but not in another. It is not the mere abstract poison of tea which deteriorates the nervous system, – though there is something even in this, – but it is the accompaniments which tea brings with it that do the greatest mischief. Pianos, parasols, Edinburgh Reviews, and Paris-going desires . . . are the true sources of nervousness and mental ailments, and not merely this or that specific article of food or drink.[13]

To Dr Benjamin Rush of Philadelphia Willis confided in 1796 some particulars of his treatment. Although Willis's letter is lost, Rush referred to it in his own correspondence:

My late success in the treatment of mania has brought me an increase of patients in that disorder. My remedies are frequent but moderate bleedings, purges, low diet, salivation, and afterwards the cold bath. I have lately received a polite letter from Dr. Willis containing a short detail of his mode of treating madness. It accords in some particular with mine, but differs from it materially in others. He does not seem to view the disease as a fever, and that it requires the same remedies as any other fever.[14]

In his *Medical inquiries and observations upon the diseases of the mind*, published in Philadelphia in 1812, Rush recollected that Willis had said he preferred to apply blisters 'to the ancles in this disease, instead of the head or neck' as was customary. To Rush this

immediately suggested a principle . . . from which I have derived great advantages, not only in the treatment of madness, but of several other diseases. In the first stage of tonic, or violent madness, the disease is intrenched, as it were, in the brain. It must be loosened, or weakened, by depleting remedies, before it can be dislodged, or translated to another part of the body. When this has been effected, blisters easily attract it to the lower limbs, and thus often convey it at once out of the body.[15]

The witty Uwins, somewhat ahead of his time, called Rush's method of treatment by 'exciting a sort of vicarious irritation' on the skin by blistering or in the gut with vomits and purges, 'the principle and practice of setting up disorder in one part, for the purpose of knocking it down in another'.[13]

Another who tried to discover how Willis achieved his results was Philippe Pinel, founder of the French school of psychiatry, who symbolically and literally struck the chains off his patients at the Bicêtre in 1793. He was disappointed not to derive greater practical help from his English colleagues. For him, as for so many at home and abroad, the name of Willis inspired a new hope because of its promise of successful treatment. 'I have for the last fifteen years,' wrote Pinel in 1801, 'paid considerable attention to the subject, and consulted all the works which have appeared upon it in the English language, as well as reports which its physicians and travellers in that country have published about their establishments for the insane . . . I have found no secret although all attest their success.' He lamented in particular that Willis had not made available 'an account of the development of his general principles of cure, and their application to the characters, varieties and degrees of intensity of mania'. He himself had lost 'faith in pharmaceutic preparations', having found that 'insanity was curable in many instances, by mildness of treatment and attention to the state of mind . . . I saw, with wonder, the resources of nature when left to herself, or skilfully assisted in her efforts.'[16] Besides, he agreed with Battie that 'altho' Madness is frequently taken for one species of disorder, nevertheless, when thoroughly examined, it discovers as much variety with respect to its causes and circumstances as any distemper whatever: Madness therefore, like most other morbid cases, rejects all general methods.'[17] Whenever a 'specific antimaniacal' was vaunted, it lessened the chances of discovering a rational, that is aetiological as opposed to symptomatic, treatment. 'The [natural] history and distinctions of the disease were neglected through excessive infatuated attention to the remedy,' wrote Pinel.[16] A useful piece could be written on the wishful credulity of medical men on 'psychiatric treatments which have worked' – if only for a season, and the pages of psychiatric journals over the last thirty years alone would furnish ample material for it.

But Willis was not to be goaded into print, not because he had a nostrum to hide but because he had nothing to reveal. His methods were no different from everybody else's. Not even the jibes of the apothecary of Bethlem succeeded. From the admission books of that hospital Haslam found only about one-third had been discharged 'cured' and even this proportion declined with patients' age. 'When the reader contrasts the preceding statement with the account recorded in the report of the committee, appointed to examine the physicians who have attended his majesty,' wrote Haslam,

he will . . . require some other evidence, than the bare assertions of the man pretending to have performed such cures. It was deposed by that reverend and celebrated physician, that of patients placed under his care . . . nine out of ten had recovered; and also that the age was of no signification, unless the patient had been afflicted before with the same malady . . . I must acknowledge, that my mind would have been much more satisfied as to the truth of that assertion, had it been plausibly made out, or had the circumstances been otherwise than feebly recollected by that very successful practitioner.[18]

It was not until 1822, almost a quarter of a century later, that a Willis set out to vindicate old Dr Willis. His claim had been based on nothing 'but the fair and natural result of superior skill and great experience', his grandson Dr Francis Willis junior told the assembled fellows of the Royal College of Physicians. He had simply failed to make himself clear before the parliamentary committees because 'as Mr. Pitt well observed . . . "The severe cross-examinations he experienced were calculated to puzzle simplicity, and leave the coolness, which ought always to accompany the delivery of evidence, too unguarded".' What he had really meant to say, said his grandson, was not that he cured nine out of ten patients indiscriminately, but

nine out of ten of that species of the disorder, namely, *delirium and derangement cum febre* [with fever], under which the exalted patient more particularly laboured, had recovered if brought under his care within three months after the attack of the disease . . . It is to this, that, in his answers, he is alone referring . . . He did not comprehend in them that determined and settled case of insanity, where the mental faculties alone are distractedly engaged, exclusively of any participation with the body. He did not intend when he delivered this opinion, to comprise the *mens insana in corpore sano*.[2]

Two visitors penetrated to Greatford and left eye-witness accounts of

what they saw and of their interviews with the Doctor and his son Dr John
– his other medical son Dr Robert Darling Willis lived and practised in
London and acted as the family's representative there. The first, in 1796,
was told:

The time it takes to cure patients varies from about six weeks to eighteen
months; on an average they are cured within six months. On their arrival
Dr Willis [senior] merely observes them and regulates their natural functions
with appropriate medicines. All heating foods, warm drinks, tea and coffee
are forbidden, but patients are exercised as much as possible. If they are
delirious, they are put into a strait-waistcoat in which they can neither hurt
themselves nor others. It has the further advantage of inculcating salutary fear
so that on later occasions the mere threat of it will make them control themselves. The rare case requires stronger coercive measures such as tying up
with ropes. The emotion of fear is the first and often the only one by which
they can be governed. By working on it one removes their thoughts from the
phantasms occupying them and brings them back to reality, even if this en-
tails inflicting pain and suffering. It is fear too which teaches them to judge
their actions rightly and learn the consequences. By such means is their
attention brought back to their surroundings.[9]

The other visitor went in 1803 to see 'the man who has achieved universal fame for his treatment of the insane but of whose methods nothing is
really known'. Dr John Willis told him that a knowledge of the human
heart was the most important part of success. One had to gain the patient's
confidence and esteem. The strait-waistcoat was the best way to tame the
violent. It was rarely necessary to hit a patient, but when it was, the blow
should be struck by doctor rather than keeper to produce the best result. All
activities must be regulated and favourite pastimes allowed only as rewards.
Madness which came on suddenly was the easiest to cure, especially in the
presence of physical disease. Dr John denied they had ever claimed to cure
nine out of ten of all their patients. Under certain circumstances he said 'we
exceed this number, in others we do not reach it'.[19]

But by this time psychiatry was well on the road to advancement and
Willis's slogan 'nine out of ten cured' had given it the necessary impetus to
encourage both doctors and patients. 'There have been, and still are, a few
medical artists no less successful in the cure of insanity than the late veteran
Willis,' wrote Dr George Nesse Hill of Chester in tribute to the Reverend
Doctor, who had died in 1807. 'The writer of this essay is enabled to corro-
borate the affirmation of Dr. Willis from the sources of considerable experience.'[20] Mr Thomas Bakewell, the Staffordshire madhouse keeper, likewise gave Willis 'full credit for the truth of his statement, without ascribing
to him any superior methods; it being borne out by what I have myself seen
of success in practice'.[21] And in 1820 Dr George Man Burrows added the
weight of his authority:

We might have been convinced, thirty years ago, that insanity was cured in a ratio equivalent probably to what is experienced in most disorders. But it was the predicament of the late celebrated Dr. Willis, in his evidence before a Committee of Parliament . . . to be discredited when he stated, that *nine* out of *ten* cases of insanity recovered. Doubts of his veracity were implied by his coadjutors, the physicians attending on his Majesty; and consequently by many others . . . Probably, those who derided Dr. Willis, had neither his experience in this malady, nor his opportunities of treating it in its early and therefore most favourable stage; and few, I am confident, ever so fully possessed the essential auxiliaries to success as that physician. We now see, that, in situations less promising, eight in ten, and even six in seven *recent* cases are reported, and believed to have actually recovered.[22]

In 1822 the compiler of a four-volume system of medicine reviewed 'recent advances' in the 'medical and moral' treatment of insanity. 'Both have undergone a very great improvement within the last twenty or thirty years' since the illness of 1788, he wrote, 'the first by being considerably simplified, the second by being more thoroughly studied and raised to a higher degree of importance.'[23]

However rash Willis's claim, with it he gave psychiatry the last leg up to respectability by removing the stigma of 'once a lunatic, always a lunatic'. He not only brought hope to the patient but also removed the excuse for neglect which therapeutic pessimism had fostered for centuries. As Francis Bacon wrote two hundred years earlier: 'This very sentence of *Pronouncing Diseases to be incurable*, enacts a law, as it were, for sloath and negligence, and redeemes ignorance from Discredit and Infamy.' It was Willis's achievement to have propounded however unwittingly '*the cures of Diseases held incurable*', the remedy which the learned Chancellor had prescribed so that the 'faculty may be awakt and stirred up'.[24]

18

Coercion and Restraint

Before 1788 public unease about the private madhouse system had centred on the danger to the liberty of the subject it entailed. There was less concern with how patients were treated once inside. Thus Alexander Cruden, author of *A complete concordance to the Holy Scriptures* (1738), which is still in print, took offence at having been 'in a most *unjust* and *arbitrary* Manner sent . . . to a *Private Madhouse*' and being 'Imprisoned' there, rather than at being '*Chained, Handcuffed, Strait-Wastecoated*'. This attitude changed after the King's illness, when the revelations of his sickroom lifted the veil from professional practice in the mad-business. A feeling of revulsion arose at the idea of the monarch in a strait-waistcoat, and the realization grew that the same fate awaited any gentleman or woman, however high-born, suffering from the same affliction. Finally, concern began to be felt about how the poor and mad fared.

Before the King had fallen ill, Professor William Cullen of Edinburgh, His Majesty's 'Principal Mediciner' or first physician in Scotland, had laid down in the standard and most widely read textbook of the time, three main principles for governing 'maniacs': intimidation, isolation and restraint. These were the essentials of the plan on which George III was treated, as agreed among the royal physicians and put into effect by Willis. Cullen wrote:

> Fear being a passion that diminishes excitement . . . it has appeared to me necessary to employ a very constant impression [of it] . . . and therefore to inspire them with awe and dread of some particular persons, especially of those who are to be constantly near them. This awe and dread is . . . to be acquired in the first place, by their being the authors of all the restraints that may be occasionally proper; but sometimes it may be necessary to acquire it even by stripes and blows . . .
>
> Restraining the anger and violence of madmen is always necessary for preventing their hurting themselves or others; but this restraint is also to be

considered as a remedy. Angry passions are always rendered more violent by the indulgence of the tempestuous motions they produce . . . Restraint, therefore, is useful, and ought to be complete . . . and the strait waistcoat answers every purpose better than any other . . .

The restraint mentioned requires confinement within doors, and it should be in a place which presents as few objects of sight and hearing as possible; and particularly, it should be removed from the objects that the patient was formerly acquainted with, as these would more readily call up ideas and their various associations. It is for this reason that the confinement of madmen should hardly ever be in their usual habitation . . . [and] that maniacs should be without the company of any of their former acquaintance; the appearance of whom commonly excites emotions that increase the disease.[1]

In fairness to Cullen it must be said that he had little experience of treating the insane, for apart from twelve 'cells' in the basement of the Edinburgh Infirmary and a bedlam attached to the city workhouse there was no provision for the insane in Edinburgh until the Royal Asylum opened in 1813. Furthermore, his views on treatment were in accord with his theory of madness: to bring down the patient's nervous excitement and turbulent spirits and allow 'right reason to return' it was necessary to abstract him from all affecting stimuli, restrain him physically by mechanical means and mentally by opposing the powerful passion of fear. At the same time the body's natural powers were reduced by bleeding, purging, vomiting and a low diet. Cullen's 'antimaniacal' regime exemplifies the old confusion between treatment and restraint, the former benefiting the patient by removing the cause of his illness, the latter controlling its manifestations for the sake of environment at whatever cost to the sufferer. Even today this distinction is not always kept in mind in considering the effects of 'treatment', and the results of one may be mistaken for the other.

Even the kindly Dr Thomas Percival, whose book on medical ethics of 1803, written with the help of and dedicated to his friend Sir George Baker, set the standard of medical practice for the period and who gave much thought to 'the *medicina mentis*' – the medicine of the mind, that is psychological treatment – praised the strait-waistcoat as a 'modern' advance over beating patients, which might otherwise be necessary.

The law justifies the beating of a lunatic [he advised aspiring doctors] in such manner as the circumstances require. But it has been before remarked that a physician, who attends an asylum for insanity, is under obligation of honour as well as of humanity, to secure the unhappy sufferers, committed to his charge, all the tenderness and indulgence compatible with steady and effectual government. And the strait waistcoat, with other improvements in modern practice, now preclude the necessity of coercion by corporal punishment.[2]

Chains too were still widely used for confining patients, as they had been since the sixteenth century. At Bethlem they continued to be preferred to

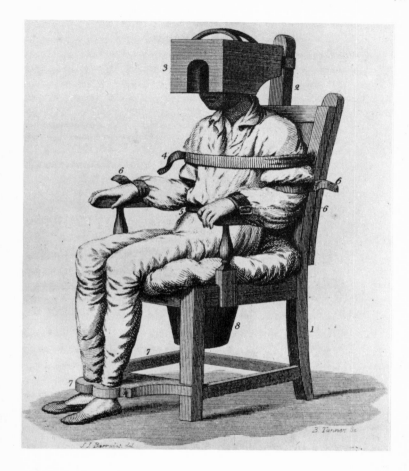

15. *The restraining chair devised by Dr Benjamin Rush, one of America's great physicians and a signatory to the Declaration of Independence. It was recommended to the royal physicians for George III in 1811 but declined.*

the strait-waistcoat. But they were considered fit only for paupers and when there was a shortage of attendants, as there always was. 'Chains are fit only for pauper Lunatics,' Dr Thomas Monro told Mr Rose's Committee in 1815 in defence of their practice. 'If a gentleman was put into irons, he would not like it . . . The more keepers there are, the less the necessity I should think for restraint [and] the less the number of irons . . . In Bethlem the restraint is by chains . . . They are generally chained to the wall with them . . . there is no such thing as chains in my [private] house.'[3] It must be stressed that such horrifying methods were not expressions of any conscious cruelty. They were in keeping with a much harsher spirit of the times, from which the insane were not exempted by their infirmity. For instance there were still something like 120 offences which carried capital punishment, and executions were public spectacles.

Even the philanthropic Dr Thomas Arnold advised the governors of the Leicester Infirmary in 1792 that their proposed lunatic block for twenty patients would need to be furnished with '20 strait waistcoats, as well as a great number of appropriate Straps, Locks, and other fastenings, and securities; besides Chairs of a peculiar construction for particular purposes, and common Chairs for common use' and a special room would be required 'to receive the various instruments of security which are not in use'.[4] By 1809, with over forty years' experience in his own private madhouse, and fifteen years' of running the Leicester Lunatic Asylum, his tone was somewhat mollified. In that year he published his *Observations on the management of the insane; and particularly on the agency and importance of humane and kind treatment*, the title of which is significant enough in itself of changing attitudes since the royal malady. He wrote it 'to urge the importance of mild and indulgent treatment . . . and to evince the great value and efficacy of good nourishment and assiduous nursing'. Yet so firmly entrenched was the class system even in psychiatric care – to an extent never known in any other branch of medicine – that he added that '*Chains* should never be used but in the case of poor patients, whose pecuniary circumstances will not admit of such attendance as is necessary to procure safety without them.'[5]

Of course there were isolated voices crying in the wilderness against such practices like that of Dr William Pargeter, who left medicine to become a naval chaplain during the Napoleonic wars and whose definition of madness has already been quoted. He inveighed not only against '*chains* and *cords* . . . and other galling manacles', whatever the patient's circumstances or mental state, but also against '*beating* . . . a practice formerly much in use in treating the insane'. He was both

sorry, and surprized to note, that some authors, of very late date [this was written in 1792], have countenanced such unnatural and brutish violence. But I will boldly and positively venture to declare, that such usage is on no occasion necessary . . . for if maniacs are not to be subdued by *management* . . . beating will never effect it . . . and therefore, I at once condemn this practice, as altogether erroneous, and not to be justified upon any principles or pretences whatsoever.

He condemned equally giving patients 'large doses of stupefying liquor, or narcotic draughts, that drown their faculties'.[6] The practice of keeping patients quiet or tranquillized by chemical means instead of physical or mechanical restraint and regarding it as treatment may be dated from that time.

Pargeter's way of managing patients was simple and harmless. It became known as 'catching them by the eye'. (We have seen that Dr Willis was adept at controlling patients by his gaze.) By this means he hoped to establish reassuring contact, subdue excitement by assuaging anxiety and so gain co-operation for whatever medical and nursing procedures were necessary.

This method symbolized a new relationship between doctor and patient, a relationship involving the doctor's personality and not only his medical skills. And this became increasingly important as mechanical restraint was abandoned in favour of moral treatment and with it the sanative influence of sane on insane mind.

Against this background of accepted medical practice as taught by the leaders of the profession, it is easier to understand why it was the royal family and the public, and not the King's physicians, who were revolted at the thought of their monarch bundled up in Willis's strait-waistcoat and tied to his bed or secured in a restraining-chair. It was this part of his treatment which so hurt and shamed the King and which his loyal Queen could never forgive.* Willis realized this himself:

When I was first summoned to attend George III, I gave great offence to the Queen by my method of treating his malady. As death makes no distinction in his visits between the poor man's hut and the prince's palace, so insanity is equally impartial in her dealings with her subjects. For that reason, I made no distinction in my treatment of persons submitted to my charge. When, therefore, my gracious sovereign became violent, I felt it my duty to subject him to the same system of restraint as I should have adopted with one of his own gardeners at Kew: in plain words, I put a strait waistcoat on him. . . . The strait waistcoat was the offence to her pride which the Queen never could, and never did, overcome. On that account, I was turned off, and not in the civillest manner.

He was even inclined to blame the Queen for William Pitt not fulfilling the inducements he had offered the doctor to bring him down from Lincolnshire. Willis 'declared that he had not kept faith with him; for that,

* The need for a drug with 'sedative powers, specifically such . . . to soothe and calm the perturbations of the human mind' (J. Ford, *Three Letters on Medical Subjects*, 1803, p. 28) was felt particularly when it became known that George III had been confined in a strait-waistcoat. It so stirred the 'patriotic . . . feelings' of Dr Edward Sutleffe, an obscure practitioner in the City of London, that he suggested to Dr Reynolds in 1801 and to Dr Simmons in 1804 a trial of his 'herbaceous tranquillizer' – the juice of Ground Ivy – on the King. So was introduced to psychiatry the name for a group of drugs which figure prominently in present times. (E. Sutleffe 'Observations on the Utility of Hedera Sylvestris (Ground Ivy) in the Treatment of Mania', *London Medical and Physical Journal*, 1819, vol. 42, p. 197; *Medical and Surgical Cases*, 1824, pp. 4–5.)

when he had evinced great reluctance to take charge of George the Third's person, he [Pitt] promised him, if he would consent, a baronetcy and a pension of £1,500 a year; neither of which he ever obtained.'[7]

Paradoxically as it may seem today, it was not this aspect of Willis's treatment with which the royal physicians quarrelled. Remarkably those frightened men took offence at the liberty Willis allowed the King. His experience gave him a fearlessness and assurance in dealing with patients which they lacked. Willis's most outspoken critic, perhaps because the most jealous and hot-headed, was Dr Richard Warren, 'that black spirit' the sight of whom always agitated the Queen 'very much'.[8] He told the Parliamentary Committee that on Willis's first coming on 5 December there had been a meeting of all the medical attendants at his house:

It was there first settled as a Principle, that Quiet of Body and Mind were to be endeavoured to be obtained by every Means possible; and that every Thing should be carefully kept from His Majesty that might tend to prevent this desirable Acquisition. It was settled that a regular Coercion [the strait-waistcoat] should be made use of – that every Thing should be kept from His Majesty that was likely to excite any Emotion – that though His Majesty had not shewn any Signs of an Intention to injure Himself, yet that it was absolutely necessary, considering the sudden Impulses to which His Distemper subjects People, to put every Thing out of the Way that could do any Mischief.

Yet Willis had allowed the King to see the Queen and his children, had given him a book to read – Shakespeare's *King Lear*, of all things, said Warren, 'which affected me much, and immediately determined me to bring a Charge against Dr. Willis, for what I thought bad Practice'. Worst of all in Warren's eyes, Willis had 'put a Razor into His Majesty's Hand, and a Penknife'.[9]

'Do you remember your having put a Razor and Penknife into the Hands of His Majesty, the Day after the Consultation?', that is 6 December, demanded the indignant members of the Parliamentary Committee of Willis, and he answered:

His Majesty had not been shaved for a long While, perhaps a Fortnight, or Three Weeks; and the Person that had been used to shave Him [Mr Papendiek, husband of the writer of the journal[10]], could not complete the Parts of His upper and under Lips; and, being confident, from the Professions and Humour of His Majesty at that Moment, I suffered His Majesty to shave His Lips Himself . . . His Nails also wanted cutting very much; and . . . I suffered Him to cut His own Nails with a Penknife.[11]

To justify himself further he added:

It is necessary for a Physician, especially in such Cases, to be able to judge, at the Moment, whether he can confide in the Professions of his Patient; and I never was disappointed in my Opinion.

In similar circumstances he explained he had even trusted them 'with a Knife and Fork'. None of the other physicians had protested at his 'indulging the King in the Use of sharp Instruments'. He had subsequently withdrawn the privilege, he said, partly because if indulged in one particular the King might take it amiss not to have all his wishes gratified and the passions thus roused might aggravate his already excited state. For instance, immediately after shaving himself, the King 'took it ill that I would not let him go up Stairs to see His Family,' said Willis, 'and many other Things, which I found it would not be prudent to do.' This at least was his face-saver. What really happened was that he had been hauled over the coals by the Lord Chancellor, to whom Warren had gone to tell tales. Warren had first turned to his old master the Prince of Wales, who 'desired me, as he had done in every Case of Difficulty that had happened, from the Beginning of the Illness, to lay the Affair before the Lord Chancellor'. Lord Thurlow intervened, went to Kew and reminded Willis 'that the Rules of the Consultation should be strictly obeyed'.[9] Warren had been the Prince of Wales's doctor before he was called to George III[12] and belonged to the Carlton House circle and Thurlow was busy ingratiating himself with the Regent-to-be.

'Good Heavens!' exclaimed a disgusted Fanny Burney in her diary, 'what an insult does this seem from parliamentary power, to investigate and bring forth to the world every circumstance of such a malady as is ever held sacred to secrecy in the most private families! How indignant we all felt here no words can say.'[13] George III grew to dislike Warren almost as much as Willis. Being asked in continuation of his examination by the Parliamentary Committee 'Whether His Majesty has ever shewn any Signs of Dislike towards you?' Warren replied 'Not lately...I was in great Disfavour at Windsor – it continued for some Time after His Majesty came to Kew; – it began to diminish soon after Dr. Willis came.' Two days earlier the King, in confinement at Kew, had picked a knave from a pack of cards and on it wrote 'Sir Richard Warren Bart First Physician to the King'.[14]

Yet these revelations of the sickroom, however afflicting to the family and embarrassing to the King after his recovery, served to guide a wider circle of doctors in the management of patients under similar circumstances. Even today the practice of removing what are colloquially called 'sharps' from patients on admission to a psychiatric unit is still widespread; and not until the past two or three decades have patients uniformly been allowed the use of knife and fork of ordinary construction, such has been the fear of psychiatrists that patients under their care might commit suicide. Their precautions, as Willis seems to have realized, often must have suggested the possibility to their patients, or at least such obvious marks of their doctors' mistrust and anxiety must have communicated itself to them and so increased their own. Willis's courage – his colleagues called it foolhardiness –

in handing George III his razor echoed round the medical world, because it allowed the patient a sense of dignity which confinement and restraint otherwise deprived him of. It was in this sense that the American psychiatric pioneer Dr George Parkman, the first from his country to undertake post-graduate study in the subject in Europe and more particularly Pinel and Esquirol's first American student,[15] repeated the story in his little manual *Management of lunatics, with illustrations of insanity* published at Boston in 1817, from 'a narrative I received from a physician to whom Dr. Willis communicated it'.

The King proposed one day to shave *himself*. Dr. W. feared to hesitate in assenting, lest he should seem to suspect the King of intended suicide, and give him dangerous notions, of the pre-existence of which there was no certainty. Dr. W. called for the razors, and in the mean time engaged the King about some papers on the table. The razors were put on the same table, the King still attended to his papers, which encouraged Dr. W. to believe suicide was not intended. After shaving, the King returned to his papers; the razors were not removed immediately, lest Dr. W.'s anxiety about possible mischief should appear, and occasion a dangerous train of thought.[16]

From allowing patients the use of razor, knife and fork, it was but one step, albeit a greatly courageous one, towards placing in their hands the tools of trade. This Hallaran did at Cork, the Tukes at the York Retreat and Ellis developed into a thriving business at Hanwell. In this way occupational and industrial therapy as a vital adjunct to normalizing the life of patients in institutions, rehearsing their intellectual and physical skills and retaining their self-respect, was born.

But in naming Ellis, psychiatry's first knight, in connexion with this important improvement in the life of the insane, it must not be thought that he was equally enlightened in other departments, least of all in 'treatment', a paradox which occurs time and again in the history of psychiatry. As late as 1838 in *A treatise on the nature, symptoms, causes, and treatment of insanity, with practical observations on lunatic asylums, and a description of the pauper lunatic asylum for the county of Middlesex at Hanwell*, the book in which Ellis summed up his life's work the year before he died and which had the honour of being translated into French, 'enriched' with notes by the great Esquirol, he wrote in his chapter on treatment:

Happily the whip has for some time, at least in this country, ceased to be allowed in any Lunatic Asylums; and the more human and rational plan of punishment, by deprivation and confinement, has been substituted in its place. It sometimes however happens, that patients are met with who are so obstinate and incorrigibly perverse, that these means alone are not sufficient. The shock of the electrifying-machine, which is often found beneficial in cases where the powers want rousing, is, in cases of determined obstinacy and bad conduct, equally useful. The terror of the machine will often overcome the vicious inclination.[17]

By coincidence the method of treating patients with nervous disorders by means of shocks and sparks was first popularized the year George III came to the throne by John Wesley in his *The desideratum: or, electricity made plain and useful. By a lover of mankind, and of common sense.* Wesley intended it as a companion piece to his *Primitive physick: or, an easy and natural method of curing most diseases*, published three years earlier and the most popular 'home doctor' of the reign. Serious electrification of patients with psychiatric disorders did not start until George Adams junior, 'Mathematical Instrument Maker to His Majesty, and Optician to His Royal Highness the Prince of Wales', invented a more powerful machine from which the current could be applied directly to the head.[18] With it Mr John Birch, surgeon to St Thomas's Hospital in London, stunned the first 'depressed' patients in the late 1780s.[19] By 1793 there was founded in that great charitable age The London Electrical Dispensary 'with a view to afford a new benefit to the lower orders of mankind'.[20]

The attitude towards restraint had changed radically by the end of the reign, thanks largely to the practice having been brought before the public in 1788 and George Rose and his colleagues making it one of the central issues of their inquiry in 1815 during the King's declining years. They reported that they had heard of many instances of 'Restraint of persons much beyond what is necessary, certainly retarding recovery, even beyond what is occasioned by the crowded state of the house . . . In the course of the Evidence there will be found opinions unfavourable to the use of strait waistcoats, as more oppressive to the Patient even than irons.'[21]

It could not be expected that a parliamentary report would from one day to the next reverse generally accepted and widespread medical practice, but at least from then on doctors and keepers had to justify themselves to a critical public. And gradually from the examples of the Retreat at York and its imitators a competition developed for minimizing the use of restraint, and evolving other methods of treatment. By 1827 Mr Robert Gordon's Select Committee 'appointed to inquire into the State of the Pauper Lunatics in . . . Middlesex' divided the treatment of the insane into three parts: 'physical treatment', embracing all those features of Cullen's restraint system already detailed; 'mental treatment', by which they meant 'the active engagement of the mind' by 'amusement' and 'employment' such as is today called occupational and industrial therapy; and 'moral treatment', comprising all means to encourage patients' 'own efforts of self-restraint in every possible way, by exciting and cherishing in them feelings of self-respect, by treating them with delicacy . . . and generally by maintaining towards them a treatment uniformly judicious and kind, sympathizing with them, and at the same time diverting their minds from painful and injurious associations.'[22] Mr Gordon's *Report* was followed the next year by the Act to Regulate the Care and Treatment of Insane Persons in England (1828), in which the policy of Parliament to encourage a milder treatment of patients was given official expression. Doctors were required to make a weekly return of every patient in restraint for inspection by the Commissioners in Lunacy in London or Quarter Sessions Visitors in the country.

There remained only the final hurdle – the total abolition of all mechanical restraint. To this perfection the Victorian asylums, organized on lines suggested by Mr Wynn's Parliamentary Committee of 1807, were devoted. This bold innovation, successfully introduced against great odds by Dr John Conolly at the Middlesex County Pauper Lunatic Asylum at Hanwell in 1839, has rightly been acclaimed as one of the great medical advances of the nineteenth century, alongside anaesthesia and antisepsis. 'There is nothing more striking in the course of medical science than the improvement in the treatment of the insane by the abolition of restraint . . . It has placed us first amongst all nations as physicians of mental disease, and has yielded the best literature on insanity that has ever been produced,' commented an eminent Victorian medical scientist.[23] It also put patients in the best way to spontaneous recovery, unimpeded by afflicting methods of control, and so for the first time allowed the natural history of mental diseases to be observed undistorted by aggravating interference. And with it the keepers of old went out and mental nursing as a profession began.[24]

'If that little book of 1813 [Samuel Tuke's *Description of the Retreat*] had done nothing more than inspire Conolly to undertake his work, it would not have been written in vain,' generously commented the son of its author.[25] And in November 1853 the first number of the new *Asylum Journal*, which later became the *Journal of Mental Science* published by the Royal Medico-Psychological Association and which is now the *British Journal of Psychiatry*, opened with these words:

From the time when Pinel obtained the permission of Couthon to try the humane experiment of releasing from fetters some of the insane citizens chained to the dungeon walls of the Bicetre, to the date when Conolly announced, that in the vast Asylum over which he presided, mechanical restraint in the treatment of the insane had been entirely abandoned, and superseded by moral influence, a new school of special medicine has been gradually forming.[26]

19

Nervous Disorders and Insanity

'Fashion has long influenced the great and opulent in the choice of their physicians,' observed the cynical Dr James Makittrick Adair of Bath,[1] that famous spa to which people of fashion resorted in health and came away even better, as Horace Walpole of equal wit remarked. 'But,' continued Adair, 'it is not so obvious how it has influenced them also in the choice of their diseases', and no better example than the group of 'nervous' disorders or 'lowness of spirits . . . spleen, vapours, or hyp', as they used to be called.

'The Princess, afterwards Queen Anne,' Adair wrote, 'often chagrined and insulted in her former station, and perplexed and harassed in the latter, was frequently subject to depression of spirits . . . This circumstance was sufficient to transfer both the disease and the remedy to all who had the least pretensions to rank.'

And with this diagnosis they remained content, without having 'the least idea that they had nerves', until Dr George Cheyne in 1733[2] and Professor Robert Whytt in 1765[3] published their treatises on nervous disorders. Physicians to 'persons of fashion' began to tell they were 'nervous; the solution was quite satisfactory, the term became fashionable, and spleen, vapours, and hyp, were forgotten'. Not quite, that is, because as late as 1841 the Chevalier De Montallegry published at Paris a book with the title *Hypochondrie-Spleen* named after the eighteenth-century Englishman's favourite malady. It had become known the world over as 'the English disease', perhaps a tit-for-tat for syphilis being called 'the French disease'. However that may be, so widely was melancholy identified with these islands that Dr Cheyne had called his book *The English Malady*. This 'Set of Distempers' he wrote, 'scarce known to our Ancestors' had become so rife in his time as 'to make almost one third of the Complaints of the People of Condition.' A distinguished visitor to England in 1765, the inquiring if somewhat credulous French scholar P. J. Grosley, gained the impression that 'the English Melancholy', a propensity to suicide and the great numbers of 'Madmen and Lunatics', were so much part of the national scene that he devoted whole chapters to them.[4] The cause of this nervous tendency he traced to the mixture of fogs, beef and beer which made up the average native's external and internal environment, aggravated by the rigours of non-conformity and the tedium of the English Sunday. Here, he wrote, even 'the principal festivals of the year', which elsewhere were joyous occasions, brought with them only 'an increase of sadness'. Stern laws had been enacted against suicide but had not stemmed the tide: 'nature is too powerful for laws' he explained and not even the stone balustrade which obstructed his view of the Thames had prevented the citizens of London from precipitating themselves into their river in considerable numbers.

Fashion and fable aside, the 1780s saw an upsurge of interest in 'nerves' for a number of reasons. It started with the appearance of the third (enlarged) edition of Professor Cullen's First lines of the practice of physic (Edinburgh, 1783), one of the most influential of later eighteenth-century medical texts. In the third volume, devoted largely to nervous disorders, Cullen gave them medical respectability and scientific status by the simple expedient of clothing them in classical garb. He called them 'neuroses', which he defined as all those affections of movement or sensation occurring without fever and not dependent on local disease in the part affected. Cullen's term soon became synonymous with functional as opposed to structural disease of nerves, although really very little of either was known. Later, 'functional' was equated with imaginary rather than real – hence the prefix 'psycho' favoured by Freud.

This psycho-neurotic bias was not intended by Cullen but owed its original impetus to events then taking place at Paris. There the Viennese expatriate Franz Anton Mesmer's doctrine of animal magnetism was at the height of its popularity. Mesmer claimed the human body possessed healing powers which could be passed from one individual to another. He likened its action to magnetism and called it animal magnetism, to distinguish it from its mineral counterpart. His lectures and demonstrations, his followers and his 'cures', caused such a stir that in 1784 Louis XVI set up a commission of top scientists to inquire into it. Among them were Antoine Lavoisier, founder of modern chemistry, Benjamin Franklin, American Ambassador to the Court of France, and the humane Dr Guillotin. They concluded that as a biological force Mesmer's 'fluid' was a myth, and explained the undoubted effects on patients they witnessed as the result of imagination reinforced by passions or emotions called forth by the ceremonial of the occasion. Never before had they witnessed that 'active and terrible power' so nakedly displayed in all its 'astonishing effects'. In 1785 the Report of Dr. Benjamin Franklin, and other commissioners, charged by the King of France, with the examination of the animal magnetism, as now practised at Paris, appeared in English translation. The same year the Medical

Society of London, sensing that the emotions might also be used to cure disease by orthodox doctors, announced as the subject for the first Fothergillian prize essay to be awarded in 1786 'What diseases may be mitigated or cured, by exciting particular affections or passions of the mind?' It was awarded to Dr William Falconer of Bath, whose *Dissertation on the influence of the passions upon disorders of the body* appeared in 1788. In 1790 incidentally, Falconer wrote a book on 'the Medicinal Properties of the Bath Waters' which he dedicated to the King with the double hope 'that your Majesty's reign may be long and happy' and of attracting him to Bath should unhappily the need arise again for him to take mineral waters, as in 1788.

In 1787 mesmerism was brought to England by a number of itinerant 'professors of that science', received a boost from the drama of the royal malady and reached its peak in 1789–90, when 'it was credibly reported that 3,000 persons have attended at one time, to get admission at Mr. Loutherbourg's [lecture-demonstrations] at Hammersmith' and a black market in tickets sprang up at 'from One to Three guineas each'.[5] In early Victorian times Mr James Braid, surgeon of Manchester, aimed to give mesmerism medical and scientific status. A necessary prerequisite was to remove the implied charlatanism associated with its name. He therefore replaced it by combining the Greek words for nerves and sleep into *Neurypnology; or, the rationale of nervous sleep* (1843). But realizing that so cumbersome a term might not find general acceptance, as Cullen's neuroses had done, he offered the shortened form by which hypnotism and hypnosis have come down to us today.

By the 1790s the neuroses were firmly established in the medical mind as psychosomatic conditions in the modern sense and the question in any given case was 'to determine whether the state of the body is to be attributed to that of the mind, or the latter to the former'.[6] Time was now ripe for another popular exposition, and this was presented by Dr Thomas Trotter of Newcastle, retired physician to the Channel Fleet. His book, *A view of the nervous temperament; being a practical enquiry into the increasing prevalence, prevention, and treatment of those diseases commonly called nervous*, was published at Newcastle in 1807. The following year it was reprinted at New York and so achieved the distinction of becoming the first psychiatric treatise to appear in America. Trotter's aim was to bring Cheyne's *English Malady* up to date, so to speak. 'The last century has been remarkable for the increase of a class of diseases but little known in former times,' he wrote:

They have been designated in common language, by the terms Nervous; Spasmodic; Bilious; Indigestion; Stomach Complaints; Low Spirits; Vapours, &c. . . . In the present day, this class of diseases forms by far the largest proportion of the whole, which come under the treatment of the physician. Sydenham at the conclusion of the seventeenth century computed fevers to constitute two thirds of the diseases of mankind [one hundred years it should be added, before the clinical thermometer by which this symptom could be detected with any degree of accuracy]. But, at the beginning of the nineteenth century, we do not hesitate to affirm, that *nervous disorders* have now taken the place of fevers, and may be justly reckoned two thirds of the whole, with which civilized society is afflicted. Dr Cheyne . . . makes nervous disorders almost one third of the complaints of people of condition in England: from which we are led to believe, they were then little known among the inferior orders. But from causes, to be hereafter investigated, we shall find, that nervous ailments are no longer confined to the better ranks in life, but rapidly extending to the poorer classes . . . It is probable the other countries of Europe do not exhibit such general examples of these diseases; as many of their causes are to be traced to the peculiar situation of Britain; its insular varieties of climate and atmosphere; its political institutions and free government; and above every thing, its vast wealth, so diffused among all ranks of people.[7]

Even though it became the trend in Georgian England to suffer from 'nerves', the successor to the melancholy of the Elizabethans, frank derangement requiring isolation from society was a different matter. The loss of the most noble faculty, that of reason, which 'sinks unhappy Man below the mute and senseless Part of the Creation', as the preacher said, was equated with 'Sin and Ignorance' as a 'third Sort of Blindness' of the mind or soul.[8] To it there remained attached, as Dr Cheyne complained, 'some Kind of Disgrace and Imputation'. Yet this calamity too was regarded as peculiarly English as the spleen. Even Dr Thomas Arnold of Leicester, one of Cullen's star pupils in this field, could not shake himself free from the belief. Indeed he opened his scholarly two volumes of *Observations on . . . insanity* (Leicester, 1782–6) – 'Dr. Arnold's very entertaining work' which James Boswell recommended to 'whoever wishes to see the opinions both of ancients and moderns upon this subject, collected and illustrated with a variety of curious facts'[9] – with a chapter 'Whether Insanity prevails more in England than in other Countries'. He pointed out that Sauvages, the great French classifier of disease, had 'among the species of Melancholy . . . one under the title of Melancholia Anglica, or English Melancholy; by which he means that disposition to suicide so frequent among the English'. Even his revered teacher Cullen had a place for it in his nosological system and what is more had suggested that because it was so common it could hardly be counted as morbid: 'Perhaps, among the English, weariness of life does not always depend on disease.'[10] It may just have been Cullen's Scottish sense of fun, but Arnold took it seriously and tried to analyse the possible causes. To those listed by Cheyne and Grosley he added 'commerce, and the various passions which attend the desire, pursuit, and acquisition of riches, and every species of luxury, and all violent and permanent

attachments thereto'. Insanity, he wrote, is 'an uncommon disorder in proportion, as wealth and luxury are but little known. In Scotland, where the
inhabitants in general are neither opulent nor luxurious, Insanity, as I am
informed, is very rare: nor is it more frequent in the poorer, and less culti-
vated parts of Wales.' The conclusion was inescapable: 'I can see no other
way of accounting for this vast increase of the disorder,' he wrote regret-
fully, 'than by attributing it to the present universal diffusion of wealth
and luxury through almost every part of the island.'[11]

Then came 1788 and George III's first attack of derangement, played
out in a blaze of publicity such as has probably never before or since been
accorded the illness even of a monarch, and it brought with it a fundamental
change of attitudes. No longer could insanity be equated with ignorance or
sin or superstitition. If it was possible for the highest in the land to be
struck down after an utterly blameless life of devotion to duty, to country
and to family, to have all the confidences of his sickroom revealed to the
world, to make a remarkable recovery and have the courage to resume his
dignities and station, surely such an illness could not be anything but
natural, demanding of sympathy and amenable to medicine as any other?
The lesson was quickly learnt. Much of what had gone for knowledge was
revealed as idle speculation. No longer could the sufferer be blamed for
succumbing to weakness or acceding to unbridled passion. Insanity ceased
to be a matter of shame or blame. Furthermore, as Willis had proclaimed,
it could be cured, and 'insanity proved curable' became the slogan which
attracted doctors to the specialty and patients to doctors. And as those
whose business it is to provide medical and social services know only too
well, supply creates demand. The result was that the number of patients
admitted to private madhouses rose sharply in the years immediately
following. So did the number of private madhouses. In the London area
there were twenty-two in 1788. By the time of George III's death their
number had more than doubled and something like eighty new licences had
been granted out of a total of 122 issued between 1774 and 1828, when a
new Act of Parliament transferred the keeping of a register from the Royal
College of Physicians to the Metropolitan Commissioners in Lunacy.[12]

A new scare now arose. Insanity was feared to be on the increase, a curious conceit not unknown to the present age and explained as the price for
the complexity of advancing civilization and the decay of morals.

Dr Richard Powell, secretary of the commissioners of the Royal College
of Physicians charged under the Act of 1774 to licence and inspect London's
private madhouses and to keep a register of all patients admitted in
England and Wales, was the first to produce figures from his books to substantiate what until then had been only an impression. In 1810 he read at
the College a paper 'Observations upon the comparative Prevalence of Insanity, at different Periods'.[13] It was the first attempt to relate the incidence

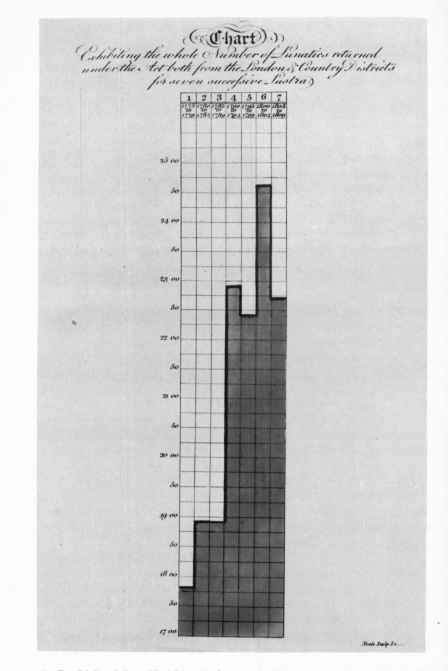

16. *Dr Richard Powell's 'Chart' of 1810, or histogram as it would be called today, showing the 'Number of Lunatics returned' by 'Lustra'. Note the jump in the five-year period 1790–94 immediately following the royal malady which gave rise to unnecessary fears that 'insanity' was on the increase.*

of mental disease to national affairs. It was also the first time that histograms were used for the presentation of numerical data in medical literature. How novel this was for his readers may be seen by the detailed instructions Powell gave for how his 'charts' were to be read – 'Each line which passes horizontally from left to right. . . The spaces as they are divided perpendicularly' etc. His figures showed a remarkable increase in the number admitted in the lustrum or five-year period following the royal recovery.

He was, he said, moved to undertake

the examination of these registers for the purpose of trying how far the relative numbers contained in them would support the popular opinion respecting the rapid increase of that most difficult, delicate, and important disease, and also of trying whether any analogy or connection could be established upon more solid grounds, between the number of insane persons and the political circumstances of the times, or any known variations in the seasons of different years.

It remained for Dr George Man Burrows in 1820[14] to draw valid conclusions from Powell's data:

Unquestionably many important causes, physical and moral, have supervened since the origin of the register (1775), and greatly influenced the number of entries in the different lustra. Obvious as they appear, nevertheless such causes have been, I believe, quite overlooked . . . Thus the late King's first illness, at the end of the third lustrum (1788–9), an event which induced a universal and deep sympathy, produced also an unusual interest in the condition of all similarly affected; and this effect was much heightened by the publishing of the examination of the attending physicians, on the nature and probable issue of his Majesty's malady. The result superadded an unprecedented number of entries to the fourth lustrum, which commenced in 1790.

The only like rise, he pointed out, occurred in the years 1809 and in the lustrum 1810–14, immediately following, and it was due to a similar circumstance:

In 1807, Parliament appointed a Committee to investigate the state of pauper and criminal lunatics; and an Act, commonly called Mr. Wynne's passed in 1808, for the better care and maintenance of them. This inquiry and the report thereon, like all others relating to the subject, incited fresh attention to the condition of the insane of all ranks; and hence a vast number, before dispersed, and of course unregistered, were sent into asylums and licensed houses, and greatly augmented the returns. The result was an increase of entries in 1809, which closes the seventh lustrum: it continued from the commencement of the eighth (1810), arrived at its maximum in 1813, and declined in 1814; before the Reports of the Parliamentary Investigation in 1815–16 were published.

But, asked Dr Burrows, if the incidence of insanity had really been increasing, why did the College register not show a steady increase?

The truth is, – the causes being temporary, so likewise the effects. The contingencies noticed appear to be the real causes of the accession to the entries in the register; and as the effect of each subsided, a consequential gradual declension of the returns of lunatics followed.

The question whether insanity was on the increase Dr Burrows therefore answered with a definite no. Furthermore he was able to show from figures of admissions to public asylums on the European Continent that the disease was no more common here than there. The anonymous reviewer of Burrows' book in the *Quarterly Review* in 1820 noted his conclusions with particular satisfaction. 'Insanity is considered by foreigners in general as the opprobrium of England'; the results of Dr Burrows' investigations were in consequence particularly 'gratifying to those who feel interested for the happiness, and jealous of the character, of their countrymen'. This particular ghost had at last been laid and was not heard again.

Medical Arithmetick and Universal Prognosticks

Advances in knowledge often depend on appreciating what is not known. This is precisely what the parliamentary committees 'appointed to examine the Physicians who have attended His Majesty, during his Illness' achieved when they sat in December 1788 and again in January 1789. Their simple but searching questions revealed areas of ignorance of which not even the profession was aware, and bringing them to notice was the first step to progress. Chief among them was what chance had the King of recovering? How easy it would have been for the royal physicians to answer this question if, instead of having to rely on a few cases dimly remembered from their own experience, they had been able to consult a series accumulated over years from many sources. This would have allowed them to estimate not only how frequent the different varieties of mental disorders were (their morbidity) and how often they caused death (their mortality), but it would have provided for the first time a basis from which to assess the prospect before their patient (the prognosis).

Each of the King's seven doctors in turn was asked 'What Hopes' he had 'of His Majesty's Recovery' and whether he could 'form any Judgment, or probable conjecture, of the Time which His Majesty's Illness is likely to last'. To the second question none could make answer. To the first they responded in hopeful but vague terms.[1] Warren said 'there is a Probability that His Majesty may recover'. Baker and Gisborne simply hoped he would, Willis had 'great Hopes', Addington 'very good Grounds of Hope', and Reynolds 'well-founded Hopes'. Pepys regarded the situation as very much like that arising in any other disease 'of which I knew that the Majority labouring under it did recover'.

Questioned further on what they based their answers, they either mumbled generalities or recollected a few cases from private practice. Baker fell back on what he had been taught as a student: 'I was formerly a Pupil of Dr. Batty's [Dr William Battie of St Luke's], who attended an Hospital,

where I had an Opportunity of seeing many Instances of this Disorder.'
Dr Battie had retired from hospital practice in 1764, the year he was elected
President of the Royal College of Physicians, the only 'psychiatrist' ever
to be so honoured.[2] In other words Baker was drawing on knowledge he had
acquired more than twenty-five years earlier. Addington went back even
further. His experience 'of the particular Species of Disorder with which
His Majesty is afflicted', as it was delicately phrased, was gained in the
years 1749–54 before he settled in London. He had looked after 'from 8 to
10 Patients . . . usually at a Time' in a house he had built for the purpose at
Reading. Warren excused his ignorance on the plea that he 'always called in
Persons who make this Branch of Medicine their particular Study', as
psychiatrists were referred to darkly in the proceedings, 'and have sometimes attended in Conjunction with them, but have oftener left the Patients
to their Care.'

Only two founded their reply on recent experience. Reynolds said: 'I
have been almost Twenty Years in Business, and in the Course of that Time I
have seen a great Number under this Disorder'. Unlike Warren, he did not
consider special skills necessary and therefore did not relinquish the case
unless 'Restraint or Coercion' became necessary. This he left to those
'Gentlemen, who have dedicated themselves to that particular Object of
Practice', most of whom owned 'Houses of Reception for Patients so circumstanced'. Willis said he spoke from an experience extending over '28
years; I imagine I have never had less than 30 Patients every Year of the
Time'. Being pressed to substantiate his claim that nine out of ten had
recovered, he unfortunately could not recollect how many patients had
been under his care and confessed he had kept no notes to refer back to.
'My first Calculation and Observation, concerning the Number cured,'
he admitted in January 1789, referring to the optimistic forecast he had
given the previous month, 'was from my remarking that the first Fifteen
were cured; and I had often recollected, upon Retrospection, that Ten had
gone together, and that I very rarely missed curing any that I had so early
[within the first three months] under my Care: I mean radically cured.' No
one thought to ask him how long his cures lasted.

At their second examination, questions about the King's chances of
recovery were coupled with specific inquiry about patients who were 'at
His Majesty's Time of Life', that is fifty years old. Being uncertain how
many patients in general recovered from derangement, the royal physicians
could hardly be more precise about a specific age group. Again only two
attempted an answer. Willis was unruffled and in his optimistic way said,
'I do not judge that the Age is of any Signification, unless the Patient had
been afflicted before with the same Malady' – which George III had not.
Warren realized that the matter could be settled only by recourse to numbers. He said he had 'been making an Enquiry lately, in order to satisfy my

own Curiosity respecting this Question; and I believe it will be still Two Days before I can give a satisfactory Answer'. Asked 'Where are you making that Enquiry?' he answered, 'By examining the Books of Bethlehem Hospital.' Two days later he was still not in a position to make a statement, but promised if possible to hand it in before the committee broke up. He never did, but a postscript in what may be called the Whig version of the parliamentary examination of the royal physicians, referred to earlier, purported to do so: 'Dr Warren is said afterwards to have prepared his Calculations of the Chances after Fifty. They were found to be about Three to One against the Recovery; but this Information was thought to be too late.'[3] By then the King was well on the way to recovery.

There was however one doctor in London, unconnected with the royal malady and of the lowest rank in the College of Physicians, who had foreseen that the most momentous decisions for King, country and government hung on the prognosis. He realized, too, when others did not, that it was impossible to answer such crucial questions from a personal stock of dimly remembered cases, and that the issues were far too serious for anecdotalism. This was Dr William Black. Just before the King fell ill he had published his picturesquely entitled *A comparative view of the mortality of the human species, at all ages; and of the diseases and casualties by which they are destroyed or annoyed* (1788). As he later rightly claimed, it contained 'the only certain and numerical data that ever have been published in any age or country, by which to determine the probabilities of recovery, of death, and of relapse in every species of disorder'. In the book itself he wrote:

I have made . . . laborious efforts, to rescue a momentous part of active medicine from the conjectural stigma with which the whole profession has been branded in the lump. And, however it may be slighted as an haeretical innovation, I would strenuously recommend . . . the science of Medical Arithmetick and Universal Prognosticks . . . as a guide and compass through the labyrinth of Therapeuticks.

When at the beginning of December 1788 it became generally apparent that measures might become 'necessary to be adopted in consequence of that melancholy and new event in English history' – the King's mental incapacity and the establishment of a regency – Black wrote an open letter to Pitt, the Prime Minister, and to Fox of the Opposition, drawing attention to his chapter on 'Insanity, lunacy, mania, melancholia, and complex insanity' as providing the only prognostic 'compass to direct Parliamentary arguments, conclusions, and political remedies, both palliative and radical'. He told how he set about gathering the information, and his account explains why Warren had not been able to get the figures. The simple reason was that none were available, since no casebooks or registers were kept at Bethlem. But the apothecary or resident medical officer was suffi-

ciently interested to keep his own notes on patients, and these he had lent
to Black. They contained details of nearly 3,000 patients admitted to
Bethlem between 1772 and 1787.

'I had long since procured the printed annual reports of Bedlam during
thirty years, from 1750 to 1780,' wrote Black, but they recorded only admissions, discharges and deaths.

I was anxious to extend my enquiries to a vast variety of particulars, not
one of which could be learned from them or the crowd of authors, good, bad,
and indifferent, whom I perused for this purpose, from the remote era of the
Greek and Roman Catholicon, the Hellebore, down to the present time.
Chagrined with this unprofitable research* I waited upon the learned and
venerable physician of Bedlam, Dr. [John] Monro; who, with his accustomed
liberality and affability, recommended me to his son [Dr Thomas] upon whom
the principal medical department of Bedlam now devolves ... [He] introduced me to Mr. Gonza [correctly John Gozna], the apothecary of Bedlam
[he was succeeded in 1795 by John Haslam]; whose curiosity and learning
induced him to keep a private register of all the patients; and with all which
Mr. Gonza most obligingly furnished me. It is from the records of this respectable and well-informed gentleman, especially on the subject of insanity, that
I am enabled to form all the following Tables and data respecting a disease,
wherein, except to the few high-priests of those temples, the rest of the Esculapian train are nearly as ignorant as the ancients; and the unenlightened
mass of the community stare with superstitious amazement as the Israelites
formerly on the epilepsy.

Black's letter, dated 1 December, appeared in the *Morning Chronicle, and
London Advertiser* on Monday, 8 December, the day on which the House
selected the committee to examine the royal physicians and the day before
they actually did so.

Sir [he wrote], As it is no longer a secret that the subject of Thursday's
deliberation in Parliament will turn upon the disorder of a Great Personage,
and the measures necessary to be adopted ... I flatter myself the general facts
relating to that malady, herewith transmitted, in the printed publication, (*A
Comparative View, &c.,* page 232) will not be thought obtrusive nor useless
... For as to any partial prognosticks in the usual mode of deductions, from
symptoms and causes, none I maintain can be found in this disease, above all
others in the morbid catalogue. The opinions, therefore, of Medical individuals, as to the consequence or duration of the malady, are as far inferior to
numerical calculation in ascertaining truth or probability, as the Oracles of
old were to the demonstrations of Euclid. I shall not further transgress upon
your time; but you will perceive, to use the language of the calculators and
annuitants, that the odds in this malady are as follows: Against cure, within
one year, about 3 to 1; against death, in the same period, from 6 to 9 to 1;
against relapse when cured 5 to 1; but after two years continuance of the

* This is the first time the word research occurs in a psychiatric context.

disease without any lucid intervals, the odds will be multiplied far beyond the duplicate ratio, and will be from 50 to 100 to 1 against cure.

Whether Black's calculations made any impression on the political scene is doubtful; the royal physicians certainly were unmoved and continued to pronounce 'as the Oracles of old' did. Yet his unpretentious contribution, called forth by a 'complicated question of politics and medicine', was the first attempt to apply the new numerical or statistical method to psychiatric problems, in particular to prognosis. So important did this aspect become that more than a hundred years later outcome and prognosis were made the focal point of psychiatric classification, when Kraepelin made it the yardstick by which he distinguished two main clinical groups, the manic-depressive psychoses and dementia praecox (which Bleuler later renamed schizophrenia).

More significant, though lost sight of in the welter of treatments with which the insane were plied, was that Black drew attention to what happens to the mentally ill without treatment, that is the natural history of mental illness, unknown till then and perhaps even today neglected. Two-thirds of all patients in the first attack will recover within twelve months 'if left to the unassisted efforts of nature' as the phrase went.[4] Black's law, as it may be called, is best expressed as the law of thirds and is borne out by general experience. Of 100 psychiatric patients taken at random, one third will recover completely, one third will recover but not to their previous level, and one third will remain impaired or get worse.

Black's claim to have pioneered the numerical or statistical method in medicine was consolidated in the second 'corrected and improved' edition of his book which appeared in the summer of 1789, twelve months after the first. It was now more soberly and scientifically entitled *An arithmetical and medical analysis of the diseases and mortality of the human species*. In it he drew attention to the fact that the method derived from two medical problems in particular which were insoluble without it: the assessment of the value of arm-to-arm inoculation in the prevention of small-pox (this was ten years before Jenner introduced vaccination or the inoculation of cow-pox); and the elucidation of prognosis in 'insanity' – a problem highlighted by the illness of the King. Indeed he suggested

that it would be a most fortunate circumstance for medicine and mankind . . . were the parliament of Great Britain to examine physicians on every disease, as they have lately done on the unfortunate malady of a Great Personage. The utility of the arithmetical system would then be as universally conspicuous throughout every disease . . . as it was in insanity.

In a new section on relapses and the chances of recovery (which he found as favourable as in the first attack) and their likely duration (which was no longer) he commented: 'Medical and political reasons render this an

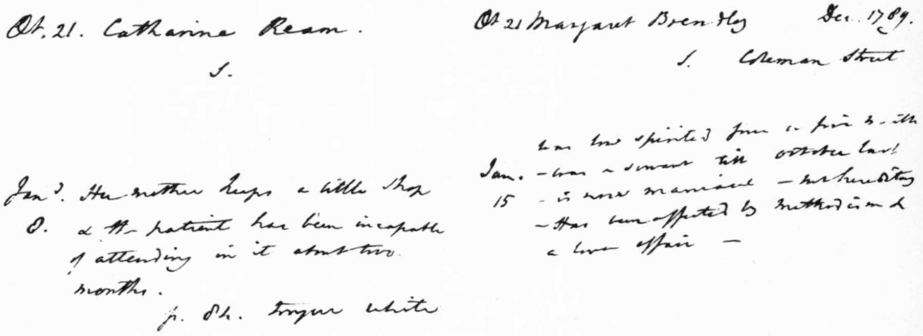
Oct. 21. Catharina Ream.
S.
Jany. 8. Her mother keeps a little shop & the patient has been incapable of attending in it about two months.
p. 84. Tongue white

Oct 21 Margaret Brently Dec. 1789.
S. Coleman Street
Jan. 15 has been low spirited from a fever [illegible] — was a servant till October last — is now maniacal — not hereditary — Has been affected by Methodism and a love affair —

Mr. Finch keeps a book, in which are registered the peculiarities of the disease of every patient, and the mode of treatment which has been adopted. His certificate is also in an admirable form.

[*The paper was put in, and is as follows:*]

Name of the Patient admitted?

Admitted?

Physicians or Apothecary's name, who signed the certificate?

Names and residence of the friends by whose direction the patient is received?

How long afflicted?

Previous symptoms?

If any occurrence took place previously to the attack, as the probable cause of the disease?

If hereditary? Age?

Constitutional structure and general appearance?

Bodily health?

If any lucid intervals? Religion?

Habits of life?

Mode of living?

Soil, climate?

Diseased ideas?

General remarks during the progress of the disease.

TRANSCRIPT OF SIMMONS'S NOTES:

Catharine Ream. Single. Her mother keeps a little shop and the
patient has been incapable of attending in it about two months. Pulse 84.
Tongue white.
Margaret Brendly. Single. Was low spirited from a fire 3 months – was
a servant till October last – is now married – not hereditary –
Has been effected by Methodism and a love affair.

17. *What doctors observe about their patients is an indication of how much is
known and therefore observed. Dr Samuel Foart Simmons's notes (above) of
two patients admitted to St Luke's Hospital for Lunaticks in 1789 show how
primitive case-taking was at the time of the king's first illness. By 1815 the
form of register kept by Dr William Finch (below) at his 'Asylum for insane
Persons', at Laverstock in Wiltshire and exhibited to Mr Rose's Committee,
shows that much more about patients' medical and social background was
gathered and also about their 'diseased ideas' and 'the progress of the disease'.*

*The Finch family illustrates too how the specialty was handed down in families
and the unqualified keeper of a madhouse in the eighteenth century turned into
the asylum doctor of the nineteenth and the psychiatrist of the twentieth.
Laverstock House and a number of other establishments dating from the reign of
George III, like Brislington House belonging to the Fox family, and Brooke
House, Hackney, belonging to the Monros, as well as Perfect's at West Malling,
Kent, were in continuous use as private asylums until the Second World War.*

interesting problem to be determined.' How right events proved him to be.

Before the numerical method could make a real contribution to psychiatry, sufficient clinical data had to be assembled. Records of detailed and prolonged observation of patients were its raw material. In Black's time they did not exist. Major centres like Bethlem Hospital kept no case notes and Black could not even have come by the basic figures had not the lowly apothecary of that hospital kept a private journal. Some fifteen years later Dr Thomas Percival pleaded that regular case notes should be kept in 'Asylums for Insanity.[5] He pointed to the clinical advances which could only be made from their accumulated case material if proper records were kept:

It is a circumstance to be regretted, both by the faculty and the public, that the various diseases which are classed under the title of insanity, remain less understood than any others ... Hospital institutions furnish the best means of acquiring more accurate knowledge of their causes, nature, and cure. But this information cannot be attained ... by the ordinary attention to single and unconnected cases. The synthetic plan should be adopted; and a regular *journal* should be kept of every species of the malady which occurs ... with a full detail of its rise, progress, and termination; of the remedies administered, and of their effects in its several stages. The age, sex, occupation, mode of life, and if possible hereditary constitution of each patient should be noted: And, when the event proves fatal, the brain, and other organs affected should be carefully examined, and the appearances on dissection minutely inserted in the journal. A register like this [he concluded with the turmoil of 1788 in mind], in the course of a few years, would afford the most interesting and authentic documents, the want of which, on a late melancholy occasion, was felt and regretted by the whole kingdom.

Such figures as he was able to give for his local mental hospital, the Manchester Lunatic Hospital, substantially confirmed Black's law. Of the 1,575 patients admitted from its opening in 1766 to 1802, '627 have been cured; 212 have been relieved; 488 have been discharged at the request of their friends; 171 have died; 8 have been deemed incurable; and 69 remained in the house.'

In 1816 Sir Henry Halford echoed Percival when he told the parliamentary committee on madhouses, with Mr Rose in the chair:

We have much to learn on the subject of mental derangement, and I am of opinion, that our knowledge of insanity has not kept pace with our knowledge of other distempers, from the habit we find established, of transferring patients under this malady ... to the care of persons who too frequently limit their attention to the mere personal security of their patients ... We want facts in the history of this disease, and if they are carefully recorded, under the observation of enlightened physicians, no doubt, they will sooner or later be collected in sufficient number, to admit of safe and usefull induction.[6]

Pinel described the first 'register' of this kind, which was in use at the

Charenton Asylum in France at the turn of the nineteenth century.[7] The idea was introduced into the Quakers' Retreat at York by Samuel Tuke soon after the publication of his *Description of the Retreat* (1813).[8] In 1841 one of the first tasks of the newly founded Association of Medical Officers of Asylums and Hospitals for the Insane (now the Royal Medico-Psychological Association) was to devise a standard form of note-keeping.[9] And in 1845 that monument of Victorian legislative philanthropy, the Act for the Regulation of the Care and Treatment of Lunatics, made it obligatory that 'there shall be kept . . . a "Case Book" in which the Physician . . . shall from Time to Time to make Entries of the mental State and bodily condition of each Patient'. The store of clinical data thus assembled in asylums became the basis of much of what we know or think we know about mental diseases today.

With the appearance of Dr F. Bisset Hawkins' *Elements of medical statistics* (1829) which he defined as 'the application of numbers to illustrate the natural history of man in health and disease', Black's 'numerical' method came of age. It was not the fault of the method that it did not fulfill its promise or help psychiatry to free itself from speculation, hypothesis and empiricism.

The enlightened American psychiatrist and stern critic of the spurious Dr Isaac Ray, author, as we shall see, of the first psychiatric study of George III, pointed out that statistics were only as reliable as the raw material on which they are based[10]:

Statistics implies something more than a process in arithmetic. It is, or should be, a profound, philosophical analysis of materials carefully and copiously collected, and chosen with an enlightened confidence in their fitness for the purpose in question . . . It is probably because statistical facts have met with too easy a faith, that conclusions drawn from them have so often been swept away by the subsequent progress of knowledge. To those accustomed to the close and careful examination of facts that characterizes other departments of natural science, it is inconceivable what slender materials have served as the foundation of very important deductions in this we are now considering.

He singled out three areas in which psychiatric statistics were likely to be misleading. First, in the assessment of results of treatment:

Whether the change is a real cure of disease, or a state where diseased manifestations are absent merely from want of a suitable opportunity of displaying them, or a temporary intermission of disease . . . these are questions which every individual will answer by the aid of his own experience and judgement, and consequently with all the diversity which is utterly incompatible with statistical accuracy.

Second, in ascertaining causes of breakdown:

Here, if anywhere, it will appear whether our studies have led us to a higher philosophy than that which consists in repeating catch-words and echoing the popular voice . . . [they] often reflect the peculiar views of their respective framers, so easy is it to find whatever we think we ought to find . . . Many of the emotions and incidents that are set down as causes of insanity, such as 'fear of poverty', 'religious doubts', 'anxiety', &c., would often be more justly regarded as its effects. They are the first symptoms that arrest the attention; and, by means of that common disposition to confound the *post hoc* with the *propter hoc*, they are placed in the relation of causes to the subsequent aberrations.

Third with respect to the classification and terminology of psychiatric ills:

No one . . . can be sure that by monomania, melancholia, moral insanity, and many other terms that are used to designate different forms of mental derangement, he understands precisely what his neighbor does, and that there would be no discrepancy between them in referring such cases to their respective classes. Indeed it could hardly be otherwise . . . Another equally fatal [objection] to such attempts at classification . . . is the fact that in a large proportion of cases the form of the disease changes in the course of its progress. The same case, at different periods [and not only to different observers, it should be added] may present the aspect of melancholia, monomania, and dementia. To which of them is it to be referred?

Substitute current psychiatric terminology – 'depression', 'schizophrenia', and 'organic brain syndrome' – and Ray's objections still stand.

'A language the terms of which are so precise and well defined as to convey the same idea to every mind, in every time and every land' is still lacking. One might add that psychiatric statistics must remain unconvincing while diagnosis remains tied to the software of the psychiatric interview based on psychological and social theory, and while results of treatment are assessed by a like subjective process. When in time these will have been replaced by the hardware of physical examination and laboratory investigation, and causes rather than symptoms can be treated, a body of psychiatric knowledge may accumulate which will bear statistical analysis and stand the test of time. When such objectivity is achieved in a terminology which all may understand, assessment of incidence of disease or efficacy of treatment will become a matter of fact rather than of opinion.

MacFlogg'em : The Study of Mania

The growing importance of mental illness is reflected in the space allotted to the subject in medical courses. Fortunately this can be assessed from the 'Outlines' or 'Heads of Lectures' which private teachers and schools published to attract students. In 1787, the year before George III fell ill, William Black issued a brochure, *Outlines of a course of medical lectures*. These he gave five days a week at 17 Harley Street, beginning in October and ending the April following. His arrangement of subjects was partly by symptoms, in which 'Fevers' figures largely; partly according to systems of the body, for instance bladder and kidneys. In part he dealt with diseases by anatomical regions in the style of the seventeenth century, so that 'Insanity furious and melancholy' appears at the end of a paragraph beginning with 'Nasal Hemorrhage, Head-ache, Nightmare, Lethargy'. 'Hystericks' was considered among 'Diseases principally ranged under Obstetricks' and 'Hypochondriasm' under gastro-intestinal disorders.

Less than twenty years later Drs William Babington and James Curry published the syllabus of the medical course at Guy's, *Outlines of a course of lectures on the practice of medicine, as delivered in the medical school of Guy's Hospital* (1802–6). It was almost a textbook in itself. Of its 207 pages, the last six are taken up by 'Insanity' defined as 'False perceptions, or erroneous conclusions, continuing during the waking state, leading to various acts not natural and customary with the patient, often dangerous either to his own, or to others' personal safety; and not immediately depending on violent anger or intoxication, or on fever, inflammation, or other morbid state speedily threatening life.' Psychiatric terminology was abundant and confused even at that time, as the synonyms for insanity which they listed show: '*Deliria* of Sauvages:– *Paranoiae* of Vogel:– *Mentales* of Linnaeus:– *Vesaniae* of Sagar and Cullen:– Anglice *Madness, Lunacy*.' Treatment was divided into '*corporeal* or *mental*' and 'confinement and restraint'. An important part of the mental treatment was 'privation or indulgence, as punishment or reward. Necessity of impressing awe from conviction of superior power ... Modes of counteracting capricious resolutions, by exciting sensations and motions incompatible with them, and which the patient cannot resist.' These were a mixture of the shock and aversion or conditioning treatments which have come back in our own time.

Drs Babington and Curry ended gloomily with 'Reasons why improvement in this branch of Medicine is accompanied with peculiar difficulties', which their epitome of the subject did nothing to lessen. Like most textbooks it perpetuated the past by retailing facts accumulated on erroneous theory and soon overtaken by scientific advances.

To form a just estimate of what may be called 'academic psychiatry' at that time, the amount of knowledge required from the medical student in this subject must be compared with that in medicine as a whole. It is possible to do this because Dr (later Sir) Alexander Morison left one of the very few records of an encounter with the examiners of the Royal College of Physicians of London to whom he presented himself in March 1804 for admission as a licentiate. This entitled him to practise within their jurisdiction, that is in London and a radius of seven miles around.[1]

Appeared before the President & 4 Censors of the Royal College of Physicians first showed my [Edinburgh] Diploma, then was asked what my purpose was in appearing before them, I said to be admitted a Licentiate of the College, the President asked me if I wanted nothing else. I said no. He then in Latin desired me to read part of Celsus [a medical authority of the second century A.D.] 2 sentences which I was at a loss to translate. Sir Lucas Pepys the president however very kindly by giving me the beginning of it enabled me to get thro' with it.

Then he asked me 'The situation of the Liver' ... 'Its use' ... 'The use of the Bile & its nature' ... [and] 'The ducts by which it was conveyed'.

The other 'examinators', as Morison called them, asked him the 'site' and use of the stomach, the urinary bladder, the brain and the heart, and to describe the circulation of the blood.

He was before them for about twenty minutes and although he 'forgot at the moment the Latin name of the kidneys' was allowed to proceed to the next part two weeks later. On that occasion he had to read 'a few lines from Sydenham', the great English clinician of the later seventeenth century who was denied the fellowship of the College ostensibly because he held only the degree of Bachelor of Medicine. Next he was asked 'The Symptoms of Hepatitis' and 'Is not Cough a Symptom'; 'When there is a stone in the Biliary duct what are the Symptoms' and 'What are the Symptoms of Diabetes'. There followed a number of questions no candidate today could attempt although a medical historian might, for instance 'In what does Hysteric Urine differ from that in Diabetes', 'What are the Symptoms of Enteritis' contrasted with those of 'Dysentery', and whether 'Hernia' was 'a cause of it'.

In part three of the examination, which lasted only 'about seven minutes', he answered successfully questions 'on the Treatment of Nephralgia [pain in the kidney], Icterus [jaundice], Pneumonia, Measles, Apoplexy, Ophthalmia [inflammation of the eye], Rheumatism & Colica Pictonum [lead poisoning], Cholera Morbus', a feat which every modern medical student may envy. He then paid the not inconsiderable fee of £43 4s. 6d. and was 'admitted a Licentiate & got my Diploma. Took the usual Latin oath & knelt whilst Sir Lucas Pepys administered the form of Admission.'

The student's view of psychiatry was caricatured by 'Peter MacFlogg'em', a pseudonym it has unfortunately proved impossible to penetrate but which may hide the satirical pen of John Wolcot M.D. In his *Aesculapian secrets revealed* (1813), addressed to all aspiring members of the profession, he lampooned in particular the royal physicians:

You will no doubt recollect in a recent disastrous case of mania, by which the people of these realms have been considerably agitated and distressed . . . a set of physicians, possessing the most exalted abilities, and alike eminent in every branch of medical knowledge . . . have exposed themselves to a considerable share of pleasantry and ridicule, for advancing . . . a sentiment by no means rare or singular, that with regard to mental diseases, no very great degree of superfluous wisdom, no extraordinary length of study or experience are required, for moderate talents competently to attain . . . no great proportion of discrimination will be found indispensible, for being acquainted with all that is at present known on the subject.

Therefore he advised,

as mania is a disease usually, though erroneously considered rather distinct and unconnected with the study and pursuit of the general practitioner, and as it should be your invariable maxim to take all fish that come to hook, waving the Aesculapian wand with equal facility and address *in all* diseases; every honourable means should be resorted to, for the purpose of dissipating so serious and groundless a prejudice, as that lunacy must require any particular quantum of medical skill and penetration, to manage successfully; particularly when you recollect that from some unforeseen happy freak of the blind goddess, who can say but that your splendid talents may luckily be transplanted from the purlieus of Bedlam or St. Luke's, to the precincts of a palace ?

Two conditions were necessary 'to effect this grand design'. First, 'you will, by every art in your power, procure an appointment of physician in ordinary or extraordinary to some branches of the high and mighty'. The budding doctor need not be deterred by a sense of his own ignorance for 'if you have address enough to flatter the pampered vices of the noble, nothing is to be apprehended on the score of real abilities'. Second, he should seek to gain fame 'by publishing very copiously as well as frequently, your singularly rare observations on the particular treatment and management of lunatics'.

MacFlogg'em's advice did not go unheeded by Dr Morison. Not only by devious means did he get himself appointed physician to Prince Leopold and Princess Charlotte, although he never met either, but later also physician to the household of the Duke of York. With these titles secured, he cast around for a specialty to make his own, and what better for one with royal connexions and seeking more, than mental diseases? Accordingly, with the financial support of Mrs Burdett Coutts and under the patronage of 'the Duke of York, (the guardian of his father, King George the Third, during his long and melancholy illness)' he launched in 1823 a 'Course of Lectures on the Cure and Prevention of Mental Diseases' at London and Edinburgh, his *alma mater*.[2] He had had no practical experience of the insane except a dozen or so annual statutory tours of inspection of private madhouses as physician accompanying the Surrey magistrates. In 1825 he published the first ever *Outlines of lectures on mental diseases*. It was based on the 'Heads of Lectures' he had circulated 'on the institution of the Mental Disease Lectureship' in 1823, expanded to seventy-two pages.

With a keen eye on public relations he had canvassed the leading physicians for letters of approval which he published with it. They give a picture of what was thought of the subject and the lecturer. Sir Henry Halford responded with 'I think some Lectures on Insanity would be a great addition to what is taught in the different branches of Medical Education and I shall be glad to hear of their being given to full classes'; Dr Matthew Baillie wrote: 'From the experience you have had in this class of diseases, and from the information you have collected from books, I believe you will give a very instructive Course of Lectures upon this subject'; Sir Matthew Tierney: 'With your connections . . . I hope you will have no difficulty in carrying it into effect'; Sir Alexander Crichton: 'It is rational to suppose that this difficult branch of Medicine is more likely to be improved by one who dedicates his time and talents almost exclusively to such subjects than by any other whose time is taken up by a diversity of objects'; and Dr William Maton: 'The Lectures which you propose to deliver would be extremely useful to our profession, and would be likely to be well attended, if there be no established Lecturer already giving instruction fully on the same subject, and I am not aware that there is.'[1]

As Morison's ambition grew, he tried to link his personal lectureship with Edinburgh University, hoping ultimately to be made professor of mental diseases. Dr Andrew Duncan senior, as might be expected from his interest in the subject, seemed to be in favour, but a conversation with Dr Thomas Charles Hope, Professor of Chemistry and Medicine and a powerful voice in the councils of the University, quickly dashed his ambition. 'He is averse to it as there is not broad enough ground for a separate establishment,' Morison lamented in his diary, 'and is unwilling to fritter away the subjects of the different professorships . . . said his objection had nothing personal to me in it – any old dropsical gentleman might muse to leave a fund for a separate Lectureship on Dropsy or Liver disease if some line was not drawn and the attention of students distracted.' Although he protested that 'Mental Disease was certainly more distinguished from the General Practice than any other branch as Eyes', it was of no avail. Psychiatry had to wait another hundred years for its first chair, symbol of its recognition as on a par with other branches of medicine.

Three years after Morison's book appeared, Dr John Conolly, first Professor of Medicine in the newly founded University of London, expressed the hope that it would be possible not only to cover the theoretical aspects of mental diseases in his lectures, but also to provide 'practical instruction' in 'their forms and management'.[3] But psychiatry was still the Cinderella of the medical sciences and Conolly failed to get support from his colleagues. It was not until 1842, when he was resident physician at the Middlesex County Asylum at Hanwell, that he obtained permission to hold clinical classes for medical students of the London hospitals and walk his wards with them.[4]

22

Crime and Insanity

Eighteenth- and nineteenth-century medical writers spent a good deal of time and effort trying 'to define true madness'. By precise description of its types, they hoped to build up a nosology, or 'doctrine of the classification of diseases',[1] which, like Linné's botanical system, would provide a scheme for clinical observations and advance. Lawyers too clamoured for a more meaningful terminology as they became more aware of the connexion between insanity and crime. Strange to say, the treatment of the lunatic by the courts of Georgian England was often more merciful than that meted out by doctors and keepers. Mary Lamb, for instance, was temporarily confined in 1796 in a Hoxton madhouse after stabbing her mother, not in the blaze of publicity of an Old Bailey trial but quietly and surely on a coroner's warrant.[2] Dr William Perfect, one of the most respectable of provincial madhouse keepers, of West Malling in Kent, had a patient, a young man, committed to his care under similar circumstances in 1779.[3]

MARGARET NICHOLSON

George III displayed the same enlightened attitude to the criminal insane and, unlike his granddaughter Victoria, even when his life was endangered. This is well shown by how Margaret Nicholson was treated. On the morning of 2 August 1786 this deluded spinster in her early forties made to stab him on the pretence of presenting a petition while he was alighting from his carriage at St James's. The weapon was an old desert knife 'worn very thin', and the blade merely bent against the King's body without inflicting a wound. As she tried to repeat her thrust, a yeoman of the guard caught her arm and wrested the weapon from her, exclaiming 'She has a knife – is your Majesty hurt?' The King 'instantly replied, stroking his hand on his waistcoat – "No, I am not hurt – take care of the woman – do not hurt her, for she is mad." '⁴ She was conducted to the Queen's antechamber 'where she remained from twelve till near five, during which time, though spoken to by several of the nobility, she did not once condescend to open her lips, but appeared totally unmoved by any representations of the atrocity of her crime.'⁵ At five o'clock she was taken before the Board of Green Cloth for examination by amongst others Mr Pitt, the Attorney-General and the Solicitor-General. 'Dr. [Thomas] Monro, being sent for, said it was impossible to discover with certainty immediately whether she was insane or not.' She was therefore committed to the custody of Mr Coates, a King's Messenger, to await further examination of herself and her background, and the Lord Chancellor provided money for a wardrobe for her. Meanwhile, 'the attempt circulated through the city with amazing rapidity, and gathering as it flew, a thousand fictions were added. The instant publication of the Gazette Extraordinary stopt at once their mischievous effect.' There had also been sent for, in addition to Dr Monro, 'three elderly matrons, who examined into her sex, and declared her to be a woman. This was thought a necessary step, as it was apprehended by some that she was a man, and had assumed the female habit to facilitate her design.'

The next day she was interrogated by Mr Justice Addington, and on 4 August was brought before the Privy Council, which was attended by the Archbishop of Canterbury, three dukes, a marquess, two earls, a viscount and two barons.⁶ They took depositions and adjourned until 8 August, when they were joined by Pitt and W. W. Grenville, another future Prime Minister. Evidence of her birth, parentage, upbringing and years of domestic service were given, of her previous quiet and steady manner of life, her talent as a needlewoman and her ability to read and write (the only book found when her lodgings were searched was a spelling dictionary). Margaret herself told the Privy Councillors that she had contemplated 'Regicide about a week' and explained that she had a right to 'a property due to her from the Crown of England' which 'if she had not ... A Woeful War would ensue'. Her numerous petitions having failed to secure it, she had made this demonstration 'not to kill the King but merely to shew the Cause'.

The Doctors Monro, father and son, who had seen her daily since her apprehension, were called, when

Dr. Monro acquainted their Lordships, that he never in his life had seen a person more disordered; that her Language was perfectly unintelligible and it was impossible to relate it; that she appeared to have a consciousness of what she had done, but did not seem sensible of having committed any Crime; that in his conversation yesterday she burst out without any apparent cause into a fit of Laughter so violent as to make it necessary for her to support herself against the back of a chair; that he thinks from her account she must have been in this situation about ten years; that she always got upon the subject of

her right to the Crown & the mystery; that he had not the least suspicion
that her Madness was Counterfeited; that he hardly ever saw a clearer case of
Insanity.

Mr Coates, in whose house she had been confined, deposed that one evening
he 'had made a party for her at Cards', namely a game of whist. The Doctors Monro were recalled and asked 'whether it was usual for Persons insane to be capable of Playing at Cards ?' Yes, they said, 'they frequently
were capable.'

Had any doubt remained in their minds from what they had seen and
heard, their lordships were convinced by the expert medical witnesses.
They concluded 'clearly and unanimously' that 'Margaret Nicholson, in
custody for an attempt on His Majesty's Person ... was and is Insane.'
The following day, 9 August, the papers 'were laid before his Majesty, for
his consideration', in consequence of which Lord Sydney, Secretary of
State (who the same year authorized the transportation of convicts to
Australia and in whose honour Sydney was named two years later), ordered
that she be taken to Bethlem Hospital 'to be confined for life; to be supported in case of sickness; but while in health to be employed, and made useful', her 'insanity' being 'of that kind as not to affect her manual operations'.[5]

On arrival the steward of the hospital

invited her and the company to dine with him which they did, and during the
whole time she appeared perfectly collected, except when the name of the
King was mentioned, she continued saying, she expected him to visit her ...
At six o'clock she was conducted to her cell ... and a chain was put around
her leg, and fastened to the floor.

Thus secured she ended her brief career of public notoriety. Contemporaries rightly commented she had been fortunate 'that her dealings were with
so generous a King, and so merciful an administration'.[4] The next weekly
levée was unusually crowded with notables anxious to congratulate the
King on his providential escape. Even old Sir John Sebright made a special
effort to attend, as he wrote to a friend: 'My hand shakes, (for I am Old),
and I am going to the Drawing-room with Lady Sebright, to assure their
Majesties that we did not instigate our quondam housemaid, Margaret
Nicholson, to attempt his sacred life, which God preserve.'[7] It was at Sir
John's table that Margaret Nicholson first set eyes on George III.[4]

She survived for more than forty years and all the other actors in the
drama. As an observer who saw her in 1823, a sprightly, deaf old woman
addicted to snuff, philosophized:

Addresses of congratulations to his Majesty, upon his happy escape, were
voted by the City of London; the loyal example was followed by all the cities,
corporations, and other great public bodies throughout the kingdom, and
many knighthoods were conferred on the occasion. It is, however, worthy of

remark, that Margaret has not only outlived all the knights then created, but even the venerable monarch himself, who in a very old age, and after the longest reign ever enjoyed on the throne of these realms, died after many years of deplorable insanity.[8]

She died in May 1828, immortalized among the great in the *Dictionary of National Biography*; and in medico-legal writings, because despite the gravity of the offence – no less than high treason – such was the royal mercy that she was not arraigned, but simply and without fuss conveyed to a place of safety.

JOHN FRITH

In 1790 one John Frith, who thought he was St Paul, threw a stone at the royal coach. Unlike Margaret Nicholson he was arraigned. While awaiting trial he was seen by Dr (later Sir) Francis Milman, at that time physician to the King's household. Lord Kenyon, the presiding judge, pointed out 'The humanity of the law of England . . . has prescribed, that no man shall be called upon to make his defence at a time when his mind is . . . not . . . capable of doing so . . . the inquiring into his guilt must be postponed to that season, when, by collecting together his intellects . . . he shall be able so to model his defence as to ward off the punishment of the law.'[9] The jury found Frith unfit to plead by reason of insanity and he was 'remanded for the present' until fit to stand trial. Whereupon the Attorney-General informed the court

that he was in possession of the king's sign manual, by which his Majesty consented to the prisoner being discharged from the gaol of Newgate, upon condition, that security was given, that he should be confined in some proper place as a lunatic, or in some other manner taken care of, so as to answer his Majesty's most gracious intentions. Bail was accordingly produced, and the prisoner ordered to be liberated.[10]

JAMES HADFIELD

Another ten years later occurred the most notorious attempt on the King's life. It led to an immediate change in the law and ultimately in 1843 to the McNaughton Rules, which still influence the courts when a plea of insanity has been entered. The trial of Hadfield is also renowned for Mr (later Lord) Thomas Erskine's speech for the defence which 'contains one of the most sound and able disquisitions on the subject of insanity, as a matter of defence against a criminal charge, that is anywhere to be found' – praise indeed from that other great advocate Lord Brougham, who like Erskine also reached the pinnacle of his profession as Lord Chancellor.[11]

On 15 May 1800, as the King entered the royal box at Drury Lane Theatre, a man in the pit, later identified as Hadfield, discharged a pistol at him. He was seized and taken to the musicians' room backstage, followed by the Duke of York and Sheridan, who was the manager and chief proprietor. At the trial six weeks later, the Duke deposed that when he entered Hadfield said, 'God bless you; I know your royal highness; you are the Duke of York; I served under you.' The Duke on his part recognized Hadfield as one of his orderlies during the Flanders campaign. The interview lasted nearly three quarters of an hour. Hadfield appeared composed and rational. Asked why he had attempted 'the foul deed', he said 'he was tired of life, that he thought he should be certainly killed if he were to make an attempt upon his majesty's life'.[12]

Erskine praised the impeccable conduct of the King:

It appears, that upon the 15th day of May last, his Majesty, after a reign of forty years, not merely in sovereign power, but spontaneously in the very hearts of his people, was openly shot at . . . in a public theatre in the centre of his capital, and amidst the loyal plaudits of his subjects, yet not a hair of the head of the supposed assassin was touched. In this unparalleled scene of calm forbearance, the king himself, though he stood first in personal interest and feeling as well as in command, was a singular and fortunate example. The least appearance of emotion on the part of that august personage, must unavoidably have produced a scene quite different, and far less honourable than the Court is now witnessing; but his majesty remained unmoved, and the person apparently offending was only secured, without injury or reproach, for the business of this day.

He then reviewed the range of cases in which the question of insanity had been raised and made the point that a direct 'relation between the disease and the act' must be established to 'deliver a lunatic from responsibility to criminal justice'. The defence had to prove 'that the act in question was the *immediate, unqualified offspring of the disease*'. The plea of insanity had rightly failed at the trial of Earl Ferrers in 1760. He had shot his steward in a fit of rage and, argued Erskine, the law 'cannot allow the protection of insanity to a man who only exhibits violent passions and malignant resentments, acting upon *real circumstances*'. He went on to discuss the particular difficulties when delusion was confined to one topic and insanity partial. In such cases considerable skill was sometimes necessary to demonstrate that the accused was ill. In illustration he quoted from the action brought in the middle of the eighteenth century by Mr Wood, a former patient, against Dr John Monro for having detained him unlawfully 'as a prisoner . . . in a madhouse at Hoxton'. To the court the plaintiff appeared sane, and the case was going against Monro when Lord Mansfield called Dr William Battie to sit beside him on the bench. By judicious and expert questioning

Battie drew Wood on the subject of his delusions and laid bare a complex paranoid system which the patient had successfully concealed.

The prisoner at the bar, said Erskine, suffered from such a delusional system while to all appearances sane on other subjects. His insanity was caused by severe battle injuries while serving in Flanders under the Duke of York. Sabre cuts had penetrated the skull and damaged his brain. He was left for dead but by a miracle survived. 'The effects of the prisoner's wounds were known by the immediate event of insanity . . . We are here not upon a case of insanity arising from the spiritual part of man, as it may be affected by hereditary taint, by intemperance, by violent passions,' he stressed, 'but with a species of insanity . . . where a man has become insane from violence to the brain, which permanently affects its structure.' From then on, Hadfield 'imagined that he had constant intercourse with the Almighty Author of all things; that the world was coming to a conclusion; and that, like our blessed Saviour, he was to sacrifice himself for its salvation . . . that he must be destroyed, but ought not to destroy himself.' This is what he had meant when he told the Duke of York immediately after the deed 'that all was not over; that a great work was to be finished'.

Erskine called Mr Henry Cline, surgeon to St Thomas's Hospital, who described Hadfield's injuries. 'It frequently happens,' said Cline, 'that after injury of the brain, there is some derangement of the understanding; the mental faculties are variously affected; sometimes by loss of memory, at other times of some particular sense, and very frequently that derangement taking place which is commonly called insanity.' Dr (later Sir) Alexander Crichton, physician to Westminster Hospital, author of *An inquiry into the nature and origin of mental derangement* (in two volumes, 1798), believed Hadfield 'insane' but 'not a maniac'. He 'labours under mental derangement of a very common but a particular kind . . . When any question is put to him, he answers very correctly; but when any question . . . relates to the subject of his lunacy, he answers irrationally.' The subject of his delusions was religion and salvation, and his illness partial insanity, which in the nineteenth century was called monomania and nowadays a paranoid psychosis.

Such was the force of Erskine's argument and eloquence that without hearing more witnesses or even the Attorney-General's closing address for the prosecution, Lord Justice Kenyon put it to the jury 'whether you will not find that the prisoner, at the time he committed the act, was not so under guidance of reason, as to be answerable for this act, enormous and atrocious as it appeared to be'. The foreman announced: 'We find the prisoner is Not Guilty; he being under the influence of Insanity at the time the act was committed.'

After some discussion how the court should proceed, since all parties were agreed 'that the prisoner, for his own sake, and for the sake of society at large, must not be discharged . . . but . . . be taken care of, with all the

attention and all the relief that can be afforded him', Hadfield was remanded 'to the confinement he came from'. He remained at Newgate prison
until one month later when Parliament hurriedly passed the Act for the
Safe Custody of Insane Persons Charged with Offences (1800). This enacted

> That in all Cases where it shall be given in Evidence upon the Trial of any
> Person charged with Treason, Murder, or Felony, that such Person was in-
> sane at the Time of the Commission of such Offence, and such Person shall
> be acquitted, the Jury shall be required to find specially whether such Person
> was insane at the Time of the Commission of such Offence, and to declare
> whether such Person was acquitted by them on account of such Insanity;
> and if they shall find that such a Person was insane at the Time of committing
> such Offence, the Court . . . shall order such Person to be kept in strict
> Custody, in such Place and in such Manner as to the Court shall seem fit, until
> His Majesty's Pleasure shall be known.

And in order to provide for Hadfield the Act was made retrospective:

> in all Cases where any Person, before the passing of this Act, had been
> acquitted of any such Offence on the Ground of Insanity at the Time of the
> Commission thereof, and has been detained in Custody as a dangerous Person
> by Order of the Court . . . it shall be lawful for His Majesty to give the like
> Order.

Hadfield, accordingly, like Margaret Nicholson, was sent to Bethlem
Hospital, where he survived until 1849.

In 1807, following the *Report of the Select Committee* 'appointed to
enquire into the State of the Criminal and Pauper Lunatics', Lord Sidmouth, Secretary of State for the Home Department, entered into a formal
agreement with the governors of Bethlem Hospital to add two wings for
sixty criminal lunatics to their new hospital which opened in St George's
Field in 1815. Its centre block, incidentally, survives as the Imperial War
Museum. In 1838 this accommodation had to be doubled, and by the 1850s
more than one hundred of the country's 436 criminal lunatics were housed
in Bethlem. In 1864 they were brought together in Broadmoor, the new
State Criminal Lunatic Asylum.[2]

How great a stir the trial of Hadfield made in medical and legal circles
may be judged from the reaction of a leading physician in the Midlands, Dr
John Johnstone of Birmingham. It stimulated him to write the first English
book on the medical or psychiatric aspects of crime, *Medical Jurisprudence:
On madness* (Birmingham, 1800). He rightly called it 'one of the most
momentous cases on which a jury was ever impanelled' and regarded it as
most auspicious for the future of British justice that, thanks to the able
advocacy of Thomas Erskine, 'all the light of science' had been admitted 'to

elucidate the fact of sanity or insanity of mind'. Of the verdict itself he wrote:

> When we reflect upon the political station of the great personage attacked, upon the decision itself, not merely as it related to the accused, but as implicating a question of incalculable importance, and upon the prejudices that would naturally hang about it, I do not know of any trial in which the accusers, the defenders, and the judges, ever merited greater honour for their calmness, discernment, and impartiality.

But unfortunately the horror felt by the nation at the attempt gave renewed life to the equation of madness with violence which had been partly responsible for the harshness with which the insane had been treated for centuries, just when humane and liberalizing influences were making headway against the stern repressive measures of what Samuel Tuke called 'the old terrific system'. It caused a reaction even in the level-headed Dr James Parkinson, although he was by no means a royalist. He had in fact been associated with the London Corresponding Society whose aims were inspired by the French Revolution and whose leaders were tried for treason in 1794 for what became known as the Pop Gun Plot. At that trial Erskine also acted for the defence and Parkinson appeared as his witness, so deeply was he implicated. In his guide book for the medical student written in the year of the trial, *The hospital pupil; or, an essay intended to facilitate the study of medicine and surgery* (1800), Parkinson referred to the implications of Hadfield's attempt when a practitioner was called to a case of alleged insanity. Discussing the often harassing decision 'when to separate a man from society' who is presented to him as insane (p. 122), he wrote:

> The task of consigning the unhappy maniac to confinement, is, by the law of the land, given to medical men: but the frequent difficulty of decision, and the great degree of responsibility with which it loads them, renders it highly desirable that some alteration might be made, in this respect. The late shocking attempt on the life of the King, and some other dreadful occurrences of a similar kind, have rationally excited a considerable degree of alarm, in the friends of those persons who have manifested symptoms of lunacy. Nor is it to be wondered at, that those, who were before satisfied in allowing those to be at liberty, who had enjoyed lucid intervals of considerable length, are now apprehensive of dreadful consequences from such permission.

This 'apprehension of dreadful consequences' cast by the shadow of Hadfield's deed, and reinforced by the knowledge that 'insanity' tends to recur, paradoxically led to a hardening of attitude towards the insane who were not offenders. The question when to discharge a patient became almost as 'momentous' as when to admit him. Dr Francis Willis junior, grandson of the Reverend Doctor, warned against declaring a patient sane because he is 'capable of saying the Lord's prayer, repeating the multiplication-table, or playing a game of whist',[13] or indeed because 'he converses quietly and rationally upon general subjects'. His standards of recovery were much stricter than those of today, which are couched not in terms of the patient's insight, but his social acceptibility. 'No man,' he stated, 'can be considered sane, until he freely and voluntarily confesses his delusions.'

In this climate it is not surprising that to be detained during his Majesty's pleasure amounted to a life sentence spent either in a county gaol, a lunatic asylum, or Bethlem Hospital. This was in many instances manifestly unjust, as Sir George O. Paul pointed out in his famous letter of 1806 to Earl Spencer, Secretary of State for the Home Department, which provided the ammunition for the setting-up of the Parliamentary Committee of 1807.[14] 'The antipathies and reigning conceits of a madman' rarely justified 'a perpetual confinement,' he maintained. Nor was it proper to lock them up in county gaols when the Act expressly exempted them from punishment, without medical attention and without hope of release. In no case, as Sir George pointed out, had 'His Majesty's pleasure ... been signified'. Furthermore, keeping persons 'who really labour under an habitual insanity, in a greater or less degree' in the manner of 'convicted felons, is unjust for any man acquitted on trial, and, regarding madmen, is wholly inconsistent with their situation, unless it were intended to heighten not repress the symptoms of their disorder.' As a remedy Sir George proposed that special wards should be set aside in 'extensive and independent Institutions', independent that is of existing gaols or hospitals. These were created by Mr Wynn's Act of 1808 as county pauper lunatic asylums, and, as has been shown, owed their existence in no small measure to Hadfield's crime and the problem of what to do with 'this unfortunate class' in an increasingly enlightened age.

JOHN BELLINGHAM

But reaction set in, as it was bound to do. In May 1812 the Prime Minister, Spencer Perceval, was assassinated in the lobby of the House of Commons. The shot which killed him was fired by John Bellingham, a forty-two-year-old merchant, father of twelve children, who for years had nurtured a growing delusional resentment against the Government for having failed to save him from, and obtain redress for, years of imprisonment and humiliation as a bankrupt in Russia. In the confusion following the deed, he remained calm, voluntarily submitted himself as the perpetrator, and said unmoved, 'It is a private injury. I know what I have done. It was a denial of justice on the part of the government.' From Newgate prison he wrote: 'For eight years I have not found my mind so tranquil as since this melancholy but necessary catastrophe.' Within seven days of the crime, from the

Monday when it was committed to the Monday following, he was tried, convicted, sentenced and executed. His counsel pleaded in vain for time. Witnesses to his abnormal state of mind could not reach London. He had failed to obtain 'the assistance of two of the ablest and most celebrated men . . . in those disorders': Dr S. F. Simmons 'stated that it was impossible for him to appear this day' and Dr Thomas Monro 'returned no answer'.

The prisoner was left without defence. In his own address to the jury, he expressed gratitude to his counsel for having raised the plea of insanity. 'I am convinced the attempt has arisen from the kindest motives,' he said. But he felt 'great obligation to the Attorney-General for the objection which he had made to the plea . . . I think it is far more fortunate that such a plea as that should have been unfounded, than it should have existed in fact . . . That I am, or have been insane, is a circumstance of which I am not apprised, except in the single instance of my having been confined in Russia.' During his summing-up Lord Chief Justice Mansfield, now in his seventy-ninth year, wept openly when he came to speak of the victim – 'a man so dear and so revered'. He begged the jury to consider the case 'unbiassed by any unfair indignation' and to try Bellingham 'as if he were arraigned for the murder of any other man'. The question of the prisoner's sanity had been raised, though not by himself. 'With respect to this the law was extremely clear,' declared Lord Mansfield, 'a man deprived of all power of reasoning . . . could not certainly commit an act against the law.' In all other cases, whatever the alleged species of insanity, 'the single question was, whether, at the time this act was committed, he possessed a sufficient degree of understanding to distinguish good from evil, right from wrong, and whether murder was a crime not only against the law of God, but against the law of his country.' It took the jury less than fifteen minutes to find Bellingham guilty.[15]

DANIEL MCNAUGHTON

'A generation passed away, and the hand of the moody assassin morbidly brooding over imaginary wrongs was again uplifted against a stranger quietly walking in the public street, equally amiable with Perceval, and equally unoffending.' But however striking the similarity of the crimes of John Bellingham and Daniel McNaughton – 'both fired at unoffending strangers in the prime of life, who had done them no [real] wrong; to whom their very persons were unknown, – in the most public place, and in the most open manner' – 'still more striking [was] the dissimilarity of the manner in which those crimes were visited by the law.' The trial of Bellingham was indecently rushed and fired by revenge and fear; that of McNaughton for the murder of Edward Drummond in mistake for his chief, Sir Robert Peel, the Home Secretary, was delayed and conducted in the spirit of mercy. Nine medical men, including Dr Edward Thomas Monro, successor at Bethlem to his father Dr Thomas, and Sir Alexander Morison, were involved. Each of them, observed the editor of *Modern State Trials*,[16] 'seemed anxious to surpass his predecessor in the tone of decision and certainty; each tried to draw the bow of Monro, and shoot, if possible, still further into empty space.' Counsel for the defence likened McNaughton's act to Bellingham's: 'All I can say of that case,' he said, 'is, that I believe, in the opinion of the most scientific men who have considered it, there now exists no doubt at all that Bellingham was a madman.' Unlike the unlucky Bellingham, McNaughton was found 'Not Guilty, on the ground of insanity'.

And as in Hadfield's case a period of public disquiet followed and it was questioned whether the law as it then stood was sufficient to distinguish the responsible from the irresponsible. In order to bring it up to date and obtain clearer guidance for the courts, the Lord Chancellor submitted to a panel of judges five questions relating to legal tests of insanity. Their answers, known the world over as the McNaughton Rules, still provide the framework in doubtful cases. Following Lord Mansfield's ruling in Bellingham's case, they shifted emphasis from the presence of delusions and linking them with the crime, as Erskine had done, to establishing whether the accused could tell right from wrong. Thus they substituted an intellectual or moral test of insanity which had neither medical nor psychological foundation.

We are of opinion [they stated] that, notwithstanding the party did the act complained of . . . under the influence of insane delusion . . . he is nevertheless punishable . . . if he knew, at the time . . . that he was acting contrary to the law . . . To establish a defence on the ground of insanity, it must be clearly proved that . . . the party was labouring under such defect of reason, from disease of the mind, as not to know the nature and quality of the act . . . or . . . did not know he was doing what was wrong.[16]

Clearly, had the McNaughton Rules been applied to Hadfield's state of mind, he, like Bellingham, must inevitably have been found guilty.

The law, like its partner psychiatry, does not always progress, nor will their often troubled co-operation end until in this difficult field the insane state ceases to be a matter of legal definition and becomes one of medical diagnosis in precise terminology. 'If no rules can be laid down with respect to the quality of mind which shall excuse and that which inculpate the perpetrator of a criminal act, in what manner is murder to be distinguished from madness, felony from fatuity, crime from disease ?' asked Dr (later Sir) John Charles Bucknill in 1857. 'Truly by Medical Diagnosis, founded . . . upon all those circumstances which enable a skilful and experienced physician to decide upon the existence or absence of disease of the brain affecting the mental functions.' He foresaw that only by relinquishing the 'tangled web of subtleties' and the unfounded hypotheses of 'the metaphysical or spiritualist theory of insanity' would 'the recognition of mental unsoundness' become and remain as it ought to be 'a question of Medical Diagnosis'.[17] Psychiatry still has a long way to go to achieve this.

Much medico-legal argumentation about absolving insanity was rooted in the horror at the death penalty. Since capital punishment has been suspended, this emotive pressure has been removed and the climate created for more dispassionate, less disputatious and more scientific discussion of criminal responsibility. Society may now well reorientate its attitude to offenders of all kinds more on sociological rather than penal principles and divide them into those who require detention in a place of safety for society's sake and into those who can be rehabilitated or treated either in or out of prison or hospital. When that time comes, psychiatrists and lawyers will find themselves working together on common ground towards a common goal.

23

Private Madhouses: 'A Fine Trade'

'The progress of insanity has, of late years, been truly astonishing. People unacquainted with the fact . . . can have but faint conceptions of the ravages of this dreadful malady.' So wrote Benjamin Faulkner, owner of a Chelsea madhouse, in *Observations on the general and improper treatment of insanity: with a plan for the more speedy and effectual recovery of insane persons* (1790). Faulkner's pamphlet, coming so soon after the events of 1788–9, provides a focal point for surveying the influence of private enterprise in the growth of the mad-business in Georgian times.

In fact little had been done to keep pace with the demands of a growing and increasingly industrialized population. The insane poor were still mostly left at large or confined in parish workhouses. For the few there was accommodation in charitable hospitals like Bethlem and St Luke's in London, but they could take only a limited number of chronic cases; or they were farmed out by their parishes to private madhouses. Subscription hospitals which took fee-paying patients and paupers, like those at Manchester and York and the one proposed at Liverpool, were few and new ones slow to be established. And the provision of asylums by district or county had to wait another twenty years to become reality. In the circumstances private enterprise continued to meet the need, as it had done for a century, until in the middle of the nineteenth century Victorian legislative control administered by a central body of Commissioners in Lunacy effectively turned the care of the insane both in and out of hospital into a nationalized corporation.

Meanwhile the public remained as suspicious of what went on behind the scenes in private madhouses as they became of what went on behind the walls of county asylums. Chief reasons for disquiet were the lack of safeguards against illegal detention and financial exploitation. Doctors were accused of confining patients to line their own pockets, since in most cases they were also the proprietors. If they were not, they often received a retaining fee to bring in patients from those who were, as, for instance, John Haslam, apothecary of Bethlem Hospital, who was paid £100 a year by Sir Jonathan Miles and Dr R. D. Willis, who had an arrangement with Mr Warburton.[1] Curing patients, it was suspected, took second place to the more profitable business of caring for them. And there was ever present the danger that the sane might be confined without redress.

The private madhouse trade in fact started with the practice of doctors taking private patients into their homes. The first to do this of whom there is record was Dr Helkiah Crooke, one of James I's physicians and physician to Bethlem Hospital in 1613–34.[2] Soon it became a flourishing business. 'You've a fine trade on't, Mad-men and Fools are a staple Commodity,' commented Middleton and Rowley in *The Changeling* (1653). By the eighteenth century it was concentrated in two centres in and around the metropolis, one at Hoxton, the other at Chelsea. Daniel Defoe, in *Augusta triumphans: or, the way to make London the most flourishing city in the universe* (1728), was the first of a long line of public-spirited and freedom-loving citizens to expose the abuses to which these houses lent themselves, for instance in getting rid of inconvenient relatives. He unleashed his wrath and his imagination particularly on husbands who, aided by unscrupulous doctors, had their wives locked up on the pretence of madness, and painted a lurid picture indeed of

the vile Practice now so much in vogue among the better Sort, as they are called, but the worst sort in fact, namely, the sending their Wives to Mad-Houses at every Whim or Dislike, that they may be more secure and undisturb'd in their Debaucheries: Which wicked Custom is got to such a Head, that the Number of private Mad-Houses in and about *London*, are considerably increased within these few Years. This is the heighth of Barbarity . . . a clandestine Inquisition, nay worse . . . If they are not mad when they go into these cursed Houses, they are soon made so by the barbarous Usage they there suffer . . . Is it not enough to make any one mad to be suddenly clap'd up, stripp'd, whipp'd, ill fed, and worse us'd? . . . our Legislation cannot take this Cause too soon in hand .

In my humble Opinion all private Mad-Houses should be suppress'd at once, and it should be no less than Felony to confine any Person under pretence of Madness without due Authority. For the cure of those who are really Lunatick, licens'd Mad-Houses should be constituted in convenient Parts of the Town, which Houses should be subject to proper Visitation and Inspection, nor should any Person be sent to a Mad-House without due Reason, Inquiry and Authority.[3]

Powerful support came from Dr Tobias Smollett, who dramatized how the liberty of the subject could be infringed with impunity. He had the eponymous hero of his *Sir Launcelot Greaves* confined in a madhouse and soliloquize:

THE

London-Citizen Exceedingly Injured:

OR A

BRITISH

INQUISITION

DISPLAY'D,

In an Account of the UNPARALLEL'D CASE of a *Citizen* of *London*, Bookseller to the late Queen, who was in a moſt *unjuſt* and *arbitrary* Manner ſent on the 23d of *March* laſt, 1738, by one *Robert Wightman*, a mere Stranger, to a *Private Madhouſe*.

CONTAINING,

I. An Account of the ſaid CITIZEN's barbarous Treatment in *Wright*'s Private Madhouſe on *Bethnal-Green* for nine Weeks and ſix Days, and of his rational and patient Behaviour, whilſt *Chained, Handcuffed, Strait-Waſtecoated* and *Impriſoned* in the ſaid *Madhouſe*: Where he probably would have been continued, or died under his Confinement, if he had not moſt *Providentially* made his Eſcape: In which he was taken up by the Conſtable and Watchmen, being ſuſpected to be a Felon, but was unchain'd and ſet at liberty by Sir *John Barnard* the then Lord Mayor.

II. As alſo an Account of the illegal Steps, falſe Calumnies, wicked Contrivances, bold and deſperate Deſigns of the ſaid *Wightman*, in order to eſcape Juſtice for his Crimes, with ſome Account of his engaging Dr. *Monro* and others as his Accomplices.

The Whole humbly addreſſed to the LEGISLATURE, as plainly ſhewing the abſolute Neceſſity of regulating *Private Madhouſes* in a more effectual manner than at preſent.

Brethren, pray for us, that we may be delivered from unreaſonable and wicked Men, 2 Theſſ. iii. 1, 2.

LONDON:
Printed for T. COOPER at the *Globe* in *Pater-noſter-Row*, and Mrs. DODD at the *Peacock* without *Temple-Bar*, 1739.

How little reason have we to boast of the blessings enjoyed by the British subject, if he holds them on such a precarious tenure: if a man of rank and property may be thus kidnapped even in the midst of the capital; if he may be seized by ruffians, insulted, robbed, and conveyed to such a prison as this . . . immured for life under the pretext of lunacy . . . and subjected to the most brutal treatment from a low-bred barbarian, who raises an ample fortune on the misery of his fellow-creatures.[4]

In the meantime a Bill had been drafted in 1754 to provide some control on the lines suggested by Defoe. It proposed 'among other Matters that the Licensing and Visiting of private Madhouses should be by the President and other officers of the College of Physicians'.[5] Unfortunately the College at that time declined to cooperate, possibly because of the vested interest of some of its fellows. In January 1763 Charles Townshend M.P., President of the Board of Trade and later Chancellor of the Exchequer, was instrumental in having appointed a committee of the House 'to consider the state of private madhouses' and became its chairman.[6] He was said also to have written a pamphlet on regulating private madhouses which appeared at the same time and strengthened his hand.[7] The committee heard evidence from several ex-patients who considered themselves to have been illegally confined, and also from Drs Battie and Monro, who confirmed its conclusion 'that the present State of the Private Madhouses in this Kingdom requires the Interposition of the Legislature'.[8] Leave to bring in a Bill was granted, but strangely none was introduced. Said Horace Walpole, 'Charles Townshend took great pains in that business, distinguished himself, was content, and dropped it'.[9] Eventually in 1774 there was passed the Act for Regulating Madhouses which remained in force for nearly fifty-five years.

Paradoxically its main aim was not to protect the insane but to safeguard the sane from illegal confinement. It provided for the licensing and inspec-

18. *Alexander Cruden's title-page – serving also as a table of contents – conveys graphically what it was like to be apprehended and confined as a lunatic in a private madhouse in eighteenth-century London before the Act of 1774 brought some order into the admission of patients. Incidentally in this book the word strait-waistcoat appears for the first time in print. Cruden's 'Dr. Monro' was Dr James Monro, first of a line of five generations of Monros, who from 1728 to 1853 ruled in succession at Bethlem – the hospital, wrote Alexander Pope, 'where Folly holds her throne, And laughs to think Monro would take her down'. Cruden's encounter with Dr James's son John Monro, when he was confined in a 'Chelsea Academy . . . for the Confinement of such as are supposed to be deprived of the Exercise of their Reason', led to another book,* The adventures of Alexander the Corrector . . . *during his Chelsea-Campaign (1754).*

tion of private madhouses by five commissioners of the College of Physicians in London and by Quarter Sessions in the country, keeping a central register at the College of all patients admitted, with severe penalties for receiving a person 'as a Lunatic, without having an Order, in Writing, under the Hand and Seal of some Physician, Surgeon, or Apothecary', the last being the style of the general practitioner of the day. So began the system of 'certification' and to be 'certified' and 'certifiable' became synonymous with 'mad'. Having gone so far, it is curious that the Act did not debar doctors from pecuniary interest in the madhouse to which they sent 'certified' patients.

Because the law anciently was more concerned to protect property than persons, the provisions of the Act were further limited to private, fee-paying patients who were liable to be exploited. It did not extend its protection to the much larger number of the poor and mad. To remedy this Thomas Bakewell, himself the owner of a private madhouse in the provinces, advocated before Mr Rose's Committee legislative reform which 'should recognize every Lunatic as a Child of the State' to be cared for in 'National Hospitals, for the Cure of Insanity'.[10]

Fifteen years later this movement found a champion in John Conolly, who proclaimed 'That all persons of unsound mind should become the care of the State' and 'Every Lunatic Asylum should be the property of the State, and be controlled by public officers'.[11] In brief, in the field of mental health there was proposed a national health service long before its advantages in other branches of medicine were realized, and more than a century before it came into being.

As far as the second loophole in the 1774 Act, doctors' financial interest in private madhouses, was concerned, Faulkner suggested that a clause be added 'exacting an oath from every physician, surgeon, etc., that he has *no interest whatever* in recommending a patient to any particular house, and for imposing a severe penalty on such as may be found to have such interest.' Not only would this prevent the too ready consigning to a madhouse of patients suffering from 'the phrenzies and deliriums incident to bodily disorders', but it would also put madhouse keepers on their mettle to cure rather than keep, and so 'would tend very much to the prevention of insanity, and to clear the houses already crowded'. As it was, 'The house to which the patient is recommended, usually belongs either totally, or in part, to the physician, whose charges for board, lodging, and attendance, too frequently preponderate against the same of speedy cure.'

Faulkner's recommendation was in fact incorporated in the Act to Regulate the Care and Treatment of Insane Persons (1828): 'No Physician, Surgeon, or Apothecary shall sign any Certificate of Admission to any House of Reception for Two or more Insane Persons, of which he is wholly or partly the Proprietor, or the regular professional Attendant.' This Act

19. *The first purpose-built private madhouse, Brislington House on the London road near Bristol, was opened in 1804 by Dr Edward Long Fox, physician to the Bristol Royal Infirmary and also a Quaker who had provided the Tukes of York with the first matron of their Retreat. In 1811 he was approached but declined to take charge of the King's management and Willis's son John took over. In September 1814 Mr Edward Wakefield, one of George Rose's closest collaborators in the parliamentary enquiry into madhouses in 1815, visited Brislington House on a fact-finding tour of the West Country and reported:*

'Dr. Fox has laid out a very large sum of money upon building an establishment, being a series of houses for the purpose of classification. . . . To each building is a distinct and separate yard, at the end of which are cells for refractory and dirty patients. . . . There is a separate bed-room to each patient, all well ventilated, whitewashed, and cleaned: the patients tranquil, without coercion, but not allowed to remain in bed. In this part of the buildings there is an infirmary for those in bodily ill health. . . . Those who pay most occupy the upper part of his own house. . . . The doctor does all he can to lead them to occupy themselves. Those who have been used to trades or farming occupations easily take to gardening, farming, or jobs about the house; but he remarked it was much more difficult to give employment to gentlemen.'

was the first legislative advance since that of 1774. It also marked the beginning of a shift of emphasis away from preventing illegal confinement of the sane, to ensuring proper care and treatment of the insane whether rich or poor.

Until such time as the law was improved, Faulkner recommended the safeguards offered by a '*free house*' like his own, 'by which is to be understood a house into which *any* physician may be called, where any friends may visit, and where the patient is attended by those who can only follow the directions of his physician, whose best advantage results from a speedy cure'. Instead of 'resigning the patient to the care of a *mad doctor* . . . let them avoid sending for such as may receive benefit from any thing but their advice . . . Let them consult a Fordyce, a Baker, a Warren, or a Reynolds; men whose knowledge cannot be surpassed, whose integrity is unimpeachable, and who can derive no advantage from the local situation of the afflicted.' In other words, he advocated independent nursing homes for the mentally ill in which they could be treated by physicians of their own choosing. So confident was he of the superior results of his system from his five years' experience (which started in 1785, according to the registers of the Royal College of Physicians[12]) that he offered to take in any 'under the influence of this disorder in its *first* stage, and before any of the class of mad doctors have been consulted, to board, lodge, and attend for *Six months . . . free of all expence whatever*' unless he should have cured him within that time.

This striking a bargain of the 'no cure, no money' variety was not just the gimmick of a quack. On the contrary, it had an honourable place in medical practice of earlier centuries. The best known of such agreements, because it is preserved in its original form, is one entered in 1702 by Dr David Irish, a Surrey practitioner, with one

Joseph Chitty for the Cure of his Wifes Hipocondriak melancholy Madness, as follows, that is to have payd down in hand five pounds . . . & when cured to have five pounds more with this provision ye said David Irish practicinor of physick do use his utmost endaevours to compleat the cure within ye terme of three or four months otherwise to have no more money.[13]

Faulkner's insistence that the patient must be in the 'first stage' of the illness merely reflected what was general knowledge, namely the longer a patient had been ill the less likely was spontaneous recovery to take place. The Reverend Dr Francis Willis too realized this when he stated how much better his results were if patients came for treatment 'within Three Months after they had begun to be afflicted with the Disorder'.

24

The Poor and Mad

Like other movements for social reform, that to improve the lot of the in-sane can also be traced to the last decades of the eighteenth century. As far as psychiatry is concerned one can be more specific and say it started in 1789. The sympathy aroused by the royal malady opened people's minds and eyes to the whole field of mental derangement and stirred the national conscience about the fate of the poor and mad. So began that period of psychiatric history which reached its full flowering in Victorian times under the aegis of the chairman of the Commissioners in Lunacy, the 7th Earl Shaftesbury. It may properly be called the 'asylum era', for in and around the new county lunatic hospitals much of what we know or think we know about mental illness developed.

At first the movement was confined to building local lunatic hospitals in provincial cities on the model of those already in existence at Manchester (1766) and York (1777). Liverpool led the way and there the active spirit was Dr James Currie, celebrated in the history of medicine for his careful thermometric investigation of 'fever' when this was still considered a dis-ease by itself. In the autumn of 1789 he made a number of appeals through the local newspaper:

A late national distress has . . . forced the subject upon general attention and . . . [should his appeal succeed, there was reason to hope that their example would] speedily be followed by several of the principal cities in the kingdom, and among the happy consequences of the issue of that calamity, future times will probably enumerate a more general provision for and hu-man treatment of this hapless class of our fellow creatures.[1]

Currie proposed that their hospital should cater for the poor, supported by their parishes, and also for those who could afford to pay: and should take in both recent and long-standing cases:

In the institution of a Lunatic Asylum there is this singularity, that the

z

interests of the rich and poor are equally and immediately united. Under other diseases the rich may have every assistance at their own homes, but under insanity, relief can seldom be obtained but from an establishment for the treatment of this particular disease. Hence the objects of a Lunatic Asylum are two-fold – to provide accommodation for the poor . . . and . . . those of superior stations . . . The objects of such an institution are two-fold in another sense: It holds out a shelter both for the curable and incurable. To the first it proposes the restoration of reason, and while it relieves society from the burthen of the last, it covers the hapless victims themselves from the dangers of life.

THE INFIRMARY, DISPENSARY, AND LUNATIC ASYLUM, MANCHESTER

20. *Manchester set the example followed by Liverpool and Leicester of building a 'lunatic hospital' next to its infirmary, which had been in existence since 1752. It opened in 1766 with 'cells' for twenty-two patients. Here, in the early 1790s Dr John Ferriar made the first realistic assessment of many time-honoured anti-maniacal treatments. In the 1830s under the patronage of William IV it became the Manchester Royal Infirmary and Lunatic Asylum. Meanwhile, following the recommendations of the Wynn Committee in 1807, the link of psychiatry with medicine was broken by the movement to build asylums by counties – an unfortunate development which caused psychiatry to grow away from medicine. Even Manchester went back on its original vision and the Asylum, separated from the Infirmary, reopened in 1848 as an independent institution in the country as the Cheadle Royal.*

He added that the governors of Liverpool Infirmary had welcomed the proposal provided the initial outlay could be raised.

In his second letter he countered objections to building the lunatic hospital next to the Infirmary:

> Some warm supporters of the Lunatic Asylum are of opinion, that it ought to be a distinct institution, placed in the country ... with a considerable space for the amusement of the patients ... and for their healthful employment.

He did not deny the attractions of such a situation, but thought the links between body and mind and their diseases so close that infirmary and asylum should be administered by the same officers and served by the same doctors with access to the same facilities:

> By combining the Lunatic Asylum with the Infirmary there will not only be an immense saving of expense in the building itself, but in the annual disbursements. The same offices, apothecary and board of oeconomy will serve both ... The institutions themselves are closely allied in their nature; the first affords relief to diseases of the body, the second to diseases of the mind. That these are more nearly connected than is commonly imagined it would be easy to show ... Madness indeed can only be called a disease of the mind, because its most striking symptom is the derangement of the intellect. The disorder, it is reasonable to suppose on every theory, is seated not in the agent but in the instrument of thought [the brain].

At Liverpool Currie's view prevailed, and in the record space of three years the Lunatic Hospital opened in the grounds of the Infirmary. He was opposed, however, by the more influential Alexander Hunter, whose dictum was 'An Asylum for Lunatics should always be a separate and independent charity; an union with an Infirmary is unnatural,'[2] and it was this policy which came to be officially adopted. Dr Hunter had founded the York Asylum and ran it from when it opened in 1777 until he died in 1809. At the time he conceived his plan of a large lunatic hospital with a hundred beds as a Bedlam of the northern counties, there were only two independent establishments of the kind in the provinces. One was Bethel, the little charitable foundation at Norwich which had been receiving patients since 1725; the other, at Newcastle, had been established in 1764. Both were little known and neither influenced the development of psychiatry. Hunter, on the contrary, publicized his asylum widely and was himself well known for his agricultural writings, for which he was elected Fellow of the Royal Society. When the Lunatic Hospitals at Liverpool and Leicester were contemplated, he was the recognized authority to whom Currie and Arnold turned for advice. His fame was such that when the government of France was planning an asylum system for their country in 1790, the Comité de Mendicité applied to him.[3] In 1792 he published an account of 'the origin, progress, and design' of the York Asylum, giving an account of its domestic arrangements and its three divisions of patients according to whether they were self-supporting, paid for by their parish, or subsidized by the charity itself.[4]

All was not well with it, however. As early as 1789 the Reverend William Mason had published *Animadversions on the present government of the York Lunatic Asylum* in which he suggested that its financial policy required urgent investigation. Hunter was able to ward him off, but his successor who inherited his system had to pay the penalty for both of them when it was exposed in 1814. How important an institution it was can be seen from the fact that when it became the subject of first local and then parliamentary inquiry it contained nearly 200 patients, against about 120 in Bethlem and around 300 at St Luke's.[5]

Disturbed by the disappearance of one of their flock in the York Asylum, the Quakers of York, led by the Tuke family of tea-dealers, founded in 1792 their own 'Retreat . . . for Insane Persons of the Society of Friends', which opened its doors in 1796. It set an example to the rest of the civilized world by demonstrating that humane treatment on moral principles was not only possible but gave better results than the old 'terrific' system generally practised elsewhere. At Edinburgh, too, Dr Andrew Duncan senior, an admirer of the Retreat, physician to King George III in Scotland, President of the Royal College of Physicians of Edinburgh, was busy initiating a fund for an asylum which opened in 1813 as the Edinburgh Royal Lunatic Asylum.[6] George III had granted it a royal charter in 1807, the year Dr Duncan issued his further *Address to the public, respecting the establishment of a lunatic asylum at Edinburgh:* 'We are now encouraged to this effort by knowing, that the prepossession against the efficacy of medicines and medical treatment, in this malady, have been generally conquered. It is now incontestably established by experience,' he claimed, sensible of the perennial attraction of the slogan 'insanity is curable' to which Dr Francis Willis had given professional sanction, and the wisdom of encouraging generosity with the prospect of returns, 'that, in a large proportion of cases, skilful practice, in an appropriate institution, will either totally remove this complaint, or, to a desirable degree, will soften its violence.'

In Ireland the first public asylum, that at Cork, was established by Act of Parliament, and started to admit patients in 1789. There Dr William Saunders Hallaran made his mark by organizing for the patients 'such employment' as 'might produce attention without anxiety', as Dr Battie had advocated in the middle of the century,[7] and so founded what is nowadays called occupational therapy. How he did this is described in *An enquiry into the causes producing the extraordinary addition to the number of the insane, together with extended observations on the cure of insanity; with hints on the better management of public asylums for insane persons* (Cork,

1810). His book also has the distinction of being the first psychiatric treatise published from Ireland.[8]

The year 1792 also saw stirrings of social conscience about the fate of the poor and mad in two other major provincial cities. At Leicester the governors of the Infirmary invited their physician, Dr Thomas Arnold, to organize an asylum in a building adjoining it to provide facilities available until then only in his own private madhouse. It opened two years later for ten patients at eight shillings a week for 'board and medicines'.[9] At Gloucester Sir George Onesiphorus Paul tried to do the same, was obstructed by the local doctors and failed. In January 1792 he persuaded his fellow governors to pass a resolution 'To extend the utility of the Infirmary Charity to insane persons'. It was referred for consideration to 'the Gentlemen of the Faculty' – that is their medical staff. They reported back six months later that 'the idea . . . was entirely impracticable, on account of the great expence which would attend such an establishment'.[10] Since they did not have to find the money it must be presumed it was a cover for their real opposition. Either they did not care to undertake the additional duties it involved, or they regarded it as below their dignity. Above all they may have feared that it would compete with the two flourishing private asylums already in the county: Dr Edward Long Fox's Brislington House near Bristol and Dr Joseph Mason Cox's two houses at Fishponds and Stapleton.[11] Despite repeated efforts Sir George was thwarted and Gloucestershire had to wait another thirty years for its asylum.

His disappointment, which he made no attempt to hide,[12] made him realize that what was needed was a medico-social service on a nation-wide scale. It could not be left to local initiative, private enterprise or voluntary subscription. Accordingly in October 1806 he addressed a letter to Earl Spencer, Secretary of State for the Home Department, proposing that the Government should establish district asylums for pauper and criminal lunatics where they could be treated at their county's expense. He pleaded the plight of insane offenders languishing in prisons 'until His Majesty's pleasure be known' although acquitted on the ground of being insane at the time of committing the offence, and described vividly the neglect of the poor and mad in his county:

I believe there is hardly a parish of any considerable extent, in which there may not be found some unfortunate human creature of this description, who, if his ill treatment has made him phrenetic, is chained in the cellar or garret of a workhouse, fastened to the leg of a table, tied to a post in an outhouse, or perhaps shut up in an uninhabited ruin; or, if his lunacy be inoffensive, left to ramble half naked and half starved through the streets and highways, teased by the scoff and jest of all that is vulgar, ignorant, and unfeeling . . . Of the number of these forlorn objects, I know that your Lordship has endeavoured to inform yourself . . . It is, however, enough for my argument to say, generally, that of all the Lunatics in the kingdom, the one half are not under any kind of protection from ill treatment, or placed in a situation to be relieved from their malady. Yet, if there be a disease which is a natural misfortune, unmixed with consequence of immoral life, this is that disease . . . Now, my Lord, cannot we unite the police intention with the efforts of humanity and provincial economy, and by that union create a mutual support ?[13]

Not a visionary but a far-seeing planner, Sir George was confident that such district asylums would also attract eminent medical men to the subject: 'There is little doubt even of a competition of men of science in the profession, for the management of such Institutions where respectably established.' This statesman-like letter was printed as an appendix to the *Report from the Select Committee* 'appointed to enquire into the State of the Criminal and Pauper Lunatics . . . and of the Laws relating thereto' which the House of Commons set up in January 1807.

The moving spirit behind the formation of this committee was Charles Watkin Williams Wynn, Under-Secretary of State for the Home Department in his uncle Lord Grenville's Ministry of All Talents. The committee, with Wynn in the chair, consisted of a galaxy of reformers: George Rose, Sir Samuel Romilly, William Wilberforce and Samuel Whitbread. They sat in February and March and published their *Report* in July 1807. They received written evidence from Dr (later Sir) Andrew Halliday, physician to William IV and author of a history of the house of Guelph, who maintained a life-long concern for the insane. His inquiries into the fate of pauper lunatics and idiots in the counties of Suffolk and Norfolk confirmed the urgent need for 'Public Asylums . . . in every county'. They heard Sir George Paul in person, besides receiving his letter. To inform themselves on the management of a well-run establishment they called Mr Thomas Dunston, who as master of St Luke's Hospital combined the office of head nurse and steward. Mr John Nash, the Regency architect, told the committee that he had 'turned' his 'thoughts to the construction of a Lunatic Asylum' and had planned the asylums at Hereford and Exeter, and gratuitously the one Sir George Paul hoped to build at Gloucester.[14] He presented an estimate of £7,760 for an asylum for fifty patients to include 'cisterns and water-closets' and 'hot and cold bath'. Dr Robert Darling Willis, in his capacity as commissioner of the Royal College of Physicians empowered to licence the private madhouses of London under the Act of 1774, spoke of the need for inspection and the advantage of having 'a medical person' in 'daily attendance'.

The committee concluded that

the measure . . . most adequate to ensure the proper care and management of these unfortunate persons, and the most likely to conduce to their perfect cure, is the erection of Asylums for their reception in different parts of the kingdom; a measure which has already been adopted with great success by private subscription at York, Liverpool, Manchester, Exeter, Hereford, Norwich, and Leicester. To this the public opinion appears to be so favourable, that it may be sufficient for the Legislature, at least in the first instance, rather to recommend and assist, than to enforce the execution of such a plan.[15]

Compulsion, they feared, was more likely to provoke resistance than the encouragement of voluntary cooperation. They therefore proposed that county magistrates be empowered to build asylums, to house no more than three hundred patients, there to be maintained at the charge of their parishes. Wynn's Act, as it came to be called, 'for the better Care and Maintenance of Lunatics, being Paupers or Criminals' received the royal assent in 1808. But they were too optimistic in making it permissive. By the 1840s only a dozen or so counties had availed themselves of their new

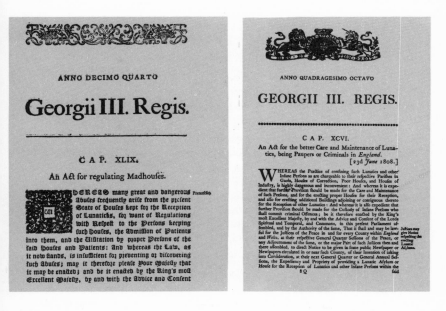

21. *The two most important Acts of Parliament of the reign which helped to put psychiatry on a proper footing were the Act for Regulating Madhouses of 1774 and Mr Wynn's Act for the Better Care and Maintenance of Lunatics of 1808. The first laid down that fee-paying patients could only be confined if properly 'certified' as insane by a medical man and provided for the licensing and inspection of private madhouses. The second enabled counties to build lunatic asylums, but it was not until 1828 that legislative protection was extended to the admission and treatment of paupers.*

powers and the Act of 1845 had to make the erection of county asylums compulsory.

Compassion for the insane was kept alive not only by the recurrences of George III's illnesses. Major scandals involving gross maltreatment of patients at York Asylum and Bethlem Hospital, two of the biggest and most respected institutions in the country, brought the whole issue back into the limelight in the years 1813 and 1814. The result was that a parliamentary inquiry was set up in 1815 which was far more comprehensive than that of 1807. From its findings developed, step by step, all the lunacy legislation of the century which dominated and even largely shaped psychiatry right up to the present time.

One of the most exciting and dramatic episodes in the history of the insane started at York in 1813, innocuously enough with the publication in June of Samuel Tuke's now classic *Description of the Retreat, an institution near York for insane persons of the Society of Friends*. He gave an account of their treatment of patients by kindness, moral management and the encouragement of self-control which they had evolved. It brought into sharp relief their 'mild' methods, which accorded mental patients the dignity of sick human beings and placed the Retreat at once in the forefront of the new era of institutional care. Dr Andrew Duncan wrote after a visit in 1812:

> The fraternity denominated Quakers have demonstrated, beyond contradiction, the very great advantage resulting from a mode of treatment in cases of Insanity, much more mild than was before introduced into almost any Lunatic Asylum, either at home or abroad ... In the management of this Institution, they have set an example which claims the imitation, and deserves the thanks, of every sect and every nation ... It may be asserted, that the Retreat at York, is at this moment the best-regulated establishment in Europe, either for the recovery of the insane, or for their comfort, when they are in an incurable state.[16]

The appearance of Tuke's book alarmed the officers of the nearby York Asylum. Dr Charles Best, the late Dr Hunter's former pupil, friend and successor, sensed implied criticism of himself and conditions at the York Asylum and brashly rose to defend himself by accusing Tuke of defamation:

> When an attempt is made to injure the reputation and interests of any public body, or private individual [a reference to the effect Tuke's book might have upon his private practice], it is of little moment to the assailed party, whether the measure be accomplished by open libel or masked insinuation ... In an account of the Quakers' Retreat ... some highly indecorous and injurious insinuations were thrown out against other Establishments ... the intended application of which no one could misunderstand.[17]

A bitter newspaper war developed with support coming in on both sides.

Tuke countered Best by stating that 'It was neither affirmed nor insinuated in the work which has given so much offense, that bad practices exist in all establishments.' But, he hastened to add, 'If anything which is said in the "Description of the Retreat" is calculated to *sap* or *undermine* that detestable system of treatment to which the insane are too frequently exposed, I shall sincerely rejoice.'[18] Best returned by declaring that to speak of 'the practicability of introducing a system of mild treatment' generally into asylums was tantamount to 'a direct assertion that such a system had not been introduced into *any* establishment of the kind – a sufficient proof that it was the author's intention to include a neighbouring institution in his sweeping censure.'[19]

Soon the accuser found himself in the position of the accused. Two influential public figures, long aware that cruelty, severity and neglect flourished unchecked at the Asylum but impotent to achieve reforms, joined forces with the Tukes and their supporters: Godfrey Higgins, county magistrate, who ruthlessly exposed the evils and pressed for a public inquiry; and William Samuel Nicoll, recorder of Doncaster, whose cool legal brain devised the strategy.

They, with Tuke and ten more of their party, gatecrashed the meeting of the Court of Governors on 10 December 1813, paid the requisite donation to the charity of £20 each and uninvited took their seats as new governors. 'It would be difficult to conceive the surprise occasioned by this unexpected incursion,' wrote an eye-witness. 'Considerable indignation was naturally felt and expressed; but the impartial and dignified conduct of the chairman (the Archbishop of York) contributed to restrain the meeting within the bounds of decorum.'[20] They managed to force the setting-up of a small committee of inquiry into a number of cases of abuse which had come to their notice. While it was sitting, on 28 December fire broke out in a detached wing of the Asylum and destroyed it. A number of patients chained up or locked in perished in the flames and also many records. 'I have never been able to divest my mind of suspicions of the most horrible kind respecting its cause,' wrote Higgins two years later.[21]

This was the signal for the reformers to mount their final offensive. At the next meeting on 7 January 1814 no less than forty of their contingent presented themselves. They outnumbered the old governors by two to one. Between them they had paid £800. Samuel Tuke and his venerable grandfather William Tuke, founder of the Retreat, were not intimidated by the taunt that, although their donations made them governors, they 'did not make them gentlemen'.[22]

The Archbishop . . . opened the business by a most able, humane and candid speech, in which he confessed the change which had taken place in his sentiments in regard to the state of the Asylum, by an investigation of the cases of complaint . . . It was . . . resolved that a committee be appointed to examine into the rules, management, and state of the Asylum ... The decided numerical superiority of the reformers ... who had entered for the sole purpose of benefiting the charity by restoring it to its original intention ... prevented any attempt at opposition and thus resolutions, which three months ago would have been spurned with disdain, were carried unanimously.[23]

Tuke and Higgins inspected every nook and cranny of the Asylum. Tuke found that 'Upward of twenty patients were shut up together in very small day-rooms which had not convenience for air, exercise, or natural wants. The appearance of the men was pitiable beyond description. Most of their faces were very hollow, and their complexion sallow.' In a wash-house he saw a patient 'on a wet stone floor ... without any clothes whatever ... apparently in the last stage of decay'.[24] Higgins discovered a secret block of cells 'about eight feet square, in a very horrid and filthy situation, the straw ... almost saturated with urine and ... the walls ... daubed with excrement'. In a room 'twelve feet by seven feet ten inches ... there were thirteen women ... I became very sick, and could not remain longer.' Neither the Archbishop nor the other governors knew of these cells.[25] Everywhere except among the patients of the richer sort, neglect, starvation and disease were rampant. They also found that funds had been misappropriated on a large scale and that 144 patients were unaccounted for; it was presumed they had died, but in the books they were entered as 'discharged cured'.

At the decisive annual general meeting held in August 1814, which lasted two days, Higgins held forth in thunderous terms:

In the name of all those persons, whose violent deaths are so stated in your books as to disguise the facts from you, I call for justice ... I call upon you to clear the house of every individual, who has neglected or abused his authority. I call upon you to cleanse the Augean stable from top to bottom.[26]

And this they did: every officer, keeper and nurse was removed. Dr Best was allowed to resign. A new code of conduct was drawn up and the managers of the Retreat took over the running of the Asylum until new staff was found. 'What strenuous efforts fruitlessly combined to accomplish, a little volume in which the Asylum was scarcely mentioned, has at once achieved – I need hardly mention Mr. S. Tuke's *Description of the Retreat*,' Nicoll wrote of this stirring episode in social and medical history.[22]

The inquiry into conditions at York Asylum was only the first of many into the affairs of hospitals for the insane in the nineteenth century. Always the question arose, how could such abuses prevail under the very eyes of a board of respectable and public-spirited magistrates or governors? And always the answer was that they did not know what was going on in their own institution. They blindly trusted their officers and what they were shown and told. The question how such malpractices could be avoided, or

'Who is to keep the keepers?' as the phrase went, was answered by formulating more stringent methods of 'visitation' and 'inspection'. Regulations to this end became an essential feature of lunacy legislation. Nicoll, who had been so active in prising open the walls of York Asylum, devoted a whole book to it. 'The keeper must himself be kept,' he maintained, otherwise 'an asylum is likely to be little beyond an alternation of reciprocal violence between the prisoner and the gaoler.' On the affairs at York he wrote: 'There was nothing local, nothing accidental, nothing attributable to individual character; all was in the regular course of human institutions.'[27]

It was not to be supposed that the campaign to liberalize and humanize the treatment of the insane would long remain a local matter. The experience of the Retreat was an expression of the new attitude to the welfare of the underprivileged and repressed at a time when many of the old tyrannies were assailed – of social order, of religion, of slavery. It found a ready echo in the minds of progressive men in the metropolis, some of whom have already been named. Among them was Edward Wakefield, land-agent and philanthropist.* He gathered a committee to found a 'London Asylum' modelled on the Retreat where 'humanity' was to 'form a leading principle in the treatment of patients'.[28] Wishing to inform themselves on the running of existing establishments, they visited the lunatic wards at Guy's Hospital, founded for incurable patients under the will of Thomas Guy in 1725, St Luke's Hospital, and Bethlem.

Like the reformers at York, they at first had difficulty in gaining access to Bethlem, which was still housed in the building put up by Robert Hooke in 1676, with wings added for long-stay or 'incurable' patients, as they were called. What they discovered on 2 May 1814 made history, just as Higgins's visit to York Asylum had done scarcely six weeks earlier.

One of the side rooms contained about ten [female] patients, each chained by one arm to the wall; the chain allowing them merely to stand up by the bench or form fixed to the wall, or sit down on it. The nakedness of each patient was covered by a blanket-gown only ... Many other unfortunate women were locked up in their cells, naked, and chained on straw ... In the men's wing, in the side room, six patients were chained close to the wall by the right arm as well as by the right leg ... Their nakedness and their mode of confinement gave this room the complete appearance of a dog-kennel.[29]

Wakefield was so horrified that he took a party of Members of Parliament to see for themselves and an artist to make a pictorial record of the patient

---

* 'Mr Wakefield, the land surveyor ... is in the first employment in his line, and is steward to many persons of great property,' wrote George Rose (*Diaries*, 1860, vol. 2, p. 443). He 'appears extremely intelligent, very conscious of it, and to be just saved from being a democrat by the power of his judgment and integrity over his presumption'.

22. *James Norris, 'an insane American . . . Rivetted alive in Iron & for many years confined in that state by chains 12 inches long to an upright massive bar in a Cell in Bethlem'. Drawn from life by C. Arnald at the request of Mr Edward Wakefield in June 1814 and exhibited to Mr Rose's Committee the following year. Norris died in February 1815 soon after he was released, from 'a very considerable disease of the lung; a consumption' and became a* cause célèbre. *His offence had been that he had threatened John Haslam the apothecary and*

most cruelly chained and fixed in irons hidden in a basement cell. Their visit had indeed furnished them with 'the strongest grounds for recommending a new asylum, to be conducted after the simple and mild . . . plan of the "Friends' Retreat" '. But in the end they achieved much more and their planned asylum became unnecessary. They had provided the parliamentary lobby headed by Rose and Wynn with the incontestable evidence they needed to force a much wider inquiry into the whole field of provision for and supervision of the insane in England, Scotland and Ireland.

A new select committee was appointed 'to consider of Provision being made for the better Regulation of Madhouses'. It was destined to become a landmark between the old private madhouse and private profit system and the new asylum era. They inquired into the state of the York Asylum, Bethlem Hospital, St Luke's, the Nottingham County Lunatic Asylum – the first built under Wynn's Act – the condition of the insane in workhouses and private madhouses at Hoxton and in the provinces. They called witnesses from all over the country, medical and lay, keepers and magistrates, patients and governors. There was no aspect of the whole vast field of the care of the insane which they did not touch. Most of the meetings were chaired by Rose, the remainder by Wynn and Lord Robert Seymour. Their questions were searching and insistent.

By July 1815 they had published their 'minutes of evidence' in four parts with an appendix of documents and plans of buildings. In February 1816 they published two more reports and in June a separate one dealing with conditions in Scotland, followed in 1817 by a similar inquiry into 'the lunatic poor in Ireland'. The three-part *Report from the committee on madhouses*, a folio of over five hundred closely printed pages with tables and plans, remains a historical source of the first importance, a monumental documentary of psychiatry in practice which no treatise on the subject can ever do justice to. It gave rise to a fresh spate of psychiatric literature, just as the King's illness had done.

The committee drew only general conclusions – the need for legislation was the most important – evidently feeling that the facts they had so laboriously assembled spoke for themselves. They condemned particularly the

---

attacked a keeper. Mr Rose scathingly asked Dr Thomas Monro, the hospital's physician, 'Do you think a person could have had about him a weight of iron, say six or eight-and-twenty pounds; that he could have been confined to his bed without being allowed to turn round for nine years, or without being able to get out and sit on the edge of the bed, being chained by the head by a chain only twelve inches from the iron stantion, and that that would have no effect upon his general health?' (Etching by George Cruickshank published July 1815.)

evils of indiscriminate restraint, overcrowding, lack of medical care, and shortage of keepers and nurses, and they urged legislative control of admission and supervision of those confined.[30]

On the strength of his committee's findings Rose introduced a Bill in 1815 and again in 1816, and his colleagues introduced another in 1819, after his death. Each time the Lords rejected it. How strongly private enterprise resisted state control of the 'mad-business' was made blatantly clear when Lord Chancellor Eldon made his notorious objection to the proposals on the last occasion Mr Rose's Bill came before the House of Lords: 'There could not be a more false humanity than over-humanity with regard to persons afflicted with insanity.'

'The evidence taken before Mr. Rose's committee . . . must be fresh in the recollection of every one,' wrote Sir Andrew Halliday in *A general view of the present state of lunatics and lunatic asylums* (1828):

He was at great pains to prepare a bill which . . . was well calcuated to remedy every evil either ascertained or anticipated. The subject was dispassionately canvassed in the lower house, and his bill passed by the Commons, almost unanimously, three or four several times; but it was uniformly rejected by the Lords, and after Mr. Roses' death [in 1818], it got into Chancery [a reference to Eldon's opposition], and there it has slept for the last nine years.

It was not until yet another select committee, this time moved by Lord Robert Seymour, had inquired into the state of the poor and mad of the county of Middlesex and their maltreatment in the Hoxton madhouses where they were farmed out[31], that the two Acts of 1828 were passed 'To amend the Laws for the Erection and Regulation of County Lunatic Asylums, and more effectually to provide for the Care and Maintenance of Pauper and Criminal Lunatics' and 'To regulate the Care and Treatment of Insane Persons'. It was the first legislation since the Act of 1774 and the first which extended legal protection to the poor and mad. It was followed in 1845 by the great Lord Shaftesbury Act 'For the Regulation of the Care and Treatment of Lunatics' by which a national register and inspectorate, the Commissioners in Lunacy, was set up.

Protecting the sane from unlawful confinement and the insane from maltreatment and exploitation, safeguarding his property and affairs, controlling his admission and discharge, even laying down how often his physical and mental state had to be examined and what clinical notes had to be kept, these became matters of law. A veritable cocoon of legislation was spun around the 'certified' patient and his psychiatrist. Ultimately it became more important not to fall foul of it and to satisfy the Commissioners in Lunacy than to investigate and treat the patient. No other branch of medicine had to bear such stifling weight of legal regulation and control. In the long run what was in its time a major advance, social and medical, acted as a brake on advances in knowledge and so against the best interest of patient and psychiatry alike.

It is in fact no exaggeration to say that in its early decades lunacy legislation grew faster than the specialty itself. The size of legal guidebooks which appeared bears this out. A. Highmore's *Treatise on the law of idiocy and lunacy* – the first since J. Brydall's little tract *Non compos mentis* of 1700 – appeared in 1807 on the heels of Wynn's committee. In 1812 followed G. D. Collinson's two-volume work on the law of lunacy. By 1847 the dependence of psychiatry on the law had reached such proportions that L. Shelford's *Practical treatise of the law concerning lunatics, idiots, and persons of unsound mind* contained 1,116 closely printed pages. This was little short of twice the length of any book on mental diseases yet published.

To return to 1815. Even without new legislation Rose's Committee speeded the movement to provide proper hospital conditions for the insane throughout the kingdom. Wherever he could Rose himself made sure practical effects followed. He approached the governors of Bethlem Hospital, for instance, drawing their attention to the damaging evidence brought out by his committee about their hospital. Haslam, their apothecary, revealed in *A letter to the governors of Bethlem Hospital containing an account of their management of that institution for the last twenty years* (1818) that Rose had directly 'intimated his wish that the medical officers should not be re-elected'. Neither he nor Monro,* the physician, was reappointed by the governors at their next annual general meeting in 1816,[32] although both had been invited to prepare answers to the allegations.[33]

The governors could hardly have acted otherwise: not only had patients been most cruelly maltreated, but the art of medicine had been prostituted into a mere arm of coercion. How backward Bethlem still was can also be seen from the fact that Rose had been unable to obtain any information about illnesses and deaths of patients because even as late as 1815 'no Register of Diseases' was kept.[34] But to the governors' credit conditions rapidly improved. By 1817 it was fit for a visit by the Duke and Duchess of York and the Duke of Gloucester, who expressed 'the highest satisfaction . . . in the accommodation and treatment of the patients' in their new premises in St George's Fields. And the following year the Duke of Kent wrote in the visitors' book: 'Nothing can exceed the cleanliness and good order of the whole establishment, and I conceive it does the highest credit to all concerned with it. I state this after a very minute inspection of three

---

* If Thomas Monro did not gain a place in the history of psychiatry, he is remembered as the founder-patron of the British school of watercolourists and numbered among his protégés Turner, Girtin and Peter de Wint. He was himself no mean artist.

hours.'[35]*

'Recent circumstances, of great publicity,' wrote Hallaran of Cork in the second, 1818, edition of his book re-titled *Practical observations on the causes and cure of insanity*, summing up the effect of the royal malady in stimulating public interest in and concern for the poor and mad, 'have tended to excite sentiments of the most generous nature in behalf of the insane, which do honour to our country, and which have . . . materially contributed to direct the attention of the community to the unabating necessities of this retired portion of our afflicted fellow-creatures.'

* George III's sons played an impressive part in encouraging the study and treatment of 'insanity'. We have already seen how the Dukes of Kent and Sussex supported the therapeutic trial of Messrs Delahoyde and Lucett's process. The Duke of Clarence, as William IV, was a staunch well-wisher to the advances in patient care at the Middlesex County Pauper Lunatic Asylum at Hanwell. In 1835 the services 'rendered . . . to the insane' by its medical director were brought to his notice and he promptly conferred the honour of knighthood on him and so created Sir William Charles Ellis, psychiatry's first knight. Indeed, 'so much interest was excited in the monarch's mind by the graphic details of the events passing at Hanwell . . . that he resolved to go and see for himself'. But his ministers intervened and the visit did not take place.

William IV's Queen, Adelaide, followed his example by lending her name and giving a donation to the fund for rehabilitating recovered patients discharged from Hanwell, which was instituted the same year as Ellis's knighthood. As Queen Adelaide's Fund it still distributes relief and aid. Three years later, in 1838, William IV also dubbed Sir Alexander Morison for his indefatigable pursuit of enlightenment in the same subject. Morison had given the first course of formal lectures on psychiatry in this country in 1823 under the patronage of Frederick Duke of York.

PART FIVE

Later Studies of George III's Illness

25

The Asylum Era: Acute Mania

When the insane were raised to the status of patients and hospitals were built for them and doctors took an interest in 'insanity', a new specialty was launched, which was later named 'psychiatry' or 'psychological medicine'. For many reasons it was and has remained a very special speciality. Unlike any other branch of medicine, it owed its existence to the efforts of dedicated laymen whose aim was social betterment and justice and not to the initiative of the profession or an awareness of medical needs.

The policy laid down during this formative period determined, for good and ill, the lines of its future development. Many advances and improvements were made in the 'asylum era' which followed, but the policy also had fateful consequences from which psychiatry still suffers. By isolating the mental patient it created artificially two orders of disease, each with its own specialists, the physical and the mental, and so set psychiatry apart from medicine and divorced psychiatrists from physicians. This unfortunate separation has determined in some measure the development of psychiatry since those heroic Georgian days and has greatly influenced the views of later generations on George III's illness, as the two main studies devoted to it, one written in the middle of the nineteenth century and the other in the middle of the twentieth, illustrate.

Asylums were built in the country, where land was cheap, the air was pure and there was ample space for occupation and recreation. There they became largely self-supporting communities, living on their own produce and industry from workshops, kitchen gardens and farms. Always the pressure was to keep costs down, whether it was parsimonious parish officers, county magistrates or Regional Hospital Boards under the National Health Service who had to find the money. At the end of the eighteenth century for instance the York Asylum charged eight shillings per week for a pauper lunatic. In the 1830s Sir William Ellis at the Middlesex County Pauper Lunatic Asylum prided himself on cutting this to less than six shillings.

'Pauper' lunatic asylums even carried this stigma in their name. The number of patients was always so great that the smallest saving per head was worth while. Even today, while something like half of all available hospital beds are for the mentally ill or incapacitated, the money spent on them amounts to only ten per cent.

The all-powerful motive of economy hit asylums in yet another way, when it was realized that costs could be further reduced by increasing the number of patients congregated in one institution. Wynn's committee in 1807 had recommended on medical and humanitarian grounds that the number should not exceed three hundred in any one hospital. In 1839 Dr Conolly took over nearly a thousand patients at Hanwell, which had been built less than ten years earlier for three hundred. By the end of the nineteenth century some county asylums had populations of two or three thousand patients, and some even more. Wing after wing was added to the original buildings, to which their higgledy-piggledy appearance still bears witness. The perennial curse of overcrowding was laid.

'A gigantic asylum is a gigantic evil,' wrote one of Conolly's pupils, Dr J. T. Arlidge, in his book *On the state of lunacy* (1859). Administration of necessity became authoritarian and regimented under all-powerful superintendents. While the number of patients increased, staff did not. One doctor had – and still has – hundreds of patients to look after. In these circumstances medical care perforce became perfunctory and still more so because there was not the money for laboratory and other investigatory facilities, such as turned nineteenth-century workhouse infirmaries into twentieth-century hospitals. A mental hospital patient was even barred by statute from entering a general hospital, and this made the separation of diseases of the mind from that of the body almost complete. The good name of a mental institution was reckoned in terms of cheapness, avoidance of accidents and suicides and escapes, and low death rate, when all the time it should have been the recovery and discharge rate, and could have been the overriding need and opportunity offered for advancing by research knowledge and understanding of the diseases of their 'inmates'. The result was that asylums were rightly reproached for being places of 'care not cure'. Psychiatrists became medically qualified keepers, and as 'alienists' lost interest and caste. These trends are reflected in the name 'asylum', which in the nineteenth century replaced the earlier 'lunatic hospital'; now the trend has been reversed and the official name is 'mental hospital'.

For these reasons medical advances have left psychiatry far behind. While medicine kept pace with the basic sciences of physiology and biochemistry, and theories and systems were gradually made redundant by facts, in psychiatry they continue to flourish, indeed more than ever, and schools divide psychiatrists into opposing camps such as medicine has not known since the early eighteenth century. While medicine became biological, investigative and diagnostic and acquired a precise terminology, psychiatry grew more speculative, metaphysical, esoteric and sociological, and the gulf between them widened still more. While medical therapeutics became rational and aetiological, in psychiatry empirical treatments – which suppress symptoms by impairing brain function or altering brain structure – still hold the field.

With the passing of the Mental Health Act, 1959, the old legal shackles were removed and patients can now enter and leave hospital without formality. The psychiatrist gained sole clinical and legal responsibility for his patient which other specialists had always had. At the same time has become official policy to join psychiatric departments with general hospitals, as Currie had proposed in 1789. The road, however long, has opened for psychiatry to find its way back to medicine.

By the middle of the nineteenth century the asylum era was in full swing and from this background came the first medical history of George III. In May 1855 the incoming president of the Association of Superintendents of Insane Hospitals (now the American Psychiatric Association) chose as the subject of his inaugural address 'The Insanity of King George III'.[1] Dr Isaac Ray, of Butler Hospital at Providence, Rhode Island, a founder member,[2] was internationally known for *A treatise on the medical jurisprudence of insanity*, published at Boston in 1838 and reprinted at London and Edinburgh the following year. His paper, 'Statistics of Insanity', has already been mentioned.[3]

He approached the royal malady from experience gained in the newly established asylums of observing the manifestations of the 'insane state'. Psychiatry had not reached the stage of concerning itself with causes, that is diagnosis. Patients were simply divided into the manic, the melancholy and those with gross brain disease. A mere recital of what they said and did sufficed to describe all there was to be known and make the type of illness clear. He wrote:

To the mere pathologist, the insanity of a prince is not more interesting than that of a peasant; but to the historian, to the medical jurist, to all who are engaged in the care of the insane, the attacks of George III are invested with peculiar interest. He was a prominent figure in a period that teemed with great men and great events, whose memorials are yet around us; and twice the recurrence of his disorder gave rise to a degree of political feeling that has seldom been equalled, and to political discussions that settled for ever a vital principle in the British constitution.

He considered 'the form of disease', that is diagnosis, only in relation to the royal physicians' distinction between delirium and insanity. They 'said it was more allied to delirium than insanity – meaning that it was characterized by mental excitement rather than by fixed, definite delusions . . .

The form of disease which they had in view is common enough; and though the progress of science may have contributed nothing to our knowledge of [its] nature or of its treatments, it has certainly improved our nomenclature.' In an expanded version of his paper, with quotations from memoirs and correspondences published in the meantime, he amplified this remark. The royal physicians

sought no doubt to give the impression that it was simply a case of delirious wandering produced by bodily disturbance, which would readily pass away with the condition on which it depended. It is impossible to see any ground for this opinion. This attack [1810] closely resembled the others. It was manifested by hurry, restlessness, caprices, indiscretions, violence, and delusions. In one word, it presented all the characters of ordinary acute mania.[4]

'Mania' was no more specific a description of an abnormal mental state than 'fever' was of an abnormal physical one. Ray somehow sensed that there was more to the King's illness than the term implied or he was able to fathom. He expressed this in a significant *caveat*, which unfortunately was later not heeded:

Few men would have seemed less likely to be visited by insanity. His general health had always been good; his powers were impaired by none of those indulgences almost inseparable from the kingly station; he was remarkably abstemious at the table; and took much exercise in the open air. Insanity had never appeared in his family, and he was quite free from those eccentricities and peculiarities which indicate an unbalanced mind.

Among his countrymen Ray's presentation of the medical history of America's last king could not but create a sensation, and a lively discussion followed. Dr Luther V. Bell, the outgoing President whose name is still recalled in some psychiatric textbooks for his description of 'acute delirious mania' – whatever that may be by modern diagnostic standards[5] –

could not willingly allow a paper of such extraordinary interest to be passed over without expression of his deep gratification and thanks to its author. While few in our speciality had not had some knowledge of the insanity of George III, as a historical incident, it was certain that here was a body of information far more complete and extended than had ever before been aggregated on that subject: and regarding the tenderness with which that topic had ever been handled by the English writers, he could not have thought that it would have been practicable, at this late day, to have collected so full a detail of almost every day's history of that sovereign's attacks.

Dr. Bell thought that this paper would occasion a very considerable sensation in England. It would lay open a vein of the most interesting portion of their own history, till now concealed in a vast mass of rubbish, parliamentary reports, public papers, political squibs, diaries of persons about the court, tittle tattle sent to other nations, &c. The British nation, in which the idea of the hereditary danger of insanity was always more prominent than with us, must have a constantly recurring fear of the same malady reaching the throne. We know, indeed, that the present most exemplary and virtuous Sovereign is constantly hinted at as being in danger of suffering under her grandfather's malady, with no other foundation, probably, than the popular idea that the hereditary predisposition is much more intense than facts would warrant ... While it is true that, pathologically, the insanity of a monarch is no more interesting than that of a peasant, yet there are many circumstances which, politically and historically, give a weighty importance to the mental diseases of those entrusted with high rule and the control of nations.[6]

Dr Joseph Workman, medical superintendent of the Provincial Lunatic Asylum at Toronto, who in a venerable old age was known as 'the Nestor of Psychological Medicine in the Continent of America',[7] spoke

as the only representative of British institutions for the insane ... He had no doubt the paper would excite great interest in England, albeit there might be a degree of sensitiveness manifested upon it ... Two great events ... had their birth in consequence of that insanity. One was no less than the confede-ration of these States. He, George III, was unquestionably a good man, and beloved by his subjects, as his grand-daughter is by hers. Another important fact originating at that time was the attention of the world and especially of the medical profession, to the subject of insanity and its treatment. Although it was unfortunate for the British nation that their monarch was so severely afflicted, it was, probably, in its results, fortunate for humanity.[8]

Ray's paper was published in the July 1855 number of the *American Journal of Insanity*, and at the special request of members was also 'printed in pamphlet form for general circulation'.

In England its younger sister journal, the *Asylum Journal of Mental Science* edited by Dr J. C. Bucknill, who was in the habit of reporting American news and meetings, on this occasion maintained a stony silence. The 'degree of sensitiveness manifested upon it' which Dr Workman had predicted was also exhibited by the *Journal of Psychological Medicine and Mental Pathology*, then in its ninth year of publication. In the January number of 1856, its founder-editor, Dr Forbes Winslow, prince of psychia-tric journalism and trained as a reporter on *The Times*, gave Victorian rectitude full rein:

'The American Journal of Insanity', July 1855, contains a history of the several attacks of insanity under which his Majesty King George the Third suffered. These particulars, which have not hitherto been published in any collected form in this country ... have now been embodied in the form of a narrative by Dr. Ray ... We take leave, however, to question whether the result is worthy of all the labour it must have cost. We were in England too well aware of the melancholy fact of the King's insanity at the time, if not familiar with all the details. We have had too much reason to regret the conse-quences thereof to wish to revive so painful a subject. We are very well convinced that much indirect good has also been providentially educed from that national affliction, by the countenance it gave to improvement in the general principle of the treatment of the insane. Nevertheless, so much being taken for granted, we fail to perceive the benefit that can accrue to psychological medicine from a revival of scenes so painful, and from a history which, after all the laborious research of Dr. Ray, is still imperfect.

Our transatlantic brethren may probably trace in the results of the mental disorder of George the Third, their own elevation to a national status. We may be disposed to concur in the inference, but content to submit with the best grace we may to the dispensations of Providence, we would not raise the veil that screens the domestic griefs of royalty – in the belief that a sovereign has as inalienable a right to have his home held sacred as has the meanest citizen of a republic. And notwithstanding we may incur the imputation of a squeamish tenderness, we hold that such a narrative as the history of the insanity of the King goes very near to trench upon the inviolability of professional confidence. In the ordinary publication of cases by medical men, names are usually suppressed – and where for the ends of justice both names and particulars must be made known, still no more than is required for the furtherance of judicial objects is usually laid bare to public gaze. Why, then, should not the same measure be meted out to the most exalted member of society ?[9]

Twelve months and four issues later the old reporter in Dr Winslow asserted himself and he reprinted Ray's paper in full and without comment.[10] Here it was noticed by the editors of the leading German psychiatric journal, *Allgemeine Zeitschrift für Psychiatrie*, published by the German Association of Asylum Doctors. They commissioned a translation by Dr H. Laehr 'because of its exceptional interest in particular for the psychiatric viewpoint and also its general historical and political importance. The illness carries many lessons for all who have to deal with such cases and diseases.' It appeared in their pages three years later in 1861.[11] Laehr incidentally numbered George III's illness among the outstanding events of psychiatric history.[12]

Ray's study was not superseded for almost one hundred years. Even passing mention of the royal malady is rare. One of the few British physicians who touched on it was Dr Arnold Chaplin in his *Medicine in England during the Reign of George III* (1919). He sympathized in particular with George III's double misfortune in being sick and royal, contrary to the general notion that the best people have the best medical attention. Far from it:

> The lot of kings when stretched upon a bed of sickness is far less enviable than that of humbler mortals. Politics and the august presence of royalty seem to conspire together to paralyse the efforts of physicians, and it may be doubted if the prognosis in cases of illness among kings can ever be regarded in so favourable a light as in those of more lowly beings.[13]

For Dr Chaplin the King's 'malady presented no unusual feature. It was a case of delusional insanity attended with exacerbations of mania followed by periods of melancholia.' Whether the learned doctor spoke with his tongue in his cheek or really thought he was making a diagnosis is not apparent. But it does show how the profusion of psychiatric jargon, with its confused and confusing medley of the old and the new, had by then befogged even level-headed physicians. This rash of new names sprang from the perpetual hope that a new terminology would make psychiatry more exact and scientific. Not knowing anything of aetiology or pathogenesis, not even whether they dealt with diseases of mind, body or brain, they took – as we still largely do – the mental state for the disease itself: the excited patient as suffering from mania, the depressed from melancholia or depression, the obsessional from obsessional neurosis and the anxious from an anxiety state.

The Era of Classification:
Manic-Depressive Psychosis

To bring some order to the field and to attempt to give psychiatry disease entities to deal with as medicine had, in the 1890s Professor Emil Kraepelin of Heidelberg and later Munich collected, described and defined mental manifestations and based on them a new classification, in which he linked them with outcome or prognosis and which has survived to the present day. With it psychiatry entered its classificatory or labelling era.

Kraepelin had observed, as others before him, that patients who had attacks of mental illness from which they recovered usually showed marked mood or emotional disturbance, that is they were either elated or depressed or alternated between the two. He therefore called these the group of affective disorders or manic-depressive psychoses. In contrast, patients with illnesses which ended in deterioration showed disorders of thought and perception, such as delusions and hallucinations and often also motor disturbances called catatonia. This group he named dementia praecox, analogous to dementia senilis at the other end of life.

'The application of Freud's ideas to dementia praecox' led Professor Eugen Bleuler of Zurich to rename it 'schizophrenia', to indicate that its essence was literally a 'splitting' of psychic functions with fragmentation of the personality.[1]

Again it was an American psychiatrist who brought George III's illness into line with these latest psychiatric concepts. In 1931 Dr Smith Ely Jelliffe applied the Kraepelinian criteria of excitement and recurrence, and thought it an advance on Ray's 'mania' to rename the royal malady 'manic-depressive psychosis'.[2] He could not be expected to have known that 135 years earlier the Reverend Joseph Townsend had called it 'mania melancholica'.[3] Dr Jelliffe wrote:

As an aside it may be recalled that King George III suffered from a manic-depressive psychosis . . . He had at least five recurring attacks . . . The second occurred after the Colonies had freed themselves, 1788. They were mostly of short duration . . . and the manic element was paramount.

In passing it may be remarked that Jelliffe was not the only American who thought it natural to link the loss of the colonies with George III's derangement in 1788, although by that time they had enjoyed independence for more than five years. What George III felt about this event, however painful when it happened, is clear from the manner in which in June 1783 he received America's first envoy to the court of St James's, John Adams. To him he said:

> I wish you, Sir, to believe, that it may be understood in America, that I have done nothing in the late contest but what I thought myself indispensably bound to do by the duty which I owed my people. I will be very frank with you. I was the last to consent to the separation; but the separation having been made, and having become inevitable, I have always said, as I say now, that I would be the first to meet the friendship of the United States as an independent Power. The moment I see such sentiments and language as yours prevail and a disposition to give this country preference, that moment I shall say, let the circumstances of language, religion, and blood have their natural and full effect.[4]

Even if hurtful to national pride, the eighteen years' struggle for independence bears no relation at any point to the King's illness, neither its beginning nor its end.

Seeing that the 'diagnosis' of manic-depressive psychosis was applied to George III's illness and stuck, it is important to assess what it means in terms of modern medicine. Kraepelin's ideas, like Bleuler's and Freud's, were time-bound, and his system, like all nosological systems which are not based on knowledge of disease process or cause, was doomed to be eroded by scientific advance.[5] They were formulated in the days of pre-scientific medicine and of the rudimentary neurology of three-quarters of a century ago, when patients could have such gross lesions as a brain tumour without it even being suspected. 'Mental' diseases were grouped by symptoms, not by causes, type or location of lesion, as in medicine. But clinical pictures are not constant: they change, sometimes rapidly in the course of an illness. Furthermore the same symptoms occur in widely differing conditions; and they vary, as Ray had pointed out, even with the observer. How little it was possible to maintain these divisions or psychosyndromes is obvious from such hybrid terms as 'manic stupor', 'schizo-affective disorder' and 'neurotic schizophrenia'.

Psychiatrists had to concentrate on mental symptoms and psychopathology because on the organic side they could make no headway until medical advances gave them the knowledge and the tools. While so little was known of the causes of abnormal mental states, theories of mental illness framed exclusively in somatic, psychological or sociological terms were and are, to say the least, premature. ' "*All* medical doctrines", says Dr. James Gregory, in his blunt and forcible manner, "are stark staring nonsense." '[6]

The list of investigations which the basic sciences have given to medicine since then, and psychiatrists seventy years ago had to do without, is formidable. Porphyria is an excellent example of how advances in biochemistry and medicine have discovered a disease previously unknown which causes mental symptoms varying from anxiety and depression to excitement, delirium and even convulsions. In a recent series of 50 patients suffering from porphyria 29 were found to have marked mental symptoms: 14 were 'depressed, nervous, hysterical, lacrymose, peculiar'; 9 were 'confused, hallucinated, disorientated'; and 6 had been sent to mental hospitals certified insane.[7]

Of routine laboratory tests on body fluids as we know them, they had none. There were no tests for syphilis. Cerebrospinal fluid was not examined if only because lumbar puncture had hardly come in. Next to nothing was known of the electrical activity of nervous tissue and nothing of the diagnostic possibilities of encephalography or brain waves. X-rays had only just been discovered and brain surgery was in its early infancy. The doctrine of cerebral localization of function was incomplete and psychometric testing could as yet make no clinical contribution.

Whole groups of disorders, such as deficiency syndromes and metabolic disturbances, hereditary or acquired, were unknown, and not even the mechanism of diabetes, the commonest of all, had been elucidated. Nor had virus diseases of the nervous system been described. Their importance in causing mental symptoms was only appreciated during and following the epidemic of lethargic encephalitis at the end of the First World War. The concept of extrapyramidal disorders of muscle tone, movement and posture, of which Parkinsonism is a familiar example, had not come in, and even so crucial an indicator of brain disease as the sign of Babinski had only just been described but was not yet appreciated.

From this historical perspective it is clear that the old labels like manic-depressive psychosis and schizophrenia, even the distinction between neuroses and psychoses, must sooner or later yield to advances in medicine when these are systematically applied to psychiatric patients. However convenient, they can no longer be regarded as equivalent to a medical diagnosis. Indeed they now hide more than they reveal.

The King on the Psychoanalytic Couch

In the 1930s, when Jelliffe diagnosed manic-depressive psychosis, psycho-analysis had also arrived. Like almost everyone else, psychoanalysts accepted Kraepelin's system as nature's own and his manic-depressive psychosis and dementia praecox as disease entities. They therefore set about constructing specific psychopathologies for his groups and sub-groups. In this way Freud, whose foremost aim it was to introduce a dynamic system of mental science, paradoxically helped to fossilize psychiatry on Kraepelinian lines. Psychoanalytic psychiatry became the vogue and to 'analyse' historic figures the fashion.

In this climate there appeared in 1941 the only other study of George III's illness besides Ray's, curiously again by an American psychiatrist, Dr Manfred Guttmacher's *America's last King: an interpretation of the madness of George III*.[1] It was destined to determine what modern historians and biographers made not only of the illness but of the man himself.

It was not so much a clinical history as an exposition of the tenets and methods of psychoanalysis. Guttmacher put, as it were, the King on the couch and found what he was looking for by bending the facts to the theory. He started from the premiss that the illness was manic-depressive psychosis and that attacks occurred in a predisposed personality not strong enough to withstand the strains and stresses of life and so prone to breakdowns. So confident was he that he claimed the whole illness could be understood in psychological terms: 'His five manic attacks were precipitated by political and domestic events that pierced his very vulnerable defenses and caused him to decompensate.'[1] The circular argument runs something like this: episodes of excitement equal mental breakdowns – these happen only in neurotic personalities – 'neuroticism' is due to conflict and frustration – hence breakdown. All that was needed after this was to 'interpret' the King's psychological situation whenever he fell ill:

The mental disorder which seized George III on five separate occasions was manic-depressive insanity . . . From my analysis of the events preceding George's attacks of insanity, and of the illnesses themselves, it appears that frustration was the major force behind his disorders . . . Believing that, as a king, he should be all-powerful, he became unbalanced when he found him-self impotent and unable to act . . . minor attacks followed frustration imposed on him by the outside world . . . major attacks came, as a rule when he felt that he had thwarted himself by a lack of decisiveness intolerable in a king . . . Self-blame, indecision and frustration . . . destroyed the sanity of George III . . . Had it been his lot to be a country squire, he would, in all probability, not have been psychotic.[1,2]

Whereas Ray was surprised that a man so stable, whose conduct of life was healthy and whose family free from mental disorder, became insane, Guttmacher on the same evidence found 'that he is a victim of neuropathic tainting . . . The list . . . of affected members . . . is imposing – frightening at first glance.' Twenty years later he corrected this wild statement to: 'The family history is not very impressive psychiatrically. There are instances of psychoses in remote ancestors and a maternal uncle committed suicide.'[2]

In the King's personality, too, Guttmacher discerned ample predisposi-tion to psychological illness: 'This unstable man' whose 'neuroticism . . . tyrannized' his family and his ministers, was 'harassed by profound feelings of inadequacy'. He 'took the job of kingship too seriously. The decisions which he felt called upon to make were at times too much for him. A vulnerable individual, he broke under the strain.' And again: 'This rigid, scrupulous psychological constitution was chiefly responsible for George's attacks of mental disorder. Had he been able to delegate unpleasant tasks to his subordinates, leave difficult decisions for others to make, or adopt a "come what may" attitude . . . he would not have become insane.'

To satisfy psychoanalytic tenets the King's conflicts had to be reduced to sex – no easy matter in a man whose habits were blameless and who never touched any woman but his wife. Playing the familiar psychiatric gambit 'Heads I win, tails you lose' Guttmacher regarded this as particularly sinis-ter and clear evidence of suppressed desires. As proof he singled out, from all the subjects the King's delirious mind rambled about, his declarations of love for Lady Pembroke and his reflections on marriage:

From the nature of George's utterances about Lady Pembroke during his illness, it seems likely that the psychosis resulted partly from his emotional relationship with her. The delusion in which the simple wish-fulfilment mechanism is clearly intelligible – the belief that all marriages had been annulled – is significant . . . During the first part of 1788 the King must sud-denly have realized that he was again greatly attracted to her. Immediately an inward conflict arose. He loved her; he wanted her as his Queen. That was obviously impossible. He must be satisfied with being her lover. No, that could not be! He must be a King . . . He could no longer stand the constant conflict between his rigid conscience and his psycho-sexual desires. Insanity appears to have been the only way out for him.

While Guttmacher gave free rein to his fantasy in his psychological construction, he made short shrift of clinical and historical facts. These he either denied or distorted. Most important among them were the physical symptoms and signs which so pained the patient and alarmed his doctors and which identify the illness for the physician today. He dismissed them partly as fictions invented by the court to hide the 'mental' nature of the illness, and partly as imagined by the patient himself and so further evidence of his 'neurotic' and 'hysterical' make-up. The illness of 1765, during which, as has been shown, the King was not deranged, he regarded as 'purely mental' and physical manifestations, if there were any, occurred only 'as a complication' of the mental illness. However,

being milder than subsequent disorders, [it] presented a less consistent type of psychiatric picture. The later illnesses were all outspoken attacks of manic excitement.* This first attack seems to have been of mixed manic-depressive character with the depressive element dominant . . . Essentially, it consisted of a period of about six months during which the King's customary instability of mood was pathologically exaggerated.

It was of course essential for the psychological theory that the first breakdown should have occurred in young manhood. It would not have done for a 'vulnerable' individual to reach the mature age of fifty unscathed.

In 1788, according to Guttmacher, 'the Court' again started 'manufacturing reports of various baffling symptoms' which if not 'entirely invented', were 'at least, exaggerated further to fool the public'. The King was even accused of being a party to this deception:

The probability is that, abetted by the false interpretations of those about him, he was trying to delude himself into viewing his illness as primarily physical . . . He doubtless was fully aware of his own vulnerability to mental disease.

Fast pulse, sweating, colic, hoarseness were rated as accompaniments of manic states; pain, paresis, stupor, fits as 'hysterical'. The wheel had turned full circle, from the royal physicians on the spot wondering what physical illness had brought their patient to the brink of death and deranged his mind, to twentieth-century psychiatrists trying to explain the physical symptoms as the guise or expression of psychological ills — so far had psychiatry moved away from medicine.

The blame for falling ill was now squarely placed on the patient and his

---

* The King's physical sufferings apart, the evidence shows that his mental state lacked the cardinal feature described as characteristic of manic excitement, namely an exaltation of spirits accompanied by a heightened sense of well-being.

insufficiencies in a manner no other specialty could or would indulge in. This moralizing and patronizing attitude fostered also a strange lack of sympathy for the King and his bitter sufferings – very different from what would be felt towards a patient stricken with severe bodily illness.

All this had profound consequences on present-day views of the King's personality and actions. It opened the floodgates to unbridled speculation about the sort of person he must have been to break down. Each time he was indisposed, for whatever reason, and every occasion of real annoyance and concern were interpreted as episodes of mental disturbance. Of this contagion the 1765 illness is the most glaring example. 'The basis of mischief is already and irremoveably laid', foretold Sir William Young in the sixth week of the King's illness in 1788 of what was to become the Whig interpretation of the reign: 'In future times, designing, ambitious and profligate men may start the idea that what has been may be, and in the desperate effort of factious opposition, men venture to arraign the temper and health of mind, though it shows its perfect state.'[3] Indeed it would make an interesting study to trace the interaction of party political allegiance and psychiatric and more recently psychoanalytic theory on the historian's view of George III.

Textbook concepts of psychopathology were applied to him and a man riddled with weaknesses, conflicts and unfulfilled desires conjured up on fashionable psychological theory – not on evidence or fact. Historians and biographers seem almost to have vied with one another in a kind of free-for-all over the King's supposed deficiencies and what caused him to fall ill. There is not a single modern history or schoolbook dealing with the reign which is not disfigured by it.

A few examples will show the harm done by this type of psychiatry by defamation, if not character assassination. Watson, in the standard Oxford history of the reign, writes: 'He lacked the pliability and easy virtue of less highly strung people. When his obstinacy encountered an immovable obstacle, all his resources were at an end and the black humour claimed him . . . Madness was but this mood in an extreme form.'[4] Pares explained 'his madness as the breakdown of a too costly struggle to maintain . . . the reserve and equanimity imposed upon a hot temper and anxious nerves, to say nothing of his resolute fidelity to a hideous queen, and regimen of violent exercise and exaggerated abstinence designed to counteract strong passions and a tendency to fat.'[5] One biographer declared that the King lived in 'a state of chronic though varying disequilibrium, with recurrent crises of extreme disorder, and ending in permanent lunacy.'[6] Plumb described the King's intellectual and emotional structure as 'fissured with weaknesses' and brought his psychopathology up to date, as it were, by divining that 'His attacks of madness took the form of a total flight from reality' due to 'the sexual strain of his marriage to so unattractive a woman as the Queen'[7] – by whom, it must be added, at the time of his first derangement he had had fifteen children; and in the illness of 1765, to which this statement refers, he was not deranged. One recent narrative of the Regency Crisis went even further and claimed that 'his loquacity, the sudden variation of his mood and spirits, quick changes between elation and depression, his psycho-sexual desires – are typical of a psychotic disorder of a manic-depressive type . . . caused by an underlying conflict . . . such as is nowadays treated by psychotherapy.'[8]

Another writer elaborated: 'George himself was manic-depressive, a form of madness which . . . has a strong tendency to recur . . . The stresses on his mind were great, and in the absence of any acute political crisis in the autumn of 1788 the behaviour of his son must be considered one of the decisive factors in precipitating his mental collapse.' 'Disillusionment and overwork' also contributed.[9] Are such musings an advance on the causes to which contemporary gossip ascribed it: 'annoyance at the endeavour of the Duke of York to introduce Turkish instruments into the Band of Guards, or a discussion over dinner on the subject of murder'?[10]

Historians and biographers were of course dependent on what was the only modern study of the illness and accepted what appeared to be the last word in psychiatry of the psychodynamic kind with all it implied.

To such absurdities may historic figures be reduced when the mutterings of a delirious mind disorganized by an intoxicated brain are interpreted as wish – fulfilments and as revealing the conflicts responsible for the illness The fundamental fallacy of the psychological approach was the same as that of the classificatory – the effects of the illness were mistaken for its cause. Who would seek the cause of pneumonia in the delirious utterances of a sick child and judge its personality by them? Yet this is precisely what has been done in George III's case.

The effect of all this psychologizing has been to distort the King's image and stigmatize sterling qualities as psychopathic. Even that he was a faithful husband, which might be considered a virtue and evidence of a satisfactory married life, became grist to the mill and was interpreted as the hallmark of a 'rigid . . . superconscientious type'.[1] One shudders to think what would have been said had he partaken of the profligacy of his time. The fact that he was principled has been turned into pathological obstinacy, and that he worked hard to perform his constitutional functions to the best of his ability into a desire to be 'all-powerful' and to show a 'naive faith in the omnipotence, the infallibility of kings'.[1] How far this picture of him is removed from reality was pointed out by Billington: 'scholars have relegated the old image of George III as an ambitious tyrant to the historical ash-pan . . . That this viewpoint grossly exaggerates George's role as a policy maker is well known to historians.'[11]

Where George III might be praised for being deliberate and cautious he is blamed for 'obsessionality' and being the victim of 'neurotic doubts'.[1] 'When flour was dear [because it was scarce], he insisted on eating potato bread,' says Guttmacher, and turns even this against him: 'The King was an ascetic – he got satisfaction from disciplining himself. His parsimony had neurotic characteristics . . . and . . . its roots in self-denial.'[1] As an aside, to call the King parsimonious because his style of life was simple and unostentatious is to show ignorance of his regular and substantial gifts to charity, to science and to the arts, and the help he quietly extended to friends in need.

Looked at from a different angle, the King's long life was so troubled with national affairs, not to mention his large and unruly family, that if he had been the weak and neurotic man he has been painted, it is perhaps more surprising that he was ever sane. How is it to be explained that he survived without a flicker or suspicion of breakdown his greatest disaster, the loss of the American colonies and the eighteen years' struggle leading up to it? And that when he fell ill in 1788 the political situation was perhaps the calmest and happiest of his reign? How can the image of George III invented by modern psychiatry be reconciled with that of his people and of his early biographers, for whom he was Britain's most devoted and best-informed king, musician, book collector, patron of the arts and sciences, country-lover and family man?

George III's psychiatric symptoms were part and parcel of widespread bodily disorder, but they were the most spectacular and because of his unique position made the greatest impact. This is why they monopolized the centre of the historical stage. No conclusion can be drawn about his personality in health from the fact that when he was ill he became deranged; nor about his psychological situation at those times when he fell ill; and least of all from what he rambled about in his delirium. If modern historiography requires that psychology be taken into account, then all that can be said about George III on the medical facts is that before and after major attacks, and during minor attacks which may have passed unrecognized, he was irritable and hurried in manner and speech. Beyond this, they allow of no legitimate inference about his actions or personality. His illness was not a 'mental' one in the accepted sense of a disease of the mind, in whatever old or new terms this may be couched. His long and sorrowful malady in which he suffered severely from his affliction, pitifully from his treatments, and miserably from his management – and posthumously from vilification – demands above all sympathy and admiration for the courage with which he resumed his duties after attacks, especially in 1789. The currently accepted image of George III will have to be drastically recast.

However distressing for sufferer and nation, George III's affliction gave the mad-business the impetus which turned it into a specialty. And the development of psychiatry is reflected in what has since been made of it. His own physicians puzzled what bodily disorder had caused his mind to become deranged; in the asylum era of the middle of the nineteenth century it was simply called mania, and in the descriptive era of classification manic-depressive psychosis. In the recent past, when psychodynamics entered the field, it was ascribed to stress and conflict and with it the King's personality and character were denigrated. Reviewed in the light of modern medical knowledge and applying to it the clinical corrective of investigative science, it emerges as porphyria, an inborn error of metabolism. With this diagnosis the abnormal mental state moves from the centre of the clinical picture to take its place alongside the many other manifestations of widespread affection of the nervous system which made up attacks. After all, the periods of mental derangement added together up to his seventy-third year hardly amounted to six months.

The royal malady may perhaps again – as in 1788 – serve psychiatry by indicating the direction of its future progress.

References

Introduction (pp. xi–xv)

1 A. Duncan senior, *Tribute of veneration . . . for commemorating the reign of George III*, Edinburgh, 1821, pp. 5–6, 9–10
2 Lord Grenville to Lord Auckland, 8 October 1811. In *The Journal and Correspondence of William, Lord Auckland*, ed. R. J. Eden, 1862
3 W. W. Grenville (Lord Grenville) to Marquis of Buckingham, 20 November 1788. In *Memoirs of the Court and Cabinets of George the Third*, ed. Duke of Buckingham and Chandos, 1853, vol. 2, pp. 6–7
4 *Diary and Letters of Madame D'Arblay*, ed. C. F. Barrett, 1842, vol. 4, p. 291

Chapter 1: The Cheltenham Episode (pp. 3–13)

1 'Memoirs of the Years 1788-9. By Elizabeth, Countess of Harcourt'. In *The Harcourt Papers*, ed. E. W. Harcourt, Oxford, 1880, vol. 4, p. 2
2 George III to W. Pitt, 12 June 1788. In *Life of the Right Honourable William Pitt*, by P. H. Stanhope, third edition, 1867, vol. 2, Appendix, pp. i–ii
3 W. Pitt to George III, 12 June 1788. In *The Later Correspondence of George III*, ed. A. Aspinall, Cambridge, 1962, vol. 1, pp. 377–8
4 George III to W. Pitt, 12 June 1788. In ref. 2, p. ii
5 Princess Royal to Prince Augustus, 3 July 1788. In ref. 3, pp. 378–9
6 Queen Charlotte to Prince Augustus, 4 July 1788. In ref. 3, p. 378
7 Duke of Buckingham and Chandos, *Memoirs of the Court and Cabinets of George the Third*, 1853, vol. 1, p. 396
8 Sir N. W. Wraxall, *Posthumous Memoirs of His Own Time*, 1836, vol. 3, p. 133
9 In ref. 8, p. 138
10 A. Fothergill, *A new experimental inquiry into the nature and qualities of the Cheltenham water; with a concise account of the diseases wherein it is chiefly indicated*, Bath, 1785; J. Smith *Observations on the use and abuse of the Cheltenham waters*, Cheltenham, 1786
11 In ref. 10, pp. 13–15, 33, 56, 61
12 George III to R. Hurd, 8 July 1788. In *Bentley's Miscellany*, 1849, vol. 26, p. 337. (The month is wrongly given as June and this has been copied into J. H. Jesse's *Memoirs of the Life and Reign of King George the Third*, 1867, vol. 3, p. 32)

13 In ref. 8, p. 139
14 Diary and Letters of Madame D'Arblay, ed. C. F. Barrett, 1842, vol. 4, pp. 156–60
15 George III to Prince Augustus, 13 July 1788. In ref. 3, pp. 380–1
16 In ref. 8, pp. 139–41
17 George III to Sir George Baker, n.d. July 1788. Baker MSS
18 Sir George Baker to George III, 19 July 1788. In ref. 3, p. 383; George III to Sir George Baker, 27 July 1788, Baker MSS
19 'Diary of their Majesties late Journey to Cheltenham, accompanied by the Princess Royal (Charlotta-Augusta-Matilda), and their Royal Highnesses the Princesses Augusta-Sophia and Elizabeth'. Gentleman's Magazine, 1788, vol. 58, part 2, pp. 755–9, 883–4, 978–9, 1074–6, 1159–60
20 A. Storer to William Eden, first Lord Auckland, 8 August 1788. In The Journal and Correspondence of William, Lord Auckland, ed. R. J. Eden, 1861, vol. 2, pp. 225–6
21 In ref. 19, p. 884
22 J. Howard, An account of the principal lazarettos in Europe . . . together with . . . additional remarks on the present state of those in Great Britain and Ireland, Warrington, 1789, p. 177–8
23 In ref. 14, p. 180
24 In ref. 14, p. 212
25 In ref. 10, pp. x, 17. See also G. Hart, A History of Cheltenham, Leicester, 1965, pp. 124–58 passim; and H. Ruff, The History of Cheltenham, Cheltenham, 1803.
26 George III to Earl Fauconberg, 18 August 1788. In ref. 3, p. 388
27 R. Phillips, A guide to all the watering and sea-bathing places, 1804, pp. 150–1
28 S. F. Simmons, The medical register for the year 1783, p. 69
29 In ref. 14, pp. 220–1
30 J. Galt, George the Third, His Court and Family, 1820, vol. 2, pp. 69–71
31 George III to William Pitt, 14 August 1788. In ref. 2, Appendix, p. ii
32 In ref. 14, p. 195
33 George III to William Pitt, 22 July 1788. In ref. 3, p. 384
34 In ref. 14, p. 201
35 In ref. 14, p. 241
36 George III to Earl Fauconberg, 18 August 1788. In ref. 3, p. 388
37 Queen Charlotte to Prince Augustus, 23 August 1788. In ref. 3, p. 390
38 Report from the Bishop of Gloucester, 15 September 1788. In ref. 3, pp. 393–4
39 George III to Lord Sydney, 19 September 1788, and to William Pitt, 20 September 1788. In ref. 3, pp. 394–5

Chapter 2: Crisis at Windsor (pp. 14–46)

1 George III to Sir George Baker, 17 October 1788. Baker MSS
2 Sir George Baker's Diary, 17 October–7 November 1788. Baker MSS
3 'Memoirs of the Years 1788–89. By Elizabeth, Countess of Harcourt', ed. E. W. Harcourt. In Harcourt Papers, Oxford, 1880, vol. 4, pp. 10–12
4 Diary and Letters of Madame D'Arblay, ed. C. F. Barrett, 1842, vol. 4, pp. 270–1
5 George III to William Pitt, 19 October 1788. In The Later Correspondence of George III, ed. A. Aspinall, Cambridge, 1962, vol. 1, p. 396
6 In ref. 4, p. 272
7 George III to William Pitt, 20 October 1788. Chatham Papers, P.R.O. 30/8/103, part 2

8 George III to William Pitt, 21 October 1788. In ref. 7
9 W. W. Grenville to the Marquis of Buckingham, 22 October 1788. In *Memoirs of the Court and Cabinets of George the Third*, ed. Duke of Buckingham and Chandos, 1853, vol. 1, pp. 428–9
10 Princess Augusta Sophia to Sir George Baker, 23 October 1788. *Baker MSS*
11 *Gentleman's Magazine*, 1788, vol. 58, part 2, p. 928
12 W. W. Grenville to the Marquis of Buckingham, 26 October 1788. In ref. 9, pp. 431–2
13 Duke of York to Prince of Wales, 24 October 1788. In *The Correspondence of George, Prince of Wales 1770–1812*, ed. A. Aspinall, 1963, vol. 1, pp. 358–9
14 In ref. 4, pp. 272–3
15 George III to William Pitt, 25 October 1788. In ref. 7
16 In ref. 4, pp. 273–4
17 Duke of York to Prince of Wales, 29 October 1788. In ref. 13, p. 360
18 J. Galt, *George the Third, His Court and Family*, 1820, vol. 2, p. 73
19 *Life and Letters of Sir Gilbert Elliot First Earl of Minto*, ed. Countess of Minto, 1874, vol. 1, pp. 225–6
20 In ref. 19, p. 229
21 In ref. 3, pp. 15–16
22 'Diary of Thomas, Earl of Ailesbury. Vol. 2'. In *Historical Manuscripts Commission*, 1898, 15th Report, Appendix, part 7, p. 297
23 In ref. 22, p. 295
24 In ref. 4, pp. 274–6, 278–9
25 W. Heberden, *Commentaries on the history and cure of diseases*, 1802
26 W. Munk, *Roll of the Royal College of Physicians of London*, 1878, vol. 2, pp. 159–64
27 *Morning Chronicle*, 12 November 1788
28 In ref. 11, p. 1025
29 George III to William Pitt, 3 November 1788. In *Life of the Right Honourable William Pitt*, by P. H. Stanhope, third edition, 1867, vol. 2, Appendix, pp. v–vi
30 Duke of Gloucester to Prince of Wales, 1 November 1788. In ref. 13, pp. 363–4
31 Sir Gilbert Elliot to Lady Elliot, 4 November 1788. In ref. 19, pp. 228–9
32 In ref. 4, pp. 279–86
33 In ref. 3, pp. 21–2
34 In ref. 4, pp. 288–90
35 In ref. 3, pp. 25–8
36 In ref. 4, pp. 290–3
37 Sir George Baker to William Pitt, 6 November 1788. In *William Pitt and National Revival*, by J. H. Rose, 1915, p. 410
38 William Pitt to Marquis of Stafford, 6 November 1788. In ref. 29, vol. 1, pp. 388–9
39 In ref. 4, pp. 299–300
40 P. H. Stanhope, Earl Stanhope, *Life of the Right Honourable William Pitt*, third edition, 1867, vol. 1, p. 391
41 W. W. Grenville to the Marquis of Buckingham, 7 November 1788. In ref. 9, pp. 433–6
42 J. Crawford to Duchess of Devonshire, 7 November 1788. In *Georgiana*, ed. Earl of Bessborough, 1955, p. 138
43 R. A. Neville to Marquis of Buckingham, 8 November 1788. In ref. 9, p. 437
44 W. W. Grenville to Marquis of Buckingham, 8 November 1788. In ref. 9, pp. 438–40

45 In ref. 13, pp. 366–7
46 Prince of Wales to Lord Chancellor Thurlow, 8 November 1788. In ref. 13, p. 369
47 W. W. Grenville to Marquis of Buckingham, 9 November 1788. In ref. 9, pp. 441–3
48 In ref. 4, p. 304
49 Sir Gilbert Elliot to Lady Elliot, 8 November 1788. In ref. 19, p. 231
50 J. W. Payne to R. B. Sheridan, 8–9 November 1788. In *Memoirs of the Life of the Right Honourable Richard Brinsley Sheridan*, ed. T. Moore, fifth edition, 1826, vol. 2, pp. 21–4
51 L. Dutens, *An history of the late important period; from the beginning of his Majesty's illness . . . to the period of his Majesty's re-appearance in the House of Lords*, 1789, pp. 4–5
52 'Life of Lord Loughborough'. In *The Lives of the Lord Chancellors and Keepers of the Great Seal of England*, by J. Campbell, 1847, vol. 6, pp. 188–91
53 E. Holt, *The Public and Domestic life of . . . George the Third*, 1820, vol. 1, p. 312
54 In ref. 22, pp. 294–5
55 In ref. 4, p. 309
56 Lady Spencer to Duchess of Devonshire, 10 November 1788. In ref. 42, p. 138
57 'His Majesty's 1st Illness in the Year 1788–9'. In *The Diaries of Colonel the Hon. Robert Fulke Greville*, ed. F. M. Bladon, 1930, p. 81
58 Sir Gilbert Elliot to Lady Elliot, 11 November 1788. In ref. 19, p. 232
59 *Morning Chronicle*, 11 November 1788
60 Lord Bulkeley to Marquis of Buckingham, 11 November 1788. In ref. 9, pp. 444–5
61 W. W. Grenville to Marquis of Buckingham, 10 November 1788. In ref. 9, p. 444
62 R. A. Neville to Marquis of Buckingham, 11 November 1788. In ref. 9, p. 446
63 In ref. 4, p. 312
64 Lord Sydney to Marquis of Buckingham, 13 November 1788. In ref. 9, pp. 447–8
65 In ref. 57, p. 77
66 In ref. 57, pp. 81–3
67 *Morning Chronicle*, 14 November 1788
68 R. Warren to Lady Spencer, 12 November 1788. In 'The Manuscripts of . . . Earl Spencer'. *Historical Manuscripts Commission*, 1871, 2nd Report, p. 14
69 Marquis of Buckingham to W. W. Grenville, 13 November 1788. In 'The Manuscripts of J. B. Fortescue, Esq., preserved at Dropmore'. *Historical Manuscripts Commission*, 1892, 13th Report, Appendix, part 3, vol. 1, p. 366
70 W. W. Grenville to Marquis of Buckingham, 13 November 1788. In ref. 9, p. 448
71 In ref. 57, p. 85
72 In ref. 57, p. 86
73 In ref. 57, pp. 89–90
74 In ref. 3, pp. 54–5
75 In ref. 3, p. 51
76 In ref. 57, p. 87
77 In ref. 57, p. 88
78 In ref. 57, p. 90
79 In ref. 57, p. 101
80 In ref. 57, pp. 102–3

81 Duke of Buckingham and Chandos. In ref. 9, vol. 2, pp. 1–2
82 In ref. 37, pp. 410–11
83 W. W. Grenville to Marquis of Buckingham, 17 November 1788. In ref. 9, vol. 2, pp. 3–4
84 In ref. 4, pp. 336–7
85 In ref. 4, pp. 316–17
86 'Georgiana, Duchess of Devonshire's Diary', 20 November 1788–12 January 1789. In *Sheridan*, by W. Sichel, 1909, vol. 2, p. 403
87 Sir W. Fordyce, 'Insania'. In *Fragmenta chirurgica & medica*, 1784, pp. 55–7
88 In ref. 3, pp. 55–7
89 In ref. 57, p. 92
90 In ref. 57, p. 96
91 Lord Sheffield to Mr William Eden, 22 November 1788. In *The Journal and Correspondence of William, Lord Auckland*, ed. R. J. Eden, 1861, vol. 2, p. 244
92 *Some Particulars of the Royal Indisposition of 1788–1789*, 1804, pp. 10–11, 16–17
93 In ref. 53, p. 314
94 In ref. 57, p. 93
95 In ref. 57, p. 94
96 P. Withers, *History of the royal malady, with a variety of entertaining anecdotes*, 1789, p. 59
97 George Selwyn to Lady Carlisle, 20 November 1788. In 'The Manuscripts of the Earl of Carlisle, Preserved at Castle Howard'. *Historical Manuscripts Commission*, 1897, 15th Report, Appendix, part 6, p. 655
98 In ref. 57, pp. 97–8
99 In ref. 3, p. 59
100 In ref. 3, p. 58
101 In ref. 37, p. 411
102 W. W. Grenville to Marquis of Buckingham, 20 November 1788. In ref. 9, vol. 2, pp. 6–7
103 A. Storer to W. Eden, 28 November 1788. In ref. 91, p. 246
104 Lord Sheffield to W. Eden, 22 November 1788. In ref. 91, pp. 242–3
105 In ref. 22, p. 295
106 In ref. 57, p. 105
107 W. W. Grenville to Marquis of Buckingham, 29 November 1788. In ref. 9, vol. 2, p. 21
108 A. Storer to W. Eden, 28 November 1788. In ref. 91, p. 245
109 *Morning Chronicle*, 28 November 1788
110 Sir Gilbert Elliot to Lady Elliot, 20 November 1788. In ref. 19, pp. 233–4
111 W. W. Grenville to Marquis of Buckingham, 26 November 1788. In ref. 9, vol. 2, p. 19
112 In ref. 3, p. 9
113 J. Fosbroke, 'Contribution towards the Medical History of the Waters . . . of Cheltenham'. In *A Picturesque and Topographical Account of Cheltenham*, by T. D. Fosbroke, Cheltenham 1826, p. 156
114 In ref. 4, pp. 332, 335

Chapter 3: Confinement at Kew (*pp. 47–86*)

1 Prince of Wales to Mrs Tunstall (housekeeper at Kew), 24 November 1788. In *The Correspondence of George, Prince of Wales 1770–1812*, ed. A. Aspinall, 1963, vol. 1, p. 383

2 P. H. Stanhope, Earl Stanhope, *Life of the Right Honourable William Pitt*, third edition, 1867, vol. 1, p. 399

3 G. Tomline, *Memoirs of the Life of the Right Honourable William Pitt*, third edition, 1821, vol. 2, p. 368

4 *Diary and Letters of Madame D'Arblay*, ed. C. F. Barrett, 1842, vol. 4, p. 334

5 In ref. 4, pp. 336–7

6 In ref. 1, p. 385

7 *The Political Memoranda of Francis Fifth Duke of Leeds*, ed. O. Browning, 1884, Camden Society NS vol. 35, pp. 122–3

8 British Museum Add. MSS 28059, folio 176

9 W. W. Grenville to Marquis of Buckingham, 30 November 1788. In *Memoirs of the Court and Cabinets of George the Third*, ed. Duke of Buckingham and Chandos, 1853, vol. 2, p. 22

10 In ref. 4, pp. 337–8

11 In ref. 4, pp. 340–1

12 'His Majesty's 1st Illness in the Year 1788–9'. In *The Diaries of Colonel the Hon. Robert Fulke Greville*, ed. F. M. Bladon, 1930, pp. 107–11

13 In ref. 1, p. 388

14 In ref. 12, p. 114

15 In ref. 12, pp. 114–15

16 In ref. 12, p. 117

17 'Diary of Thomas, Earl of Ailesbury. Vol. 2'. In *Historical Manuscripts Commission*, 1898, 15th Report, Appendix, part 7, p. 296

18 In ref. 4, pp. 352–3, 358

19 'Memoirs of the Years 1788–89. By Elizabeth, Countess of Harcourt'. In *Harcourt Papers*, ed. E. W. Harcourt, Oxford, 1880, vol. 4, pp. 67–8

20 In ref. 2, vol. 2, p. 2

21 In ref. 1, p. 406

22 Lord Sheffield to W. Eden, 12 December 1788. In *The Journal and Correspondence of William, Lord Auckland*, ed. R. J. Eden, 1861, vol. 2, pp. 256–7

23 In ref. 12, pp. 118–19

24 *Diaries and Correspondence of James Harris, First Earl of Malmesbury*, ed. J. H. Harris, 1845, second edition, vol. 4, pp. 317–18

25 In ref. 17, p. 297

26 In ref. 12, p. 119

27 *Gentleman's Magazine*, 1788, vol. 57, part 2, p. 1118

28 In ref. 12, p. 186

29 In ref. 12, pp. 119–23

30 In ref. 7, p. 129

31 Public Record Office PC 2/133

32 W. W. Grenville to Marquis of Buckingham, 3 December 1788. In ref. 9, p. 31

33 In ref. 17, pp. 296–7

34 In ref. 1, p. 405

35 *Report from the Committee appointed to examine the physicians who have attended his Majesty, during his illness, touching the state of his Majesty's health*, 1788

36 Sir S. Smith to W. Eden, 30 December 1788. In ref. 22, p. 263

37 W. Battie, *A treatise on madness*, 1758. Reprinted 1962

38 E. Burke to C. J. Fox, *c.* 30 November 1788. In *The Correspondence of Edmund Burke*, ed. H. Furber, Cambridge, 1965, vol. 5, p. 428

39 W. W. Grenville to Marquis of Buckingham, 10 December 1788. In ref. 9, p. 47

40 In ref. 17, p. 298

41 J. Stockdale, *The history and proceedings of the Lords and Commons of Great Britain . . . with regard to the Regency*, 1789, pp. 12–13
42 In ref. 41, p. 15
43 J. Debrett, *A sketch of the reign of George the Third, from 1780, to . . . 1790*, 1791, pp. 98–9
44 In ref. 41, pp. 181, 198–9
45 In ref. 41, pp. 178, 183–4
46 In ref. 41, pp. 219, 221–2
47 In ref. 4, p. 367
48 In ref. 4, p. 375
49 In ref. 12, p. 122
50 Archbishop of Canterbury to W. Eden, December 1788. In ref. 22, p. 255
51 In ref. 4, p. 360
52 In ref. 17, p. 299
53 *Report from the Committee appointed to examine the physicians who have attended his Majesty, during his illness, touching the present state of his Majesty's health*, 13 January 1789, p. 69
54 In ref. 12, p. 125
55 In ref. 53, p. 58
56 In ref. 53, p. 68
57 In ref. 53, pp. 68, 67; ref. 47, p. 275
58 In ref. 53, p. 62
59 In ref. 35, p. 11
60 In ref. 12, p. 122
61 W. Nisbet, *A Picture of the Present State of the Royal College of Physicians of London*, 1817, p. 208
62 W. W. Grenville to Marquis of Buckingham, 13 December 1788. In ref. 9, p. 57; ref. 53, p. 128
63 In ref. 53, pp. 127–9
64 In ref. 53, p. 94
65 Sir S. Smith to W. Eden, 30 December 1788. In ref. 22, p. 263
66 Duke of Buckingham and Chandos. In ref. 9, p. 68
67 A. Storer to W. Eden, 16 January 1789. In ref. 22, p. 270
68 *Willis Papers*, 16 December 1788, and subsequent dates. British Museum Add. MSS 41690–1
69 In ref. 53, pp. 34–5
70 R. Hunter and Ida Macalpine, *Three Hundred Years of Psychiatry 1535–1860*, 1964, pp. 487–8
71 W. W. Grenville to Marquis of Buckingham, 19 December 1788. In ref. 9, p. 66
72 'Georgiana, Duchess of Devonshire's Diary'. In *Sheridan* by W. Sichel, 1909, vol. 2, p. 418
73 In ref. 12, p. 126
74 In ref. 12, pp. 127–8
75 In ref. 12, pp. 129–30
76 W. W. Grenville to Marquis of Buckingham, 21 December 1788. In ref. 9, pp. 67–8
77 Lord Hawkesbury to Earl Cornwallis, 6 January 1789. In *Correspondence of Charles, First Earl Cornwallis*, ed. C. Ross, 1859, vol. 1, p. 405
78 Sir W. Young to Marquis of Buckingham, 23 December 1788. In ref. 9 pp. 73–4

79 Sir W. Young to Marquis of Buckingham, 22 December 1788. In ref. 9, p. 70
80 *Morning Chronicle*, 23 December 1788
81 In ref. 12, pp. 130–1
82 In ref. 12, p. 132
83 In ref. 12, p. 133
84 In ref. 12, p. 135–6
85 In ref. 12, p. 138–9
86 In ref. 12, pp. 139–40
87 In ref. 19, p. 94
88 In ref. 12, pp. 142–3
89 In ref. 19, pp. 97–8
90 In ref. 12, pp. 145–6
91 In ref. 12, p. 149
92 Sir Gilbert Elliot to Lady Elliot, 29 December 1788. In *Life and Letters of Sir Gilbert Elliot First Earl of Minto*, ed. Countess of Minto, 1874, vol. 1, p. 253
93 *Some Particulars of the Royal Indisposition of 1788–1789*, 1804, p. 69
94 Queen Charlotte to Lord Chancellor Thurlow, 3 January 1789. British Museum *Egerton MSS* 2232 folio 71
95 L. Dutens, *An history of the late important period; from the beginning of his Majesty's illness, to the . . . period of his Majesty's re-appearance in the House of Lords*, 1789, pp. 186–7
96 In ref. 95, p. 188
97 In ref. 53, pp. 4, 8
98 In ref. 53, p. 50
99 In ref. 53, p. 103
100 In ref. 95, pp. 195–6
101 In ref. 41, pp. 368, 456–8
102 Archbishop of Canterbury to W. Eden, 16 January 1789. In ref. 22, p. 267
103 In ref. 12, p. 161
104 In ref. 68 and ref. 12, p. 172
105 In ref. 12, p. 173
106 In ref. 12, p. 175
107 In ref. 12, p. 180
108 In ref. 12, pp. 182, 185
109 In ref. 12, p. 184
110 In ref. 12, pp. 187, 189
111 In ref. 12, pp. 196, 202
112 In ref. 12, pp. 198, 200
113 *The Diaries and Correspondence of the Right Hon. George Rose*, ed. L. V. Harcourt, 1860, vol. 1, p. 94
114 In ref. 12, p. 199
115 In ref. 12, p. 224
116 In ref. 12, pp. 221, 238–9
117 In ref. 12, pp. 204, 209
118 Archbishop of Canterbury to W. Eden, 13 February 1789. In ref. 22, p. 286
119 Archbishop of Canterbury to W. Eden, 12 February 1789. In ref. 22, p. 286
120 In ref. 22, p. 286
121 *London Chronicle*, 17 February 1789
122 In ref. 12, p. 219
123 Sir G. Elliot to Lady Elliot, 12 February 1789. In ref. 92, p. 271

124 W. W. Grenville to Marquis of Buckingham, 14 February 1789. In ref. 9, pp. 106–7
125 In ref. 12, pp. 201–2
126 J. Campbell, Lord Campbell, 'Life of Lord Chancellor Thurlow'. In *The Lives of the Lord Chancellors and Keepers of the Great Seal of England*, 1846, vol. 5, p. 596
127 W. Pitt to Countess Chatham, 19 February 1789. In ref. 2, vol. 2, p. 25
128 In ref. 9, p. 115
129 W. W. Grenville to Marquis of Buckingham, 19 February 1789. In ref. 9, pp. 115–16
130 In ref. 9, p. 119
131 In ref. 12, pp. 237–8
132 In ref. 12, pp. 239, 252
133 W. W. Grenville to Marquis of Buckingham, 21 February 1789. In ref. 9, p. 120
134 'Mrs. Harcourt's Diary of the Court of King George III'. In *Miscellanies of the Philobiblon Society*, 1871–2, vol. 13, p. 13
135 Lord Bulkeley to Marquis of Buckingham, 24 February 1789. In ref. 9, pp. 122–3
136 George III to Lord Chancellor Thurlow, 23 February 1789. In *The Later Correspondence of George III*, ed. A. Aspinall, Cambridge, 1962, vol. 1, p. 398
137 George III to W. Pitt, 23 February 1789. In ref. 2, Appendix, pp. vi–vii
138 W. W. Grenville to Marquis of Buckingham, 24 February 1789. In ref. 9, p. 125
139 *London Chronicle*, 21–24 February 1789
140 A. Storer to W. Eden, 24 February 1789. In ref. 22, pp. 296–8
141 Lord Sydney to Earl Cornwallis, 21 February 1789. In ref. 77, p. 406

Chapter 4: Restored to Health (pp. 87–98)

1 'Mrs. Harcourt's Diary of the Court of King George III'. In *Miscellanies of the Philobiblon Society*, 1871–2, vol. 13, pp. 21–2
2 *Willis Papers*, 23 February 1789 and subsequent dates. British Museum Add. MSS 41690–1
3 In ref. 1, p. 17
4 'His Majesty's 1st Illness in the Year 1788–9'. In *The Diaries of Colonel the Hon. Robert Fulke Greville*, ed. F. M. Bladon, 1930, p. 259
5 Sir N. W. Wraxall, *Posthumous Memoirs of His Own Time*, 1836, vol. 3, p. 362
6 Lord Sheffield to W. Eden, 19 February 1789. In *The Journal and Correspondence of William, Lord Auckland*, ed. R. J. Eden, 1861, vol. 2, p. 288
7 In ref. 4, p. 253
8 Countess of Pembroke to George III, 8 April 1789. In *The Later Correspondence of George III*, ed. A. Aspinall, Cambridge, 1962, vol. 1, pp. 405–6
9 *The Political Memoranda of Francis Fifth Duke of Leeds*, ed. O. Browning, 1884, Camden Society NS vol. 35, p. 141–2
10 George III to Prince Adolphus, 6 March 1789. In ref. 8, p. 399
11 J. Stockdale, *The history and proceedings of the Lords and Commons of Great Britain . . . with regard to the Regency*, 1789, 'Debates in the House of Lords', p. 186
12 In ref. 5, pp. 369–70
13 Sir G. Elliot to Lady Elliot, 11 March 1789. In *Life and Letters of Sir Gilbert Elliot First Earl of Minto*, ed. Countess of Minto, 1874, vol. 1, p. 281

14 J. H. Jesse, *Memoirs of the Life and Reign of King George the Third*, 1867, vol. 3, p. 114

15 *Diary and Letters of Madame D'Arblay*, ed. C. F. Barrett, 1842, vol. 5, pp. 8–9

16 Archbishop of Canterbury to W. Eden, 10 March 1789. In ref. 6, p. 299

17 In ref. 15, p. 10

18 George III to W. Pitt, 15 March 1789. In ref. 8, p. 401

19 George III to Lord Sydney, 15 March 1789. In ref. 8, p. 401

20 'Diary of Thomas, Earl of Ailesbury, Vol. 2'. In *Historical Manuscripts Commission*, 1898, 15th Report, Appendix, part 7, p. 301

21 In ref. 14, pp. 112–13

22 In ref. 1, pp. 25–6

23 'Memoirs of the Years 1788–9. By Elizabeth, Countess of Harcourt'. In *The Harcourt Papers*, ed. E. W. Harcourt, Oxford, 1880, vol. 4, p. 264

24 In ref. 20, pp. 299–300

25 In ref. 1, p. 37

26 In ref. 15, p. 17

27 George III to Lord Sydney, 20 April 1789. In ref. 8, p. 410

28 In ref. 4, pp. 253, 258

29 In ref. 14, pp. 116–17

30 George III to W. Pitt, 21 April 1789. In *Life of the Right Honourable William Pitt*, by P. H. Stanhope, third edition, 1867, vol. 2, Appendix, pp. viii-ix

31 Sir S. Smith to W. Eden, 24 April 1789. In ref. 6, pp. 318–19

32 Sir G. Elliot to Lady Elliot, 25 April 1789. In ref. 13, pp. 304–5

33 Bethlem Hospital Court of Governors Minute Books

34 W. Roberts, *Memoirs of the Life and Correspondence of Mrs. Hannah More*, third edition, 1835, vol. 2, pp. 144–5

35 F. Willis to George III, 13 March 1789. In ref. 8, p. 400

36 F. Willis to George III, 11 May 1789. *Hanover State Archives* Han Des 92 IV H 40 g

37 In ref. 1, p. 26

38 *Parliamentary Register*, 1790, vol. 27, p. 634

39 *Baker MSS*

40 George III to W. Pitt, 27 August 1789. *Chatham Papers*, P.R.O. 30/8/103, part 2

41 G. D. Collinson, *A treatise on the law concerning idiots, lunatics, and other persons non compotes mentis*, 1812, vol. 1, p. 496

42 F. Winslow, *Physic and Physicians*, 1839, vol. 2, p. 175

43 In ref. 1, p. 31

44 George III to W. Pitt, 1 May 1789. In ref. 40

45 George III to W. Pitt, 5 May 1789. In ref. 30, p. x

46 George III to W. Pitt, 29 May 1789. In ref. 40

47 In ref. 15, p. 28

48 In ref. 15, pp. 35–6

49 In ref. 1, p. 29

50 Queen Charlotte to Prince Augustus, 24 September 1789. In ref. 8, pp. 442–3

51 George III to W. Pitt, 22 September 1789. In ref. 40

52 C. L. H. Papendiek, *Court and Private Life in the Time of Queen Charlotte*, ed. V. D. Broughton, 1887, vol. 2, pp. 215–16

53 George III to W. Pitt, 22 December 1795. In *The Later Correspondence of George III*, ed. A. Aspinall, Cambridge, 1963, vol. 2, p. 439

54 George III to Duke of Portland, 23 December 1795. In ref. 53, p. 441

55 George III to Duke of Portland, 27 December 1795. In ref. 53, p. 447

56 *The Diaries and Correspondence of the Right Hon. George Rose*, ed. L. V. Harcourt, 1860, vol. 1, p. 322

Chapter 5: *What Other Doctors Thought* (*pp. 99–107*)

1 J. Brown, *The elements of medicine; or, a translation of the elementa medicinae brunonis*, 1788, vol. 1, p. 65
2 J. B. Friedreich, *Historisch-kritische Darstellung der Theorien über das Wesen und den Sitz der psychischen Krankheiten*, Leipzig, 1836, pp. 51–7
3 J. Graham, *The general state of medical and chirurgical practice, exhibited*, Bath, 1778, 6th ed., appendix, p. 14
4 J. Graham, *The guardian of health, long-life, and happiness: or, Doctor Graham's general directions as to regimen, &c.*, Newcastle upon Tyne, 1790, pp. 28–9
5 J. Graham, *A clear, full, and faithful portraiture, or description, and ardent recommendation of a certain most beautiful and spotless virgin princess, of imperial descent! To a certain youthful heir apparent … Most humbly dedicated to His Royal Highness George, Prince of Wales, &c. And earnestly recommended to the attention of the members of both Houses of Parliament*, Bath, 1792
6 J. Graham, *A new and curious treatment of the nature and effects of simple earth, water, and air, when applied to the human body*, 1793, p. 4
7 W. Withering to the Reverend W. Scholefield, 11 November 1792. *Osler Bequest MSS*, Royal Society of Medicine, London

Chapter 6: *The Return of the Willises: 1801* (*pp. 111–30*)

1 J. H. Jesse, *Memoirs of the Life and Reign of King George the Third*, 1867, vol. 3, p. 245
2 *Diaries and Correspondence of James Harris, First Earl of Malmesbury*, ed. J. H. Harris, second edition, 1845, vol. 4, pp. 28–9
3 *The Diaries of Sylvester Douglas Lord Glenbervie*, ed. F. Bickley, 1928, vol. 1, p. 185
4 George III to H. Addington, 16 February 1801. In *The Later Correspondence of George III*, ed. A. Aspinall, Cambridge, 1967, vol. 3, p. 502
5 George III to H. Addington, 16 February 1801. In *The Life and Correspondence of the Right Honble Henry Addington, First Viscount Sidmouth*, ed. G. Pellew, 1847, vol. 1, p. 308
6 *Willis MSS*, British Museum Add MSS 41692–3
7 In ref. 2, p. 46
8 In ref. 4, pp. 507–8
9 In ref. 2, p. 15
10 *The Diaries and Correspondence of the Right Hon. George Rose*, ed. L. V. Harcourt, 1860, vol. 1, p. 314
11 *The Diary and Correspondence of Charles Abbot, Lord Colchester*, ed. C. Abbot, Lord Colchester, 1861, vol. 1, p. 243
12 In ref. 11, p. 242
13 In ref. 2, p. 16
14 In ref. 11, p. 244
15 P. H. Stanhope, *Life of the Right Honourable William Pitt*, 1867, third edition, vol. 3, pp. 294–5
16 Lady Malmesbury to Lady Minto, 23–25 February 1801. In *Life and Letters of Sir Gilbert Elliot, First Earl of Minto*, ed. Countess of Minto, 1874, vol. 3, pp. 202–3

17 In ref. 10, p. 311–12
18 In ref. 10, pp. 320–1
19 In ref. 15, pp. 296–7
20 Duke of Buckingham and Chandos, *Memoirs of the Court and Cabinets of George the Third*, 1855, vol. 3, p. 144
21 In ref. 2, p. 17; ref. 15, pp. 294–5
22 In ref. 2, pp. 19–20
23 In ref. 15, p. 294
24 In ref. 10, p. 315
25 In ref. 10, p. 319
26 In ref. 2, p. 18
27 In ref. 11, p. 245
28 In ref. 10, p. 318
29 In ref. 11, pp. 245–6
30 In ref. 11, p. 247
31 *The Correspondence of George, Prince of Wales 1770–1812*, ed. A. Aspinall, 1967, vol. 4, p. 203
32 In ref. 10, p. 322
33 In ref. 11, p. 248
34 In ref. 2, p. 27
35 In ref. 11, pp. 249–50
36 In ref. 10, pp. 324–5
37 In ref. 11, p. 251
38 In ref. 2, p. 32
39 In ref. 10, p. 328
40 In ref. 11, p. 252
41 In ref. 2, pp. 33–4
42 In ref. 11, p. 253
43 In ref. 10, pp. 332–3
44 In ref. 10, pp. 335–7
45 In ref. 1, p. 265; ref. 15, p. 311; ref. 6
46 In ref. 2, p. 51
47 In ref. 10, p. 338
48 In ref. 2, p. 54
49 'Memorandum of the Prince of Wales', 15 April 1801. In 'The Manuscripts of the Earl of Carlisle', *Historical Manuscripts Commission*, 1897, 15th Report, Appendix, part 6, pp. 733–4
50 In ref. 10, pp. 346–7
51 British Museum Add. MSS 38190 folio 1
52 'Lord Carlisle', Memorandum, April/May 1801. In ref. 31, pp. 213–14
53 In ref. 10, p. 354
54 In ref. 11, p. 270
55 George III to Bishop Hurd, 31 May 1801. In *Bentley's Miscellany*, 1849, vol. 26, p. 516
56 Princess Elizabeth to the Reverend Thomas Willis, 9 June 1801. In *The Public and Private Life of Lord Chancellor Eldon*, by H. Twiss, 1844, second edition, vol. 1, p. 380; *Willis MSS* 41695 folio 35
57 In ref. 10, p. 355
58 Dr T. Gisborne to George III, 8 May 1801. In ref. 4, p. 531
59 Lord Eldon to George III, 21 June 1801. In ref. 4, pp. 557–9
60 George III to Lord Eldon, 21 June 1801. In ref. 56, pp. 382–3

61 *Sidmouth MSS*, Devon Record Office
62 In ref. 3, p. 236
63 George III to H. Addington, 8 July 1801. In ref. 5, p. 428
64 'Life of Lord Loughborough'. In *The Lives of the Lord Chancellors and Keepers of the Great Seal of England*, by John Lord Campbell, 1847, vol. 6, pp. 331–2
65 George III to Bishop Hurd, 24 October 1801. In *Bentley's Miscellany*, 1849, vol. 26, p. 517
66 In ref. 2, p. 65

Chapter 7: Recurrence: 1804 (pp. 131–42)

1 George III to H. Addington, 25 January 1804. In *The Later Correspondence of George III*, ed. A. Aspinall, Cambridge, 1968, vol. 4, p. 151
2 *Diaries and Correspondence of James Harris, First Earl of Malmesbury*, ed. J. H. Harris, second edition, 1845, vol. 4, pp. 292–3
3 George III to H. Addington, 24 January 1804. In ref. 1, p. 150
4 *The Diary and Correspondence of Charles Abbot, Lord Colchester*, ed. C. Abbot, Lord Colchester, 1861, vol. 1, p. 476
5 In ref. 4, pp. 479–80
6 Colonel McMahon to Duke of Northumberland, 11 February 1804. In *The Correspondence of George, Prince of Wales 1770–1812*, ed. A. Aspinall, 1967, vol. 4, pp. 490–1
7 George III to H. Addington, 24 January 1804. In *The Life and Correspondence of the Right Honble Henry Addington, First Viscount Sidmouth*, ed. G. Pellew, 1847, vol. 2, p. 247
8 Duke of Kent to Prince of Wales 9 February 1804. In ref. 6, p. 492
9 In *The Diaries of Sylvester Douglas Lord Glenbervie*, ed. F. Bickley, 1928, vol. 1, p. 364
10 Duke of Kent to H. Addington, 13 February 1804. In ref. 6, pp. 493–6
11 British Museum Add. MSS 35705 folio 105
12 Dukes of Kent and Cumberland to H. Addington, 15 February 1804. In ref. 6, p. 496
13 Prince of Wales to Duke of Kent, 21 February 1804. In ref. 6, pp. 505–6
14 'Declaration of the Queen, and Nine of His Majesty's Children', 15 February 1804. In ref. 6, pp. 501–2
15 In ref. 4, pp. 481–2
16 In ref. 7, vol. 2, p. 250
17 In ref. 2, p. 294
18 In ref. 4, p. 483
19 In *The Public and Private Life of Lord Chancellor Eldon*, by H. Twiss, 1844, second edition, vol. 1, pp. 421–2
20 In ref. 4, p. 484
21 In ref. 4, pp. 487–8
22 In ref. 4, p. 494
23 In ref. 2, p. 317
24 Colonel McMahon to Duke of Northumberland, 25 August 1804. In *The Correspondence of George, Prince of Wales 1770–1812*, ed. A. Aspinall, 1968, vol. 5, p. 89
25 Lord Carlisle to W. Pitt, 3 June 1804. In ref. 1, p. 185
26 In *The Diaries and Correspondence of the Right Hon. George Rose*, ed. L. V. Harcourt, 1860, vol. 2, p. 148

27 In ref. 2, p. 328
28 W. Pitt to George III, 16 May 1804. In P. H. Stanhope, *Life of the Right Honourable William Pitt*, 1867, third edition, vol. 4, Appendix, pp. xiv-xv
29 'Opinion of the King's Physicians', 16 May 1804. In ref. 1, p. 173
30 W. Pitt and Lord Eldon to George III, 1 June 1804. In ref. 1, p. 185
31 In ref. 26, vol. 2, p. 149
32 Duke of Kent to Prince of Wales, 17 May 1804. In ref. 24, p. 17
33 Duke of Kent to Prince of Wales, 3 June 1804. In ref. 24, p. 29
34 Duke of Kent to Prince of Wales, 9 June 1804. In ref. 24, p. 33
35 Prince of Wales to Lord Eldon, 19 June 1804. In ref. 24, pp. 37–8
36 Lord Eldon to Prince of Wales, 26 June 1804. In ref. 24, pp. 39–40
37 Prince of Wales to the Cabinet, 1, July 1804. In ref. 24, p. 44
38 Prince of Wales to Lord Eldon, 2 July 1804. In ref. 24, pp. 45–6
39 Duke of Kent to Prince of Wales, 27 July 1804. In ref. 24, pp. 63–4
40 In ref. 4, p. 522
41 W. H. Fremantle, 1 August 1804. *Cottesloe MSS*. In ref. 1, p. 221
42 George III to W. Pitt, 2 August 1804. In ref. 28, vol. 4, Appendix, p. xvii
43 George III to W. Pitt, 26 August 1804. In ref. 28, Appendix, p. xviii
44 Lord Camden to W. Pitt, 9 September 1804. *W. Dacres Adams MSS*. In ref. 1, pp. 230–1
45 In ref. 24, p. 117
46 Charles Long to Lord Redesdale, 27 September 1804. *Redesdale MSS*. In ref. 24, pp. 104–5
47 Lord Hawkesbury to Earl Liverpool, 6 November 1804. British Museum Add. MSS. 38236 folio 309
48 In ref. 9, p. 406
49 In ref. 24, p. 114
50 Lord Auckland to Lord Henley, 11 September 1804. In *The Journal and Correspondence of William, Lord Auckland*, ed. R. J. Eden, 1862, vol. 4, pp. 212–13
51 In ref. 4, p. 528
52 Lord Eldon to George III, 10 November 1804. In ref. 24, pp. 123–4
53 George III to Lord Eldon, 13 November 1804. In ref. 19, p. 472
54 T. Grenville to Marquis of Buckingham, 13 November 1804. In *Memoirs of the Court and Cabinets of George the Third*, ed. Duke of Buckingham and Chandos, 1855, vol. 3, pp. 373–5
55 W. Pitt to Lord Eldon, 12 November 1804. In ref. 19, p. 473
56 Queen Charlotte to George III, 2 February 1805. In ref. 1, p. 286
57 In ref. 26, p. 196
58 In ref. 4, vol. 2, p. 14
59 In ref. 58, p. 16
60 *Hurd MSS*. In ref. 1, p. 341
61 Lord Henley to Lord Auckland, 23 July 1805. In ref. 50, pp. 244–5
62 Queen Charlotte to Countess of Chatham, 3 August 1805. In ref. 1, p. 350
63 George III to Bishop Hurd, 10 August 1805. *Bentley's Miscellany* 1849, vol. 26, p. 522
64 In ref. 28, Appendix, p. xxvii
65 George III to W. Pitt, 15 September 1805. In ref. 28, Appendix, p. xxvii

Chapter 8: The Regency: 1810–12 (pp. 143–64)

(Unnumbered quotations in this and the following chapter are from the Queen's

Council Papers at Lambeth Palace Library and the Willis MSS at the British Museum.)

1 *Autobiography of Miss Cornelia Knight*, 1861, fourth edition, vol. 1, pp. 174–5
2 W. H. Fremantle to Marquis of Buckingham, 31 October 1810. In *Memoirs of the Court and Cabinets of George the Third*, ed. Duke of Buckingham and Chandos, 1855, vol. 4, pp. 459–60
3 D. Gray, *Spencer Perceval*, Manchester, 1963, pp. 400–1
4 Lord Grenville to Earl Grey, 29 October 1810. In 'Report on the Manuscripts of J. B. Fortescue, Esq., preserved at Dropmore', vol. 10. *Historical Manuscripts Commission*, 1927, pp. 59–60
5 W. H. Fremantle to Marquis of Buckingham, 1 November 1810. In ref. 2, pp. 460–2
6 *The Diary and Correspondence of Charles Abbot, Lord Colchester*, ed. C. Abbot, Lord Colchester, 1861, vol. 2, p. 282.
7 In ref. 6, pp. 283–4
8 *Willis MSS*. British Museum Add. MSS 41696–41736
9 Earl Grey to Lord Grenville, 9 November 1810. In ref. 4, pp. 66–8
10 T. Grenville to Lord Grenville, 1 November 1810. In ref. 4, pp. 62–3
11 Lord Auckland to Lord Grenville, 1 November 1810. In ref. 4, pp. 60–1
12 W. Munk, *The Life of Sir Henry Halford*, 1895, p. 143
13 Lord Auckland to Lord Grenville, 5 November 1810. In ref. 4, pp. 65–6
14 W. H. Fremantle to Marquis of Buckingham, 2 November 1810. In ref. 2, pp. 462–3
15 In ref. 6, p. 288
16 W. H. Fremantle to Earl Temple, 11 November 1810. In ref. 2, pp. 468–9
17 *The Diaries and Correspondence of the Right Hon. George Rose*, ed. L. V. Harcourt, 1860, vol. 2, p. 455
18 In ref. 6, pp. 290–1
19 In ref. 6, p. 292
20 T. Grenville to Lord Grenville, 26 November 1810. In ref. 4, pp. 75–6
21 In ref. 6, pp. 293–4
22 *Copy of the examination of the physicians attending his Majesty; taken . . . before the . . . Privy Council*, 29 November 1810
23 In ref. 6, p. 296
24 In ref. 17, pp. 460–1
25 W. H. Fremantle to Marquis of Buckingham, 7 December 1810. In ref. 2, p. 476
26 Lord Auckland to Lord Grenville, 11 December 1810. In ref. 4, p. 83; the same to the same, 19 February 1811. In ref. 4, p. 123
27 *Cobbett's Parliamentary Debates* 1810–11, vol. 18, pp. 128–79, 202–29
28 In ref. 6, p. 299
29 In ref. 15, p. 462
30 Lord Grenville to Marquis of Buckingham, 19 December 1810. In ref. 2, p. 483
31 Lady Bessborough to Lord Granville Leveson Gower, 23 December 1810. In *Lord Granville Leveson Gower, first Earl Granville: Private Correspondence*, ed. Castalia Countess Granville, 1917, vol. 2, p. 374
32 T. Grenville to Lord Grenville, 25 December 1810. In ref. 4, p. 92
33 Lord Auckland to Lord Grenville, 8 January 1811. In ref. 4, p. 96
34 Lord Buckinghamshire to Lord Auckland, 8 January 1811. In *The Journal and Correspondence of William, Lord Auckland*, ed. R. J. Eden, 1862, vol. 4, p. 364

35 In ref. 6, pp. 307–8
36 In ref. 17, p, 473
37 *Memoirs of the Political and Literary Life of Robert Pluner Ward*, ed. E. Phipps, 1850, vol. 1, p. 344
38 Earl Grey to Lord Grenville, 22 January 1811. In ref. 4, p. 112
39 In ref. 6, p. 310
40 In ref. 17, pp. 474–5
41 In ref. 6, p. 312
42 In ref. 6, p. 313
43 In ref. 17, p. 476
44 In ref. 4, pp. 113–15; ref. 37, pp. 372–3
45 In ref. 17, p. 481
46 *Memoirs of the Life of Sir Samuel Romilly, Written by Himself*, 1840, vol. 2, pp. 360–1; ref. 12, pp. 144–5
47 In ref. 37, p. 376
48 In ref. 6, p. 316
49 In ref. 17, p. 482
50 Queen Charlotte to Lord Eldon, 22 February 1811. In *The Public and Private Life of Lord Chancellor Eldon*, by H. Twiss, 1844, second edition, vol. 2, p. 165
51 In ref. 37, pp. 393–4
52 *Queen's Council Papers*, Lambeth Palace Library
53 Lord Ellenborough to Lord Eldon, 3 April 1811. In ref. 50, pp. 173–4
54 Lord Grenville to Earl Temple, 10 March 1811. In *Memoirs of the Court of England, during the Regency*, ed. Duke of Buckingham and Chandos, 1856, vol. 1, pp. 57–8
55 *Halford Papers*
56 Lord Auckland to Lord Grenville, 7 March 1811. In ref. 4, p. 126
57 Lord Grenville to Earl Temple, n.d. In ref. 54, p. 50
58 In ref. 37, p. 411
59 *The Taylor Papers being a Record of ... the Life of Lieut.-Gen. Sir Herbert Taylor*, ed. E. Taylor, 1913, p. 58
60 In ref. 54, p. 102
61 Lord Auckland to Lord Grenville, 23 July 1811. In ref. 4, p. 158
62 In ref. 1, vol. 2, p. 280
63 W. H. Fremantle to Marquis of Buckingham, 25 October 1811. In ref. 54, pp. 133–4

Chapter 9: The Last Years: 1812–20 (pp. 165–71)

1 *Report from the Committee appointed to examine the physicians who have attended his Majesty, during his illness; touching the state of his Majesty's health*, 13 January 1812
2 Duke of Northumberland to Colonel McMahon, 13 July 1812. In *The Letters of King George IV 1812–1830*, ed. A. Aspinall, Cambridge, 1938, vol. 1, p. 126
3 Duke of York to Prince Regent, 27 November 1819. In ref. 2, vol. 2, pp. 298–9

Chapter 10: Porphyria (pp. 172–5)

1 A. Goldberg 'The Porphyrias'. In *Porphyria – a Royal Malady*, 1968, pp. 66–8
2 G. W. Holt 'Porphyria and Neuronal Dysfunction'. *American Journal of the Medical Sciences*, 1963, vol. 245, pp. 95–107
3 E. G. Saint 'The Porphyrinopathies'. *Medical Journal of Australia*, 1963, vol. 1,

pp. 101–8

4 *Supplementary Willis MSS.* British Museum Add. MSS 54202–6

Chapter 11: Retrospect: The Illness of 1765 (pp. 176–91)

1 H. Walpole to H. Mann, 20 June 1762. In *The Yale Edition of Horace Walpole's Correspondence*, ed. W. S. Lewis, 1960, vol. 20, p. 42

2 C. L. H. Papendiek, *Court and Private Life in the Time of Queen Charlotte*, ed. V. D. Broughton, 1887, vol. 2, p. 34

3 H. Walpole, *Memoirs of the Reign of King George the Third*, ed. G. F. R. Barker, 1894, vol. 2, p. 69

4 *Grenville Papers*, ed. W. J. Smith, 1853, vol. 3, p. 73

5 H. Mann to H. Walpole, 4 May 1765. In ref. 1, vol. 22, p. 291

6 *Correspondence of King George the Third 1760–83*, ed. J. Fortescue, 1927, vol. 1, p. 74

7 H. Fox, Lord Holland, 'Memoir on the events attending the death of George II, and the accession of George III'. In *Life and Letters of Lady Sarah Lennox 1745–1826*, ed. Countess of Ilchester and Lord Stavordale, 1904, p. 67

8 H. Walpole to H. Mann, 20 June 1762. In ref. 1, vol. 22, p. 42

9 British Museum, Newcastle Papers, Add. MSS 32939, f. 190

10 *Life of Chancellor Hardwicke*, ed. G. Harris, 1847, vol. 3, p. 283

11 George III to Lord Bute, 7 June 1762. In *Letters from George III to Lord Bute 1756–1766*, ed. R. Sedgwick, 1939, p. 114

12 In ref. 9, folio 228

13 In ref. 9, folio 228

14 In ref. 9, folio 230

15 In ref. 9, folio 246

16 In ref. 9, folio 248

17 George III to Lord Bute, 9 June 1762. In ref. 11, p. 115

18 In ref. 9, folio 250

19 In ref. 9, folio 272

20 In ref 9, folio 325

21 George III to Lord Bute, 15 June 1762. In ref. 11, p. 116

22 In ref. 11, p. 119

23 P. C. Yorke, *Life and Correspondence of Philip Yorke, Earl of Hardwicke*, 1913, vol. 3, p. 397

24 H. Mann to H. Walpole, 31 July 1762. In ref. 1, vol. 22, p. 50

25 In ref. 4, pp. 115–16

26 In ref. 4, p. 116

27 In ref. 4, pp. 119–20

28 In ref. 4, p. 7

29 In ref. 4, p. 121

30 In ref. 4, p. 15

31 In ref. 4, p. 123

32 In ref. 4, p. 189

33 In ref. 4, p. 73

34 In ref. 4, p. 73

35 In ref. 4, p. 357

36 In ref. 4, p. 124

37 J. S. Watson, *The Reign of George III 1760–1815*, 1964, p. 109

38 J. H. Plumb, *The First Four Georges*, 1961, pp. 97, 105

39 R. Sedgwick, Introduction to *Letters from George III to Lord Bute 1756–1766*, 1939, pp. vii, viii, xlix

40 L. Namier, 'King George III: A Study of Personality'. In *Crossroads of Power*, 1962, p. 139

41 P. J. Grosley, *A Tour of London; or, new observations on England, and its inhabitants*, transl. T. Nugent, 1772, vol. 2, p. 228

42 C. Meigham, *A treatise of the . . . waters of Bareges*, 1764, p. 155

43 In ref. 41, pp. 223–4

44 [R. Macfarlane], *The History of the First Four Years of the Reign of George the Third*, 1783–5, second editon, vol. 1, p. 223

45 W. Belsham, *Memoirs of the Reign of George III*, Dublin, 1802, vol. 1, p. 90

46 E. Holt, *The Public and Domestic Life of . . . George III*, 1820, p. 124

47 E. Baines, *The History of the Reign of George III*, Leeds, 1820, p. 67

48 R. Huish, *The Public and Private Life of . . . George the Third*, 1821, p. 299

49 *Gentleman's Magazine*, 1820, vol. 90, p. 102

50 J. Galt, *George the Third, his Court and Family*, 1820, vol. 1, p. 288

51 N. W. Wraxall, *Historical Memoirs of My Own Time*, 1815, vol. 1, pp. 371–2

52 N. W. Wraxall, *Posthumous Memoirs of His Own Time*, 1836, vol. 3, p. 136

53 In ref. 2 and Introduction

54 R. Anderson, *The Miscellaneous Works of Tobias Smollett*, Edinburgh, 1820, vol. 1, p. 74

55 T. Smollett, *Continuation of the Complete History of England*, 1765, vol. 5, p. 444

56 *London Chronicle*, 27–30 July 1765

57 L. M. Knapp, 'The Publication of Smollett's *Complete History* and *Continuation*'. In *The Library*, 1935, vol. 16, pp. 295–308

58 L. M. Knapp, personal communication, 1966

59 J. Adolphus, *The History of England from the Accession to the Decease of King George the Third*, 1840, vol. 1, p. 175

60 *Quarterly Review*, 1840, vol. 66, p. 240

61 I. Ray, 'The Insanity of King George III'. In *American Journal of Insanity*, 1855, vol. 12, pp. 1–31

62 J. H. Jesse, *Memoirs of the Life and Reign of King George the Third*, 1867, vol. 1, p. 250

63 In ref. 62, p. 258

64 In ref. 4, p. 122

65 M. S. Guttmacher, *America's Last King: An Interpretation of the Madness of George III*, New York, 1941

66 B. Knollenberg, *Origin of the American Revolution: 1759–1766*, New York, 1960, pp. 275–81

67 Public Record Office, P. C. 2/111

68 *Additional Grenville Papers 1763–5*, ed. J. R. G. Tomlinson, Manchester, 1962, p. 247

69 In ref. 4, p. 119

70 British Museum, Stowe MS 260, folios 183, 185, 187; MS 142, folio 133

71 In ref. 68, p. 248

72 In ref. 4, p. 7

73 In ref. 68, MS 261, folio 3

74 In ref. 3, vol. 2, p. 62

75 Hanover, Niedersächsisches Staatsarchiv, K G Cal. Br Nr. 106

76 *Report from the Committee appointed to examine the physicians who have attended his Majesty*, 1789, p. 57

77 Cobbett's Parliamentary Debates, 1810–11, vol. 18, pp. 128 ff.
78 The history and proceedings of the Lords and Commons ... with regard to the Regency, 1789, p. 222
79 Lambeth Palace Library. Queen's Council Papers, Memorandum, 4 August 1811

Chapter 13: The Stuarts and the Tudors (pp. 201–22)

1 King James, Daemonologie, Edinburgh, 1597; London, 1603. R. Hunter and Ida Macalpine, Three Hundred Years of Psychiatry, 1964, p. 47
2 N. Moore, The History of the Study of Medicine in the British Isles, Oxford, 1908, p. 116
3 This summary (British Museum Sloane MS 1697, folios 42r to 51v) was printed by Moore (in ref. 2, p. 162 ff.) in the original Latin together with a partial translation which was reprinted in G. L. Keynes, The Life of William Harvey, Oxford, 1966, p. 96
4 A. Weldon, The Court and character of King James the First, 1650, p. 165
5 Sir George Baker, Diary
6 Calendar State Papers Dom. Series 1619–23, pp. 32, 33, 37, 39, 56
7 C. H. Gray, C. Rimington, S. Thomson, Quarterly Journal of Medicine, 1948, vol. 51, pp. 123–37
8 Praxeos Mayernianae, ed. T. de Vaux, 1690, p. 349
9 J. Waldenstrom, Studien über die Porphyrie. Acta med. scand., 1937, Supplement 82, p. 71
10 N. Moore, 'Sir Theodore Turquet de Mayerne'. In Dictionary of National Biography
11 British Museum Sloane MS 1697, folio 21r
12 In ref. 11, folio 19r
13 In ref. 11, folios 20v, 21r
14 In ref. 11, folios 23r, 25r, 26v, 29v
15 Calendar State Papers Dom. Series 1611–18, p. 198
16 British Museum Sloane MS 1697, folios 11r, 11v
17 British Museum Sloane MS 2063, folios 18–33
18 N. Chevers, Did James the First of England Die from the Effects of Poison, or from Natural Causes?, 1862
19 F. Peck, Desiderata curiosa, 1779, vol. 1, pp. 199–204
20 Calendar of State Papers Venetian 1610–13, p. 470
21 H. Ellis, Original Letters ... in the British Museum, second series, vol. 3, p. 247; British Museum Sloane MS 2064, folio 49
22 T. T. de Mayerne, Opera medica, ed. J. Browne, 1700, pp. 114–16
23 In ref. 21, p. 116
24 J. H. Jesse, Memoirs of the Court of England during the Reign of the Stuarts, 1840, vol. 1, p. 168
25 G. Goodman, The Court of King James the First, ed. J. S. Brewer, 1839, vol. 1, p. 247
26 In ref. 20, p. 464
27 N. Moore, The Illness and Death of Henry Prince of Wales in 1612: A Historical Case of Typhoid Fever, 1885
28 J. A. Petit, History of Mary Stuart, transl. C. de Flandre, 1874, vol. 1, pp. 120–2; C. Nau, The History of Mary Stewart, ed. J. Stevenson, Edinburgh, 1883, pp. 31–2; R. Keith, History of the Affairs of Church and State in Scotland

from the beginnning of the Reformation to the Year 1568, Edinburgh, 1844–50, vol. 3, p. 286

29 *Calendar of State Papers relating to Scotland and Mary Queen of Scots 1547–1603*, ed. W. K. Boyd, Edinburgh, 1903, vol. 3, p. 441

30 J. D. Leader, *Mary Queen of Scots in Captivity*, Sheffield, 1880, p. 56

31 In ref. 29, p. 3

32 In ref. 30, p. 255

33 Nau, in ref. 28, p. 15

34 In ref. 29, p. 435

35 In ref. 29, p. 563

36 *The Letter-Books of Sir Amias Poulet*, ed. J. Morris, 1874, p. 164

37 In ref. 29, p. 283

38 A. Strickland, *Lives of the Queens of Scotland*, 1853, vol. 4, p. 412

39 *The Tragedy of Fotheringay*, ed. M. Scott, 1895, p. 118

40 In ref. 30, pp. 163, 537

41 Antonia Fraser, *Mary Queen of Scots*, 1969

42 A. Makinson, 'Solway Moss and the Death of James V'. In *History Today*, 1960, vol. 10, number 2, p. 107

43 E. T. Bradley, *Life of Arabella Stuart*, 1889, vol. 1, p. 110

44 In ref. 43, p. 114

45 In ref. 43, vol. 2, p. 120

46 In ref. 43, vol. 2, p. 136

47 In ref. 43, vol. 2, p. 123

48 In ref. 43, vol. 2, p. 141

49 In ref. 43, vol. 8, p. 160

50 In ref. 43, vol. 2, p. 170

51 British Museum Sloane MS 4164, folio 180

52 B. C. Hardy, *Arabella Stuart*, 1913, p. 243

53 *Calendar of State Papers Domestic 1611–18*, p. 16

54 In ref. 53, p. 17

55 British Museum Sloane MS 4161, folio 55

56 R. Hunter and Ida Macalpine, *Three Hundred Years of Psychiatry*, 1963, pp. 47, 76

57 In ref. 51, folio 56

58 In ref. 55, folio 57

59 In ref. 53, p. 19

60 In ref. 43, vol. 2, p. 15

61 In ref. 43, vol. 2, p. 268

62 In ref. 52, p. 309

63 In ref. 53, p. 175

64 In ref. 53, p. 242

65 In ref. 43, vol. 2, p. 72

66 *Historical MSS Commission*, 8th Report, part 1, p. 229

67 A. Strickland, *Lives of the Queens of Scotland and English Princesses*, 1851, vol. 2, p. 417

68 *Gentleman's Magazine*, 1773, vol. 43, pp. 324–5

69 M. A. E. Green, *Lives of the Princesses of England*, 1855, vol. 6, pp. 543–90 where the illness is fully documented

70 British Museum Harleian MS 7003, folio 202, r & v

71 C. H. Hartmann, *The king my brother*, p. 217

72 J. Nada, *Carlos the Bewitched*, 1962, p. 143

73 This and the following quotations are from letters of Queen Anne to the Duchess of Marlborough and to the Earl of Oxford in *Letters of Queen Anne*, ed. B. C. Brown, 1968, pp. 66, 67, 105, 127, 353, 382, 400

74 Jonathan Swift, *Journal to Stella*, ed. H. Williams, Oxford, 1948, pp. 255, 557

75 *The Correspondence of Jonathan Swift*, ed. H. Williams, Oxford, 1963, p. 238

76 A. Strickland, *Lives of the Queens of England*, 1866, vol. 8

77 Sir A. Halliday, *Annals of the House of Hanover*, 1826, vol. 2, p. 547

78. J. H. Jesse, *Memoirs of the Court of England*, 1843, vol. 1, p. 316

79 A. W. Ward, 'Queen Anne'. In *Dictionary of National Biography*

Chapter 14: The House of Hanover (*pp. 223–46*)

1 W. H. Wilkins, *Queen of Tears*, 1904, vol. 1, p. 48

2 *Memoirs and Correspondence of Sir Robert Keith*, ed. G. Smyth, 1849, vol. 1, p. 286

3 N. W. Wraxall, *The Historical and the Posthumous Memoirs*, ed. H. B. Wheatley, 1884, vol. 4, pp. 176–212; vol. 5, pp. 397–421

4 *Correspondence of George III with Lord North 1768–83*, ed. B. Donne, 1867, vol. 1, p. 247; vol. 2, 359

5 Pastor Lehzen, *Die letzten Stunden Ihre Majestät der . . . Königin von Dännemark Caroline Matilda*, Hanover, 1775

6 Niedersächsisches Staatsarchiv, Hanover, KG Hann. 9 Caroline Matilda No. 11 and 11B

7 *Life and Times of Her Majesty Caroline Matilda Queen of Denmark and Norway*, ed. C. F. W. Wraxall, 1864, vol. 3, pp. 242 ff.

8 N. W. Wraxall, *Memoirs of the Courts of Berlin, Dresden, Warsaw, and Vienna in the years 1777, 1778, and 1779*, 1806, vol. 1, p. 87

9 Report of 9 May 1775 by Drs Leysser and von Zimmermann to the Privy Council, Hanover. In ref. 6

10 In ref. 1, pp. 191–2

11 This document was found among Sir Nathaniel Wraxall's papers after his death and was included in the appendix to his *Memoirs . . .* , ed. H. B. Wheatley, 1884

12 *Correspondence of George Prince of Wales*, ed. A. Aspinall, 1967, vol. 4, p. 41

13 *Letters of Princess Charlotte*, ed. A. Aspinall, 1949, p. 244

14 *Letters of King George IV*, ed. A. Aspinall, 1938, vol. 2, p. 485

15 In ref. 13, p. 16

16 Duke of Buckingham and Chandos, *Memoirs of the Court of England*, 1856, pp. 145, 162, 178, 181

17 In ref. 13, p. 22

18 *The Historical and Posthumous Memoirs of Sir Nathaniel Wraxall*, ed. H. B. Wheatley, 1884, vol. 5, pp. 362, 363

19 In ref. 12, vol. 1, pp. 54, 55

20 *Gentleman's Magazine*, 1787, vol. 1, p. 544

21 *The Manuscripts of . . . the Marquis of Ailesbury*, Historical MSS Commission, 1898, pp. 283, 285

22 In ref. 12, vol. 2, p. 157

23 In ref. 12, vol. 2, pp. 163/4

24 In ref. 12, vol. 2, p. 200

25 In ref. 12, vol. 3, p. 301

26 W. H. Wilkins, *Mrs. Fitzherbert and George IV*, 1905, vol. 1, pp. 337/8

27 In ref. 12, 1967, vol. 4, p. 38

28 In ref. 12, vol. 4, p. 44

29 G. de Beer and R. M. Turton, 'John Turton'. In *Notes & Records of the Royal Society of London*, 1956, vol. 12, pp. 77–79
30 In ref. 16, vol. 3, p. 41
31 In ref. 12, vol. 4, pp. 106, 132, 160
32 In ref. 12, vol. 4, pp. 488, 491
33 *The Letters of Richard Brinsley Sheridan*, ed. C. Price, 1966, vol. 2, p. 216
34 *The Diaries of Sylvester Douglas Lord Glenbervie*, ed. F. Bickley, 1928, vol. 2, p. 125
35 In ref. 26, vol. 2, p. 34
36 In ref. 12, vol. 5, p. 97
37 In ref. 34, vol. 2, pp. 125, 126
38 *Lord Granville Leveson Gower: Private Correspondence*, ed. Countess Granville, 1917, vol. 2, pp. 422, 426, 429
39 In ref. 14, vol. 1, p. 188
40 In ref. 14, vol. 1, p. 322
41 In ref. 13, p. 86
42 In ref. 14, vol. 1, p. 377
43 In ref. 13, p. 112
44 In ref. 14, vol. 1, p. 412
45 In ref. 13, p. 224
46 In ref. 14, vol. 2, pp. 222/3
47 In ref. 14, p. 231
48 *The Private Letters of Princess Lieven to Prince Metternich 1820–26*, ed. P. Quennell, 1937, p. 11
49 *The Creevey Papers*, ed. H. Maxwell, 1903, vol. 1, p. 296
50 In ref. 49, p. 297
51 In ref. 14, vol. 2, p. 306
52 In ref. 14, p. 312
53 In ref. 14, vol. 2, p. 370
54 In ref. 48, p. 150
55 In ref. 48, p. 252
56 In ref. 14, vol. 2, p. 550
57 In ref. 48, p. 266
58 *The Journal of Mrs. Arbuthnot 1820–32*, ed. F. Bamford and the Duke of Wellington, 1950, vol. 1, p. 239
59 In ref. 58, vol. 1, p. 270
60 Sir Robert Peel to Sir Henry Halford, February 1827. *Halford Papers*
61 *The Croker Papers*, ed. J. Jennings, 1884, vol. 1, p. 408
62 In ref. 58, vol. 2, p. 241
63 *The Greville Diary*, ed. P. W. Wilson, 1927, vol. 1, p. 121
64 The Duke of Wellington to Sir Henry Halford, 18 January 1820. *Halford Papers*
65 W. Munk, *The Life of Sir Henry Halford*, 1895, p. 226
66 Sir Henry Halford to Lady Halford, 21 June 1830. *Halford Papers*
67 In ref. 14, pp. 461, 467
68 In ref. 63, pp. 116, 117
69 *The Life and Time of Henry Lord Brougham by Himself*, 1871, vol. 2, p. 332
70 In ref. 14, vol. 2, p. 212
71 T. Green, *Memoirs of her Late Highness Charlotte-Augusta*, Liverpool, 1818, pp. 386–8
72 'The Princess of Wales. A Triple Tragedy'. *Journal of Obstetrics and Gynae-*

cology of the British Empire, 1951, vol. 51, p. 905
73 The above quotations are from ref. 13, pp. 28, 38, 43, 49, 51, 52
74 In ref. 14, vol. 1, pp. 285, 287, 497
75 In ref. 13, pp. 160, 169
76 *Autobiography of Miss Cornelia Knight*, 1861, vol. 2, pp. 78, 89
77 In ref. 13, pp. 161, 247
78 In ref. 14, vol. 2, p. 142
79 In ref. 14, pp. 203–5

Chapter 15: The House of Brandenburg-Prussia (pp. 247–54)

1 *Diaries and Correspondence of James Harris, Earl of Malmesbury*, ed. by his grandson, 1845, vol. 3, p. 210
2 *Annual Register*, 1821, vol. 63, pp. 118–19
3 *The Creevey Papers*, ed. Sir Herbert Maxwell, 1904, vol. 2, pp. 20–1
4 This and the following quotations are from R. Huish, *Memoirs of Caroline Queen Consort of England*, 1821, vol. 1, p. 15; vol. 2, pp. 31, 41, 52
5 Anon., *Voyages and Travels of her Majesty, Caroline Queen of Great Britain... By one of her Majesty's suite*, 1821
6 A. D. Greenwood, *Lives of the Hanoverian Queens of England*, vol. 2, 1911, p. 304
7 *Letters of King George IV*, ed. A. Aspinall, 1938, vol. 2, pp. 280–1
8 J. G. von Zimmermann, *Fragmente über Friedrich den Grossen zur Geschichte seines Lebens*, Leipzig, 1790, vol. 3, p. 18
9 C. G. Selle, *Krankheitsgeschichte des ... Königs von Preussen Friedrich des Zweyten Majestät*, 1786, p. 5
10 Frederic to Voltaire, 22 February 1747. In *Œuvres de Frédéric le Grand*, ed. J. D. E. Preuss, Berlin, 1853, vol. 22
11 This and the following quotations are from *Briefwechsel Friedrichs des Grossen mit Grumbkow and Maupertuis*, ed. R. Koser, Leipzig, 1898. Publications from the k. Preussischen Staatsarchiven, vol. 72 (in French), pp. 13, 15, 135, 149
12 *Die Briefe Friedrichs des Grossen an seinen vormaligen Kammerdiener Fredersdorf*, ed. J. Richter, Berlin, 1926, p. 96
13 This and the following quotations are from ref. 12, pp. 75, 77, 85, 95–100, 112, 114, 116, 140, 373
14 Frederic to Voltaire, 22 October; 4 December 1775; January 1776. In ref. 10
15 *Wilhelmina Margravine of Baireuth*, ed. E. Cutheil, 1905, vol. 1, pp. 63, 80, 184
16 T. Carlyle, *History of Friedrich II of Prussia, Called Frederick the Great*, 1858, vol. 2, pp. 53–5

Chapter 16: George III's Other Sons (pp. 255–66)

1 The material relating to Dr von Zimmermann is in the Niedersächsische Staatsarchiv, Hanover, Han Des 92 III B no. 5
2 *The Later Correspondence of George III*, ed. A. Aspinall, vol. 1, 1962, p. 232
3 *Correspondence of George, Prince of Wales*, ed. A. Aspinall, vol. 1, 1963, p. 134
4 In ref. 2, vol. 1, p. 74
5 In ref. 2, vol. 1, p. 162
6 In ref. 2, vol. 1, pp. 429–31
7 In ref. 2, vol. 1, p. 441
8 In ref. 2, vol. 2, 1963, p. 492
9 In ref. 3, vol. 3, 1965, p. 231

10 In ref. 3, vol. 3, p. 338
11 *The Letters of King George IV*, ed. A. Aspinall, 1938, vol. 2, p. 370
12 *The Private Letters of Princess Lieven to Prince Metternich 1820–1826*, ed. P. Quennell, 1937, p. 238
13 *Halford Papers*
14 *The Journal of Mrs. Arbuthnot 1820–32*, ed. F. Bamford and The Duke of Wellington, 1950, vol. 2, p. 28
15 R. Fulford, *Royal Dukes*, 1933, p. 77
16 The following medical information about Prince Augustus, Duke of Sussex, is translated from records in the Niedersächsiche Staatsarchiv, Hanover, KG Hann 9 Domestica No 147 and Hann 92 Domestica No 147c
17 In ref. 2, vol. 1, pp. 395/6, 493, 586
18 In ref. 3, vol. 3, 1965, pp. 13/15
19 In ref. 3, vol. 4, 1967, p. 279
20 In ref. 3, vol. 5, 1968, pp. 485, 486
21 *Letters of Princess Charlotte*, ed. A. Aspinall, 1949, p. 22
22 *Sir Joseph Banks and the Royal Society*, 1844
23 D. Firth, *The Case of Augustus D'Este*, Cambridge, 1948
24 In ref. 3, vol. 4, 1968, p. 115
25 In ref. 2, vol. 1, 1962, p. 507
26 In ref. 2, vol. 1, 1962, p. 382
27 In ref. 3, vol. 2, 1965, p. 137
28 In ref. 3, vol. 3, 1965, pp. 439, 454–5
29 In ref. 3, vol. 4, 1967, p. 59
30 Duke of Kent to Thomas Coutts, 28 September 1799. *Coutts MSS*
31 In ref. 2, vol. 3, 1963, p. 380
32 In ref. 3, vol. 4, 1967, p. 124
33 In ref. 3, vol. 4, 1967, p. 292
34 Duke of Kent to Thomas Coutts, 9 December 1802. *Coutts MSS*
35 Duke of Kent to Thomas Coutts, 26 October 1809 and 5 August 1810. *Coutts MSS*
36 In ref. 11, vol. 2, p. 304
37 *The Croker Papers*, ed. L. J. Jennings, 1884, vol. 1, p. 155
38 Dr W. G. Maton to Lord Sidmouth, 20 January 1820, Devon Record Office, *Sidmouth MSS*
39 D. M. Stuart, *The Mother of Victoria*, 1941, p. 76

Chapter 17: Dr Francis Willis: Insanity Proved Curable (pp. 269–76)

1 R. James, *A dissertation on fevers, and inflammatory distempers*, 1778, eighth edition, pp. 28–9
2 F. Willis junior, *A treatise on mental derangement*, 1823, pp. 169–81
3 F. Willis senior, 'An Account of an extraordinary Case of a Lady who swallowed Euphorbium'. *Philosophical Transactions*, 1760, vol. 51, pp. 662–9; *The Medical Museum: or, a repository of cases, experiments, researches, and discoveries, collected at home and abroad*, 1763, vol. 2, pp. 414–19
4 J. Quincy, *Pharmacopoeia officinalis & extemporanea: or, a compleat English dispensatory*, 1718, pp. 196, 221
5 J. M. Adair, *Medical cautions, for the consideration of invalids; those especially who resort to Bath*, Bath, 1786, p. 138
6 R. Hunter, Ida Macalpine and L. M. Payne, 'The Country Register of Houses for the Reception of "Lunatics", 1798–1812'. *Journal of Mental Science*, 1956,

vol. 102, pp. 856–63

7 R. Hunter and Ida Macalpine, *Three Hundred Years of Psychiatry 1535–1860*, 1964, pp. 36, 383–4

8 Anon., 'A lamentable Relation of the cruel murther committed on a Minister at Morton near Bury'. In *A terrible thunder-clap at Wangford in the county of Suffolk*, 1661, p. 3

9 Anon., 'Détails sur l'établissement du Docteur Willis, pour la guérison des aliénés'. *Bibliothèque Britannique, Littérature*, 1796, vol. 1, pp. 759–73

10 F. Reynolds, *The life and times of . . . written by himself*, 1826, vol. 2, pp. 23–4

11 H. Swinburne, *The Courts of Europe at the Close of the Last Century*, 1895, vol. 2, p. 65

12 S. Mason, *The good and bad effects of tea consider'd*, 1745

13 D. Uwins, *A treatise on those disorders of the brain and nervous system, which are usually considered and called mental*, 1833, pp. 51, 198–9

14 B. Rush to J. R. Coxe, 28 April 1796. In *Letters of Benjamin Rush*, ed. L. H. Butterfield, Princeton, 1951, vol. 2, p. 774

15 B. Rush, *Medical inquiries and observations, upon the diseases of the mind*, Philadelphia, 1812, pp. 195–6

16 P. Pinel, *Traité médico-philosophique sur l'aliénation mentale, ou la manie*, Paris, 1801. Translated as *A treatise on insanity* by D. D. Davis, Sheffield, 1806, pp. 49–50, 108–9, 254. To the German translation by M. Wagner, published at Vienna in 1801, are appended accounts of visits to the Retreat at York, Dr Willis at Greatford and Dr Thomas Arnold at Leicester from *Bibliothèque Britannique*, 1796 and 1798

17 W. Battie, *A treatise on madness*, 1758, pp. 93–4. Reprinted 1962

18 J. Haslam, *Observations on insanity: with practical remarks on the disease*, 1798, pp. 114–16; second edition as *Observations on madness and melancholy*, 1809, pp. 251–3

19 In ref. 9, pp. 759–73

20 J. Frank, *Reise nach Paris, London, und einem grossen Theile des übrigen Englands und Schottlands*, Vienna, 1804–5, vol. 2, pp. 154–71

21 G. N. Hill, *An essay on the prevention and cure of insanity*, 1814, pp. 203–4

22 T. Bakewell, *A letter, addressed to the chairman of the Select Committee of the House of Commons, appointed to enquire into the state of mad-houses*, Stafford, 1815, pp. 7–8

23 G. M. Burrows, *An inquiry into certain errors relative to insanity*, 1820, pp. 43–4

24 J. M. Good, *The study of medicine*, 1822, vol. 3, p. 100

25 F. Bacon, *Of the advancement and proficience of learning . . . Interpreted by Gilbert Watts*, Oxford, 1640, p. 195

Chapter 18: Coercion and Restraint (pp. 277–86)

1 W. Cullen, *First lines of the practice of physic*, Edinburgh, 1784, vol. 4, pp. 151–5

2 T. Percival, *Medical ethics; or, a code of institutes and precepts, adapted to the professional conduct of physicians and surgeons*, Manchester, 1803, pp. 27, 68–9

3 T. Monro, in *First report. Minutes of evidence taken before the Select Committee appointed to consider of provision being made for the better regulation of madhouses, in England*, House of Commons, 25 May 1815, pp. 95–7

4 T. Arnold, 'A Sketch of the preparations . . . [for] the Asylum'. *Leicester Infirmary Minute Books*, MS, Leicester City Library

5 T. Arnold, *Observations on the management of the insane*, 1809, p. 17

6 W. Pargeter, *Observations on maniacal disorders*, Reading, 1792, pp. 49–53, 126–32

7 J. C. Young, *A Memoir of Charles Mayne Young*, 1871, vol. 1, pp. 341–50

8 British Museum Egerton MSS 2232, folio 71

9 R. Warren, in *Report from the Committee appointed to examine the physicians who have attended his Majesty* . . . , House of Commons, 13 January 1789, pp. 92–5

10 C. L. H. Papendiek, *Court and Private Life in the Time of Queen Charlotte*, ed. V. D. Broughton, 1887, vol. 2, p. 23

11 F. Willis, in *Report from the Committee appointed to examine the physicians who have attended his Majesty* . . . , House of Commons, 13 January 1789, pp. 109–10

12 F. B. Hawkins, 'Warren'. In *Lives of British Physicians*, ed. W. Macmichael, 1830, pp. 230–34

13 *Diary and Letters of Madame D'Arblay*, ed. C. F. Barrett, 1842, vol. 4, p. 378

14 *The Diaries of Colonel the Hon. Robert Fulke Greville*, ed. F. M. Bladon, 1930, p. 164

15 E. T. Carlson, 'The Unfortunate Dr. Parkman'. *American Journal of Psychiatry*, 1966, vol. 123, pp. 724–8

16 G. Parkman, *Management of lunatics*, Boston, 1817, Appendix, p. 4

17 Sir W. C. Ellis, *A treatise on . . . insanity*, 1838, p. 227

18 R. Hunter and Ida Macalpine, *Three Hundred Years of Psychiatry 1535–1860*, 1964, pp. 534–7

19 J. Birch, 'A Letter to Mr. George Adams on the Subject of Medical Electricity'. In G. Adams, *An essay on electricity*, 1792, 4th edition, pp. 519–73

20 A. Highmore, *Pietas Londinensis: the history, design, and present state of the various public charities in and near London*, 1810, pp. 348–51

21 G. Rose and others, *Report from the Committee on madhouses in England*, House of Commons, 11 July 1815, p. 4

22 R. Gordon and others, *Report from Select Committee on pauper lunatics in the county of Middlesex, and on lunatic asylums*, House of Commons, 3 April 1828

23 Sir B. W. Richardson, 'Medicine under Queen Victoria. The first Advancement: the Treatment of the Insane'. *The Asclepiad*, 1887, vol. 4, pp. 202–14

24 J. Conolly, *The treatment of the insane without mechanical restraints*, 1856. Reprinted 1970

25 D. H. Tuke, *Reform in the treatment of the insane. Early history of the Retreat, York; its objects and influence*, 1892, pp. 51–2

26 Editorial, *The Asylum Journal*, 1853, vol. 1, no. 1, p. 1

Chapter 19: Nervous Disorders and Insanity (pp. 287–94)

1 J. M. Adair, *Medical cautions, for the consideration of invalids; especially who resort to Bath*, Bath, 1786, pp. 12–14

2 G. Cheyne, *The English malady: or, a treatise of nervous diseases of all kinds, such as spleen, vapours, lowness of spirits, hypochondrical, and hysterical distempers*, 1733, pp. ii, 260

3 R. Whytt, *Observations on the nature, causes, and cure of those disorders which have been commonly called nervous, hypochondriac, or hysteric*, Edinburgh, 1765

4 P. J. Grosley, *A tour to London; or, new observations on England, and its inhabitants*, 1772, translated by T. Nugent, vol. 1, pp. 175, 233

5 Anon., *Wonders and mysteries of animal magnetism displayed*, 1791; J. Bell, *The general and particular principles of animal electricity and magnetism*, 1792; G. Winter, *Animal magnetism*, Bristol, 1801, pp. 16–18

6 S. Walker, *A treatise on nervous diseases*, 1796, p. 213

7 T. Trotter, *A view of the nervous temperament*, Newcastle, 1807, pp. xv–xviii
8 A. Snape, *A [Spital] sermon*, 1718, pp. 9–12
9 J. Boswell, *Life of Johnson*, ed. R. W. Chapman, 1953, p. 856
10 W. Cullen, *Nosology: or, a systematic arrangement of diseases*, Edinburgh, 1800, p. 132
11 T. Arnold, *Observations on the nature, kinds, causes, and prevention of insanity, lunacy, or madness*, Leicester, 2 vols., 1782–6, vol. 1, pp. 15–28
12 Royal College of Physicians of London. *Treasurer's Account Book*, 26 October 1774–[1828], MS
13 R. Powell, 'Observations upon the comparative Prevalence of Insanity, at different Periods'. *Medical Transactions, published by the College of Physicians in London*, 1813, vol. 4, pp. 131–59
14 G. M. Burrows, *An inquiry into certain errors relative to insanity*, 1820, pp. 58–64.

Chapter 20: *Medical Arithmetick and Universal Prognosticks* (*pp. 295–304*)

1 *Report from the Committee appointed to examine the physicians who have attended his Majesty, during his illness, touching the state of his Majesty's health*, 1788, House of Commons, 10 December; House of Lords, 11 December; House of Commons, 13 January 1789
2 R. Hunter and Ida Macalpine: Introduction to W. Battie's *Treatise on madness* and J. Monro's *Remarks on Dr. Battie's Treatise*, 1758, reprinted 1962
3 *Important facts and opinions relative to the King; faithfully collected from the examination of the royal physicians, and clearly arranged under general heads*, 1789, p. 30
4 J. Gregory, *Observations on the duties and offices of a physician*, 1770, p. 163
5 T. Percival, *Medical ethics; or, a code of institutes and precepts, adapted to the professional conduct of physicians and surgeons*, Manchester, 1803, pp. 27–9, 135–6
6 Sir H. Halford, in *First report. Minutes of evidence taken before the Select Committee appointed to consider of provision being made for the better regulation of madhouses, in England*, House of Commons, 26 April 1816, pp. 13–14
7 P. Pinel, *A treatise on insanity*, translated by D. D. Davis, Sheffield, 1806, pp. 248–50
8 J. Thurnam, *Observations and essays on the statistics of insanity, and on establishments for the insane*, [1845], p. 70
9 In ref. 8, p. 69
10 I. Ray, 'Statistics of Insanity'. *American Journal of Insanity*, 1849, vol. 6. Reprinted in *Contributions to mental pathology*, Boston, 1873, pp. 66–96

Chapter 21: *MacFlogg'em: The Study of Mania* (*pp. 305–9*)

1 Royal College of Physicians of Edinburgh: Sir Alexander Morison's *Diary*, MS
2 Sir A. Morison, *A paper, suggesting the propriety of the study of the nature, causes, & treatment of mental diseases, as forming part of the curriculum of medical education*, 1844
3 R. Hunter and Ida Macalpine, 'Introduction' to reprint of J. Conolly's *The indications of insanity, 1830*, 1964
4 R. Hunter and Ida Macalpine, 'Introduction' to reprint of J. Conolly's *The*

construction and government of lunatic asylums and hospitals for the insane, 1847, 1968

Chapter 22: Crime and Insanity (*pp. 310–21*)

1 J. M. Good, *The study of medicine*, 1822, vol. 1, p. iii
2 R. Hunter and Ida Macalpine, *Three Hundred Years of Psychiatry 1535–1860*, 1964, pp. 569, 1019–20
3 W. Perfect, *Select cases in the different species of insanity*, Rochester, 1787, pp. 196–203
4 J. Fiske, *The life and transactions of Margaret Nicholson*, 1786; Anon., *Authentic memoirs of the life of Margaret Nicholson*, 1786
5 *Gentleman's Magazine*, 1786, vol. 56, pp. 708–11
6 Public Record Office, *Privy Council Minutes*, PC 2–131, folios 357–88
7 J. H. Jesse, *Memoirs of the Life and Reign of King George the Third*, 1867, vol. 2, pp. 536–7
8 Anon., *Sketches in Bedlam; or characteristic traits of insanity, as displayed in the cases of one hundred and forty patients of both sexes, now, or recently, confined in New Bethlem*, 1823, pp. 253–8
9 T. B. Howell and T. J. Howell, *A Complete Collection of State Trials*, 1820, vol. 22, p. 75
10 G. D. Collinson. *A treatise on the law concerning idiots, lunatics, and other persons non compotes mentis*, 1812, vol. 1, pp. 502–3
11 Henry, Lord Brougham, 'English Orators – Erskine'. *Works*, 1856, vol. 7, pp. 209–55
12 In ref. 9, vol. 27, pp. 1281–356
13 F. Willis junior, *A treatise on mental derangement*, 1823, pp. 150–2
14 E. Wakefield, 'Sir George O. Paul on Lunatic Asylums'. *The Philanthropist*, 1813, vol. 3, pp. 214–27
15 *A full and authentic report of the trial of John Bellingham, Esq. . . . taken in short hand, by Thomas Hodgson*, 1812
16 W. C. Townsend, *Modern State Trials*, 1850, vol. 1, pp. 314–402
17 Sir J. C. Bucknill, *Unsoundness of mind in relation to criminal acts*, 1857, 2nd edition, pp. vii, xxxiv–xxxv

Chapter 23: Private Madhouses: 'A Fine Trade' (*pp. 322–8*)

1 *First report. Minutes of evidence taken before the Select Committee appointed to consider of provisions being made for the better regulation of madhouses, in England*, House of Commons, 26 April 1816, pp. 73–4; *Fourth report. Minutes of evidence*, 26 June 1815, p. 191
2 R. Hunter and Ida Macalpine, *Three Hundred Years of Psychiatry 1535–1860*, 1964, pp. 103–8, 199
3 D. Defoe, *Augusta triumphans*, 1728, pp. 30–4
4 T. Smollett, *The adventures of Sir Launcelot Greaves*, 1762, vol. 2, pp. 228–30
5 In ref. 2, pp. 451–6
6 Sir L. Namier and J. Brooke, *Charles Townshend*, 1964, pp. 88–9
7 [C. Townshend], *Some considerations on the proper means of regulating madhouses*, 1763
8 C. Townshend and others, *A report from the Committee appointed . . . to enquire into the state of madhouses*, House of Commons, 1763
9 H. Walpole, *Memoirs of the Reign of King George the Third*, ed. G. F. Russell

Barker, 1894, vol. 1, p. 192

10 T. Bakewell, *A letter, addressed to the chairman of the Select Committee of the House of Commons, appointed to enquire into the state of madhouses*, Stafford, 1815, pp. 16, 22

11 J. Conolly, *An inquiry concerning the indications of insanity, with suggestions for the better protection and care of the insane*, 1830, reprinted 1964, p. 481

12 Royal College of Physicians of London, *Madhouses. Treasurer's Account Book*, 26 October 1774–[1828], MS

13 In ref. 2, pp. 279–81

Chapter 24: The Poor and Mad (pp. 329–44)

1 *Liverpool Advertiser*, 29 August and 12 November 1789; reprinted in *Medical reports, on the effect of water, cold and warm, as a remedy in fever and febrile diseases*, Liverpool, 1804, vol. 2, Appendix, pp. 19–43

2 A. Hunter to Sir G. O. Paul, in *A scheme of an institution, and a description of a plan, for a general lunatic asylum, for the Western Counties, to be built in or near the city of Glocester*, [Gloucester], 1794, p. 1

3 C. Bloch and A. Tuetey, *Procès-verbaux et rapports du comité de mendicité de la Constituante 1790–1*, Paris, 1911, pp. 19, 163–4

4 A. Hunter, 'York Lunatic Asylum' in W. White's *Observations on . . . phthisis pulmonalis*, ed. A. Hunter, York, 1792, Appendix, pp. 1–26

5 *First report. Minutes of evidence taken before the Select Committee appointed to consider of provision being made for the better regulation of madhouses*, House of Commons, 25 May 1815, p. 5; *Fourth report*, 26 June 1815, Appendix, pp. 207–11; *St. Luke's Hospital for Lunatics. The physician's report for the year 1850 with statistical tables for 1850 and the last century*, 1851, pp. 38, 43

6 A. Duncan, 'Some Account of the Plan for establishing a Lunatic Asylum at Edinburgh'. In *Observations on the structure of hospitals for the treatment of lunatics*, Edinburgh, 1809, Appendix, pp. 1–15

7 W. Battie, quoted in *Literary Anecdotes of the Eighteenth Century*, by J. Nichols, 1812, vol. 4, p. 268

8 R. Hunter and Ida Macalpine, *Three Hundred Years of Psychiatry 1535–1860*, pp. 648–55

9 In ref. 8, pp. 467–9

10 Sir G. O. Paul, *Minutes of proceedings relative to the establishment of a General Lunatic Asylum, near the city of Glocester*, [Gloucester], 1796, pp. 9, 65

11 R. Hunter, Ida Macalpine and L. M. Payne, 'The County Register of Houses for the Reception of "Lunatics" 1798–1812'. *Journal of Mental Science*, 1956, vol. 102, pp. 856–63

12 Sir G. O Paul, *Observations on the subject of lunatic asylums*, Gloucester, 1812

13 Sir G. O. Paul, 'Suggestions on the Subject of Criminal and Pauper Lunatics'. In *Report from the Select Committee appointed to enquire into the state of lunatics*, House of Commons, 15 July 1807, pp. 14–20

14 In ref. 10, p. 60

15 C. W. W. Wynn and others, *Report from the Select Committee appointed to enquire into the state of lunatics*, House of Commons, 15 July 1807, p. 6

16 A. Duncan, *Short account of the rise, progress, and present state of the lunatic asylum at Edinburgh, with some remarks on the general treatment of lunatics, pointing out the advantages of avoiding all severity*, Edinburgh, 1812, p. 15. Quoted by S. Tuke, *Description of the Retreat*, York, 1813, pp. 225–6. Reprinted 1964

17 C. Best, letter signed 'Evigilator', *York Chronicle*, 25 September 1813. Quoted in *Family Portraiture. Memoirs of Samuel Tuke*, ed. D. H. Tuke, 1860, vol. I, pp. 215–6

18 In ref. 17, p. 217

19 In ref. 17, p. 219

20 J. Gray, *History of the York Lunatic Asylum: with an appendix, containing minutes of the evidence on the cases of abuse lately inquired into by a committee*, York, 1815, p. 34

21 G. Higgins, *The evidence taken before a committee of the House of Commons respecting the Asylum at York; with observations and notes, and a letter to the committee*, Doncaster, 1816, pp. 42–3

22 R. Hunter and Ida Macalpine, Introduction to S. Tuke's *Description of the Retreat*, 1813, reprinted 1964

23 In ref. 17, pp. 228–9

24 In ref. 17, pp. 229–30

25 *First report. Minutes of evidence taken before the Select Committee appointed to consider of provisions being made for the better regulation of madhouses*, House of Commons, 25 May 1815, p. 1

26 In ref. 21, Appendix, pp. 12–13

27 S. W. Nicoll, *An enquiry into the present state of visitation, in asylums for the reception of the insane; and into the modes by which such visitation may be improved*, 1828, pp. 12–13

28 *Medical and Physical Journal*, April 1814, vol. 31, pp. 341–2

29 E. Wakefield, 'Extracts from the Report of the Committee employed to visit Houses and Hospitals for the Confinement of Insane Persons, with remarks; by Philanthropus'. *The Medical and Physical Journal*, August 1814, vol. 32, pp. 122–8

30 G. Rose and others, *First report from the Committee on madhouses in England*, 11 July 1815

31 *Report from Select Committee on pauper lunatics in the county of Middlesex, and on lunatic asylums*, House of Commons, 3 April 1828

32 In ref. 8, pp. 632, 696–8

33 T. Monro, *Observations of Dr. Monro, (physician to Bethlem Hospital,) upon the evidence taken before the Committee of the hon. House of Commons for regulating madhouses. Read before the governors at a Court holden on the 30th of April, 1816*

34 *Fourth report. Minutes of evidence taken before the Select Committee appointed to consider of provision being made for the better regulation of madhouses*, House of Commons, 26 June 1815, Appendix, p. 212

35 *Sketches in Bedlam . . . By a Constant Observer*, 1823, pp. 293, 296

Chapter 25: The Asylum Era: Acute Mania (*pp. 347–53*)

1 I. Ray, 'The Insanity of King George III'. *American Journal of Insanity*, 1855, vol. 12, pp. 1–31; reprinted at the Asylum, Utica

2 J. Curwen, *The Original Thirteen Members of the Association of Medical Superintendents of American Institutions for the Insane*, Warren, 1885, pp. 13–16, 17–21

3 I. Ray, 'Statistics of Insanity'. In ref. 4, pp. 66–96

4 I. Ray, 'Insanity of King George the Third'. In *Contributions to mental pathology*, Boston, 1873, pp. 433–81

5 R. P. Smith, 'Acute Delirious Mania'. In *A Dictionary of Psychological Medicine*, 1892, edited by D. H. Tuke, vol. I, pp. 52–5; D. K. Henderson and R. D. Gillespie, *A Textbook of Psychiatry*, 1950, 7th edition, pp. 242–4

6 L. V. Bell, Discussion of Dr I. Ray's paper. *American Journal of Insanity*, 1855, vol. 12, pp. 49–51

7 W. J. Mickle, 'Dr. Joseph Workman'. *Journal of Mental Science*, 1894, vol. 40, pp. 482–4

8 J. Workman, Discussion of Dr I. Ray's paper. *American Journal of Insanity*, 1855, vol. 12, pp. 51–2

9 F. Winslow, 'Foreign Psychological Literature'. *The Journal of Psychological Medicine and Mental Pathology*, 1856, vol. 9, pp. 110–11

10 I. Ray, 'The Insanity of King George III'. *Ibid.*, 1857, vol. 10, pp. 95–122

11 I. Ray, 'Der Wahnsinn Georg's des Dritten'. *Allgemeine Zeitschrift für Psychiatrie*, 1861, vol. 18, pp. 407–49

12 H. Laehr, *Gedenktage der Psychiatrie*, Berlin, 1893, 4th edition, pp. 411–12

13 A. Chaplin, *Medicine in England during the reign of George III*, 1919, pp. 109–19

Chapter 26: *The Era of Classification: Manic-Depressive Psychosis* (*pp. 354–6*)

1 E. Bleuler, *Dementia praecox or the Group of Schizophrenias*, translated by J. Zinkin, New York, 1950, pp. 1–12

2 S. E. Jelliffe, 'Some Historical Phases of the Manic-Depressive Synthesis'. In *Manic-depressive Psychosis. An Investigation of the Most Recent Advances*, ed. W. A. Davies and A. M. Frantz. *Ass. Res. nerv. ment. Dis.*, vol. 11, Baltimore, 1931, pp. 3–47

3 J. Townsend, *Guide to Health*, 1796, vol. 2, pp. 135–45

4 C. F. Adams, *The Works of John Adams*, 1850–56, vol. 8, pp. 255–7

5 Ida Macalpine and R. Hunter, Introduction to translation of D. P. Schreber, *Memoirs of my Nervous Illness*, 1955, pp. 12–17

6 D. Uwins, *A Treatise on those disorders of the brain and nervous system, which are usually considered and called mental*, 1833, p. 13

7 A. Goldberg and C. Rimington, *Diseases of Porphyrin Metabolism*, 1962, Springfield, Illinois

Chapter 27: *The King on the Psychoanalytic Couch* (*pp. 357–63*)

1 M. G. Guttmacher, *America's Last King: An Interpretation of the Madness of George III*, New York, 1941, pp. xi–xv, 26, 27, 75, 175, 188–9, 190, 194, 258–9, 281, 292

2 M. G. Guttmacher, 'The "Insanity" of George III'. *Bulletin of the Menninger Clinic*, 1964, vol. 28, pp. 101–19

3 Sir William Young to the Marquis of Buckingham, 25 November 1788. In *Memoirs of the Court and Cabinets of George the Third*, ed. Duke of Buckingham and Chandos, 1853, vol. 2, pp. 16–17

4 J. S. Watson, *The Reign of George III*, Oxford, 1960, pp. 5–6

5 R. Pares, *King George III and the Politicians*, Oxford, 1963, p. 65

6 C. E. Vulliamy, *Royal George*, 1940, p. 10

7 J. H. Plumb, *The First Four Georges*, 1956, pp. 95–7, 105, 139

8 C. C. Trench, *The Royal Malady*, 1964, p. 64

9 J. W. Derry, *The Regency Crisis and the Whigs 1788–9*, Cambridge, 1963, pp. 7–10

10 J. H. Rose, *William Pitt and the National Revival*, 1911, pp. 406–10

11 R. A. Billington, *The Historian's Contribution to Anglo-American Misunderstanding*, 1966, p. 47

Index

PRIVATE MADHOUSE